Toward a Negative Theology of Judaism

Toward *a* Negative Theology *of* Judaism

Ernest Rubinstein

CASCADE *Books* • Eugene, Oregon

TOWARD A NEGATIVE THEOLOGY OF JUDAISM

Copyright © 2025 Ernest Rubinstein. All rights reserved. Except for brief quotations in critical publications or reviews, no part of this book may be reproduced in any manner without prior written permission from the publisher. Write: Permissions, Wipf and Stock Publishers, 199 W. 8th Ave., Suite 3, Eugene, OR 97401.

Cascade Books
An Imprint of Wipf and Stock Publishers
199 W. 8th Ave., Suite 3
Eugene, OR 97401

www.wipfandstock.com

PAPERBACK ISBN: 979-8-3852-3954-2
HARDCOVER ISBN: 979-8-3852-3955-9
EBOOK ISBN: 979-8-3852-3956-6

Cataloguing-in-Publication data:

Names: Rubinstein, Ernest, author.
Title: Toward a negative theology of Judaism / by Ernest Rubinstein.
Description: Eugene, OR : Cascade Books, 2025 | Includes bibliographical references and indexes.
Identifiers: ISBN 979-8-3852-3954-2 (paperback) | ISBN 979-8-3852-3955-9 (hardcover) | ISBN 979-8-3852-3956-6 (ebook)
Subjects: LCSH: Negative theology—Judaism.
Classification: BM610 .R61 2025 (paperback) | BM610 (ebook)

VERSION NUMBER 07/24/25

Quotations from the Wisdom of Solomon are from Revised Standard Version of the Bible, Apocrypha, copyright © 1957 by the Division of Christian Education of the National Council of Churches of Christ in the United States of America. Used by permission. All rights reserved worldwide.

Quotations from the New Testament are from Revised Standard Version of the Bible, copyright © 1971 by the Division of Christian Education of the National Council of the Churches of Christ in the United States of America. Used by permission. All rights reserved worldwide.

In memory of Baruch Spinoza (1632–1677)
and for all uplifted by his life and thought

Does not Wisdom call out and Understanding gift us her voice?
—Proverbs 8:1

But we must get back to the philosophers.
—Jostein Gaarder, *Sophie's World*

Contents

Acknowledgments | ix
Abbreviations | xi
Introduction | xiii

Chapter 1: Creation | 1
Chapter 2: Suffering | 28
Chapter 3: The Jewish People | 48
Chapter 4: The State of Israel | 74
Chapter 5: History | 104
Chapter 6: Revelation | 129
Chapter 7: Ethics | 149
Chapter 8: Ritual | 179
Chapter 9: God | 211
Chapter 10: Spiritual Life | 245
Chapter 11: Conclusions | 275

Bibliography | 279
Name and Subject Index | 295
Ancient Document Index | 315

Acknowledgments

THANKS FOR THOSE WHO, as teachers, friends, or both, have over my lifetime deepened my understanding of the philosophical stream within Judaism: William A. Johnson, Nahum Glatzer, z"l, Alexander Altmann, z"l, Dan Pekarsky, Marc Saperstein, Jim Wallis, Arnold Jacob Wolf, z"l, Jeff Gresser, Barry Kogan, Alvin Reines, z"l, Shlomo Cooperstein, Nostradamus Sher, Manfred Vogel, z"l, Peter Fenves, Géza von Molnár, z"l, Michael Michlin, z"l, Virginia Burrus, Elliot Wolfson, among many others, especially the many scholars I do not know personally but from whose writings I have learned much. I thank Professor Keren Mock, of Sciences Po, Paris, for her permission to quote from a manuscript letter of Yeshayahu Leibowitz, in Hebrew, that she translated into English; and Professor Peter Fenves, of Northwestern University, for reviewing my comparison of Rosenzweig and Walter Benjamin in chapter 4. Thanks to Brandeis University, the University of Michigan, Harvard Divinity School, Hebrew Union College (Cincinnati), and Northwestern University, where at different times I studied Jewish philosophy; and to Beth Am the People's Temple (New York), Hebrew Tabernacle (New York), Drew University, and New York University for allowing me to teach Jewish philosophy in those settings. I am grateful especially to Emerita Professor Danna Fewell and Professor Catherine Keller, both of Drew University, who invited me to teach a graduate course entitled "Jewish Philosophy in Contemporary Perspective" at Drew's Theological School in the spring 2008 term. That class introduced Jewish philosophy to a largely Christian community according to topics arranged from those most to least top of mind in the collective consciousness of American Jews today. Much of this book builds on notes for that class,

ACKNOWLEDGMENTS

which Professor Fewell, who kindly took time to participate in the sessions, encouraged me to turn into a book. Needless to say, none of these teachers, friends, or institutions bear any responsibility for any errors of fact or interpretation advanced here.

Abbreviations

Abr.	De Abrahamo (On Abraham)
b. Eruvin	Tractate Eruvin of the Babylonian Talmud
b. Shabbat	Tractate Shabbat of the Babylonian Talmud
b. Sotah	Tractate Sotah of the Babylonian Talmud
b. Ta'anith	Tractate Ta'anith of the Babylonian Talmud
b. Yoma	Tractate Yoma of the Babylonian Talmud
m. Avot	Tractate (Pirkei) Avot of the Mishnah
Congr.	De Congressu Quaerendae Eruditionis Gratia (On Mating for the Purpose of Education)
Contempl.	De Vita Contemplativa (On the Contemplative Life)
Cor	Letter to the Corinthians
Det.	Quod Deterius Potiori Insidiari Soleat (The Worse Attacks the Better)
Deut	Deuteronomy
Eccl	Ecclesiastes
Exod	Exodus
Ezek	Ezekiel
E4p45c2s	*Ethics* (of Spinoza), part 4, proposition 45, corollary 2, scholium (note) [example]
Flacc.	In Flaccum (Flaccus)
Fug.	De Fuga et Inventione (On Flight and Finding)

ABBREVIATIONS

Gen	Genesis
GP	*Guide of the Perplexed*
Hypoth.	Hypothetica (Suppositions)
Ios.	De Iosepho (On Joseph)
Isa	Isaiah
Josh	Joshua
Kgs	Kings
Leg.	Legum Allegoriae (Allegories of the Law)
Legat.	Legatio ad Gaium (On the Embassy to Gaius)
Lev	Leviticus
Matt	Gospel of Matthew
Migr.	De Migratione Abrahami (On the Migration of Abraham)
Num	Numbers
Opif.	De Opificio Mundi (On the Creation of the World)
Post.	De Posteritate Caini (On the Posterity of Cain)
Prov	Proverbs
Ps	Psalms
QE	Quaestiones et Solutiones in Exodum (Questions and Answers on Exodus)
Rep.	Plato's Republic
Rom	Romans
Sacr.	De Sacrificiis Abelis et Caini (On the Sacrifices of Abel and Cain)
Sam	Samuel
Somn.	De Somniis (On Dreams)
Song	Song of Songs
SR	*The Star of Redemption*
Wis	Wisdom of Solomon

Introduction

NEGATIVE THEOLOGY IS AN esteemed tradition of thought in the history of Judaism and Christianity. According to negative theology, the only truthful approach to God is by way of negations. We can say what God is *not*, but not what God *is*. But in process of asserting the negations, a dialectical switch occurs: the indescribable God comes positively into view. A relation with God becomes possible. That makes of negative theology a natural partner with mysticism—that domain of religious experience that rises up on an old Greek word for closing the eyes and mouth: *muein*. Negative theology makes an opening that proceeds by way of closure.

Within Judaism, negative theology's paradigmatic spokesman is the medieval philosopher Maimonides (1138–1204). Maimonides's chief negation is of positive predicates applied to God. In consequence, God cannot be said to exhibit mercy and justice in recognizably human ways—an affront to much biblical and rabbinical thought about God. But God does as though *appear* to Maimonides at the end of his *Guide of the Perplexed*, and to his sympathetic readers. The lesson? Some things come into better view against a backdrop of negating other things—as the sun must be negated for us to behold the stars.

In the course of his expressly theological negations, Maimonides opens a line of questioning that could lead to negations of other key teachings, or aspects of them, such as that the world was intentionally created and that revelation comprises chiefly a body of law. This book continues that line of questioning and broadens its scope to include a host of other received notions, or aspects of them, as detailed below. The point of the negations is to clear space for some new significance or understanding of these notions or their implications to shine through, previously too

INTRODUCTION

dimmed by received tradition to hold our attention, like a daytime moon obscured by sunlight. And these might invite those who have lost touch with Jewish tradition to renew acquaintance with it—or those long ensconced in it to rethink old connections in new ways.

The Jewish negation of Judaism is nothing new. It is as old as the biblical book of Ecclesiastes. Within the Talmud, it is practiced by the learned rabbi Elisha ben Abuya. Spinoza is the modern exemplar, who paved the way for many others. Today, the small but vibrant denomination of Humanistic Judaism negates aspects of the religion. They are not alone. As David Biale has observed, "Jews throughout the world today are disproportionately more secular than their Gentile neighbors."[1] What is different about our negations of the religion as practiced in this book is that we engage them as a strategy. Negation is a method of closure intended to manifest openings, after the model of negative theology.

Such a theology of Judaism need not construct itself out of whole cloth. Theology—in the sense of sustained, rational discourse on divine matters—is largely the province of the Jewish philosophers. Why they are deemed philosophers and not theologians may relate to the breadth of topics they address apart from God, such as law. It may also reference a willingness in them, more than in the rabbis, to plumb to the point of doubt foundational notions of Judaism, as we will suggest Maimonides does. And thankfully a long tradition of Jewish philosophy is at our disposal, extending from the biblical book of Ecclesiastes to such voices in our own times as Elliot Wolfson and Judith Butler.

A constructive, negative theology of Judaism would build on the past of Jewish philosophy. We will forage among its works both for the negations we will practice and for the clearings we hope to discern in the wake of them. Our negations are less of things, persons, or events, than of doctrines, teachings, or presumed meanings. In the order of the chapters that follow, we successively negate: creation doctrine, theodicy, contentful Jewish identity, political Zionism, purposive history, discursive revelation, moderate Jewish ethics, heteronomous Jewish ritual, and the personal God. Our topics for negation stake their claims on our attention from their salience within Jewish tradition (creation, revelation, God, ritual), their commanding place within American Jewish consciousness today (Holocaust remembrance, concern with Israel), or the connective work they perform between these various notions (Jewish

1. Biale, *Not in the Heavens*, 181.

INTRODUCTION

identity, history, ethics). We hope, within the clearings, to discern: the fragility of our world, some balms on our suffering, the possibility of a re-directed Jewish state, some recourse from the horrors of history, some manifestations within an otherwise contentless revelation, a countercultural ethics, a simultaneously dispensable and commanding ritual practice, a possibility of spiritual life. A key finding we hope persuasively to articulate is of a bond between negated God and negated Jewish identity: the two in a partnership of absent content.

The topics unfold roughly in order of importance to American Jews today, as registered by the Pew Research Center 2020 poll of American Jewish opinion.[2] Stimulated by Holocaust remembrance, the topic of suffering heads the list, but we begin with creation as prelude to that, as what motivates theodicy and other defenses of suffering. Then follows the Jewish people as prelude to a second key topic: the State of Israel. Then history, for its relevance both to the memory of the Holocaust and founding of Israel. Revelation follows as prelude to the important topics of ethics and ritual. God and the spiritual life pull up the rear, as topics least important to American Jews but, we hope to suggest, potentially of great interest for recovery to Jewish consciousness.

---

2. Pew Research Center, *Jewish Americans in 2020*.

Chapter 1
Creation

LET US NOT DOUBT the centrality of this concept to Jewish thought and liturgical practice. The doctrine of creation features in the first story the Bible tells. Liturgical practices repeatedly affirm it. Rabbinic midrashim expand on it.[1] Provocatively, for us, some of those midrashim pit a pagan philosopher, skeptical of the creation story, against a wise rabbi, who invariably triumphs in their debate.[2] And for the most part, the *Jewish* philosophers are with the rabbis on this point. However great their respect for Aristotle—who was, in Maimonides's estimation, "the prince of the philosophers" (GP322)—they will not side with him on this issue of the world's origin, that it had none, since, said Aristotle, it is eternal. Philo of Alexandria (20 BCE?–50 CE?) minced no words: the teaching of the world's eternity was a "worthless and baleful doctrine" (Opif. 11), for tempting us to worship Nature itself (Opif. 7)—an outrageous idolatry. Maimonides agrees: An eternal world "reduces to inanity all the hopes and threats that the law has held out" (GP328). If God did not create the world, God does not control it; if God does not control it, God can effect no miracles within it; if God can effect no miracles within it, Judaism is false (GP332). And we cannot have that.

And yet, the rabbis themselves open a place within Gen 1 to begin to doubt if not the creation itself, at least the goodness repeatedly claimed for it. As the Midrash notes, unlike on most of the days

---
 1. For anthological samplings, see Ginzberg, *Legends of the Jews*, 1:[3]–46; Bialik and Ravnitzky, *Book of Legends*, 6–30.
 2. For example, Bialik and Ravnitzky, *Book of Legends*, 6 (no. 5).

of creation, a pronouncement of goodness over what has come into being is conspicuously absent on the second day, when God "divided the waters which were under the firmament from the waters which were above" (Gen 1:7, JPS 1917[3]). One explanation: separation is itself disunion and sorrow.[4] But even Maimonides, for all his seeming commitment to creation doctrine, allows himself to raise doubts about it. The problem for Maimonides is that there is no proof from reason for either the creation or the eternity of the world. Either might be true. If he holds to creation, it is because the revealed law of Judaism teaches it. But if he allows for the esteemed Aristotle to be right, the law is void and "a shift to other opinions would take place" (GP330).

It is a remarkable concession. Maimonides seems to open an exit route from Judaism, which others after him would take. But perhaps he was just confident that no proof of Aristotle's opinion could ever arise. But the wily Maimonides, who fears that the truths he wants to teach in his *Guide of the Perplexed* are so prey to misinterpretation by the uninformed that he must communicate them in hints, parables, and contradictions (GP15–20), which only the wise will even notice, might intend something else. For, according to Maimonides, the doctrine of creation suffers from its own problems. It seems to presuppose a time before creation happened. But time is dependent on movement. And prior to creation there would have been nothing to move. But if time comes into being with creation,[5] there was no time in which the world did not exist. Doesn't that nudge the world toward eternity if not exactly take it there? The notion of a time before which there was no time boggles the mind. Perhaps the church father Tertullian was right when he famously proclaimed against reason the absurdity (but nonetheless truth) of faith. It is creation doctrine, taught by divine revelation as given in Torah, that is self-contradictory and absurd.

But there is more, which even Maimonides does not mark for us. A circularity plagues the relation between the monotheistic doctrines of creation and revelation, as Maimonides has presented them. Unless creation is true, revelation cannot be. But it is only on the basis of revelation, not reason, that we can believe creation doctrine true. Before we

---

3. All subsequent quotations from Hebrew Scripture are from the Jewish Publication Society translation of 1917.
4. Genesis Rabbah 4:6. See Bialik and Ravnitzky, *Book of Legends*, 10.
5. Philo agrees (Opif. 26), but does not hint at the paradoxical result.

believe in revelation, we must believe in creation; but before we believe in creation, we must believe in revelation. How do we navigate that circle?

Maimonides will not articulate this circle for us. But he has accomplished something else with regard to creation doctrine. He has shown it to be a rickety teaching. It undermines itself by embroiling itself in a state of mutual presupposition with revelation even as it verges precipitously, by the logic of time, of falling into its opposite, Aristotle's view that the world is eternal. Only our faith keeps it, and us, from the fall.

But what if we accept the fall? Then we are primed to pronounce our first negation, of any divine goodness or benevolently creative intent behind the fact of the world. From outside the monotheisms, this is hardly a dramatic act. The famously agnostic philosopher Bertrand Russell opined in debate with the Jesuit historian of philosophy F. C. Copleston, "I do think the notion of the world having an explanation is a mistake. I don't see why one should expect it to have. . . . I should say that the universe is just there, and that's all."[6] Certainly he would not get much argument from Buddhist thinkers. There is simply too much pain and seemingly pointless barrenness in the cosmos for it to redound to any kind of benevolent being. No less a religious poet than John Milton could reference the "monstrous world."[7]

Once no creating and sustaining divine energy is discerned behind the world, we are freed to appreciate one standout feature of it—the magnitude of its fragility, as though to echo and match the fragility of creation doctrine itself. Even monsters suffer, as Mary Shelley showed. The vulnerability of the blue earth, suspended in an emptiness of black, is what struck the astronaut William Anders, when he photographed it in 1968 from his orbit around the moon, in what became his famous color portrait, "Earthrise." He later commented, "The view points out the beauty of Earth, and its fragility. It helped kick start the environmental movement."[8] Anders implies our care for the planet rises in sync with our awareness of its fragility. This is already a discernment within the framework of our negation.

It is no more than what Buddhism teaches when it links our awareness of the suffering of beings to our compassion for them. But this linkage, repurposed as a lens for readings in the history of Jewish philosophy, finds sympathetic response in some of it, quite apart from any

6. Russell, "Existence of God," 145, 147.
7. In his pastoral elegy, *Lycidas*.
8. Goldstein, "William A. Anders, 90," 26.

commitments in play to creation doctrine itself—which we can simply ignore. Let us return for a moment to creationist Philo. All is not as well with creation as his own negation of the world's presumed eternity might lead us to believe. The world of sense experience constitutes a fall even before Adam and Eve have sinned.

For Philo the problem with the world is that it is not exclusively an idea. Philo the Platonist was in love with ideas. Listen to Plato's account of the soul's mystical ascent to the pinnacle of reality, the Idea of the Good: she moves "into a world which is above hypotheses, . . . from ideas, through ideas, and in ideas she ends."[9] Philo is not far behind Plato in his love of ideas. Hermann Cohen, an idealist of the Kantian stripe, wondered, in response to the doubt that we could ever love a God who was in its being a sheer idea, "how is it possible to love anything but an idea?"[10] Dostoevsky's Arkady Dolgoruky, protagonist of *An Adolescent*, sustains himself through thick and thin by repeated recourse to "*my idea*, to which I will never be false," and by way of which "I shall never be alone."[11] And art critic John Russell was so captivated by a lecture he heard by art historian Meyer Shapiro, he suddenly "realized all over again that an idea is the most exciting thing there is."[12]

But Philo illustrates for all idealists their common experience of that "queer little pang of bitterness because reality seemed so different from the ideal."[13] Perhaps the Greeks discovered this even before Plato when they saw how badly their beloved ideas of beauty, love, reason, and art behaved when transformed downward into depictable, deified personifications—the gods. Plato restored them to their transcendent, purely ideational state. For Philo, creation too initially *was* an idea. He understands Day One of creation to be of the *idea* of what follows on the succeeding days. Like an architect who first draws a blueprint, "first, then, the Maker made an incorporeal heaven, and an invisible earth" (Opif. 29). And everything is downhill from there. The material heaven and earth are mere copies of the ideational original. But the matter which received the impress of the ideas was itself "without order, without quality, without soul, (without likeness); it was full of inconsistency, ill-adjustment, disharmony" (Opif. 23). "The passage from the intelligible to

---

9. Rep. (tr. Jowett) 511.
10. Cohen, *Religion of Reason*, 160.
11. Dostoevsky, *Raw Youth*, pt. 1, ch. 1, sec. 7.
12. Russell, "Scholar's Papers."
13. Maugham, *Of Human Bondage*, 156.

the sensibly discerned" (Opif. 31) is a fall, "for no object of sense is free from dimness" (Opif. 31). It seems the perfection of being requires it to realize its full plenitude in lesser states of being. As Philo puts it, "it was necessary with a view to the clear manifestation of the superior beings that there should be in existence an inferior creation also" (Leg. 3 73). That inferior creation is the one we inhabit.

We are free to say that about our world, border as it may on gnosticism, once we have negated creation doctrine. And yet, as the Buddhists might predict, this very fall of the world draws our concern for it, even before we have come in our own day so sorely to pollute it. For the sensible world, in all its dimness, is nonetheless after the divine pattern of Day One and to that extent in the image of God (Opif. 25)—*pace* much of monotheistic tradition, which reserves that epithet for humanity alone. The world exhibits a wholeness and unity within itself that copies God's, "unique and one with Himself" (Opif. 172). But never mind the prototype of God. Philo has so dignified the world in its fall as to rebuke any demand to "subdue it" (Gen 1:28).

Ancient environmentalists would have applauded Philo. For within the creation of the physical world, Philo is especially intrigued by the relation between physical land and water. According to Genesis, the dry land simply appears from the gathering together of waters (Gen 1:9), as though it were there all along, submerged. And then at God's command "the earth put forth grass" (Gen 1:11). How could this be, Philo wonders, unless some of the water remained embedded in earth, there to nourish the plants? This fruitful water must have been sweet, as opposed to the salty kind gathered into seas. On the Bible's behalf, Philo speculates that veins of sweet water from the beginning not only watered the earth, but held it together to "secure its permanence, since, when supplied in fit quantity, this sweet moisture served as a cohesive to the separate parts" (Opif. 38). It is as though the water in contact with earth becomes a muddy glue that holds the earth together which otherwise, too dry and brittle, would come apart in flakes. But the dependence of the earth on water suggests it is not so permanent after all. Without the water within it, it would come undone—which not only flags the fragility of earth but underwrites the importance of every voice raised today on behalf of clean water.

Like the world, humanity too undergoes a decline as it transposes from idea to body. We are in the image of God to extent that we are pure idea, as we were on Day One of creation, "an object of thought (only), incorporeal, neither male nor female, by nature incorruptible" (Opif. 134). But the first embodiment of humanity, Adam, was as perfect as it could be. Since then we have been in decline (Opif. 140). It is as though the decline in "space" from idea to matter reproduces in time from Adam's day to ours.

Genesis tells a different story. If we suffer now in the world we inhabit, from the toil of work and the pain of birth-giving, we have only ourselves to thank. These are divinely imposed punishments on collective humanity, represented by Adam and Eve, for disobeying God. We inherit from them a choice for knowledge of good and evil over what might otherwise have been an innocent immortality of nearness to God, represented by the tree of life. Philo nuances the story. He gets Adam and us off the hook. Adam was indeed perfect. If we suffer it is not on account of him but on account of the distance time imposes between us and him. Time is the culprit. In his perfection, Adam himself could not have done anything wrong. The garden of Eden story is not really about Adam.[14] It is an allegory about us. It is a mirror held up to our habitual choice for the lesser over the greater. The tree of the knowledge of good and evil yields a lesser good—"moral prudence" (Opif. 154)—than what we would gain from the tree of life: "reverence toward God, the greatest of the virtues, by means of which the soul attains to immortality" (Opif. 154).

Philo analyzes moral prudence into the ability "to distinguish things by nature contrary the one to the other" (Opif. 154). His allegorical interpretation of Adam and Eve's disobedience makes his meaning clearer. If the serpent who tempts Eve is pleasure; Eve, our senses; and Adam, our mind, then the story illustrates the baneful effect on us of pleasure's appeal through our senses to our mind. Pleasure in Philo's scheme of things is always bad.[15] Moral prudence seems Philo's euphemism for knowledge of what yields pleasure over pain. The story shows us how we habitually prefer that kind of knowledge to knowledge of God. And we suffer in consequence, not from divinely inflicted punishment, but from the

---

14. Philo begins his interpretation on the literal level, remarking of Adam that "since no created thing is constant, and things mortal are necessarily liable to changes and reverses, it could not but be that the first man too should experience some ill fortune" (Opif. 151). Even this implicitly absolves Adam of wrongdoing. But the biblical reference to trees of life and of knowledge gives Philo pause, since "never yet have trees of life or of understanding appeared on earth" (Opif. 154). The fantastical trees persuade Philo that the whole story is to be read allegorically.

15. It is a "courtesan and a wanton" that seduces and debases the Mind (Opif. 166).

natural consequence of preferring lesser to greater things.[16] We need not believe in God to suffer from this practice.

Why do we do this? Because we were created not by God but by "lesser beings … from the number of his subordinates" (Opif. 76). Philo infers this from the first person plural of Gen 1:26, "Let us make man in our image." When we behave badly, the cause lies back in those lesser beings (Opif. 76). It would seem that even our bad choices are not really our fault. Deprived of God as our true Maker, no wonder we fail.

Philo does not go so far as to excuse our faulty choices. But both his account of the world and of ourselves shifts the burden of both the world's and our own sorry condition off of ourselves. He pushes toward a philosophical determinism, which his distant successor in philosophical Judaism, Baruch Spinoza, will realize for us, as we shall later see, as a balm on our suffering. But Philo does more. As he probes the conditions of creation he uncovers and names for us one of our deepest rooted fears: change. On this point, Philo is certainly addressing us as much as his Alexandrian compatriots, as the many self-help books on navigating change in our own fast-changing times readily testifies.

Time is the culprit. Philo shares Maimonides's view that time is a function of motion and comes into being with creation. "Time is a measured space determined by the world's movement" (Opif. 26). And movement is a species of change. The problem of creation shows in the very name of the Bible's first book: Genesis.[17] Philo takes the Greek name Genesis to connote "becoming," "since everything that is an object of sensible perception is subject to becoming and to constant change" (Opif. 12). And Genesis is primarily about the creation of the sensible, not the ideational, world.

He does not explicitly critique that world. But he only seems to praise it. When at the beginning of his book on the creation of the world, we read of "the beauty of the ideas embodied in this account of the creation of the cosmos" (Opif. 4), we might think the beauty belongs to the cosmos. It does not; it belongs to the ideas of the cosmos which precede the creation of the physical world. More explicitly, Philo's concern is with "the beauties of the world's creation *recorded in the Laws*" (Opif. 6) (emphasis ours). He is praising Moses's *account* of creation.

---

16. Nature "rewards virtue with ease and punishes unchecked passion that eclipses reason" (Opif. 80).

17. Philo, who knew the Bible in Greek, referred to its first book by its Greek name, Genesis, not its Hebrew name, Bereshit.

Philo is especially enamored of the role of numbers in Gen 1. Even the fact of the cardinal number to name Day One (Gen 1:5) of creation and ordinal numbers for all the rest impresses him.[18] It signals the key difference in kind between the first day of creation and all the rest. Philo explains that distinction on grounds we already know, that the first day comprises the ideational blueprint for all the succeeding days. But he expends the most space on praise of the number seven. This remarkable number among the first decade of numbers is a paradigm of changelessness. For, as Philo explains, within the limits of the first decade, it neither results from any two other numbers multiplied together, nor, in multiplication with another number, produces another number. As Philo puts it, between one and ten, "it is the nature of seven alone . . . neither to beget nor to be begotten" (Opif. 100). This lends to seven a motionlessness that assimilates it to God, "for that which neither begets nor is begotten remains motionless . . . [and] there is only one thing that neither causes motion nor experiences it, the original Ruler and Sovereign" (Opif. 100). In a still more Platonic mood, Philo might have said as much of ideas themselves.

Either way, Philo has uncovered one of the qualities that uniquely characterizes divinity. It does not change. If changelessness is divine, it becomes all the clearer how far from divinity we and the world are. Philo's love of numbers is partly an inheritance from the Pythagorean tradition, already hoary in his day. But it also offers a peg on which he can hang a conceptualization of our discomfort with the world and ourselves. There is *good reason* for that discomfort. We circle back round to Aristotle and a philosophical Judaism that is perhaps more in tune with him than Maimonides would allow. For surely an eternal world—even a changing one—reflects an ideal of changelessness. Philo has diagnosed a human problem and offered us a balm. The problem is change, which we naturally receive as for the worse. Even in the worst of places, the concentration camp of the Holocaust, Primo Levi reports on a common saying in the camp, "when things change, they change for the worse."[19] The balm is the reality of changelessness, which even apart from the God Philo worships, we can contemplate in ideas, as Hermann Cohen, Arkady Dolgoruky, and John Russell model for us. Our sights on ideas

---

18. This is true in both the original Hebrew and in the Greek translation (Septuagint), which Philo would have used.

19. Levi, *Survival in Auschwitz*, 116.

that move us, even abstract numbers if we are mathematically inclined, will lessen the burden of our vulnerability to change.

We have not yet negated God, only the *creator* God. Philo effectively negates that too, since lesser beings take credit for us and the world around us. Philo sets the stage for a Jewish philosophy that extracts from his creationism key ideas implicated by it that can nonetheless stand alone: ideas, perfection, changelessness. By way of the world's fragility, in contrast with these, he authorizes a discontent that awakens at the same time our care and compassion for what is after all, as any viewer of Earthrise might say—our home. Philo's ideals of perfection may not be ours. But insofar as they serve to dim the glare of creation doctrine, they push for the world's unguaranteed state to excite our concern.

We have heard from a Platonically inspired Jewish philosopher in response to our negation of creation doctrine. Now let us hear from an Aristotelian: Maimonides. For Aristotle will allow for other revelations to appear within the space cleared of creation doctrine. Like Philo, Maimonides diagnosed the discomfort we might feel with creation and ourselves and offered balms of his own. Like Philo, he was enamored of ideas. But Aristotelian that he was, Maimonides focused more on the act of knowing than the ideas known.[20] This stands to reason from the framework of his *Guide of the Perplexed*, which seeks to help a gifted student resolve seeming conflicts between philosophy and Judaism. A frequent command within his *Guide* is "Know this" or "Learn this," which will sometimes conclude a chapter.

Maimonides has enormous faith in the healing power of knowledge. Knowledge is indeed compassionate, both toward the person who has it and, within that person, toward others. A truly knowing person deflects evil from themselves and also from their inner life. Like a Buddhist monk, they are free of harm-causing hatred (GP441). To explain why we suffer, Maimonides here unknowingly echoes the Buddhist understanding of how knowledge relates to compassion. Hatred and harm toward one another result from desire for things we do not really need for our well-being, which are very few. And the mistaken desire for non-necessities is a species of ignorance. It easily waxes infinite beyond what we can ever

---

20. One way Aristotle builds on Plato is to activate ideation. Plato's ideas rest in sublime stasis. Aristotle reconceives them in identity with God's acts of knowing and as the forms within things that cause them to be the kinds of thing they are. Ideas as formal causes help to enact reality.

satisfy (GP445). If we all indulged it, conflict would be inevitable. The truly blessed rest content with life's bare necessities (GP446).

Maimonides suggests most of the ills we suffer result from inflated desire (GP445). He implies we have only ourselves to blame for these ills. This sounds like a tack opposite to Philo's, which worked to free us of self-blame. But Maimonides has already undermined his own move by suggesting that the ills *follow* from ignorance. Like the Buddhists, Maimonides has implied a causal relation between knowledge and good behavior, on the one hand, and ignorance and bad behavior, on the other. We do not *choose* the bad we do out of ignorance. It follows from the ignorance, as smoke from fire. And so Maimonides appears to be on the same page with Philo after all, except that he appeals not to lesser creator beings to explain our bad choices, but a natural, causal connection between ignorance and ills.

Maimonides follows a similar tack to account for the sufferings we endure from the created order—our illnesses and wounds (GP441–42). Here again a causal nexus is the culprit. Matter by its very nature is subject to depredations. By its very impressionability, it suffers. As bodily beings, we too are impressionable. We cannot have material bodies without falling prey to the depredations of matter (GP443). Maimonides has placed us to revisit the fragility of the material world, "whose being it is to be a concomitant of privation entailing death and all evils" (GP440). God created the material world. But Maimonides will not, any more than Philo, attribute the ills of it to God. Still, his theodicy is subtler than Philo's. It is not that lesser beings fashioned the world. Material being, as "all being, is a good" (GP440). But privations follow of necessity from it and "privations . . . do not need an agent" (GP438). More to the point, the logic that necessitates privations on being absolves the agent of being from any blame for them. It would be as though to blame a person for the darkness of a shadow he casts when he stands in the late afternoon sun.

If we ask after the impressionability of matter we come back to the problem of change. Matter is the kind of thing that is subject to beginnings and ends. There is, within it, "no coming-to-be except through passing-away" (GP443). But this is the shadow it casts. As embodied beings, we can no more escape it than the reflection we cast when we face a mirror.

This gets God off the hook for the worldly sufferings we endure, without invoking the lesser beings Philo does. But the comfort of the logic is scant. Maimonides encourages us to take the larger view of things.

CREATION

Individuals may die but the species of things remain (GP440); nor do the other earthly realities exist for our sake (GP442–43). We might take both these observations to heart. They both console for the "privations" of being that seem necessarily to attend us as individuals.

If Maimonides has improved on Philo for a modern sensibility contemplating the disturbances within creation, it is by conforming his consolations to the science of his day, which was Aristotle. Even our modern science is still beholden to the old principle, every effect has a cause. Maimonides has naturalized what was supernatural in Philo. In the end, he unites his two complementary accounts of the sufferings we endure, whether from the world or from ourselves. Both kinds of suffering stem from privations, in the first case of matter, in the second case, of ignorance. For ignorance, too, is a privation—of knowledge (GP440). Maimonides surfaces for us a possibly consoling principle with roots in Plato: "all evils are privations" (GP439). Otherwise put, they lack real being. They are shadows. But there is no sunshine without the shadows it casts.

To modern ears, Maimonides's theory of privation may sound trite or quaint. But like Philo's antique Platonism, Maimonides's Aristotelianism lays a foundation for a modern Jewish philosophy that, in the absence of creation doctrine, allows for a clearer view onto the vulnerabilities of being. Anyone who has served on a jury knows that the seeming facts of a case are subject to interpretation. A restatement of the theory of privation might be that reality exhibits a two-fold character. It is not so much that every finite thing suffers from privations as that everything that happens is interpretable in either positive or negative ways, relative to the value schemes employed to judge the case. Even within a single value scheme, a given act or state may register positively or negatively depending on interpretation. Being is to privation within Maimonides's worldview as positive to negative interpretation within ours. If we follow Maimonides's lead, the problem is not so much of relativity as of reality itself. It is inherently dual in its amenability to opposing interpretations of itself. It is as though the sorrowful tone of Day Two of creation—the day of division—sets the mood for the whole of it, rather than the joyful tone of Day Six. For Maimonides, it may well be enough simply to *know* this for us to cope with it. For knowledge is always compassionate. Our whole purpose in being is to apprehend—most especially the nature of reality (GP446). We who know the world's self-division may work to ease it as we can, both for its sake and ours.

Between them, Philo and Maimonides have laid ancient and medieval groundworks for a non-creationist Jewish philosophy of the world. Such a philosophy opens space for the fragility of a God-free world to awaken our care for it. One more philosopher—this one inspired by Friedrich Schelling (1775–1854)—gives a *modern* take on how the world appears to us in the wake of a negated creation. It is Franz Rosenzweig (1886–1929).

Rosenzweig is no less than Philo and Maimonides a creationist, i.e., someone who believes that God created (or enabled creation of) the world. But, like theirs, his thought lays a foundation for thinking outside the framework of creation doctrine, toward an appreciation of the world's capacity to awaken our care, compassion, and—in his case—even love. But he is not a rationalist. To speak in Maimonides's terms, but against him: knowledge of privation does not convert to ideational being. A privation known remains just that—a privation. It has always been the philosophical subterfuge, says Rosenzweig, to credit ideas with more than they can do. Philosophy's tack has always been to assuage our worries and fears over the privations that assail us with the illusion "it weaves [of] the thick blue haze of its idea of the All" (SR10). Rosenzweig relies on neither ideas nor knowability to set a standard by which the world fails. He builds on the most obvious worldly privation of all: death.

Rosenzweig knew this privation firsthand as a German soldier in World War I. There is no conversion of death to consolatory idea. There is no possibility of beautifying death. Death is no abstraction (SR10). We are right to fear it. But "in [our] fear of death [we] should—stay" (SR10); not just in the sense of remain alive, against the temptation of despair to suicide, but remain with our fear, for it has something to teach. Here begins Rosenzweig's now classic text, *The Star of Redemption*, and Rosenzweig's philosophical Judaism.

Rosenzweig's philosophy begins with death. That in itself is not unusual. As David Ferrel Krell observes, "philosophy, from Plato through Schopenhauer, Nietzsche, and Heidegger, is born of the struggle to think about death."[21] The difference is that Rosenzweig has no comfort or consolation over death in store for us. Just the opposite—what death underscores for us is our singularity, for "only that which is singular can die and everything that is mortal is solitary" (SR10). What death reveals is that each of us is scarily alone.

---

21. Krell, foreword to Dastur, *How Are We to Confront Death*, x.

CREATION

In fact, we are not. We have families and friends. We belong to neighborhoods, communities, congregations, nations. We are in relationship with each other, with the world and, Rosenzweig insists, with God. How can this be in the frightful solitude death imposes?

It can be because of creation. From the very start, Rosenzweig invites a possibility of negating creation by posing "the question of the origin of the world" (SR66). More even than Maimonides, Rosenzweig makes a question, not an answer, of creation doctrine. Rosenzweig believes in creation. But he does not take it for granted. It might not have happened. And we can imagine other worlds in which it did not happen. It is a marvel of relationship between the world and its partner in being. It might have remained in its priority to being. And this is what he tries to describe for us in the first part of the *Star*.

Rosenzweig is not pellucidly clear on the ontological status of that priority. He calls it, in German, *die immerwährende Vorwelt*,[22] variously translated: The Everlasting Primordial World (SR7) or The Ever-Enduring Proto-Cosmos.[23] He asks us to think of this world in terms of "secret forces beyond all reality ever visible to us" (SR98). We are dealing here with "ghostly fogs ... devoid of light" (SR96). With this language Rosenzweig raises in our minds the image of a vaporous world, a ghost town deserted before it even comes to be. He has presented death as the entrée to this world. For no sooner has he flagged death as the start of philosophy than this *Vorwelt* comes into view. Like the existential markers of human death, what characterizes this world is that it is utterly singular, solitary, and self-enclosed.

The scientifically inclined among us might read the *Vorwelt* as Rosenzweig's take, within modern cosmology, of the universe prior to the Big Bang. Rosenzweig says of the world in its singular self-enclosure that it is metalogical.[24] He means by that a world prior to the workings

---

22. Rosenzweig, *Stern*, [1].

23. Rosenzweig, *Star*, tr. Hallo, [1].

24. Here, for ease of expression, I conflate two different senses of World in Rosenzweig's parlance. He can mean by the World all of reality, or just the component of it we might otherwise call nature. For Rosenzweig, all of reality comprises not just a proto-world, but a proto-humanity and a proto-God. The table of contents of *The Star of Redemption* clarifies that ambiguity. But for our purposes, we can elide it. Indeed the whole account Rosenzweig gives of creation is distortedly simplified here to make more plain its significance for our discussion. Hopefully the distortions do not compromise the significance. For a more faithful restatement of Rosenzweig's views on creation, see Moses, *System and Revelation*, 76–96.

of deductive reason. In no way could this world occupy the conclusion of a reasoned argument for its being. Analogously, the universe prior to the Big Bang is not an object of scientific research. But this is already a departure from Philo, for whom the world does indeed unfold from a prior, divinely reasoned blueprint for its being. For Rosenzweig, it simply *is*—or more accurately, constitutes a permanent, everlasting, priority to all that is. That makes of the Vorwelt a kind of inverted ghost—it does not linger on after death, but in a death that precedes life.

Insofar as death is a negation, so is the Vorwelt. As though in sync with our project of negation, Rosenzweig calls it "a nothing of our knowledge" (SR49), and thoughts about it a "negative cosmology" (SR49). If this were all the world was it would constitute indeed a negation of creation doctrine. But the Vorwelt is only provisional. Rosenzweig does not intend for us to linger in it for its own sake. The point of it is the prelude it makes to the actual world we know. The world of our experience emerges from the Vorwelt on the heels of its extraversion. It renounces its self-enclosure for the sake of relationship. We are standing here with Rosenzweig at just the point where creation occurs. For what Rosenzweig means by creation is a passage the Vorwelt makes from self-enclosed singularity to relation with another. Reality *is* relation, as in English an anagrammatic puzzle relating the two might reveal.

With this thinking Rosenzweig contests the Platonic tradition that so energized Philo. Even though the world does not unfold, as Philo claimed, from a priority of reasoned ideas, that notion may still help us understand the inversion of the Vorwelt. Both Day One on Philo's account of the Genesis story and Rosenzweig's Vorwelt are precedents to being. The difference is that the world that followed Philo's ideational blueprint for it is a decline, while the world that emerges from Rosenzweig's ghostly precedent is a fulfillment. The world fulfills a prediction or promise contained in its priority to itself. In that way the creation of the world is like much of the biblical story: the realization of a promise. The Jewish people in descent from Abraham, its redemption from Egypt, its home in ancient Canaan/Palestine/Israel/Judah are all fulfillments of promises. The salvific messiah is a promise still unfulfilled. Rosenzweig has extracted this paradigm from the Bible and given it even more scope than the Bible does—he has applied it to creation itself.

Here is how creation fulfills a prediction: The pre-world is already in relation with itself. Its self-enclosure comprises a duality within it of need and supply. It has needs that it itself supplies. What it has are abstract

CREATION

categories that foretell all the kinds of animal, vegetable, and mineral of our world—foretell them without being them. We might almost think of it as a kind of Periodic Table of the elements, but without the actual elements manifesting anywhere. What these abstractions need are individual instances of themselves. The pre-world supplies placeholders—foretellings—of the individuals that fill its categories in the real world, but without being them. These ghostly hints of individuals fill the spectral categories that foretell without being the real world's genera, species, and chemical groups. Rosenzweig does not want us even to try to picture these ghostly premonitions, lest we mistake them for realities. And so he represents them, as though cousins to the symbols for the elements of the Periodic Table, by algebraic symbols (x and y, A and B) connoting abstract qualities without substance. This is perhaps the most difficult part of his book, and in retrospect he encourages us to rush through it: "Above all rush! Do not stop!,"[25] he exclaims. He promises it to become clear by the end of the reading. What matters for us just now is this key feature of the Vorwelt: its promise of the reality to emerge from it.

If the pre-world had remained in self-enclosure, we would not be here to tell the tale of it. Reality as we know it would not be. But the pre-world emerged from its self-enclosure. It effectively inverted itself. Without any assurance of meeting with success, it externalized its need and supply. It looked outside itself for something to supply its need, and for something whose need it could supply. And it did indeed find them. But the miracle is not in the occurrence of a non-necessity or even necessarily in the meeting of need with supply. The miracle is in the fulfilled promise. "Miracle is essentially 'sign'" (SR104) of promise fulfilled.

The Vorwelt does not declare itself the promise of creation. It only shows itself to be that, retrospectively, once creation has occurred. It is just when the world finds outside itself a need to supply, and a supply for its need, that its prior supply of its own need, in solitary self-enclosure, shows itself for a promise. The promise is of genuine relationship, bound by matches of need with supply. Solitary self-enclosure in all its shadowy ghostliness turns out not to have been the last word, but the first word toward genuine relationship. The emergence of relational reality from the promise of it within self-enclosed singularity *is* creation.

And what does the pre-world meet when it externalizes? As Rosenzweig tells the rest, what the world's need meets when it projects

---

25. Rosenzweig, *Franz Rosenzweig's "The New Thinking,"* 73.

outward is a formerly introverted God who has likewise emerged from a self-enclosure seeking a need to supply. The extraverted God matches its supply with the world's need. The extraverted God has turned its capacity to supply a need away from itself and toward the world, which the world gratefully receives for its extraverted categories of being. But creation is a partnership to which God and world contribute complementary halves, God divine creator-ship and the world worldly creatureliness (SR143). Rosenzweig has invested the *tohu v-vohu* (formlessness and void) of Gen 1:2 with an agency equal to God's. If God brought to the relation a capacity to create, the world brought a capacity to be created. Seeming passivity is active with its own agency.

Creation *is* God's sustenance of the world's outwardly turned categories of genera, species, and families of minerals. These, now extraverted, are literally on view and we see them all around us in the world we know, thanks to the God who sustains them. Rosenzweig's picture recalls what is sometimes called the Parable of the Long Spoons, attributed to one Rabbi Haim of Romshishok, according to which a group of people seated at a table who cannot bend their extended elbows and so feed themselves, feed instead, with long spoons, their counterparts across the table.[26]

And so we are back to God. But not in the way Philo and Maimonides were as, in Philo's case, to a God so beyond the world the formation of it fell to less than perfect subordinates, or in Maimonides's case, to a God so constrained by the logic of being as to enact a pervasion of privation. The value for us in their accounts of creation was in the fragility of the world we could extract from them even despite the creation doctrine they espoused. Rosenzweig has taken a different tack. He has invested the world with partial capacity for its *own* creation. This already unsteadies creation doctrine itself, if it does not entirely negate it. To come into reality, the world need only renounce its self-enclosure and turn outward. And so it has done. It turned outward at risk of not finding a partner to supply its now exposed need. But that partner was there. And so creation happened. The God Rosenzweig has sighted is a partner, not a self-enclosure that creates out of nothing. Such a god departs enough already from creation doctrine to, perhaps, survive the negation of it. But no matter, for what matters to us now is the appearance of the world, not of God, to us on this account. The world is founded on need:

---

26. For one telling of the tale see Shazeer, "Blessing, Curse, and the Freedom to Choose."

for extraversion, for relationship. It is risky business. The risk is precisely in the relationship, in the renunciation of control.

Rosenzweig implies by this that creation is not an accomplished fact. No relationship is. Insofar as any relation involves a distinction between two, neither of which controls the other, every relation is in process and at risk. Rosenzweig invites us to think of creation in these terms, as neither Philo nor Maimonides had. In these ecologically stressed times, we might well picture ourselves (rather than God) the world's partner in creation, so far as it manifests on planet Earth, and in danger of reverting backward toward a ghostly prediction gone awry.

It is just here, too, that we recover the import of death for this picture. Death for Rosenzweig was an assurance of singularity. Only singular things can die. But singularity is also a necessary condition of relation. Relation is the bridge between two solitary singulars. Unless solitary singulars precede, relation cannot be. For self-relations are not real relations. Death assures the possibility of relation and so of creation. This sounds a little like Maimonides's theory of privations. The difference is that, for Maimonides, death *follows* on creation as one of the privations necessitated by it; while for Rosenzweig it *precedes* creation as a condition of it. For Maimonides, the fragility of creation is a consequence of it; for Rosenzweig, a condition of it. The world is fragile in its very coming to be.

Nor is the fragility ever overcome. The Vorwelt is ever-enduring. Rosenzweig means that insofar as there is creation, death is always its presupposition; but also its promise. For once creation has happened, as it has, it shows itself to have been predicted by the deathly Vorwelt, where supply met need within solitary isolation. Now, in creation, supply meets need in relationship. As though with x-ray vision, Rosenzweig espies the pre-world beneath the world we inhabit. He sees the deathly pre-world of self-enclosure beneath the actual world of relationship we inhabit. He sees the promise of the latter in the former. He is telling us the world we know could not be except by resting on the foundation of that pre-world. That is another facet of its fragility. The world is founded on death. It is effectively a cemetery. And when Rosenzweig from his philosophical perch within it looks out on it around him, what he sees is a "vast nocturnal and twilight-kingdom" (SR176). For revelation has not yet occurred.

In ways startlingly different from Philo and Maimonides, Rosenzweig has pressed upon us the fragility of the world. In a conflation of activity and passivity, the world's very agency occasions its fragility. And so, like Philo and Maimonides, he presses upon us its need of care. We cannot take it for granted, or, as creatures, ourselves. We may suffer in sync with it, compassionately, as Buddhists and Jains most especially do. Rosenzweig evokes this attitude already in some of his descriptions of the Vorwelt. In its pre-worldly state, it seems to suffer in a way it cannot name from an "unresolved problem" (SR66): it does not know relation. It seems to know it lacks reality. In its self-enclosure, it cannot conceive otherness. But it lacks the vocabulary even to name its isolated state. It is like a ghost that does not know it is a ghost and suffers unawares over its lack of self-awareness. No language is available to it at all, but an "alternation of cries and silences" (SR85). William Hallo, who translates Rosenzweig's *Schreien und Schweigen*[27] as "screaming and silence"[28] brings to mind for an image of the Vorwelt Edvard Munch's famous painting, *The Scream*. In despair of its condition, without even the language of introversion and extraversion, or any understanding of the contrast, it externalizes, for its capacities exceed its comprehensions. And to its surprise creation happens. It is like the switch from black-and-white to color in the movie classic *The Wizard of Oz*—except that, just as in Oz, life in full color brings worries of its own.

Perhaps there is still more to extract from the negation of creation doctrine. What has waxed for us in the waning of that doctrine is the fragility of the world. We have not taken into account the images of cosmic grandeur that such roving instruments as the Webb telescope have shown us. A thinker is at hand to make good on that lack. It is Abraham Joshua Heschel. Heschel is a philosophical poet of nature's sublimity. Of course, as Immanuel Kant taught, the starry heavens are not in their being essentially different from us—fragilities all in the end. But some of these are more awesome than others. Let us not leave our negation of creation doctrine without such inspiration as these may provide.

But let us be forewarned of Heschel's own agenda—to ride on the back of nature's sublimity straight into the arms of creation doctrine. We will not follow him there. As in the cases of Philo, Maimonides, and Rosenzweig, we will pull from his thought what comes into relief from our denial of that doctrine. And that will simply be: nature's sublimity. And so we will leave this chapter fueled doubly by our renewed awareness of both nature's fragility and its grandeur.

---

27. Rosenzweig, *Stern*, 83.
28. Rosenzweig, *Star*, tr. Hallo, 77.

Heschel affirms with his philosophical predecessors the non-ultimacy of the world and its consequent fragility. He infers already from Gen 1:1 "the contingency and absolute dependence of all reality."[29] But his intent here is not to arouse our compassion for it—rather, to deflect our worship of it. For he knows that from ancient Lucretius to nineteenth-century Emerson, there is a long philosophical tradition of reverencing nature. He warns us: "Pitiless is the silence of the sky. Nature is deaf to our cries and indifferent to our values [and] . . . threatens to become a source of ultimate despair" (92). Some of us avoid the nature documentaries on television, despite all we could learn from them, for fear of the inevitable scenes of animal predation we might witness. Heschel writes of history when he says, "He who accepts this world as the ultimate reality will, if his mind is realistic and his heart sensitive to suffering, tend to doubt that the good is either the origin or the ultimate goal of" it (195), but he might have had nature in mind, too. Heschel may have intended to rebuke any *worship* of nature; but these words, applied to nature, also cast doubt on creation doctrine.

Heschel is more evidently on track toward the *fragility* of nature when he sees the world through the lens of Maimonides, whom he greatly admired. Heschel wrote a popular biography of Maimonides.[30] A reviewer of it comments, "Heschel not only admired Maimonides, he identified with him, and there is a strong autobiographical dimension to the biography."[31] Heschel, who had himself acquired a Western European education atop a traditional Jewish one, with roots in Hasidism, admired the breadth of Maimonides's interest in the world, from plants to stars.[32] And he acknowledged Maimonides's love of ideas—he was an "apostle of intellectuality"[33]—but reads that with some caveats. First, there are "the limits of the intellect."[34] We've already encountered

---

29. Heschel, *Between God and Man*, 95. Subsequent citations to pages of this text are given parenthetically.

30. Heschel, *Maimonides*.

31. Marmur, "Heschel's Two Maimonides," 241.

32. "He was familiar with seven species of cedar," "the flora of the Egyptian landscape," and "cultivated astronomy with ever greater passion" (Heschel, *Maimonides*, 20, 56, 66). Reviewers of the book comment on Heschel's uncritical use of legends about Maimonides, resulting in a "somewhat apocryphal version" of his life (Marmur, "Heschel's Two Maimonides," 241). But it would be natural for any disciple of Aristotle, as Maimonides was, to take an interest in the physical world around him.

33. Heschel, *Maimonides*, 209.

34. Heschel, *Maimonides*, 26.

TOWARD A NEGATIVE THEOLOGY OF JUDAISM

one of these in Maimonides's thought—we cannot prove by reason that the world was created. And second, the intellect in Maimonides's hands was no detached faculty of sheer ideation. According to Heschel, Maimonides had a "passion for reason," he "related to thinking as to something personified," and in consequence led a "tremendous philosophical life."[35] Citing the Aristotelian idea Maimonides inherited that all of contingent reality aspires to the self-containment of God (without ever reaching it), he called it a "*pathos*—in the Greek sense: a great passion that rules the world. And the *pathetic* idea of the universe found its likeness and echo in Maimonides's *pathetic* character."[36]

A pathetic universe excites our attention. Pathos implies more than sheer fragility. We must banish all thought of "the pathetic" as anything sad that evokes our sympathy. Pathos in the Greek sense is the suffering that accrues on a noble failure against great odds, such as Oedipus's to avoid his terrible fate, or closer to Jewish home, King Saul's to avoid his. The language is suggestive in light of one of Heschel's signature ideas, expressed in his now classic text *The Prophets*, that God responds in pathos to humanity's moral failures and successes. There, he characterizes the divine pathos as "God's capacity to be moved and affected by what happens in the world," which the prophets show when they speak for God in words of "joy or sorrow, pleasure or wrath."[37] This is a startling view of God for any fan of Maimonides to hold. It already negates one standard view of the divine. But it also detours away from the path we know Heschel has ultimately in mind, toward the sublimity of nature.

Heschel evidently means pathos in the Greek, not the divine, sense when he likens the pathos of the world to Maimonides's. For both Maimonides and the world could be understood in Heschel's view to suffer from a perfection they lacked but that lured them beyond their own reach, in the world's case to attain the self-sufficiency of God, in Maimonides's, to fully understand the world. The pathos is in the passion for the perfection that, in the very nature of things, eludes. They must both fail to reach what they aspire to. Privation was indeed for

---

35. Heschel, *Maimonides*, 157, 211, 244.

36. Heschel, *Maimonides*, 148. The italics are Heschel's. One reviewer of the book, Professor Barry Kogan of Hebrew Union College, singles this passage out for its extravagance. "It is quite mistaken, if not bizarre, to suggest that the universe that found its likeness and echo in Maimonides's own character was in *any* sense pathetic" (Kogan, review of *Maimonides*, 73).

37. Heschel, *Prophets*, 224.

Maimonides the logically inescapable shadow of creation. But would he have called it a pathos?

More important for us is that Heschel would. For Heschel gives explicit expression to our modern adaptation of Maimonides's theory of privation, that it points to an ambiguous duality of good and ill within the very fabric of things. He writes, "There is nothing in the world that is not a mixture of good and evil" (193). And he asks, "is good ultimately a parasite on the body of evil? Or is it just the opposite, is it evil that lives as a parasite on the body of the good?" (195). With that question, Heschel sounds like Maimonides reflecting that if the philosophers are right about the eternity of the world, we will require "a shift to other opinions" (GP330). He opens a door to exit not only creation doctrine but the whole monotheistic world view.

If Heschel does not himself enter that doorway to wherever it leads, it is not reason that holds him back. More than a pathos of the world, or of Maimonides himself, we might cite a pathos of reason. Even a philosopher as committed to reason as Immanuel Kant noted a proneness to illusion within it, "sprung from the very nature of reason" itself, which "unceasingly mocks and torments."[38] Reason teases us with arguments for creation—that there must be a first cause, prime mover, cosmic watchmaker, highest perfection—that ultimately fail to persuade. Heschel wonders what a Judaism informed by Maimonides's intellectual pathos might have looked like had it had more influence. As it happened, it was "the commentator Rashi who became the shaper, teacher, and educator of his people.... How different the existence and accomplishment of Judaism would be if Maimonides's idea had gained wide acceptance."[39] We can only wonder.

Heschel's pathos of reason takes us back to Rosenzweig. For it is not just that, as Maimonides allowed, reason has its upward limits. In our encounter with reality, it does not even properly activate, says Heschel, until *after* the world has seized us on a pre-conceptual level (64). "Our thought is but an after-belief" (68)—a poor effort "to raise the preconceptual awareness to the level of understanding" (67). Ideas as likely distort as illuminate what they strive to capture. They "become caricatures when transposed into categories of pedestrian thinking" (48). Worse, when they aspire to normative status (as they do in Plato) they deceive:

---

38. Kant, *Critique of Pure Reason*, B397.
39. Heschel, *Maimonides*, 211.

"Ideals have a high mortality rate in our generation.... All our norms are nothing but desires in disguise" (195).

And now, a reason-occluding world is already a step toward sublimity, whose defining mark is its defiance of reason to subsume it. Heschel, who comes a generation after Rosenzweig, shares his thoughtful suspicions of thought. Both Heschel and Rosenzweig deny the old idealist credo that we can equate "concepts with things" (47), or that ideas generate reality. And they agree that "there is no thinking about the world without the premise of the reality of the world" (68). But they interpret this thesis in opposite ways. For Heschel, all our thought about the world *follows* our preconceptual awareness of its reality. For Rosenzweig, a concept of the world retrospectively *precedes* our awareness of its reality. Awakened to the reality of the world around us, and stimulated to reflect on its foundations, we find, says Rosenzweig, that it rests on a priority of self-enclosure that has opened itself up to relationship. That self-enclosed priority is the pre-real pre-world (Vorwelt) that has no existence outside of thought. It is the logical priority in thought of the thought-transcending reality we experience. Rosenzweig is trying to explain how the relationships he takes to constitute reality rest on priorities of self-enclosure. If this already sounds a bit foggy, Rosenzweig will remind us that the Vorwelt is a ghost-town—its natural complement is fog. But Heschel teasingly denies, even without a thought of Rosenzweig, "the notion that the foundations of the world lie amid impenetrable fog" (59).

For Heschel, what comes into view when reason stands silent before the preconceptual world is not fog but mystery—or *would*, but for the fogs of disillusion that have occluded our capacity to register the mysterious. "Forfeit your sense of awe, let your conceit diminish your ability to revere, and the universe becomes a marketplace for you" (53). The encompassing word for this forfeiture is disenchantment, a word that gained currency in the wake of a lecture by sociologist Max Weber, in 1918, when he reflected, rebukingly, that in our relation to the world, "there are no mysterious, incalculable forces that come into play but rather ... one can, in principle, master all things by calculation. This means that the world is disenchanted."[40] The notion was of a "rationalization and intellectualization" that, unlike Philo's or Maimonides's understandings of reason and ideas, leaves us "denuded of [our] mystical

---

40. Weber, "Science as a Vocation," 139.

but inwardly genuine plasticity" and "apt to make the belief that there is such a thing as the meaning of the universe die out at its very roots."[41] A reference book in the sociology of religion puts the case more simply: "Disenchantment does not simply mean that the world is no longer seen as filled with angels and demons, but that the category of 'mystery' is negatively valued: Mysteries are to be solved by science, technology, or other this-worldly efforts. Modern people do not wish to 'enter into' mysteries but to conquer them."[42]

Heschel's lead toward the sublimity of the world begins here, in the loss of our capacity to be moved by the world. Philo, Maimonides, and even Rosenzweig all took for granted the impressiveness of the world. That was indeed one feature of the creation doctrine we bracketed out of their thought. It is just the impressiveness of the world that witnesses to its creator. But what shone out in what remained of their thought, absent creation doctrine, was just the world's fragility. But now, says Heschel, we are inured to being moved by the world in any way at all, either by its weakness or strength. It is simply something to be technologically mastered, subjected to production, and marketed.

Of course, Heschel survived beyond Rosenzweig to witness the impact of the atomic bomb. This was the *reductio ad absurdum* of technological reason. His starting point toward creation doctrine is an extreme of de-creation. The fragility of the world at human hands is all too clear. What is needed is to revive our capacity to be awed of it.

The notion of mystery is the first of a series of terms by which Heschel advances toward an awakening of awe. Mystery is not a function of our reason to discern but of our experience, so much so that it subsumes our reason. "Even reason is a mystery to itself" (37). "Even the very act of thinking baffles our thinking" (42). More: "Every sensation is anchored in mystery" (44). Heschel is here battling disenchantment on its own turf. He might as well say that our capacity for disenchantment is itself mysterious, in just the way epistemological realists refute relativists by applying relativism to itself. But Heschel does not intend such coyness. His real subject is nature. "Nature is the ultimate mystery" (91). A sense for this is what he wants us to recover, for "the awareness of grandeur and the sublime is all but gone from the modern mind" (37).

---

41. Weber, "Science as a Vocation," 155, 148, 142.
42. Swatos, "Disenchantment."

Heschel is like all our previous philosophers, a creationist. There is no doubt, for him, that once we recover a sense for the mystery of nature, we will understand it to be God's creation. As he remarks in passing and relevant to his own confidence, "there is no word in biblical Hebrew for doubt" (96). He shows his hand quite openly when he writes that by "the essential mystery of being as being" he *means* "the nature of being as God's creation out of nothing" (45). Heschel will implicitly resist all our efforts to extract from him a godless awe of nature. He so readily slides from his signature terms of mystery, the sublime, the ineffable, wonder, awe, and amazement into incipiently prayerful allusions to God that we may well be seduced by him. Witness: (1) "the world is a mystery, a question, not an answer" (59); (2) because it is "the ultimate mystery" (91), it poses the "ultimate question" (67); (3) "in facing our ultimate question we are carried beyond the known to the presence of the divine" (101). Really? Prying Heschel away from God talk is no easy task. But it can be done. And in the process he may leave us with a more appreciative view of the world than our philosophers up to now have done.

So what *is* the mystery of nature? One thing it is not: a problem solvable by scientific method or theory. Weber put the issue rhetorically: "Who—aside from certain big children who are indeed found in the natural sciences—still believes that the findings of astronomy, biology, physics or chemistry could teach us anything about the meaning of the world?"[43] Heschel agrees. Science is not inherently disenchanting. But its purview does not extend beyond ethically neutral causal explanation: "Science does not try to fathom the mystery. It merely describes and explains the way in which things behave in terms of causal necessity" (45). Science itself confirms this in a curious way in the case of quantum mechanics. For, as a modern science writer tells us, "although physicists use it [quantum mechanics] to predict the behavior of the fundamental particles . . . it doesn't describe what's actually happening underneath nature's hood to make those results come about . . . . It's impossible to translate into words how the theory's math relates to the world we live in."[44] It is as though the mystery of nature blocks the translation of predictive symbols into narrative description.

Heschel marshals an array of terms, already just cited, to help explicate what he means by nature's mystery. Nature is sublime. That

---

43. Weber, "Science as a Vocation," 142.
44. Henderson, "Rebel Physicist."

means it is "that which we see and are unable to convey, . . . which our words, our forms, our categories, can never reach" (38). Theologian Catherine Keller helps out here by having written *On the Mystery*, where she characterizes our sense of mystery as "an attunement to that which exceeds our knowing."[45] Heschel and Keller might be referring to the impression nature makes on us when we attempt to take in the whole of it, not just all the complexity of earth's ecosystems, but all those galaxies, stars and planets in their sum. Immanuel Kant had suggested that the world so conceived resists our capacity to register it. The idea of the world is a placeholder for a wholeness we can never comprehend. And that would make it sublime.

Nature is also ineffable. This means it "offer[s] resistance to our categories" (47). That seems little advance over sublimity, except that Heschel sees in ineffability a bridge between the objective and subjective content of our experience. Heschel has been playing with this dualism all along. Sometimes he speaks of "the mystery" (45), and sometimes of "the sense of mystery" (61), as though to mark an objective reality in the first case and our subjective response to it in the second. Heschel seems sensitive to the charge that his preoccupations with mystery may be with a mere attitude of mind. He knows that if "the feeling of awe may often be the result of a misunderstanding" (54), so may be the sense of mystery. He needs to find in the *sense* of mystery he hopes to arouse in his readers a passage to the actual mystery of the world. Only then can he so casually interchange the objective and subjective expressions for the mystery.

Heschel finds this passageway within the ineffability of the mystery. For the ineffable too courses through his writing as both "the ineffable" (47) and "the sense of the ineffable" (47). But in the case of the ineffable, Heschel erects what appears to be a correlation between our sense of it and the actual reality of it. It turns out that our sense of the ineffable is not just a certain impressionability or receptivity to what defies description. It is not so merely passive. It is rather an "ability" (46) or "faculty" (46) "with which all men are endowed" (46), whose particular province is "something objective which cannot be conceived by the mind" (47). Just as our eyes imply a visible world to be perceived, so our sense of the ineffable implies the reality of the inconceivable. When Heschel asks, "How would we know of the mystery of being if not through our sense of the ineffable?" (46), he implies that our sense of the ineffable entails the

---

45. Keller, *On the Mystery*, xi.

mystery of being. Heschel's confident conclusion is: "we do not create the ineffable, we encounter it" (47); "the ineffable is there before we form an idea of it" (54). And now by extension, since the ineffable is a feature of the mystery, "the mystery is an ontological category, . . . it is a dimension of all existence and may be experienced anywhere" (45).

Heschel's tack here, of arguing to the objective from the subjective, has a long philosophical history. It was the practice of German philosophical idealism. Heschel has transplanted the subjectivity of ideas to the subjectivity of our perceptions and inferred from there an objectivity. But by this procedure he also evokes Rosenzweig. For by activating what might seem our passive impressionability for hints of the mystery, he echoes Rosenzweig's investment of the world with agency in its own creative process. Just as, for Rosenzweig, world and God join in the act of creation, so, for Heschel, do we and the ineffable work to produce the experience of the ineffable. Of course, a faculty can atrophy from lack of use. This, says Heschel, is just what has happened. Disenchantment has deactivated our sense of the mystery. And so the mystery seems no longer to exist. "Our normal consciousness is in a state of trance [and] what is higher in us is usually suspended" (62). We suffer in consequence: "The dead emptiness of the heart is unbearable to the living man" (61). Much of Heschel's writing comes in answer to this problem.

With stretches of poetic writing that interweave a bevy of evocative terms—wonder, awe, radical amazement—Heschel hopes to stimulate our sense of the mystery so that the actual mystery can return to our lives. He begins with small, quotidian things: "bread or fruit, . . . a pleasant fragrance or a cup of wine, . . . rainbow, . . . the ocean, . . . trees when they blossom" (43).[46] Wonder can already arise over these. And then the heavens: "It is hard to live under a sky full of stars and not be struck by its mystery" (91). Here wonder intensifies to awe, as Immanuel Kant reflected in his now famous words about the "starry heavens" that they "fill the mind with ever increasing wonder and awe, the oftener and more steadily we reflect on them,"[47] which Heschel himself quotes (44). The words carry special weight coming from a writer as averse to undue displays of enthusiasm as Kant was. And they remind us of philosophy's special debt to

---

46. Orthodox Judaism supplies blessings for encounters with just these things—a reminder of Heschel's own traditionalism and of his address to Jewish readers.

47. Kant, *Critique of Practical Reason*, 169.

wonder which, according to both Plato and Aristotle[48] as Heschel recalls for us (41), inaugurates the whole philosophical enterprise.

And as the mystery emerges more engagingly for us, the wonder and awe in response become radical amazement—radical because evoked now by "all of reality, not only [by] . . . what we see but also [by] the very act of seeing as well as . . . our own selves" (41). As though to recover the objective reference of our sense of the ineffable, Heschel claims for radical amazement the intellectually compelling force of sheer logic: "Radical amazement is as universally valid as the principle of contradiction or the principle of sufficient reason" (47)—universally valid, we venture to say, toward the reality of the pervasive mystery it implies. As in the case of our sense of the ineffable, "our radical amazement responds to the mystery, but does not produce it" (47).

At this maximum of subjective response to the mystery, we stand with Heschel at the threshold of God-consciousness. "The sense of wonder, awe, and mystery . . . leads to a plane where the question about God becomes an inescapable concern" (66). This is where Heschel wants to lead us. But as negaters of creation doctrine, we cannot follow him here. Even Heschel allows that "the mystery is not the ultimate" for it might be that "a demonic, blind force . . . rules the world" (50); or that nothing rules it. By granting that "God is a mystery but the mystery is not God" (49), Heschel respects our reluctance to follow his lead and allows us to savor the mystery un-theistically. Perhaps he has awakened in us, besides a sense for the fragility of the world the other philosophers have promoted, a sense for its mystery too. A walk in the woods may mean more to us from now on. Let us draw what inspiration we can from nature in preparation for the next topic in line: suffering, which has already surfaced for us as a problem within the natural order.

---

48. "This sense of wonder is the mark of the philosopher" (*Theaetetus* 155d); "It is owing to their wonder that men both now begin and at first began to philosophize" (*Metaphysics* 982b12).

Chapter 2
Suffering

Robert Gibbs has written that "suffering has pride of place in postmodern Jewish philosophy."[1] If we began our reflections with the topic of creation, that is not just because origins make a natural start, but because suffering is so deeply implicated in creation doctrine. The topic of creation has primed us to reflect on suffering, which the fragility of the world and all its inhabitants already imply. The very doctrine of creation itself can barely stand. Platonic Philo reminds us of the human predicament in a world not wholly friendly to us. "Human life is full of . . . vast confusion and disorder and uncertainty" (Ios. 143), of "grief and very fearful evils" (Abr. 202), and of "darkness" (Fug. 136). His master Plato had already opined about us that through our bodies we are, at least potentially, "disfigured by ten thousand ills" (Rep. 611).

In a culture as body-obsessed as America's, the Platonic and Philonic worry over materiality itself can barely sound. But a noted art historian, who draws our attention to the paintings of Caravaggio, finds in the vivid brutality of the scenes depicted there a stark reminder "of all the pain, loneliness, beauty, fear, and awful vulnerability our bodies have in common."[2] The beauty of the body may appear in those paintings, in the gyms and on the sports fields, but outside of that—the "awful vulnerability." It is possible to wonder whether the byzantine complexity of the US health care system and the insurers who both support and profit from

---

1. Gibbs, "Postmodern Jewish Philosophy," 21.
2. Cole, "On the Trail of Caravaggio," 67.

it, in aid of ailing bodies, is not proof enough of Plato's and Philo's view of the body as indeed a burden, a drain, a prison, a tomb.

Our negation here is of any moral or religious *justification* for this suffering. We loosely label all such attempts *theodicy*, though this term, that comes to us from the philosopher Gottfried Wilhelm Leibniz (1646–1716), more properly denotes attempts to justify an all good and powerful God who permits seemingly inexplicable suffering to happen. We are not thinking of the suffering doled out by courts in punishment for crimes, though the justification for this, too, might fall under our negation. We have in mind the kinds of suffering that Rabbi Harold Kushner was referencing when he wrote his now classic book, *When Bad Things Happen to Good People*. Importantly, the querying word is not *why*, but *when*—what can be our response *when* these things happen.

Ever since the biblical prophets, suffering had found excuse in either of two explanations, that it punished or that it purified—or both at once. Where an offense could not be identified that suffering punished, there was ample scope for suffering to purify. The distinction between the two explanations is not airtight, since the very need of purification presupposes something amiss, however indeterminate or hidden from view. This is one of the arguments of Job's friend, Eliphaz, in the book of Job, that biblical cornucopia of theodicies. "Shall mortal man be just before God? Shall a man be pure before his Maker?" Eliphaz asks (Job 4:17). A modern counterpart of Eliphaz might say to Job that however righteous he thought himself, he was in all his former wealth surely implicated in the systemic imbalances of his local society, and therefore justly punished.

But then, God in God's own self rebukes all the theodicies of Job's friends (Job 42:7). And so the book sets itself up to negate any meaning to Job's suffering. It is true that the prologue and epilogue supply a meaning: Job's suffering is a test of his fidelity to God. This is a variation on the theme of suffering as purification. But many scholars take the prose prologue and epilogue to be later additions to the poetic middle, added to endow it with piety. On its own, the broad middle of the book is a puzzle. Job receives a declaration of God's power, but not of God's wisdom, to account for the suffering. Indeed, the whole of the book can be read as an effort to draw the reader into the very suffering depicted in the middle part. Insofar as the reader is made to wonder, by the prologue, whether Job will pass his test, she is enrolled in the very suspension that holds him in thrall. While Job awaits a response from God, we await the outcome of his trial: Will he "blaspheme God and die" (Job 2:9), as his wife counsels, or ride out the storm of his distress? We are suspended at length in this drama, in echo of Job's own, like a Yom Kippur worshiper who does not know until after many pages of prayer that God will forgive his sins.

Maimonides says the point of the book is not to assure God of Job's fidelity—the omniscient God already knows that—but to broadcast the story for the edification of others (GP497–98). And certainly Job has been used to edify. But our negation of the meaning of suffering tends toward another interpretation: that the point of book is to enroll the reader in the very meaninglessness of suffering it displays—to bring home the point of its pointlessness.

That is a reading we might extract from a now classic essay by Emmanuel Levinas, "Useless Suffering." Here is what Levinas tells us about the phenomenon itself:

> Suffering is a given in consciousness, . . . unassumable, . . . what disturbs order and this disturbance itself, . . . the categorial ambiguity of quality and modality, . . . passivity, . . . more passive than receptivity, . . . a submission, . . . independent of its conceptual opposition to activity, . . . precisely an evil, . . . negative right up to non-sense, . . . the explosion and most profound articulation of absurdity, . . . [and finally and climactically] useless, . . . "for nothing," . . . intrinsically meaningless and condemned to itself without exit.[3]

At the most obvious level, what this lengthy itemization of all that suffering is implies is that it is not a mere negation, not a nothing, as Rosenzweig had also said of death. Rosenzweig asked after the being of death. And its answer to him was that, whatever it was, it was *not* nothing. It was less a recess of being than an abscess on it. This is Rosenzweig's rejection of the old idealist idea we find in Maimonides that death is a kind of absence—a privation. Death, for Rosenzweig, was *something* that shamelessly obtruded on life. The same is true for Levinas about suffering. Suffering may be *for nothing*, but in just so being constitutes *something*. It has enough presence to count for something—for being meaningless.

Rosenzweig lays some additional groundwork for Levinas. For Rosenzweig, death marked our singularity, which magnifies the horror of it by linking it to loneliness. In context of creation, Rosenzweig reflected on the protocosmic world. But in context of suffering, he reflects

---

3. Levinas, "Useless Suffering," 156–58.

in addition on protocosmic humanity. Like the world, humanity too rests on a priority to itself in a pre-humanity, which Rosenzweig calls the *metaethical*. He means by that a framework prior to the relationality that makes ethics possible in the first place. Like the protocosmos, the metaethical connotes the unrelationality to which it holds its charge—in this case, the human. Like the world, we humans too have emerged from a prior isolation into relationship. This as we shall see in our chapter on ritual has redemptive import for the world.

But before we enter into the relationships that sustain so many of our lives, we are grounded in horrific isolation. If we would ignore that fact or forget it, Rosenzweig bids us read the ancient Greek tragedies. For working within a metaphysic that failed to truly figure relationship, the ancient Greeks effectively inhabited, in thought if not in experience, the horrific isolation of metaethical humanity. Their great playwrights showed this in their tragic heroes, victims of a pitiless fate that left them utterly alone, a "self enclosed upon itself" (SR91) or as Levinas might say, "condemned to themselves without exit," and communicatively capable of little more than soliloquy. The tragic Greek hero, rather like the protocosmic world, suffers without words in an isolation of his own. The heroes of the Greek tragedies personified the non-relationality of the metaethical and the suffering endemic to any life that might find itself there.

Levinas follows here in Rosenzweig's wake. When Levinas writes of "the absolute passivity, beneath the level of activity and passivity, which is contributed by the idea of creation,"[4] he might be referencing the *tohu v-vohu* of Gen 1:2, or he might have Rosenzweig's protocosmos in mind, which lies *beneath* creation. But Levinas characterizes that priority in a way Rosenzweig does not emphasize, in terms of its passivity. And this becomes his link to suffering. For suffering is "passivity, . . . more passive than receptivity."

Levinas is even more explicit than Rosenzweig that the human self in its priority to relations *suffers*. His language of the unrelated self makes that plain. In the "dominating imperialism characteristic of it, . . . [the unrelated self is] tight in its skin, encumbered and as it were stuffed with itself, suffocating under itself."[5] "The ego is an incomparable unicity; it is outside of the community of genus and form and does not find any rest in

---

4. Levinas, *Otherwise Than Being*, 110.
5. Levinas, *Otherwise Than Being*, 110.

itself, unquiet, not coinciding with itself."[6] Its site is "null-site."[7] This language of self-enclosure recalls Rosenzweig's for the priorities to worldly and human being; and the language of nullity recalls his nothing—but nothing as obtrusion, not privation.

Levinas expresses this another way. The suffering passivity he intends is not simply the opposite of activity. He intends *absolute* passivity—a passivity so passive it lacks an opposite; or as he has already put it for us, a passivity "more passive than receptivity," "independent of its conceptual opposition to activity," "negative right up to non-sense." Insofar as we understand things by grasping what they are not, by way of their opposites, the passivity Levinas has in mind defies comprehension. And so he says: in the face of it, we do not "take cognizance" of it, we do not exercise any kind of *taking* at all, but as Richard Cohen's English translation deftly rhymes it, we suffer an "*aching* consciousness"[8] (emphasis ours). When Levinas calls suffering a "contradiction by way of sensation," and "in-spite-of-consciousness,"[9] he implies a conflation of what Kant had distinguished between: sensation, on the one hand, and, on the other, our conscious understanding of it through our categorizing reason (*Verstand*). Contradictions generally register in our consciousness between concepts. But suffering is already a contradiction on the level of sensation even before consciousness is brought to bear on it. And suffering, uniquely within our experience, is so far from privation that it registers not just at the level of sensation, not even primarily there, but at the level of consciousness to disrupt understanding. We might liken it to a paper jam in an industrial-strength library copier. It uniquely gums the whole work of knowing and the very distinction, as Kant put it, between sensation and consciousness.

Our own suffering does nothing more than that. It does nothing further to draw meaning to itself. That is the uselessness of it. It is as though to establish the aseity of suffering, its lack of need of any otherness to itself to assert itself. This is the import of Levinas's claim for suffering, already quoted, that it is "what disturbs order and this disturbance itself." As simultaneously cause and effect of itself, it gives the appearance of being self-caused. Like the pre-human of Rosenzweig, it precedes

---

6. Levinas, *Otherwise Than Being*, 8.
7. Levinas, *Otherwise Than Being*, 8.
8. Levinas, "Useless Suffering," 157.
9. Levinas, "Useless Suffering," 157.

relationality. And those of us who have suffered, especially in sickness, know the pall of the isolation it casts over our ailing self.

Such a train of thought uncovers for us the true target of Levinas's essay, which is theodicy, that is, explanatory schemas that justify suffering in relation to something else: the will of God, the whole of reality, or human free will. Levinas has no ears for any appeal to "a kingdom of transcendent ends, willed by a benevolent wisdom"[10] that ennobles our suffering. If we could say that suffering instructed us, humbled us, strengthened us, sensitized us, tested our mettle, as the poet Milton memorably put it, then we could, as Saint Paul did with death, extract the sting from it. But Levinas wants us to feel the sting. So let us have no more of Milton's effort to "justify the ways of God to men,"[11] by appeal to temptation-resisting human freedom. If as Milton puts it in his *Areopagitica*, he "cannot praise a fugitive and cloistered virtue unexercised and unbreathed, that never sallies out and seeks her adversary,"[12] that may say more about the limits of even his fertile imagination than about the nature of virtue.

For many of us, the event that presses forward to test the viability of Levinas's critique of suffering is the Holocaust. Levinas himself says as much—"The Holocaust of the Jewish people ... seems to us the paradigm of gratuitous human suffering"[13]—toward the end of his essay, under a section appropriately titled "The End of Theodicy." It is just the Holocaust that pounds the final and conclusive nail into the coffin of theodicy. The Holocaust neither punishes nor purifies nor justifies. It does nothing but confront us with a magnitude of suffering beyond belief.

Levinas does not rely on himself to make this point, but rather on the Canadian-Israeli philosopher Emil Fackenheim, whom he quotes at length. Fackenheim is one of several Jewish thinkers who underscore the pointlessness of the suffering endured over the Holocaust by deeming it a unique event. For uniqueness is in itself a challenge to explanation of any kind, whether in the service of meaningfulness or not. What is unique cannot be subsumed under a category. What cannot be subsumed under a category cannot be explained as an instance of a rule—it arrests all explanatory schemas of cause and effect or of instrumentality. It remains stubbornly resistant to all our meaning-producing efforts. Paradoxically,

10. Levinas, "Useless Suffering," 160.
11. *Paradise Lost* 1:25–26.
12. Milton, "Areopagitica," 167.
13. Levinas, "Useless Suffering," 162.

the Holocaust in all its resistance to categorization does indeed uniquely instance one category: useless suffering.

According to Fackenheim, "no thought can exist in the same space as the Holocaust."[14] It was "an eruption of demonism without analogy,"[15] "a scandal of particularity,"[16] a mania of totalizing oppression unlike "all other tyrannies."[17] To respond to it, "all past categories are inadequate."[18] Even to speak of so unique an evil strains language to the point of paradox. The more anyone "succeeds in explaining [the Holocaust], . . . the more nakedly he comes to confront its ultimate inexplicability."[19] Ordinarily, we understand whatever is real to be, or to have been, possible, prior to its realization. But in the case of the Holocaust, the relation between possibility and reality is inverted. The Holocaust was a realized *impossibility*, or, as Fackenheim puts it quoting philosopher Hans Jonas, "much more is real than is possible."[20]

Fackenheim is not alone in this view. In his book *The Tremendum*, philosophical writer Arthur Cohen, too, walks this path. He shares Fackenheim's sense that "thinking and the death camps are incommensurable,"[21] that the Holocaust was a "novelty in extremis, severed from all normative connections to historical precedent" (12), and "discontinuous with all that has been" (25). Cohen goes further than Fackenheim to name the historical break the Holocaust constitutes a *caesura*. He likens it to the break in historical time the revelation at Sinai was and is in Jewish consciousness. That obtrusion of exceptionality came from above. The caesura of the Holocaust came from below, but just as starkly establishes a Before and After: "Caesura in such a reversal can emerge from below, a verticality as infernal as incarnation may be divine" (52–53).

---

14. Fackenheim, *To Mend the World*, 191.

15. Fackenheim, *Jewish Return into History*, 29.

16. Fackenheim, *Jewish Return into History*, 92.

17. Fackenheim, *Jewish Return into History*, 258.

18. Fackenheim, *Jewish Return into* History, 109.

19. Fackenheim, *To Mend the World*, 233. Even so, there are attempts at explanation, to which Fackenheim himself contributes when he writes that what differentiates the Holocaust murders was "an unheard-of principle: that a whole group of people . . . are guilty by dint not of actions but of existence itself" (258). But is this an explanation or just a restatement of the problem? See also Katz, *Post-Holocaust Dialogues*, especially the last chapter, "The 'Unique' Intentionality of the Holocaust" (287–317).

20. Fackenheim, *To Mend the World*, 233.

21. Cohen, *Tremendum*, 1. Subsequent citations to pages of this text are given parenthetically.

If, for Fackenheim, the affront of the Holocaust to language showed in paradox and self-contradiction, for Cohen it manifests in startling reversals and inversions. The Holocaust is "a meaningless inversion of life [in] an orgiastic celebration of death" (19); an investment of the once exclusively divine power over life in "the potency of infinitized man" (18); a universalization of the particularity of Jewishness (11), since no distinctions between different kinds of Jew any longer mattered in their universal determination for death; and a particularization of what was formerly the universal category of evil (10). By this last inversion Cohen intends something similar to Fackenheim's paradox of realized impossibility. Evil was once a category that subsumed individual instances of it. With the Holocaust, the very category itself self-instantiated, in horrific inversion of the Christian idea of divine Incarnation. But, so particularized, evil ceased to serve as a subsuming category for the Holocaust. It ceased to serve as a categorizing universal at all and so lost its ability to supply meaning. The very meaning of evil itself imploded. After the Holocaust, "the judgment of good and evil seems pallid and worn-out.... How can we mean much with 'good and evil'?" (4). And so Cohen concludes, the Holocaust "is beyond the discourse of morality and rational condemnation" (8).

This is not an unusual turn for thought on the Holocaust to take. A striking feature of Elie Wiesel's now classic, novelistic memoir of the Holocaust, *Night*, is that, for all the suffering it records it barely comments, directly and overtly, on the morality of the proceedings. It fell to François Mauriac, who introduced the book,to reflect on its author's encounter at Auschwitz and Buchenwald with "absolute evil."[22] Readers sense that a mindset of moral judgment in the text would inevitably raise a conceptual wall between them and the historic sufferers, since, for the inmates, there was not the scope for thought of moral judgment, but only for the next crumb of bread. Wiesel's intent was as far as possible for the reader to identify with those who suffered in the camps and he musters all his poetic gifts to achieve that effect. But what is the philosopher to say? When I visited the Buchenwald memorial with a group of Jewish students, our non-Jewish German guide asked whether we wished his commentary on the site to accompany our visit, or whether we would

---

22. Wiesel, *Night*, 9.

prefer to register the scene, by ourselves, in silence.²³ Sometimes silence is best. And yet we continue to speak about the Holocaust.

Speaking of the unspeakable is the dark analog to describing the indescribable—a not uncommon practice of mystics in their efforts to render for non-mystics their experience of the divine and, as noted in the introduction to this book, a natural partner to negative theology. A negative theology of the Holocaust denies it meaning but not a capacity to be felt and heard across time. Jewish writers and memorialists of those who died or otherwise endured the Holocaust imitate the writer of Job, at least on our reading of that text: They aim to enroll the reader in the very suffering described. We shall see later on how Levinas shapes this gesture into a foundation of ethics. But this works less to endow with meaning the suffering described than, however minutely, to ease the burden of it. Useless suffering may resist explanation or justification; it is not immune to balms.

For Cohen, the Holocaust "resonates endlessly, without end" (48); it "makes claim upon us" (30); it is "so charged a reality as to require that the extremities of subjectivity and passion be engaged in its evocation" (40). Otherwise put, we cannot remain detached from those who died in the Holocaust when we think of them. To the extent possible, we must be with them, "hear the witness as though I were a witness, . . . be with the witness as though I were a witness" (23). This does not restore the deceased to life. But it rescues their deaths from oblivion.

Fackenheim takes the image of hearing further. For the Holocaust does indeed speak. It says to the surviving Jewish people: Remain Jewish! What emerges from any Jewish encounter with the Holocaust, philosophical, historical, or otherwise is "what I will boldly term a 614th commandment: the authentic Jew of today is forbidden to hand Hitler yet another, posthumous victory."²⁴ Jews augment that victory whenever they cease to affirm their Jewish identity. The affirmation need not be through halachic observance. On the contrary, the 614th commandment addresses both agnostic and believer, secularist and devout.²⁵

We are "to remember in our very guts and bones the martyrs of the Holocaust."²⁶ With this qualification, Fackenheim points away from the violence of execution to the dead themselves. For it is not really the

---

23. Rubinstein, "New German-Jewish Identity," 11–12.
24. Fackenheim, *Jewish Return into History*, 22.
25. Fackenheim, *Jewish Return into History*, 23.
26. Fackenheim, *Jewish Return into History*, 23–24.

Holocaust that speaks; it is those who died within it. In that way, those who might have been mere objects of our attention become subjects of the command they issue. So, they do indeed effectively re-live. We reduce ourselves to objects for the sake of their restored subjectivity.

If what rose into view from our negation of creation doctrine was the fragility of the presumed creation itself, what now appears in the wake of our negation of meaning to suffering are the balms available to bear it. Cohen and Fackenheim have been articulating those that manifest in remembrance of the Holocaust. But Levinas was not as convinced as they of the uniqueness of the suffering they described. The Holocaust may forefront a "paradigm of gratuitous suffering," as we already quoted him, but one that nonetheless "can be given a universal signification."[27] That is really the point of Levinas's essay. Suffering is *in itself* a uselessness. But it is not without balms. Here is how pastoral counselor Emily Click puts it for us, reflecting on what help she could be over the socially distanced time of the COVID-19 pandemic: "Once my eyes were opened to the universality of suffering, I relaxed from trying to ease it. . . . I was bearing witness to suffering in the human community. . . ."[28] But we would suggest the very bearing of witness works to ease the pain of those who suffer.

There is one Jewish philosopher who centered his thought on the quotidian ubiquity of human suffering and its balms: Baruch Spinoza. More precisely, the problem of our suffering occupies two central books of his magnum opus, *The Ethics*: part 3, "Concerning the Origin and Nature of the Emotions," and part 4, "Of Human Bondage, or the Nature of the Emotions." The concluding part 5 articulates a cure: "Of the Power of the Intellect, or of Human Freedom."

It is not that Spinoza did not have historical horrors of some piece with the Holocaust to endure. His family had fled the Portuguese Inquisition, whose roving eyes continued to regard with inimical intent the Sephardic *converso* refugees inhabiting the then United Provinces of the Netherlands. History, however, was not his concern, but rather geometry, optics, and the rising natural sciences. He openly confesses his resolve in *The Ethics* to examine our emotional lives "just as if it were an investigation into [geometric] lines, planes, or bodies."[29] Indeed,

---

27. Levinas, "Useless Suffering," 164.

28. Click, "Minister Cultivates Abiding," 18.

29. Spinoza, *Ethics*, 103. This is from the preface to pt. 3 of the *Ethics*, abbreviated E3preface. Further citations to the *Ethics* are given in this abbreviated form within the

the whole of *The Ethics*, written in Latin, the scholarly language of his day, follows the pattern of Euclid's geometry text, *The Elements*, in its treatment of everything from God to the good life by way of Euclidean definitions, axioms, propositions, and proofs.

That works in service of our negation of any *meaning* to emotional pain. It has no point or edifying goal to improve us in any way. If Levinas's target in his attack on the meaning of suffering was theodicy, Spinoza's was teleology—the Aristotelian notion much defended in his day that part of the cause of a thing was its goal in being. That reality moved toward goals filled it with meaning. But, for Spinoza (and the rising natural sciences), things did not have goals. They only had what Aristotle called efficient causes: predecessors that by necessitarian law issued in them, like fire resulting in heat, or ice in cold. As Rebecca Goldstein helpfully observes of Spinoza, he "managed to get the teleology out of physics by displacing Aristotle's final causes with Plato's mathematical conception of causality."[30] Emotions, like motions of any kind, "are assignable to definite causes through which they can be understood" (E3preface). That is their absence of meaning, but also the foundation of the balm for them, or better, our release from the burden of them.

It is an obvious premise for Spinoza that human life is full of emotional pain. His one autobiographical reference to this introduces his *Treatise on the Emendation of the Intellect*, an early work that preceded *The Ethics*. There he wrote of the "hollowness and futility of everything that is ordinarily encountered in daily life."[31] The sentiment echoes elsewhere: Our lives are "fraught with uncertainty and hazard";[32] we "are infinitely surpassed by the power of external causes" (E4p32s) much greater than us. That is another import of the starry heavens and the forces that govern them, as helped to fuel our denial of creation doctrine.

The problem of the emotions emerges from two key assumptions Spinoza makes, both of them much indebted to his predecessor in the so-called rationalist school of European philosophy, René Descartes, whom Spinoza admired and interpreted: that the more self-determining we are, the better off we are; and that emotions bridge the divide between body and mind—they are simultaneously bodily and mental. Now we can be

---

text. In the citations, *a* stands for axiom, *c* for corollary, *d* for definition, *p* for proposition, and s for scholium (note).

30. Goldstein, *Plato at the Googleplex*, 53.
31. Spinoza, *Ethics*, 233.
32. Spinoza, *Theological-Political Treatise*, 171.

very self-determining, as indeed Descartes was, in matters purely of mind. After all, if Descartes's famous *cogito* is true, "I think therefore I am," each of us enacts ourselves through sheer exercise of mind. That makes us, as mental beings, fairly self-determining. We can trace this view back to Plato's on the soul, which was also capable of a purely self-determined existence apart from the body. But our bodies are another story. They are prey, as Plato also said, to ten thousand ills, from sickness, natural disasters, violence suffered from war, conflict, criminality.

The problem of the emotions is that we are largely passive in our experience of them; they simply happen to us, mostly as effects of causes beyond our control. Their alternate name, *passions*, makes that clear. And the reason for the passivity they impose on us relates to their bodily aspect. As bodily phenomena they, like our bodies in general, are subject to external forces. Maimonides said as much, too. But as they are simultaneously psychological, the suffering they subject us to in body also impacts our mind (E3p11). When we suffer in body we suffer also in mind.

Many of us will find nothing remarkable in this claim. It is not so different from Levinas's view that suffering confuses the Kantian distinction between sensation and the understanding. We know from the attested phenomenon of psychosomatic suffering that mind and body do suffer in sync. Spinoza is suggesting that there is more of this than we realize and that it is as much the body impacting the mind as the reverse. And therapeutic applications of neuroscience draw our attention to correlations between chemical transactions in the brain and our own moods. By his preoccupation with the emotional side of the mind-body interaction, Spinoza could be said to have foretold the very field of neuropsychology.

To the extent that Spinoza was a rationalist like his mentor Descartes, he understood our reason and not our emotions to be our life's best guide. In that, he resembles Maimonides and Philo. Both would approve the final chapter of his book, "Of the Power of the Intellect." But Spinoza departs from Maimonides and the whole reason-loving tradition in a key way in that he identifies the body with the mind. This too has philosophical precedent in such materialist philosophies as ancient Stoicism. But Spinoza does not mean that the mind is material, composed perhaps of a refined kind of matter. He means that mind and body are parallel expressions of the same reality. As he provocatively puts it: "The order and connection of ideas is the same as the order and connection of things" (E2p7). It is as though we ourselves are a bilingual book that has the same text in different languages on facing pages. We live continuously in the simultaneous translation of the two languages of body and mind.

Spinoza intended this view to answer a problem he inherited from Descartes, who had separated mind and body as thoroughly from each other as they could possibly be, and so provoked the problem of how they could interrelate as they seem so clearly to do in our daily lives. For Spinoza, they are very different, but also identical, like two identical twins on opposite poles of a personality spectrum. In consequence, Spinoza departs from the disparagements of body we find in Philo and Maimonides. For a body identified with mind, in all its potential for self-determination, is suddenly ennobled. Spinoza associates the complexity of the human body with the larger capacities of the human mind: the one enables the other (E4p45c2s, also E4appendix27). For Spinoza, philosophers have not sufficiently credited the body, which amazes the mind with all it can do (E3p2s). As palliative care physician B. J. Miller puts it, "the body houses more than we can express."[33] Spinoza advocates more than a sound mind in a sound body; he associates our bodily complexity with our capacity for intellectual complexity. The body is such a wonder that he cannot fathom "why matter should be unworthy of the divine nature" (E1p15s). And this allies him more with Rosenzweig, whose enormous respect for the reality of death—its obtrusiveness into life—indirectly tributes the importance of the body. If its ending is truly a grief, its ongoing life must be a joy. And indeed, Spinoza encourages us to enjoy the energizing pleasures of life, from the sensual to the aesthetic and intellectual (E4p45c2s).

But only *in moderation*. The beginnings of our body-induced suffering is that we are typically *immoderate*. This had been Maimonides's complaint about us, too. In particular, "love and desire can be excessive" (E4p44) to the point of obsession. Surely Somerset Maugham had these theses in mind when he told Philip Carey's wrenching story of obsessive, unrequited love in *Of Human Bondage*, named after the title of part 4 of Spinoza's *Ethics*. Philip suffered terribly from jealousy, as Spinoza might have predicted, according to his analysis of that emotion (E3p35s). And Spinoza himself may have experienced unhappiness in love.[34] But jealousy is just one of a host of unattractive emotions that Spinoza analyzes, including contempt, derision, disparagement, envy,

33. Miller, "What Is Death?," 4.
34. Nadler, *Spinoza*, 126.

revenge, cruelty, dissipation, avarice, and lust (E3definitions of emotions 5,11,22,23,37,38,45,47,48).

It is not that there is not also joy, benevolence, courtesy, and compassion (E3definitions of emotions 16,24,35,43), but these do not predominate in our lives. We find them only in those guided by reason, who are rare (E4p17s). We are more generally prone to dislike (E4p35c2s), greed (E1Appendix), revenge over perceived slights (E3p41s), and a tendency to bore others with our self-centeredness (E3p55s) or vanity (E3p30s). What passes for humility is often concealed envy (E3definitions of emotions 29). And so it goes. If we are looking for an unapologetic exposure of how suffering manifests in human depravity—what Christians might call original sin—Spinoza obliges.

Even the more attractive emotions make a poor showing in Spinoza. Those of us accustomed to high estimates of love, such as we find in Saint Paul, at 1 Cor 13, will be disheartened to learn that "love is merely pleasure accompanied by the idea of an external cause" (E3p13s). That "merely"—*nihil aliud*—already demotes the emotion of love. But then, by Spinoza's reductive account of the emotions, all of them reduce to pleasure, pain, and desire (E3p11s) in some combination with each other and the things that cause them. Emotions are psychosomatic experiences of either raised or lowered energy (E3d3); when of raised energy they instance pleasure; when of lowered energy, pain (E3definition of emotions 2,3). Desire is simply the endeavor endemic to us as far as possible to experience raised energy (E3definition of emotions 1, E4p59). From these three primal emotions, Spinoza derives forty-five others, neatly defined at the end of part 3 of his *Ethics*, some of which we have already named. But even more of them exist unnamed and beyond what can be numbered (E3p59s).

It stands to reason that with so many emotions potentially at play within us, some of them will conflict with others. For instance, we self-divide over the love we receive from someone we dislike (E3p41c). Some opposite emotions spring from the same source, such as compassion and envy (E3p32s), grounded alike in susceptibility. The same is true of hope and fear (E3p50s). No wonder Spinoza likens us to storm-tossed vessels on this sea of emotion (E3p59s), drowning in our lack of direction and focus (E3definition of emotions 1).

And yet, by this very account, Spinoza has begun to turn us in at least one direction: away from emotionality as such. The seemingly unfeeling starkness of his approach to emotional life is part of the treatment of them as though they were "lines, planes, or bodies" (E3preface). But it is also the first step toward our freedom from bondage to them. For insofar as we suffer them, as we largely do, we fail in the high desideratum of self-determination. Spinoza's descriptions of the emotions subtly wean us from attachment to them, as a Buddhist or Stoic meditation on them might do. His largely negative characterization of them serves to negate a negative—our accustomed emotionality of envy, dislike, boredom, vanity, and obnoxiousness. And a negative negated is a positive.

Spinoza's account of the mind/body relation, that each is the other in a different language, serves in the weaning process. For it comes as a liberative surprise to learn that neither of these can really affect the other (E3p2). In the resemblance of their paradoxical relation to a bilingual text, mind and body cannot intermingle, any more than the German, say, on one side of a dual-language translation into English from the German properly mingles, lexicographically, with the semantically identical English on the other side. A bodily reality cannot figure in the causal sequence that produces a thought any more than a German word can figure—without italic typeface or quotes around it—in an English sentence. This is counterintuitive. When a neighbor says something that hurts me, it seems like a bodily presence outside me, my neighbor, has impacted my inner sanctum of thought—my self-esteem. But no: what has happened is that a bodily chain of causation involving mouth motions in my neighbor, sound reaching my ear, fluids flowing in my body, nerves being stimulated, and brain cells activated has resulted in a lower bodily energy for me. Parallel with that, and by a purely mental causal chain perhaps beyond my ken, a thought of my neighbor's, in identity with his bodily act, has impacted a thought of mine that results in lower psychological energy. But my neighbor as bodily being has no effect on my mind. I have misconstrued the source of my mental hurt. A thought outside me has affected a thought inside me. That is all. My bodily neighbor standing there is innocent of my mental hurt.

Of course, such a train of thought radically reconfigures my own identity, and also my neighbor's. My neighbor is one or the other, or both, of two: a body and a mind, as am I. His body interacts with mine; his mind with mine. But not his body with my mind. This suggests an order of bodies relating to each other in one world alongside an order of minds interacting in parallel within another world. We straddle the two worlds, like a single stick half submerged in water that appears to the eye with two identities: one that dwells in water, the other in air. But for Spinoza, this is true of everything. It is just that inanimate physicalities have less of mental correspondence than we and other animals do. Spinoza employs a helpful metaphor to explain us to ourselves when we think we are minds governing bodies (as Descartes thought): dreaming with our eyes open. Minds are no more the *agents* of bodily acts than I am when I dream with my eyes open.[35] Rather, my mental acts *are* my bodily acts in the dual text I am.

And now a third feature of minds and bodies unfolds to distance us yet further from our emotions. If minds are not the agents of bodily acts, who or what is?—simply other bodies. A body moves or rests in consequence of the impact on it, or not, of other bodies (E2p13Lemma3). The same is true of the denizens of our minds, which are ideas—a term that for Spinoza covers imageless abstractions, images, and emotions insofar as they are mental (E2p48). Ideas impact other ideas. Part of the reason our emotional lives are so rich is that images can take the form of memories of things from our past that affect us emotionally as though they were present (E3p18). But the point is that whatever we are feeling at the bodily or psychological level is caused by antecedent bodies or ideas (E1p28). If everything is caused, there is no contingency (E1p29); and if no contingency, no free will (E2p48). There is no more room for freedom in this vision of ourselves than there is in the unfolding of a mathematical proof. This is, in the end, what it means to treat emotions as geometric lines and planes.

Insofar as ethics in our common understanding of the term presupposes the freedom that enables responsibility, Spinoza's book *The Ethics* is ironically named. Whatever will we have is itself necessitated and necessitating, never free (E1p32). And we soon learn that our moral terms, too, have no meaning that cannot be reduced to a base emotional ground. "By good I mean that which we certainly know to be useful to us" (E4d1), i.e., to raise our energy. Spinoza sacrifices an ancient, Platonic understanding of ethics, by which a vision of Goodness climaxes the ethical life, for a deterministic view he assures us is of happier consequence. For a deterministic worldview fosters a tranquil and patient mind, free of the turbulent emotions attendant on the illusion of free will.

---

35. See E3p2s and E3p26s. Spinoza employs this metaphor to other ends in both these cases, but it serves just as well to capture the illusion of causal efficacy between mind and body. He also suggests that sleepwalking proves that the mind does not cause the body's acts (E3p2s).

Perhaps this is the outcome of any deterministic philosophy we might embrace. What *must* be, by its very resistance to possibility, disarms our whole emotional life of stress and worry (E4appendix32). In our resignation to the determinations of being, we are freed from all the negative emotions Spinoza has cataloged. But we can receive Spinoza's ethics in another spirit, not so much of resignation as of gratitude for the sheer starkness of his presentation. There is relief in an honest diagnosis, however harsh, even before the therapeutic cure begins. If we follow Levinas's advice to banish all theodicies, then along with them we renounce all false consolations for the human condition. Like the fence around the law the rabbis built, to keep us from inadvertently breaking any rules, we can take Spinoza to have distanced us enough from our emotions not to be tempted by any false comforts they promise.

But let us follow Spinoza's therapy a little further. As it happens, the emotions as a group do offer one substantive pleasure, that of lending themselves to being understood. As necessary effects, or passions, they are understood through their causes. This understanding is already freeing for us (E5p6). Any emotion understood effectively converts from a passion to an action (E5p3), from a kind of suffering to an act of self-determination. For Spinoza, the act of understanding is itself a self-determinative act. It is self-determined because our own reason is the direct cause of anything we understand. However much it may itself be determined by prior causes, when our reason understands something it has only itself immediately to thank for that accomplishment. Things flourish in the exercise of their own nature. Since understanding is the whole point of reason, its success in that act precipitates a psychosomatic rise in energy for the whole reasoning organism (E4p63). Indeed, Spinoza insists that reason is never a source of pain (E4appendix3), as knowledge never was for Maimonides.

There is more to the energy we can derive from understanding our emotions. But it takes us more deeply into Spinoza's metaphysics and epistemology. For instance, we learn near the start of his system that we are simultaneously much less and much more than we think we are—much less, in that we are modes of something else; much more, in what we are modes of. My individual body turns out to be part of a larger corpus of causally connected bodies that constitutes a whole greater than its parts, called extension. And my mind turns out to be part of a corpus of mental activity embracing all that was, is, or ever will be conceived, called thought; and extension and thought are attributes of God. We are embedded in God, like a cell in our body. Spinoza's God, which is not a creator God and so unnegated by our negation of creation doctrine, is available to us both as a release from emotional pain and as focus of spiritual life. But that is for chapter 10. Up to now, Spinoza has served us more simply by discerning in the negation of any meaning to our negative emotions a release from the burden of them.

Levinas has little truck with Spinoza. Spinoza was a disturbance to him, as to several modern Jewish philosophers. He wrote that Spinoza was "guilty of betrayal," for the fact that "he subordinated the truth of Judaism to the revelation of the New Testament."[36] In his *Theological-Political Treatise* Spinoza did indeed write warmly of Jesus, who, he suggested, "communed with God mind to mind,"[37] which is just about the highest praise anyone could win from Spinoza. But Spinoza is even more disturbing for his exorbitant rationalism. For Levinas, reason's role in the uselessness of suffering is to be stymied by it, not energized toward healing it. Suffering, far from enlisting a help from reason, gums up its works, as Emil Fackenheim and Arthur Cohen underscore for us in the case of the Holocaust. And perhaps Spinozist reason is too austere a help for many of us. Let us close with one more discernment that may be provoked to view by negating the meaning of suffering, and which bypasses the debate over rationalism: the consolations of art. Two thinkers especially come to mind here: one of the oldest in the tradition of Jewish philosophy, the biblical writer Ecclesiastes (Kohelet), and one of the most recent, Rosenzweig, who has already helped us to negate creation doctrine.

Ecclesiastes did not expressly negate it, but might as well have, for all the nihilism of his worldview. From the standpoint of meaning, the world is a barren place, past finding out (3:11, 8:17) and, famously, fraught with vanity. God may have created the world (12:1) but is not visible behind or above it. The causal connections of the world that work therapeutically for Spinoza only dumbfound Ecclesiastes. Contradictions abound. The good suffer and the wicked prosper (7:15); labor is in vain (2:18–19); "He that diggeth a pit [for a grave, say] shall fall into it [himself]" (10:8), says Ecclesiastes in a foretelling of slapstick comedy. Comparative religionist Jack Miles finds in Ecclesiastes "as thoroughly secular a worldview as can be imagined."[38] And biblical scholar R. B. Y. Scott

---

36. Levinas, *Difficult Freedom*, 108.
37. Spinoza, *Theological-Political Treatise*, 14.
38. Miles, *God*, 353.

opines, in welcome support of our own project, that what Ecclesiastes offers up is in its breadth a "philosophy of negation."[39]

And yet, this book of vanities closes with one of the loveliest poems in the whole Tanak. As though in echo of the author's own closing life (he self-presents as aged), the book itself ends in a meditation on death: "Remember . . . the days of thy youth, before the evil days come, and the years draw nigh, . . . in the day when the keepers of the house shall tremble . . . and the mourners go about the streets . . . and the dust returneth to the earth as it was" (12:1–7). It is a series of metaphors for death and dying. But the beauty of the poem carries compassion for its readers. The form of the poem belies its content. By its very beauty, it negates the theme that "all is vanity" (1:2) since it itself is far from vain, but an early instance of consolatory art. Long before Saint Paul, Ecclesiastes extracted the sting of death by the beauty of his words on it. It is as though from compassion toward his mortal listeners and readers, the writer would beautify death or wreath it in loveliness. It is like one of the Schubert lieder, *Wiegenlied*, a lullaby, which seems to put a child to sleep but actually to his eternal rest: "Schlafe, schlafe, in dem süssen Grabe" [sleep, sleep, in the sweet grave].[40]

And now comes Rosenzweig to theorize the consolations of art, which manifest most visibly against a backdrop of meaning denied to suffering. For Rosenzweig, like Levinas, has no ears for theodicy. "Art overcomes suffering only by giving it figurative shape and not by denying it" (SR399). Rosenzweig has the Christian cross in mind which, whether or not a crucifix, holds the attention of Christian worshipers at the head of processions, at the altar, on the very robes of the clergy. It "represents" (SR399) suffering without canceling it out, and so as to ease it. In the easement it even assumes a comic form, as it might at Mardi Gras, and as Ecclesiastes may have had in mind when one of his images for the "ever-present poverty and deficiency of existence"—Rosenzweig's words (SR399)—was a grave-digger accidentally fallen into the grave. "Art as representation is tragic and comic in one" (SR399).

But there is Jewish art too. A metalworker at a medieval arts fair, who made crosses of nails, once fashioned for me a Star of David made of the same material. It is a transposition of the suffering the cross configures onto the star, the very symbol for Rosenzweig's magnum opus.

---

39. Scott, *Proverbs, Ecclesiastes*, 206.

40. The same is true of "The Brook's Lullaby" that closes Schubert's song cycle, *Die Schöne Müllerin* (Schubert, *Complete Song Texts*, 177–78, 363).

Ritual objects make a redoubt of safety in the memorable film *Madame Rosa*, directed by Moshé Mizrahi, in which a Holocaust survivor played by Simone Signoret finds rest from her painful memories of World War II among her stash of menorahs and Sabbath candleholders stored in the basement of her building. And in a poem that celebrates the artistry of stained glass windows designed by Jacob Landau and installed at Reform Congregation Keneseth Israel, in Elkins Park, Pennsylvania, Tanak scholar Danna Nolan Fewell reflects, in a poem entitled "Stained Windows," on the power of stained glass to figure suffering within a framework of beauty.[41] In this series of windows celebrating the biblical prophets, one of them, unexpectedly, takes its cues from the book of Job, who by standard Jewish reckoning was less prophet than Wisdom writer. But it gave the artist an opportunity he considered, but in the end rejected, to illustrate a theme from that book, that God "destroyeth the innocent and the wicked" (9:22)[42]—an implicit denial of logic to suffering that Professor Fewell also references in her poem. Fewell credits Rosenzweig for the idea that art, alternatively, can *structure* suffering without presuming to explain it. We would add, it is just the refusal to otherwise negate what Rosenzweig called the "deficiency of existence" that allows that structure to come into view.

---

41. Fewell, "Stained Windows," 87.
42. Herrstrom, "*Prophetic Quest* of Jacob Landau," 113n2.

Chapter 3
The Jewish People

JEWISH IDENTITY IS MYSTERIOUS. I can spend a lifetime seeking it out, as Ecclesiastes did the meaning of life, and never find it. I can practice Judaism; join synagogues; advocate for the State of Israel; contribute to Jewish philanthropies; learn Hebrew, Yiddish, and Ladino; study Jewish history; express pride in my ancestors; enjoy lox and bagels—and still miss the core of the identity. For I can also cease to do all these things and find myself just as Jewish as before. I can even join another religion. The Jewishness remains, but undefined.

The noted scholar of Jewish philosophy Harry Austryn Wolfson (1887–1974) implies a thought-experiment: Imagine, he writes, "we could start on a given day with a new generation of Jews and raise them in absolute freedom from all traces of Jewish influence." Imagine all preconceived notions of Jewishness pared away. "You cannot go on annulling without having something left of Judaism. There will always be a residuum of Judaism that will make you uncomfortable and demand some sacrifice."[1] But that residuum of Jewishness appears to resist all definition and, for all the sacrifice it demands, deflect from itself all content.

German playwright Max Frisch makes the same point, in reverse, within his play *Andorra*, about a community ridden with anti-Semitism. In that drama, one of the characters, Andri, is taken for Jewish by birth, even by himself, when he is not. But qualities stereotypically associated with Jews are imputed to him to the point that he believes he actually has them. Only Andri's father knows his true, non-Jewish birth. In the wake of

1. Wolfson, *Escaping Judaism*, 4, 49.

the anti-Semitic jibes Andri suffers, the father advises him to stop "believing what they [the townspeople] say. Just remember there's nothing in it."[2] He could be critiquing either anti-Semitism itself, or, very indirectly, the lie that Andri is Jewish. Or, for our purposes, he could be suggesting that the content of Jewishness is nothing. An inference from the story is that the attribute of Jewishness carries with it no distinct qualities.

The word *Jew* does not explain itself. It is like the pawprint left by a creature we cannot identify. It has shape without content. Still, it calls out to some of us and we respond. It is a little like the God who appears in the biblical book of Job. Job beseeches God to explain Godself. God refuses. Instead, God supplies a display of power. The little collection of words, Jew, Jewish, Jewishness, behaves just that way. They won't explain themselves. They simply hold in thrall those who hear their call. Whether we do or not can be a matter of life or death, as it was in Europe during the 1940s, or of privilege or prejudice, as in the State of Israel today.

Consider the case of the French Jewish philosopher Simone Weil (1909–1943). She lived during a time when Jewishness was a death warrant. Under the Vichy regime in France, Weil lost her teaching position in the French lycées. In an astonishing act of bold naiveté, she wrote the Minister of Education protesting that to suspend her from teaching on account of her presumed Jewishness was absurd, since the concept did not apply to her. "I do not know the definition of the word, 'Jew'; that subject was not included in my education. . . . I have never been in a synagogue and have never witnessed a Jewish religious ceremony. . . . I myself . . . have certainly inherited nothing from the Jewish religion. . . . Mine is the Christian, French, Greek tradition. The Hebraic tradition is alien to me, and no statute can make it otherwise."[3] The letter had no effect, and if Weil had not fled France with her parents for New York in 1942, she and they surely would have perished.

Weil was entirely sincere. That Weil was held to her contentless Jewishness by others highlights another feature of it, that it is unchosen. Weil herself admits as much when, in the same letter, she reflects that if "the law insists that I consider the term, 'Jew,' whose meaning I don't know, as applying to me, I am inclined to submit, as I would to any other law."[4] Leave aside that it is French (or German) rather than Jewish law that she would submit to—the point is the submission. It is

---

2. Frisch, *Andorra*, 32.
3. Weil, "What Is a Jew," 79–80.
4. Weil, "What Is a Jew," 80–81.

as though the word claims adherents even over their inability to understand what it wants of them. Perhaps this is part of what rabbinic tradition captured when it defined Jewishness by birth. Just as we are born to parents we have not chosen, so we are to Jewishness. We enter the world ensconced in it, as in (hopefully) our parents's love. Rosenzweig drew out this feature of Jewish identity in contrast with its Christian complement and counterpart. For Christians acquire their religious identity (SR418), while Jews are born into theirs (SR419).

This is true even of converts. The adoptive parents, Abraham and Sarah, project a fiction of born Jewishness onto the convert. The fiction tells a truth of *all* Jewish self-consciousness, that Jewish identity is always found within, never acquired or assumed, like the Sabbath candles that appear to their candle-lighter as though already lit when, having lit them and closed her eyes, she opens them onto the little flames, which seem without anyone's work to have brightened the beginning of the Sabbath rest. Some go so far as to say that the conversion ceremony itself is just an afterthought to a prior sense of already being Jewish, quite apart from parental identity. As Gershom Scholem wrote in his own reflection on Jewish identity, "I do not think Jewish descent is the only element. . . . Jews . . . are entitled to define themselves according to their own needs and impulses. . . . Jewish identity is not a fixed or static."[5] He does not go so far as to say that Jewishness is a matter of self-declaration, regardless of birth. But Israeli writer Amos Oz does: "A Jew, in my vocabulary, is someone who regards himself as a Jew."[6] We would only add: so regards himself because he finds Jewishness, howsoever contentless, within himself, as Rosenzweig suggested. The givenness of Jewishness precedes the affirmation of it the convert practices, and it remains given, whether affirmed or not.

But now consider the case of Israeli historian Shlomo Sand, who might beg to differ. From disgust over the Israeli government's policies toward Palestinian inhabitants of Israel, the West Bank, and Gaza, Sand authored the book *How I Stopped Being a Jew*. Sand knows the received view that "a Jew is a Jew and . . . there is no way a person can escape an identity given at birth."[7] But Sand opines that, absent its religious core, Jewish identity is so empty of content as not to exist. For, he suggests, there is no unifying *secular* identity of Jewishness. Sand is like a

5. Scholem, "Who Is a Jew?," 138, 139.
6. Oz, "Meaning of Homeland," 19.
7. Sand, *How I Stopped Being a Jew*, 1.

Buddhist who interprets the Hindu claims for the soul, that in its absence of qualities it cannot be defined, as evidence that it does not exist at all.[8] Jewishness is a collectively imagined identity whose seeming givenness is itself part of its fiction. An individual Jew may assume that fiction, but need not. Sand writes of his Jewishness, "I am today fully conscious . . . that such an imaginary characteristic lacks any specific basis or cultural perspective and . . . now, having painfully become aware that I have undergone an adherence to Israel, have been assimilated by law into a fictitious ethnos of persecutors and their supporters, . . . I wish to resign and cease considering myself a Jew."[9]

Unlike Weil, who would submit to the French law of her Jewishness if she understood it, Sand rejects the Jewishness imposed on him by Israeli (and rabbinical) law. He will renounce the privileges of Jewish identity if they come at the expense of Palestinian suffering. But does he really renounce them? He characterizes his renunciation as a *wish*. There is no doubt he has rejected the policies of the Israeli government. But that government will hold him to his Jewishness, as will most of his readers. An ironic rejoinder may even sound: His very rejection of his Jewishness is itself Jewish! Jews are, after all, as the Bible insists, a stiff-necked people. Jewish identity is not so easily shed.

This chapter reviews the elusiveness of Jewish identity as it shows in Jewish tradition and history; then explores what comes to light when we expressly deny of Jewish identity any descriptive content. A provocative finding: Jewish identity shows an affinity with the God of negative theology. That affinity has implications we explore for two relational features of Jewish identity, as traditionally understood, that take their bearings from the idea of God: that the people are exceptionally chosen and that they enjoy a definitive covenant with God. These concepts, examined through a negative theological lens, appear also in a new light.

Most of us know the standard account of what it means to be Jewish: to have been born of a Jewish mother. Even converts become Jewish by adoption into the Jewish people. This is according to Jewish law, but is also a very common understanding. The problem, as historian Shlomo Sand implies, is that this definition of Jewishness pushes the content

---

8. The doctrine of *anatta*, or no-soul, is a fundamental teaching of Theravada Buddhism, in rebellion against a teaching of the Hindu Upanishads that the soul is too infinitesimally small to have discernible qualities at all (Svetasvatara Upanishad 5:8–10, in *Thirteen Principal Upanishads*).

9. Sand, *How I Stopped Being a Jew*, 97.

TOWARD A NEGATIVE THEOLOGY OF JUDAISM

of the designation continuously backward, "until the dawn of time,"[10] where it remains elusive. Perhaps we need not go so far. If the Bible is any guide, we might take the first Jewish mother to have been Sarah; except that historians give no assurance Sarah ever existed. Perhaps she and the stories about her are meaning-disclosive myths that emerged, after her presumed time, from a collective Jewish consciousness trying to understand itself.

Shaye J. D. Cohen has traced the quandary of Jewishness back to the ancient world. "Jewish identity in antiquity was elusive and uncertain.... There was no single or simple definition of Jew."[11] Matters have not much changed. Cohen confesses of Jewishness generally that "I cannot claim to have penetrated to the inner mystery of Jewish identity or 'Jewishness,' the qualities that make a Jew a Jew."[12] There is "no empirical, objective, verifiable reality to which we can point and over which we can exclaim, 'This is it!' Jewishness is in the mind.... We are speaking of an 'imagined community.'"[13] Emmanuel Levinas puts it most simply and boldly when he references "the mystery of Israel."[14]

If Jewishness is the product of a collective imagination, it is no less real than if it arises from shared DNA, a notion that has been floated but never definitively established. The challenge of Jewish identity in either case, whether imagined or biological, is to fill in the mere outline that recourse to the imagination and/or biology supplies. What are the features of that identity? Levinas speculates that "Judaism cannot even be called a culture, it is a vague sensibility made up of various ideas, memories, and emotions together with a feeling of solidarity towards Jews who were persecuted as Jews."[15] It would not even be questioned but for its precipitous loss, suggests Levinas: "The very fact of questioning one's Jewish identity means it is already lost. But by the same token, it is precisely through this kind of cross-examination that one still hangs on to it."[16] But what is hung onto?

Let us dispense with any appeal to physical characteristics. For all the loose reference among both Jews and non-Jews to a Jewish physicality

10. Sand, *How I Stopped Being a Jew*, 2.
11. Cohen, *Beginnings of Jewishness*, 3.
12. Cohen, *Beginnings of Jewishness*, 3.
13. Cohen, *Beginnings of Jewishness*, 5.
14. Levinas, *Difficult Freedom*, 24.
15. Levinas, *Difficult Freedom*, 24.
16. Levinas, *Difficult Freedom*, 50.

or appearance, in facial features or skin color, we all know there are always exceptions to these stereotypes, as Jews who passed for gentiles in Nazi Germany attest. Shaye Cohen is explicit about at least the ancient world: "Not a single ancient author says that Jews are distinctive because of their looks, clothing, speech, names, or occupations."[17]

Perhaps the problem here is perspectival. It may be the word *Jew* has no meaning in the singular, like the word *troops*. Is there ever a single troop sent abroad to right some wrong? Perhaps the three letters of this word only carry meaning in the collective of the Jewish people, or Israel. Israel, itself the divinely given name for the patriarch Jacob, functions to name not only the collectivity of the modern State of Israel, but all the putative descendants of Jacob himself. It is the biblical name for the Jewish collective, often rendered biblically as the Children of Israel. Perhaps Jewishness is properly a collective, not an individuality.

Shaye Cohen helps us here, too. At the collective level, the Jewish people is or would certainly pass for an ethnic group. Sociology has indeed roughly defined that term, as Cohen channels for us. An ethnic group is "a social group whose members share a sense of common origins, claim a common and distinctive history and destiny, possess one or more distinctive characteristics, and feel a sense of collective uniqueness and solidarity."[18] Once again, we have the outline of an identity but not its content. Cohen's task is to supply that, or at least identify the obstacles to supplying that. And now on the collective level, just as on the individual, there proves to be one. It is not that no content shows forth, but that two do in confused relation with each other. The word itself, *Jew*, only gained currency in late Hellenistic times. On the one hand, a Jew was a Judean—someone who inhabited or descended from inhabitants of the Hellenistic and then Roman region of Judea, once the ancient Jewish kingdom of Judah. The term referenced a geographic identity. That was the point of common origin and the basis for the sense of solidarity, collective history, shared characteristics. But in time, especially in light of the large Jewish diaspora of the time, the term took on religious overtones. It also and alternatively referenced the set of religious practices that distinguished the followers of the law of Moses. Now the point of origin extended back further to a prior Judah, the son of Jacob, and indeed to Jacob himself under his divinely given name, Israel. The sense

---

17. Cohen, *Beginnings of Jewishness*, 28.
18. Cohen, *Beginnings of Jewishness*, 6.

of solidarity, collective history, and shared characteristics were now religious and biblically, not geographically, based.

The result was confusion in the ancient world over just who or what the Jewish people were. And that ambiguity within Jewish ethnicity over a joint geographic and religious grounding has persisted through history.

Shlomo Sand makes much of this. He targets especially the ancient, geographic basis of Jewish identity as a foundation for Jewish identity today. His point is that there is not only no DNA evidence for a continuous line of descent from the ancient Judeans of either the Jewish state or the Roman province to the Jews of today, neither is there historical evidence for it. On the contrary, birth-giving among those who have historically identified as Jews over time has involved a multiplicity of different ethnic groups. Sand's key defense of this claim turns on what he takes to be a much larger phenomenon of conversion into Judaism over time than Jewish self-consciousness typically allows. The biblical book of Esther, howsoever mythic, may tell a truth of Persian conversion to Judaism (8:17). But Sand cites literary and/or historical evidence of ancient conversion into Judaism under the Maccabean rulers of the temporarily restored Jewish kingdom; under Queen Helena of the kingdom of Adiabene (first century CE); and under the Roman emperors, up until the fourth century CE, when Rome went Christian under Constantine. The story picks up massively with the conversion of the medieval Khazars "between the mid-eighth and mid-ninth centuries,"[19] whose descendants, Sand suggests, became the Jews of Eastern Europe—which would make them, he wryly comments, closer to "the Hun, Uigar and Magyar tribes than to the seed of Abraham, Isaac, and Jacob" (239).

Sand argues that population estimates of ancient Jewry—perhaps as many as eight million Jews worldwide in the first century CE (146)—could only have come about through massive conversion,[20] and that the universalist streams of later scriptural writings, in the books of Isaiah, Ruth, Jonah, and Judith (151), also attest indirectly to gates opened wide for converts. If many Jews today deny that Jews ever proselytized that only shows, Sand suggests, how much the story Jews have invented

---

19. Sand, *Invention of the Jewish People*, 221. Subsequent citations to pages of this text are given parenthetically.

20. Sand quotes (in translation) from a 1965 doctoral dissertation (in Hebrew) by Uriel Rapaport: "Given its great scale, the expansion of Judaism in the ancient world cannot be accounted for by natural increase, by migration from the homeland, or any other explanation that does not include outsiders joining it" (Sand, *Invention of the Jewish People*, 154). See Rapaport, "Jewish Religious Propaganda."

about themselves as an ethnic group has taken hold of them—so driven are they to make sense of their identity in genealogical and geographic terms. A genealogically continuous ethnic group of such ancient provenance, grounded in ancient Judea, and back further, in the patriarch Judah and his siblings, the Children of Israel, would indeed be a point of pride, to say nothing of a basis, as we shall see in the next chapter, for a modern nation-state of the Jewish people. But Sand will have none of it: "The people known to the world as Jews . . . have never been, and are still not, a people or a nation" (21) as commonly understood.

What are Jews, then?—an association, Sand opines, of "significant religious communities that appeared and settled in various parts of the world" (22). Sand blames the nationalist Jewish historians of the nineteenth century for the fiction of a three-millennia old continuous Jewish genealogy. Only one of the older historians, he suggests, Isaak Jost (1793–1860), got the history right when he identified the Jewish people, in Sand's paraphrase, as "a scattering of religious communities" (91) of diverse ethnicities. Sand argues that, in any case, the bond of religion offers a much better explanation for long-term Jewish survival than ethnicity does. "Religions survived through the ages," he writes, "while empires, kingdoms, principalities and peoples rose and fell" (56). How true. But how strange in this day and age of secular or cultural Jewishness to identify Jewishness with religion. Was it not the scholar David Biale who told us in the introduction to this book that Jews today are disproportionately secular?

If it is religion that has held the Jewish people together, its absence spells the end of Jewish identity entirely. There is no "secular" identity to fill the breach. For it already follows from Sand's denial of Jewish ethnicity that "there has never been a secular Jewish culture common to all the Jews of the world" (285). And so we are back to the notion of contentless identity which we already encountered at the level of the individual Jew, but now at the level of the Jewish people. Sand insists that the lack of content for Jewish ethnicity means it does not exist at all. What exists is a loose confederation of religious thoughts and practices that goes under the name *Judaism*. Where this has fallen away, all that makes for Jewish identity is a sense of attachment to the memory of it—hardly enough to constitute an identity.

We do not go so far as to deny a nonreligious Jewish identity entirely. Our negative theological approach merely denies it definitive content. Let us then grant for our starting point a contentless Jewish identity. What comes to light in the wake of this negation? The Jewish philosophers offer up some candidates. The first we consider comes by way of analogy and may take us by surprise. For there is one other term within the Jewish repertoire of concepts that, according to a significant strain within the philosophical tradition, lacks any content we can specify. And that is God.

To follow up this lead, we need to go back to Philo's etymology for the word *Israel*, the other name for the Jewish people. Biblical names often carry meanings apart from the sheer sound of them. A standard Torah commentary will relate the name Israel to the biblical Hebrew verbal root for striving, *s-r-h*, in accord with the story of the name's origin in Jacob's struggle or striving with an angel (Gen 32:29)—"Thy name shall be called no more Jacob, but Israel,[21] for thou hast striven with God." This story helps bolster a stereotypical view of Jews even among Jews as lovers of argument. But Philo reads for the name a different etymology, based on the verbal root for seeing: *r-ʾ-h*. For Philo, Israel is "that which sees God" (Leg. 3 186). It is not a matter of striving but of mystical vision. This etymology casts a very different light on the Jewish people. For as many mystics will tell us, Philo among them, what is seen in the vision of God cannot be described. Like the Jewish people, God's identity is without definable or describable content. In echo of the divine name—*I am that I am*—revealed to Moses at the burning bush (Exod 3:14), God for Philo is simply The Existent, *to on* in Greek (Det. 153). Beyond that, language reduces to silence in the face of God. There is a coincidence of absent essence in both the Jewish people and the biblical appearance of God to Moses.

It might give us pause that, faced with our own contentless identity, the counterpart in contentlessness that rises up most readily from the tradition to partner with us in that status is God. We have negated creation doctrine, but not the notion of God as such. What if Jewishness is a microcosm of contentless identity and God the macrocosm of it? The natural affinity between the two becomes a gateway to a philosophical understanding of Jewishness we are poised to explore. The notion of God becomes a mirror in which Jewish identity can see and recognize its contentless nothingness as something.

One of the most remarkable understandings of a God-illumined Jewish identity comes from the medieval Jewish philosopher Judah Halevi

---

21. "That is, *He who striveth with God*," according to Hertz, *Pentateuch and Haftorahs*, 124.

(1075–1141). Indirectly, Shlomo Sand already pointed this way in his reference to the medieval Khazars, the Turkic people whose leaders converted to Judaism, so the history books attest: "In the early Middle Ages, the Jewish faith gained additional adherents when many members of the ruling class of the Khazar kingdom on the estuary of Volga to the Caspian Sea, headed by their king, adopted Judaism as their religion."[22] Halevi, the Andalusian philosopher and poet, imagined the thought process that persuaded the Khazar king to adopt Judaism over the rival bids for his affections from Christianity, Islam and, perhaps most interestingly, philosophy, understood as a spiritual path apart from the religions. Halevi's book *The Kuzari* pictures the king briefly in dialogue with a philosopher, a Christian, and a Muslim, before turning to the rabbi who, over the course of the book, persuades him to adopt Judaism.

Halevi's presentations of Judaism's rivals are remarkably sympathetic, a witness, perhaps, to the success of the Andalusian *Convivencia* of the monotheisms that has stimulated so much warm, if idealized, memory of that place and time. The king has had a dream in which he learns from a divine voice that "Thy way of thinking is indeed pleasing to the Creator, but not thy way of acting."[23] So the king seeks guidance on how to behave. The philosopher is too enamored of sheer contemplation to have much advice on action; the Christian and Muslim both presume miraculous events—the Incarnation of God, the Revelation of the Quran—that strain the king's credulity. Only the rabbi offers a way of acting, the Jewish way, that persuades the king on grounds of the believable evidence for the divine sanction of it: the over six hundred thousand Jews who actually witnessed the revelation of the law, according to Num 1:46, with their eyes and ears, the memory of which they reliably bequeathed to their descendants over the millennia.

Never mind that the witness of the six hundred thousand only carries weight for those who already, on some other grounds, accept the reliability of the Bible, evidence for which cannot, without circularity, be the six hundred thousand themselves. What endears about Judah Halevi is how much of a loner he was within the medieval Jewish philosophical ambiance of reason-veneration, which Maimonides has already instanced for us. For Halevi, reason already shows its weakness in that it cannot prove creation doctrine. Maimonides flagged that too for

---

22. Ben-Sasson, "Middle Ages," 395.

23. Halevi, *Kuzari*, 35. Subsequent citations to pages of this text are given parenthetically.

us—worriedly, in light of the threat to Judaism any persuasive disproof of creation would be. But Halevi is not worried. The argumentation of philosophy, especially on this "obscure" point of the world's origin, is mere "speculation founded on analogies" (54), "open to many doubts" (45), and quite beside the point. For the truth of creation is already guaranteed by those six hundred thousand sets of eyes and ears that received via Moses the creation story in Gen 1–3. For Halevi, what guarantees our claims to significant knowledge is what we receive through our *experience*, not our reason. Those ancient six hundred thousand effectively *experienced* the truth of creation and of everything else in the Torah at the foot of Mount Sinai and passed the experience down to the rest of us between the lines of the biblical text.

With this account, Halevi already lends clarity to who or what the Jewish people might be: experts in a kind of *experience*—the experience of God. But who or what is this God? God is a being (if even *being* is an appropriate descriptive) "too high, holy, and exalted for the mind still less for the senses to grasp" (54), "exempt from complexity and divisibility" (85), "high above any attribute of created beings" (203). We are back to Philo's abstraction from all *qualities* of being, to Being itself. Once again, the divine name, *I am that I am*, carries the absence of definitive content. The point of it, Halevi suggests, is not to supply a meaning, for "its meaning is hidden," but "to prevent the human mind from pondering over an incomprehensible but real entity" (201, 202). That name names a "real entity"—even this is too descriptive—that can enter our experience without our being able to describe, categorize, or analyze it in any way. And it is the whole point of our existence, Halevi suggests, to accommodate that entry.

Halevi, writing in Arabic, the Andalusian language of scholarship, has a name for this presence-of-God to us: *amr ilahi*, which is literally: divine thing. We will follow Hartwig Hirschfeld's more communicative translation: divine influence. The divine influence resembles some other ideas sometimes encountered in Jewish thought—the *Shekhina* in the rabbinical literature, the *sefirot* in the mystical literature—that serve to mediate between God and the Jewish people. Philosophers like Halevi gravitate to mediating ideas, too, when their notion of God is so "high, holy, and exalted," for how else connect with it? A consequence of the mediating role, though, is that the mediating presence can blur the boundaries between the mediated and its recipients. In the case of Halevi, the divine influence sometimes seems part of God, sometimes part of humanity. So Halevi can write that God "allowed His influence" to rest "wherever something is arranged and prepared to receive" it (64, 102). But once received, it raises in whomever it dwells to a higher level of humanity, to a "divine and seraphic degree" (48). Such elevated specimens of humanity themselves instance the divine influence. The divine influence in them takes the shape of a faculty reserved for them alone: "an inner eye which sees things as they really are" (207).[24]

And now the import of these views for the Jewish people: within all of humanity, *only* the Jewish people are equipped with this inner eye. The *amr ilahi* rests on them alone. Scholar Harold Davidson calls it "a divine aura enveloping the Jewish nation,"[25] which raises them above the rest of humanity. "The divine influence connected with Israel himself and the whole of his posterity,"[26] "which made of them, so to speak, an angelic caste."[27] A secular Jew can only receive such a self-understanding the way she might the adulation directed her way by an earnestly Christian fundamentalist who meets in her, for the first time, a member of the biblical Chosen People—that is to say, with self-deflecting indulgence for the exalted part she is put to play in someone else's heartfelt story of her. But consider what the Jewish people chiefly sees with their inner eye: the "high, holy, and exalted" God beyond description and on that account contentless. Halevi has suggested that an identity without content may be so not from deficiency of being, but a surfeit of meaning that cannot be contained, for that would be God. As much as the Jewish people themselves, God may be just a character in the story Halevi tells. But that story buoys a Jewish identity that has its contentless counterpart in God.

This idea of a meeting between God and the Jewish people over contentless identity has implications for part of what seems negated in any denial of content to Jewishness: the notion of a chosen people. For chosenness implies a distinction between one people and another—"us and them"—that imputes a distinguishing content to the chosen. Up to a point, Jewish tradition itself questions that concept if it does not expressly negate it. The Torah itself never expressly designates the Children

---

24. For a helpful exposition of the *amr ilahi* see Davidson, "Active Intellect," 381–95.

25. Davidson, "Active Intellect," 392.

26. Halevi, *Kuzari*, 203.

27. Halevi, *Kuzari*, 73. Halevi accepts what to many would be a disturbing consequence of this view, that no one can really convert into Judaism. As the rabbi in *The Kuzari* puts it: "Any Gentile who joins us unconditionally shares our good fortune, without, however, being quite equal to us" (47).

of Israel the chosen people. God is said to have chosen them (Deut 14:2), but this does not issue in any nominalization of that act, toward a chosen people. The Children of Israel are indeed God's *treasured* people, *am segulah*, according to Exod 19:5, which is a "prime source for the concept of the Jews as a 'chosen people.'"[28] But even there, they are treasured only on condition that "ye will hearken unto My voice indeed, and keep My covenant" (Exod 19:5). They are not treasured from any innate capacity they have for spiritual vision. Famously, Maimonides refrained from listing the doctrine among his thirteen principles of Jewish faith.[29] It counts against the whole rational stream, which favors universals over particulars, reasoned choice over unfounded preference.

But Halevi's account of the relation between God and the Jewish people, or at least our interpretation of his account, allows for the idea of a chosen people to expel from itself any conscious choice of one people over another. God really does not *choose* Israel "from among all peoples" (Exod 19:5). It is more the case of a natural match between the Divine Influence and the "inner eye which sees things as they really are." Insofar as both God and the Jewish people, who carry the inner eye, are uniquely contentless in their respective spheres of the cosmos and humanity, they gravitate to each other as like to like, more in illustration of natural law than divine preference. On this reading, the focus is less on chosenness than the mutual attraction between contentless identities across levels of being.

If this picture is too couched in an implicit Neoplatonism to register persuasively with most of us, it finds modern expression in the thought of Franz Rosenzweig, who took Halevi for his spiritual kin across the centuries. Rosenzweig drew attention to Halevi the poet, whose philosophy of Jewish exceptionality reads more gently, movingly, even poignantly in verse.[30] For in poetic form, the doctrine mutes before the actual experience of God, via the inner eye, that the poet so heartfully craves. One short poem, entitled "At Night," recounts a vision that comes to the poet in response to having longed for the Divine, who appears to penetrate his being.[31] Philosophically translated: how wonderful that my inner eye and your Divine Influence could meet in the middle of the night. Halevi underscores the *experience* of this by framing it, at the start, in thoughts that

28. Sutcliffe, *What Are Jews For?*, 11.
29. Maimonides, "Helek," 401–23.
30. Thanks to Professor Virginia Burrus for suggesting this reading of Halevi to me.
31. Halevi, "At Night," 12.

prepare the ground for it and, at the finish, in meditations that, succeeding it, move him toward ritual prayer. But neither the thoughts nor the ritual prayer are the heart of the experience, which is visionary. Philosophy lacks the proper vocabulary to capture the tender intimacy of so remarkable a meeting between the macro- and microcosm, and so it resorts to grades of human being of which the Jewish people occupy the top tier, nearest God. But, once again, it is almost as though the meeting happens naturally, without any deliberate decision, in analogy with the natural law of gravitational pull, by which each of two bodies attract each other, rather than by way of an intentional choice of the one for the other.

Rosenzweig singles Halevi out among the medieval philosophers for his willingness overtly to state the doctrine of the chosen people. Rosenzweig himself asserts quite baldly that the teaching of Israel's chosenness "wholly permeates Judaism [and] . . . alone can explain the preservation of the Jewish people. . . . It becomes word, meaning, form, but never a dogmatic formula . . . with the great exception of Jehuda Halevi's *Kuzari*."[32] Linked to the survival of the people, the doctrine takes on the aspect of a protective shield, still another tenor for it. Rosenzweig suggests that the reason it is not usually articulated is that Jewish consciousness identifies with it so deeply it cannot distance it enough to analyze it, and only does so when provoked by non-Jewish thought to articulate it. As Rosenzweig puts it, "No one became a Jewish thinker within the private domain of Judaism."[33] Even to think about chosenness, as opposed to simply living in identity with the concept, required a Jew "to be drawn to the border of Judaism,"[34] where he would not likely want to remain, so distant from the center. Halevi's informed and sympathetic treatments of Judaism's Andalusian rivals—philosophy, Christianity, Islam—suggest that is just where he was: on the borders. But as Rosenzweig might have predicted, he did not remain there but according to the biographical record moved himself bodily at the end of his life to the center of Jewish earthly yearning, the land of Israel, where he died.

Rosenzweig is no less shy than Halevi to speak of Jewish chosenness: the Jew, "as God's well-beloved, as Israel . . . knows he is chosen by God" (SR326). But this relation shares with Halevi's account an openness to another reading, of a meeting between God and the Jewish soul that comes about because of an inherent fitness to it, rather than

32. Rosenzweig, "Apologetic Thinking," 265.
33. Rosenzweig, "Apologetic Thinking," 267.
34. Rosenzweig, "Apologetic Thinking," 267.

deliberate choice or intention. It is rather a natural consequence of a feature of revelation, which is not properly our subject until chapter 6. But for now: Revelation complements the act of creation within Rosenzweig we have already encountered. Creation happens when the passive agency of God, which seeks a partner to sustain, and the active passivity of the world, which seeks a sustainer, meet. But alongside that meeting another occurs, between humanity and God. In that encounter, the active passivity of God, which seeks a partner to love, meets the passive activity of humanity, which presses itself forward to be loved. And that is revelation. But it is no more a single, intentional act of God than creation is. Rather, humanity partners with God in the act of revelation. The roles of giver and receiver are so intertwined as to mesh. It is as though the logic of revelation sets a place for two agencies to fill and God and humanity rise to the occasion of filling them, by the need of one to love and the other to be loved.

This requires a division of labor within humanity, between one collective agent who lives that love in the restricted space of their communal life, attesting to the joy of it, and another who spreads it worldwide, expanding the circle of it, so that ultimately all participate in it. Jews are the former agent, Christians the latter. The Jewish people are like a puzzle piece that fits the gap made for it in a jigsaw picture of love's mechanics. Humans do not self-generate love. They can only transmit a love they have received. Jews receive the love; Christians transmit it. God, Jews, and Christians all take up their appropriate place in the mechanics of love without any deliberate acts of choice, but according to the requirements of love itself. Appropriately, the biblical book that holds attention at the center of the *Star* is not Exodus, where the doctrine of chosenness roots, but the Song of Songs, the Bible's great tribute to love, to which we return in chapter 6, on revelation.

But Rosenzweig echoes Halevi in another way. The loving relation Jews enjoy with God culminates in a visionary experience that blinds them. Toward the end of the *Star of Redemption* Rosenzweig imagines an appearance of God's face most especially to the Jewish people, but for all people, as though to illustrate that beautiful plea of the priestly blessing: May "the Lord make His face to shine upon thee" (Num 6:25). Rosenzweig goes so far as to reference the features of the divine face, from forehead to mouth (SR445–46).

It is a vision that Rosenzweig says happens "beyond words" and even "beyond life" (SR408, 439).[35] It must be beyond life, since "man shall not see Me and live" (Exod 33:20). We have entered "the divine sanctuary where no man can remain alive" in a "life beyond life" (SR446). In this inkling of the Beyond, it is no light of the everyday that shines but one that overwhelms all attempts to see. In this light, "it is too bright for us yet to behold the countenance" of God (SR404). Our eyes are blinded—in German, *geblendeten*[36]—by this light. God's "hidden aspect remains all the more hidden" (SR404) even in the disclosure. We encounter a darkening light that enables unseeing vision. What we "see" is as good as nothing—*das Nichts*[37]—to our senses and our thought. To underscore the point, Rosenzweig highlights as well the utter silence of the experience: "The word grows silent in the afterworld and supra-world" (SR441) of the vision. It is "the last silence" (SR407).

Rosenzweig suggests that the high holy day of Yom Kippur positions Jews each year to experience this vision. He is struck by the unique liturgical posture of that day, of prostrating (SR343). This is the only appropriate posture to take in such proximity to God. But the position also accords with what Rosenzweig understands Jews to see in that vision: a surfeit of reality that blinds. If their faces are to the ground, the worshipers are not seeing in any ordinary sense. With just this posture, the distinction any notion of chosenness implies falls away. The very posture of self-diminution vacates space for the rest of humanity to fill, who join in the vision (SR349).

Rosenzweig in liturgical-mystical mode has given us, once again, an image of emptiness for the God of experience, just as Halevi did. But Rosenzweig is even more explicit than Halevi over the emptiness of our own selves mirrored in the vision. In the midst of the vision, the Jewish people have effectively ceased to be; in it, they have sunk and vanished (*sank und schwand*[38]). There is already a foretelling of this in the everyday life of the Jewish people who, according to Rosenzweig, stands out among peoples for lacking all the identity-conferring marks of a people: their own land, language, and law. For, to Rosenzweig's mind, the land of Israel, the Hebrew language, and the halacha do not so much confer ethnic

35. The vision is "jenseits der Worte" and "jenseits des Lebens." Rosenzweig, *Stern*, 428, 462.
36. Rosenzweig, *Stern*, 464.
37. Rosenzweig, *Stern*, 433; SR412.
38. Rosenzweig, *Stern*, 427.

identity as efface it before the divine. The land is Israel's only as an object of longing, which they could ever only inhabit as strangers (SR319); the Hebrew of its liturgical life lives outside the rough and tumble of worldly identity (SR321);[39] the Jewish law extracts them from history entirely (SR323). By virtue of the vision that holds it in thrall, the Jewish people's past is "really not at all past, but eternally present" (SR323). In short, by some key standards of ethnic identity, Jewish ethnicity is as empty as God's own being, and the two connect as naturally in Rosenzweig's vision of Jewishness as in Halevi's or Philo's.

Rosenzweig would not have us linger in these heady regions. This life-beyond-life is not for daily living. So let us descend from here. (We return here in ch. 10.) We do not yet even have in our sights the player key to this vision of Jewish identity: God. All that we have pulled from these three accounts of divine emptiness—Philo's, Halevi's, Rosenzweig's—is a macrocosmic mirror of Jewish emptiness. But to the extent a divine Nothing looks back at Jewish identity when it sees itself in the mirror, we are already on to a nothing that is something.

Our negation of content to Jewish identity has lit the notion of chosenness with a darkening light. Being chosen is less a privileging, preferencing, or otherwise distinguishing mark than an emptying. There is one more term traditionally attached to Jewish identity, especially in connection with God, that may newly appear under this same negating light. It is the notion of covenant.

Even apart from the Bible, the word *covenant* carries warm connotations within American history. The early colonists distinguished covenantal relationships from contractual ones on grounds that they issued in a more tightly knit community than a contract does, and that they implied a witness of high stature to their making, either God or the king.[40] Bill Clinton adopted the word to distinguish his message from Newt Gingrich's Contract with America, back in his 1992 presidential campaign, and to connote a "higher moral force"[41] than Gingrich's

---

39. Rosenzweig was not active in the Zionist movement or the revival of Hebrew as a language of everyday life. But even so, Shlomo Sand suggests that what we call modern Hebrew is so different from its biblical namesake that it is only "incorrectly called 'Hebrew' [and] . . . it would be far more appropriate to . . . define it as 'Israeli.'" Sand, *How I Stopped Being a Jew*, 42.

40. Lutz, "Evolution of Covenant Form," 38–39.

41. Van Der Slik and Schwark, "Clinton and the New Covenant," 887.

contract. It is a term we might prefer to keep for Jewish identity, even under the light of negation.[42]

The problem with covenants is that they are full of content. Covenants course through Hebrew Scripture like trout upstream. A concordance to the Hebrew Bible will show over two hundred and fifty uses of the word, from the beginnings in Genesis to the ending in Malachi. And as Daniel Breslauer observes, the usage is very broad. There are "covenants between human beings, between human beings and God, covenants with individuals, covenants with communities, unilateral covenants, stipulative covenants, unconditional covenants."[43] And they typically contain stipulations that define them.

For example, the centering covenant of Torah has already crossed our path within the framework of chosenness, at Exod 19:5, which declares, "If ye will hearken unto My voice indeed and keep My covenant, then ye shall be Mine own treasure from among all peoples." This is a stipulative covenant: it is to hold between God and the six hundred thousand gathered at Sinai (and their descendants). They will be God's treasure *if* they follow the laws about to given, which come to 613 by rabbinical reckoning. Later on, the covenant intensifies by the lists of rewards for keeping it (Deut 28:1–14) and punishments for breaking it (Deut 28:15–68). And the Children of Israel accept the provisions: "All that the Lord hath spoken will we do and obey" (Exod 24:7). That mass response already bonds the individuals at the foot of the mountain into a compact of "we"—a community—under the higher witness of God, in anticipation of how the American colonists would understand their covenants several millennia later.

Like the concept of chosenness, that of covenant invites a distinction between insiders and outsiders that threatens to undermine the negation of content to Jewish identity we are practicing. Certainly Exod 19:5 makes a point of separating out the Children of Israel "from among all peoples." And the laws that follow do indeed supply a content to the covenant that applies uniquely to people Israel. Jewish identity fills with the content of

---

42. Covenantal accountability is also hidden in plain sight within the federation structure of Jewish philanthropy. The Jewish Federations of North America is a federation of philanthropic Jewish federations. And, as Daniel Elazar helpfully informs us, the root meaning of *federation*, implying a collaboration of independent agencies or, in political theory, a separation of powers, from the Latin *foedus*, is covenant. Elazar, "Covenant," 9.

43. Breslauer, *Covenant and Community*, 1. Perhaps the tenderest covenant to appear in Tanak is the one between Jonathan and David (1 Sam 20).

those covenant-defining laws. What impact might our negation of content to Jewish identity have on such a covenant? Can covenantal thinking be so universal and inclusive, so non-differentiating among peoples, as *not* to entail a distinctive content? In places the Bible, especially the prophets, suggests so. When God says to the Children of Israel, via the prophet Amos, "Are ye not as the children of the Ethiopians unto Me?" (Amos 9:7), or, via the prophet Isaiah, "Blessed be Egypt My people and Assyria the work of my hands, and Israel mine inheritance" (Isa 19:25), what can the biblical writers be thinking but that covenants expand toward the whole of humanity, either by way of a single one, all-embracing, or a federation of distinct, covenantal communities?

There is ready to hand a rabbinic means of universalizing the covenant idea, by way of the doctrine of the Noahide laws. The rabbis taught that at the conclusion of the flood, God not only promised Noah that there would be no more such floods, but commanded a set of seven laws for all humankind.[44] This creative interpretation hangs on Gen 9:1–17, where God both issues some laws, such as not to commit murder (Gen 9:5) and proclaims "my covenant with you and with your seed after you" (Gen 9:9) that "waters shall no more become a flood to destroy all flesh" (Gen 9:15). As the addressee is Noah, a second primal origin of all humanity after Adam, "your seed" means everyone. So God has issued a universal covenant in context of some laws. And, winsomely, the rainbow serves to signify that.

The pairing between law and covenant is natural to the Bible. One way to understand the fact that the first of the Ten Commandments, as numbered by Jews—"I am the Lord thy God who brought thee out of the land of Egypt" (Exod 20:2)—lacks the form of a command is that it serves implicitly to recall the covenant, by which God in God's love for Israel redeemed them from Egypt. The Ten Commandments remind observant Jews that the law comes to them within the framework of a prior love relation with God. The law contextualized by covenant loses the frown it sometimes carries in the popular imagination, and wears a smile. The covenant that contextualizes the Noahide laws fits the pattern to a tee: it is a rainbow, after all, which from the standpoint of heaven is indeed a smile. But for many of us, the covenant of the Noahide laws disappoints. It is just seven laws, compared to the 613 delivered to Jews. It cannot but seem both law- and love-lite—less than what God both demands of and delivers

---

44. On the negative side, not to commit idolatry, blasphemy, murder, stealing, sexual impropriety, or animal cruelty; on the positive side, to establish courts.

to the Israelites. So for Jews seeking a truly universalized covenant, that mutes distinctive content to the covenant idea, the covenant of the rainbow, for all its winsome beauty, will not do.

A philosopher who extracts from rabbinic thinking on covenant a more generous account of its scope is Emmanuel Levinas, in his short essay "The Pact," which is an ingenious reading of a passage from the Talmud. The Talmudic passage, from b. Sotah 37a–b, addresses a question the Mishnah raises about the languages appropriate for speaking a variety of ritual prayers, blessings, and curses. As is typical within rabbinic reasoning, a discussion of one thing—the *sotah*, or woman accused of adultery (based on Num 5:11–31), and of the curse pronounced upon her if found guilty—sparks a tangential discussion of another thing: the language not only appropriate to pronouncing *this* curse but various other ritual locutions. And this in turn opens onto a still larger discussion of the covenantal relations implied by the very promise of blessings and curses as given at three places in the Torah, according to the Talmud, at Mount Sinai (Exod 23:20–33), in the plains of Moab (Deut 28:1–68), and later, under Joshua's aegis, on Mounts Ebal and Gezerim (Deut 27:11–26 and Josh 8:30–35). According to the Bible, Moses or Joshua recited the law to the Israelites on each of these occasions, incorporating each time a set of blessings and curses (or, at a minimum, curses) contingent on Israelite behavior, whether or not faithful to the law.

Levinas identifies at the start of the Talmudic passage he discusses the very issue that troubles us: "the problem of the relationship between the particular case of Israel and the universal state of mankind."[45] For this issue is implied by the debate over language, whether the various ritual locutions must be spoken in the language of the Bible (Hebrew) or may be pronounced in any of the languages of the world. That the rabbis raise the question at all shows their own concern to relate the particularity of the Israelites to the universality of the world. Levinas traces a movement from particular to universal over the course of the way the scene on Mounts Ebal and Gezerim, where the law is delivered for the third time, is portrayed. At the predictive set-up of the scene (Deut 27:11–26), when Moses is merely commanding it as a future performance, those intended to hear the law and its accompaniment of here curses only, include all the Israelites; at the second portrayal of the scene, in its actual occurrence, the strangers sojourning with the Israelites are also included (Josh 8:33,

---

45. Levinas, "Pact," 213.

35); finally, according to the Mishnah, where the scene receives a third telling, the law is to be inscribed in all the languages of the world, i.e., the seventy languages the rabbis believed exhausted the whole of them (m. Sotah 7:5). That is how the rabbis interpreted Moses's command to write the law out *very plainly* (Deut 27:8). Levinas interprets the progression to illustrate an increasingly inclusive Jewish movement from the already expansive community of the biblical Israelites to the rabbinical "reaching out to humanity as a whole."[46]

Both the rabbis and Levinas press covenantal thinking into service of this universalizing trend. As Levinas draws them out, the Talmudic rabbis suggest that, in addition to the covenant that precedes the giving of the law in total, each of the individual laws given is embedded in a prior covenant of its own; and that each of the Israelite (men) gathered to hear the law—all 603,550 of them, to be precise, according to Num 1:46—receives within his own hearing of each law an embedding covenant specific to him. The number of covenants involved rises even more as the rabbis consider the various dimensions of the law, whether taken as an organic whole or in its itemized aggregation; whether learned, taught, observed, or carried out, as prescribed at Deut 5:1 and 11:19; and whether carried out on the positive side, by doing what is prescribed, or the negative side, by not doing what is *pro*scribed. Each of those dimensions comes embedded in its own covenant. As Levinas reflects on the resulting totality of covenants, he wryly comments, "it is a large number."[47] But the point for him is that this bursting the bounds of quantity implies one of quality as well, especially when joined to the multiplication of languages in which the law is to be written. Those for whose sake the law is given and observed expands to all humanity, howsoever qualified (Jew or gentile). "The Israelites [are] more correctly described as men participating in a common humanity. . . . The Torah belongs to everyone: everyone is responsible for everyone else."[48] It is almost as though so great a multiplication of covenants requires more than just the whole of Israel to participate in them all; it requires the whole world. At the same time, such a multiplication of covenants and the laws they embrace stymie the mind and attenuate their content to the near point of erasure.

It is true that we are looking to the Jewish philosophers, not the rabbis, for guidance on our Jewish journey. But by way of Levinas, the

46. Levinas, "Pact," 217.
47. Levinas, "Pact," 225.
48. Levinas, "Pact," 225.

rabbis oblige us with a universalist reading of covenant that multiplies the instances of it beyond all conceiving, which is effectively to negate the content of it, in accord with the intent of this chapter. We can negate the describable content of the covenant by magnifying it beyond conception; we can accomplish the same end by reducing it to zero. This is the approach of Martin Buber.

Martin Buber's *I and Thou* is a poetic reverie on inter-subjectivity: how at moments of life we receive an other to us—whether human, animal, vegetable, or mineral—as a location of subjectivity that reciprocally receives us in the same way, so that neither is merely sizing the other up as an object of use or abuse. This is the I-Thou relation. It is in contrast to the I-It relation, which is the default relation of mutual categorizing and use that characterizes many of our daily interactions. Buber understands the I-Thou and I-It relations to constitute two different ways we take in the same reality we inhabit—the first supplies the meaning of our lives, the second our physical and social perdurance in being. We must have both. They alternate in our lives and, sadly, for all the import of the I-Thou relation, it invariably subsides into I-It. But we will have much more to say about these two kinds of relation in succeeding chapters.

For now, what is key about I-Thou relations is how difficult they are to write about. This is in part because, for Buber, the I-Thou relation is prior in reality to the two for whom it comes about. It is hard to talk about a relationship that precedes in being those that it relates. It seems a case of cart before the horse, but so it is. What is more, the relation defies the subject/object form of grammar. "Whoever says [Thou] does not have something for his object."[49] So I cannot really even say, within the framework of this relation, "I see you"—even taking "see" in its most deeply metaphorical sense. Buber admits the problem: what he is talking about, "I cannot . . . describe" (61). Still, he musters a family of terms to indicate his meaning. In the I-Thou relation, each receives the other in their "whole being" (54), "unmediated" (62), "unique and devoid of qualities" (68) and of "any rules" (162), "present exclusively" (90), "uncanny" (84).

---

49. Buber, *I and Thou*, 55. Subsequent citations to pages of this text are given parenthetically. Kaufmann makes the choice to translate the German *Du*, in *Ich und Du*, as You, rather than Thou—to my mind, a rational but poor choice, since *Thou*, though archaic, captures better for Buber what has become, in his view, the exceptionality of I-Thou relationship in our time; and "*You!*" in American parlance often works as a rude affront.

Revealingly, most of these terms communicate meaning negatively, in terms of absences: of mediation, of qualities, of rules. Even "whole being" takes much of its clarity of meaning from *not* being its opposite: an "aggregate of qualities" (69). It is as though the I-Thou relation depends for its being on a certain kind of clearing away. "Measure and comparison have fled" (83); so has action as we normally understand it. "An action of the whole being must approach passivity" (62). There is "no prior knowledge and no imagination, . . . no purpose, . . . no greed and no anticipation, . . ." (62–63). Buber obliges our project of negation with a string of negatives that echo our denials of content to both Jewish identity and God. Now the I-Thou relation takes up its position with them.

But the book *I and Thou* challenges anyone seeking insights from it on the distinctive idea of covenant. The problem with the book for many Jewish readers is that in reaching for universal truths of the human condition it seems indifferent to the distinctiveness of Jewishness entirely, especially to those features so central to Levinas's analysis of covenant: revelation and law. But the notion of covenant is important to Buber in both his personal life and, most especially, his biblical writing. Paul Mendes-Flohr, in his appreciative biography of Buber, quotes from a letter Buber wrote his wife, hoping that his grandson would be circumcised, even over objection of his son-in-law, on grounds that "this primordial sign of an affiliation," prescribed by the Bible for Abraham's descendants (Gen 17:10–14), is "the only one available to us," especially within the diaspora, that will "let the 'covenant' . . . continue on a personal plane."[50]

In his biblical writing on covenant, Buber takes us back to the covenantal prelude to the giving of the Ten Commandments: Exod 19:5. He explicates more carefully what it means for the Children of Israel to be God's treasure—*segulah*. The Hebrew term connotes "a possession set apart from the common property of the tribe for special disposition and

---

50. Mendes-Flohr, *Martin Buber*, 93. Buber, writing from Israel, hopes that this primal Jewish ritual can help sustain the bond of covenantal connection among diaspora Jews, who lack the encompassing communal environment of Jewishness Israel guarantees. The comment impresses, coming from Buber, who downgraded ritual, as he does even here by enclosing the word *covenant* in quotes. But he also points toward another content of Jewish identity by way of what is sometimes now in the scholarship termed *carnality*. For what could be more carnal than circumcision to symbolize the covenant? See, for example, Wyschogrod, *Body of Faith*; Boyarin, *Carnal Israel*; Eilberg-Schwartz, *People of the Body*. Of course, such body-focus on Jewish identity will receive little welcome from the likes of Philo and Maimonides, who took circumcision to be a symbolic negation or at least constriction of the body and its sexuality.

use;"⁵¹ or, even more precisely, "a possession which is withdrawn from the general family property because one individual has a special relation to it and a special claim upon it."⁵² He analogizes the concept to the related one of "first fruits," that prime of a harvest that is to be dedicated to God. According to Jer 2:3, which Buber cites, "Israel is the Lord's hallowed portion, His first-fruits of the increase." Buber elaborates: "It is a part selected from the whole for a sacred purpose, a hallowed portion."⁵³

On the surface, our recourse to covenant by way of Buber has reburdened us with chosenness. But Buber reads these ideas of special selection against the grain. He is not interested in the standard inference from them of a "chosen people." Rather, he highlights the whole from which the part has been selected, which provides the context for it to be *selected* in the first place. The selected people belongs to the whole of peoples, all of whom are God's; the first fruits come from the whole of the harvest, which all redound to the Creator. And now it is this whole of things that confers upon the chosen people the one thing special about them—that they are called to muster the whole of themselves in their dedication to God. What God asks of Israel is "with *all* its substance and *all* its functions, with legal forms and institutions, with the *whole* organization of its internal and external relationships, [to] dedicate itself to YHWH"⁵⁴ (emphasis ours). Paradoxically, it is just the presupposition of select status, that it come from a larger whole, that in this case underwrites the selection.

The word *whole*—not selected part—recalls the language of the I-Thou relation. And following Buber's lead, we soon find ourselves in its vicinity. For the covenant that yields the treasured first-fruit of Israel is "not a contract but an assumption into a life-relationship, a relationship comprehending the entire life of the men involved."⁵⁵ Like President Clinton in response to Newt Gingrich, Buber distinguishes covenant from contract. "The original meaning of *brith* [covenant] is not 'contract' or 'agreement'; that is, no conditions were originally stipulated therein, nor did any require to be stipulated."⁵⁶ Conditions on a covenant would import contingency into the covenantal relation,

---

51. "Election of Israel," in Buber, *Martin Buber Reader*, 28.
52. "'Upon Eagle's Wings,'" in Buber, *Writings of Martin Buber*, 176.
53. "Election of Israel," in Buber, *Martin Buber Reader*, 26.
54. "'Upon Eagle's Wings,'" in Buber, *Writings of Martin Buber*, 178.
55. "'Upon Eagle's Wings,'" in Buber, *Writings of Martin Buber*, 175.
56. "'Upon Eagle's Wings,'" in Buber, *Writings of Martin Buber*, 174.

when what God wants at Exod 19:5 is "an unconditionally committing union with Him."[57] For Buber, what makes a covenant unconditional is not irrevocability, for it will be revoked if Israel fails in its part, but the quality of the commitment asked: It must be total, whole, without restraint. Buber has rethought covenants on the model of an I-Thou relationship. Wanda Warren Berry makes the point succinctly: There is a "continuity between Judaism's understanding of covenant existence and Buber's picture of I-Thou existence."[58] Daniel Elazar puts it this way: "the covenant relationship is to social and political life what Buber's I-Thou relationship is to personal life."[59]

Buberian covenant supplies content to what has been our undefinable Jewishness. But it does so in sync with that very want of definition when it affiliates covenant with the I-Thou relation. For that, too, lacks definition in otherwise than negative terms. In a three-way mirror, God, Jewishness, and I-Thou each reflects the other within a different frame, respectively, of macrocosm, microcosm, and relationality. They all defy language to capture them. They all undermine their own seeming intent to supply descriptive content for themselves. Buber will find God an implicit third in every I-Thou relation. But God is still several chapters ahead of us. For now, Buber bids us discern in our Jewishness a special gift for the I-Thou relation. That is the sum of our covenantal identity. "I am far from wishing to contend that the conception and experience of the dialogical situation [i.e., the I-Thou relation] are confined to Judaism. But I am certain that no other community of human beings has entered with such strength and fervor into this experience as have the Jews."[60] We are prototypically Jewish not when we observe the law, buy Israeli bonds, or remember the Holocaust, but when we open ourselves maximally to I-Thou relations. In such a life, every being we encounter is potentially a special treasure, a *segulah*.

---

57. "Election of Israel," in Buber, *Martin Buber Reader*, 24.

58. Berry, "Judaism Without Covenant," 42. Berry notes that if the word *covenant* does not explicitly appear in *I and Thou*, a German variant on it does in the term *Verbundenheit*, containing *Bund*, German for covenant. Kaufmann translates *Verbundenheit* as association, but comments that it "is hard to translate" (Buber, *I and Thou*, 165n).

59. Elazar, "Covenant," 6.

60. "Faith of Judaism," in Buber, *Writings of Martin Buber*, 255–56. Daniel Elazar makes the same point more practically for the Jewishness of covenant: "the Jewish people is one of those societies that stand out in their utilization of partnership devices, all of which also have their roots in the covenant idea" (Elazar, "Covenant," 32).

Buber has not only modeled his idea of covenant after the I-Thou relation. We could say, in reverse, he has modeled the I-Thou relation after his idea of covenant. That would make the whole of *I and Thou* a vision of covenantal life. The universal availability of the I-Thou relation then transfers to covenantal life, too, just as, for Levinas, covenantal particularity expanded to include all humanity. Israel may be, for now, the select people of God, most open to the I-Thou relation, but a time will come "when the whole world appears . . . as such a people" in a "becoming-perfect of the creation."[61] That's the promise of the liturgical prayer "In that day, God will be one and God's name will be one." In the meantime, Israel models for all people who would take up the challenge a mustering of the whole national self to the highest possible end of I-Thou relationality. Buber hoped for Jews to model that mustering "on a basis of political and social realism,"[62] that is, in the form of what would become the nation-state of Israel in 1948. Did he hope in vain?

---

61. "'Upon Eagle's Wings,'" in Buber, *Writings of Martin Buber*, 180.
62. "'Upon Eagle's Wings,'" in Buber, *Writings of Martin Buber*, 177.

Chapter 4
The State of Israel

BUBER HELD A HIGH ideal for the state of Israel. It was to be "a union of persons living together, a union founded on the direct relation of all to all."[1] In accord with the biblical vision, there was to be "communal ownership of the land (Lev 25:23), regularly recurring leveling of social distinctions (Lev 25:13), guarantee of the independence of each individual (Exod 21:2), mutual aid (Exod 23:4). . . ."[2] This would be a "true people, that is, a people that realizes in its life the basic meaning of the concept *am* (people), of living one *im* (with) another."[3] Buber takes advantage of the consonantal spelling of Hebrew words to identify *am*, for "people," with *im*, for "with." In Hebrew only the vowels, which do not show, differentiate the two. To be a people is to experience the import of being *with* one another, as in I-Thou relations.

This is a utopian vision for any state, Jewish or Marxist—and most literally utopian, *without place*, either in the ancient or modern worlds. Anyone who held Israel to this standard, and faulted it for failing it, would be (rightly) accused of expecting more of it than was reasonable, or was expected of any other nation-state. But then, this is just the problem with nation-states. They sorely disappoint, which becomes the foundation for the negation that guides this chapter: the negation of political Zionism. Increasingly, this is not a radical stance among Jews, especially of the younger generation. But it has precedent within Jewish philosophy even post 1948,

---

1. "On National Education" in Buber, *Writings of Martin Buber*, 287.
2. "Land and Its Possessors," in Buber, *Writings of Martin Buber*, 283.
3. "Holy Event," in Buber, *Writings of Martin Buber*, 167.

as Jonathan Graubart limns for us in his *Jewish Self-Determination Beyond Zionism: Lessons from Hannah Arendt and Other Pariahs*. Visions of alternatives to political Zionism are increasingly non-pariah.

Political Zionism, after the vision of Theodor Herzl, sought through diplomatic means to establish a Jewish state, the only space it understood to guarantee freedom from anti-Semitic violence. From one point of view, political Zionism has already negated itself. For the Jewish state it sought now exists. In fulfilling its goal, political Zionism simultaneously completes and ends itself. So negated a Zionism, far from negating the existing State of Israel, indirectly affirms it, or at least presupposes it. But then our question becomes: In the wake of negating political Zionism, what appearances come into view that may shed light on actual Israeli realities? Certainly one of those appearances is that very utopia that motivated Buber's vision of a Jewish homeland, better known as cultural or spiritual Zionism, and now largely forgotten as an historical curiosity.

Before we revive cultural Zionism for the illuminations we hope from it, we might probe more deeply our negation of political Zionism. For we mean by this more than a terminating self-fulfillment. The problem with political Zionism is the *political* itself. At least, so Martin Buber instructs us. According to Buber, if there was any block to the realization of his utopian vision of a Jewish homeland, it was not the Arab population already inhabiting Palestine, but politics. For Buber, the notion of a nation-state of Jews embroiled the Jewish people in a quicksand of political machination, just the opposite of I-Thou relationality. The nation-state could not but erect that very divide between *us and them* that undermined covenantal ideals. He wrote of "the pernicious effects of an evil which afflicts humankind perhaps more than any other evil, ... the current exaggeration, indeed glorification of politics in our world ... out of all proportion to what is truly important in life."[4] And so Zionism was not for Zionistic Buber primarily a political movement. Out of the organic emergence of covenantal communities in Ottoman and later British Palestine a political organization of Jews and Arabs would naturally build, but it would not be a Jewish or Palestinian state.

> The Arab population does not need an Arab state in order to develop its potential freely, nor does the Jewish population need a Jewish state to accomplish this purpose. Its realization on both sides can be guaranteed within the framework of a

---

4. Buber, *Land of Two Peoples*, 194.

joint bi-national socio-political entity, in which each side will be responsible for the particular matters pertaining to it, and both together will participate in the ordering of their common concerns. The demands for an Arab state or a Jewish state in the entire Land of Israel fall into the category of political "surplus," of the desire to achieve more than what is truly needed.[5]

Buber spoke these words as part of a speech he delivered on Dutch radio, in June 1947, only a few months before the UN would issue its partition plan for Palestine on November 29 of that year. So he was on the losing end of the debates over the future of Palestine. Paul Mendes-Flohr writes of Buber, "A self-conscious outsider in the context of pre- and post-1948 Zionism, he was by the end of his life inured to being branded unpatriotic."[6] His critiques of "modern national egoism," "patriotic bombast," and "empty self-assertion,"[7] might certainly have registered as unpatriotic with some. Buber was not persuaded by considerations of national security to support any of the disempowerments practiced by the State of Israel on Palestinians. Any nation devoted primarily to "preserving and asserting itself [most especially at the price of justice] . . . deserves to pass away."[8] This was a bold claim, in 1941, when he wrote it, before the State was founded; much more so, today.

But even before the founding of Israel, there were philosophical Jewish voices that questioned the wisdom of statehood as such. Two of those were Franz Rosenzweig and Walter Benjamin who, within quite different ideational frameworks, and unbeknownst to each other, mounted similar critiques of the nation-state. Rosenzweig did so in context of his magnum opus, *The Star of Redemption*; Benjamin as part of his now much referenced "Toward the Critique of Violence." But both put a bold question mark to any notion of a Jewish state.

Rosenzweig lived in Germany between 1886 and 1929. Over that time he experienced with all of Europe the trauma of World War I. He served stoically on the German side, without any of the nationalist fervor that galvanized much of Germany. But the anti-Semitism that motivated political Zionism was not uppermost in his experience; nor did he suffer from a spiritual vacuum that Zionism presumed to fill, since he came to find fulfillment enough in his own existential practice and study of

---

5. Buber, *Land of Two Peoples*, 199.
6. Mendes-Flohr, *Martin Buber*, 319.
7. "Hebrew Humanism," in Buber, *Writings of Martin Buber*, 295, 296.
8. "Hebrew Humanism," in Buber, *Writings of Martin Buber*, 296.

rabbinic Judaism. So he lacked the motivation to take up any kind of Zionism with any conviction. Of Zionism he wrote, with his customary wit, "Zionism, diagnostician of genius but most mediocre healer, has recognized the disease but prescribed the wrong treatment."[9]

So far as nation-states were concerned, what impressed Rosenzweig was their proneness to violence. This is what World War I demonstrated. He reflected on the willingness of individuals and peoples to sacrifice their "self-preservation" to the hold on them of "pledged allegiance[s]" to states (SR349).[10] A paradox underlay this willingness. On the one hand, a people, like any organic being, would left to its own devices grow, mature, decline, and perish. This was a lesson any student of ancient peoples could not but glean from their rise and fall. And so, as though to arrest their own inevitable demise, peoples ensconce themselves in structures of law that seem to promise a future continuity. Mechanisms of law enforcement give rise to states that enact pledges of allegiance. But then, when states in conflict with each other mobilize for war, the very impulse that gave rise to them, to arrest decline, defeats itself in death.

But the paradox cuts deeper. Rosenzweig likens the natural life of a people to the flow of a river, always in motion in response to changing environment (SR353). The state artificially and violently dams the flow, in an illusion of peaceful stasis (SR353). State law arrests a people's life. The arrest offers promise of ongoing life even as it curtails that life. "This is the meaning of all violence, that it founds new law" (SR353), under pretense of preserving the old, as though the law were unchanging and eternal. A people in the grip of a state—a nation-state—constricts itself to save itself. But the state and its laws take on a life of their own. They will not save the people. The people is an organism and it will die. The state does not confer eternity, but only seeming, at best temporary suspensions of change (SR354). It would be as though an armored knight of the Middle Ages never doffed his protective suit in hopes to live forever.

So states are inherently both violent and false. They lure peoples into them with the "all too worldly illusory eternity of their lies" (SR355). In a way, this is what the prophet Samuel implied when he advised the ancient Israelites not to follow the neighboring nations by appointing over themselves a king. For God was their king. But then, Rosenzweig does not presume by this critique of the state to free peoples of them. For

---

9. Rosenzweig, *On Jewish Learning*, 64.
10. "Pledged allegiance" translates *verpfändetes Treuwort* (Rosenzweig, *Stern*, 366).

most peoples of the modern world, there is no alternative to states. The point is to live in them in full awareness of what they exact, which should on its own dampen the enthusiasm for the wars they enact.

For Rosenzweig, the stateless Jewish people enjoyed an advantage over the rest of the nations on earth. For their statelessness was the outward sign of an eternity they truly enjoyed in their inward life and that "had no need of the sword" (SR355). For Rosenzweig, the standard marks of a people—its own language, land, and law—were in the sole case of the Jewish people unsuitable to construction of states. Its language was liturgical, its law was heavily ritualistic, and its land was longed-for, not possessed. The three in concert lifted the people out of time into an eternity of their own. But it was not as though the Jewish people could not instate themselves in temporal Palestine, like an immaterial soul that assumes a body. (Toward the end of his life, Rosenzweig grew more open to Zionism.) But if they did, they could only avoid the violence of their bargain by maintaining a critical distance from it, as though to withhold their full assent to it. The goal would be for the Zionists in Palestine "to become homeless within time and to remain wanderers, even over there,"[11] i.e., to translate the customary eternity of the Jewish people into a timeless temporality, within a state they simultaneously disowned—a paradoxically self-undermining self-instatement. That would be no easy task.

In fact, a fellow German Jew, scholar of repute, and committed Zionist, Gershom Scholem, who had moved to Palestine in 1923, came to see a truth in Rosenzweig's fears for a Jewish state. In celebration of Rosenzweig's fortieth birthday, in 1927, his friends wrote letters of tribute to his life and thought. Scholem picked up on Rosenzweig's fears for a humanly instated, rather than God-fashioned, Jewish state. He did so by way of what would become a defining feature of that state: a revived, secularized Hebrew language. But Scholem sensed a danger here. The problem was precisely what Rosenzweig honored in that language: its sanctity. It could not be secularized without cost. Scholem, who virtually founded the academic study of Jewish mysticism, seemed to sense in the secularization of Hebrew the same dangers the rabbinical tradition suspected in the careless and premature study of mysticism: a disastrous explosion of sacred wrath. And so he wrote,

---

11. "... heimatlos in der Zeit zu werden und auf der Wanderschaft zu bleiben, auch dort." Rosenzweig to Gertrud Oppenheim, May 1, 1917, in Rozenzweig, *Briefe*, 200.

> This country is a volcano, and language is lodged within it. . . .
> That sacred language on which we nurture our children, is it
> not an abyss that must open up one day? . . . The secularization
> of the language is no more than a manner of speaking. . . . Shall
> not the religious power of that language explode one day? . . .
> We are seized with fear when, amidst the thoughtless discourse
> of a speaker, a religious term suddenly makes us shudder. . . .
> This Hebrew is heavy with impending catastrophe. . . . The
> day will come when the language will turn against those who
> speak it, . . . when all the presumptuousness of our enterprise
> is suddenly revealed.[12]

Modern Hebrew is a human creation. In his birthday letter, Scholem calls it an Esperanto. But it is a presumption in a way Esperanto is not, for modern Hebrew forces a sacred language into a secular mold. It is in analogy with humanly reframing the inherent statelessness of the Jewish people in the form of a state. Did the ancient Jewish monarchies fail in the Bible's eyes simply *because* they were human- rather than God-initiated? The Bible knew the human temptation to willfully transpose the sacred to the secular, and forbade it in the third of the Ten Commandments, not to take God's name in vain. For that yields what we commonly call profanity. Scholem suggests that modern Hebrew is a kind of profanity. Eventually that Third Commandment will wreak its vengeance on those who speak it. And they will face a choice put to them by the outraged language "either to submit [to its sacrality] or to perish"[13] in defiance of it. Violence, it would seem, is unavoidable in the humanly established Jewish homeland.

Scholem himself grew disillusioned with the State of Israel, though he died and is buried there. Despite his worry over the secularization of Hebrew, he shared Buber's hope for a revival of Jewish spirit in Israel, in bi-national partnership with the native Palestinians. He opined that the Nazi catastrophe thrust Palestine too precipitously into the role of Jewish homeland before it had sufficiently matured into a center of Jewish culture. And in 1948 it was pushed into statehood before its time, subject to all the violence that attends states, their founding and preservation, without the countervailing and moderating force of revived Jewish culture. Though Scholem had written harshly of Germany's Jews for trusting too much in the relation they imagined they had with

---

12. Scholem, "On Our Language," 97–98.
13. Scholem, "On Our Language," 99.

German culture, toward the end of his life he grew nostalgic for the old, Weimar era Germany of his youth. In his later years, he accepted academic awards from German institutions and visited Berlin, the city of his childhood, several times. One of his biographers, Noam Zadoff, suggests that Palestine came to function best as a Jewish homeland, for Scholem, in the subjunctive mood, as an object of longing, as it does in the Passover liturgy, rather than as possession. His last visit to Berlin, toward the end of his life, allowed him to re-experience in purity, from afar, the old longing for Zion. As Zadoff puts it, "this journey symbolizes both Scholem's return to a familiar world and his departure from Jerusalem and from the effort to realize the Zionist dream, which had disappointed him for so many years."[14]

Scholem was close friends with another German-Jewish lens on the idea of a Jewish state: Walter Benjamin, who knew and admired the work of Franz Rosenzweig. In 1921, the same year that Rosenzweig's *Star of Redemption* appeared, Benjamin published his short essay "Toward the Critique of Violence." The unprecedentedly violent disruptions of World War I were still vivid in memory. Michael Steinberg observes that "the present moment began for the mature Benjamin with the Great War."[15] This was equally true for Rosenzweig, whose response to it was to extract Jews and Judaism from the war-laden mess of history entirely and ensconce them in a world beyond time. In such a space, the Jewish people would not think much of Zionism. Benjamin, who admired Rosenzweig, did not follow him here. But his evaluation of statehood and the violence it implicates is remarkably close to Rosenzweig's. His essay on violence, in concert with Rosenzweig's paragraphs on it in the *Star*, raise the volume of this non-Zionist critique of statehood to a pitch that holds our attention.

To follow their thought, we must grant these two philosophers two assumptions: that states depend for their existence on the laws they enact; that violence does not simply or even necessarily manifest in breach of law, as we might think, or in the punishments triggered by that, but more importantly at the very foundations of law. Rosenzweig as we just saw wrote that in the context of states, violence "founds new law." Benjamin largely agrees: "all violence as a means is either law-positing or

---

14. Zadoff, *Gershom Scholem*, 249. See also Zadoff, "'Zion's Self-Engulfing Light,'" 272–84.

15. Steinberg, "1921," 403.

law-preserving."¹⁶ The law violently preserves itself when it punishes violation of itself. The law violently enacts itself at the foundation of states through the punishment threatened over its violation, but also, as Judith Butler opines, by the sheer proclamation of itself, rather than inference of itself from some antecedently and universally accepted value scheme.¹⁷ "It does this [self-enactment] by fiat, as it were, and this is part of what is meant by the violence of this founding act. In effect, the violence of law-instating violence is summarized in the claim that 'this will be law' or, more emphatically, 'this is now the law.'"¹⁸

To those of us accustomed to venerate law as peace-preserving, these thinkers respond, in words Judith Butler again helpfully supplies for them, "it is not possible to treat law as the alternative to violence."¹⁹ They ask us to invert our understanding of the relation between law and violence. Violence does not follow on (breach of) law. Rather, law follows on the heels of violence. We could find precedents for this view in currents of Marxist and anarchist thought we will not pursue here.²⁰ But we can also find them in the disillusionment over the failure of statehood that World War I seemed to represent. What Rosenzweig might

---

16. Benjamin, *Toward the Critique of Violence*, 48. Benjamin adds the caveat on law-founding violence that it function as a means. He suggests that in the realm of law "the most elementary basic relation . . . is the one between ends and means" (39). But violence can also function more immediately, outside the context of means and ends, as a sheer manifestation, in which case rather than founding law it can as "divine violence" actually annihilate it. "This violence is not a means but a manifestation" (54). Benjamin's distinction between violence as means and as manifestation anticipates an analogous distinction we will encounter under the rubric of revelation, between a *communication* that is intelligible and an *expression* (of someone or something) that is not. The distinction relates as well to one between phenomena subject to our control and manipulation, because of their intelligible location in cause-effect sequences, and those that are not.

17. By way of underscoring the polarity Benjamin sees between law and any universal value scheme from which it might be deduced, Peter Fenves puts it concisely on Benjamin's behalf, "where there is justice, there is no law, and where law, no justice." The two are "mutually repugnant" (Benjamin, *Toward the Critique of Violence*, 28).

18. Butler, *Parting Ways*, 71.

19. Butler, *Parting Ways*, 69.

20. Scholars cite George Sorel's *Reflections on Violence* (1908) as a key source of Benjamin's thought. But for a full, scholarly treatment of the essay's precedents, see Benjamin, *Toward the Critique of Violence: A Critical Edition*, edited by Peter Fenves and Julia Ng, which includes a helpfully orienting introduction by Professor Fenves, relevant fragments from Benjamin, a substantive afterword by Professor Ng that traces the after-currents of the essay, and excerpts from the sources of Benjamin's thought, each served by a scholarly introduction.

have called the pledges of allegiance that bind individuals to states, and states to conflicting alliances, unveiled the explosiveness of law that founds and perpetuates states. Benjamin opens our eyes to this view of law as violently coercive when, decades before the success of the films *Bonnie and Clyde* and *Thelma and Louise*, he remarked on "how often the figure of the 'great' criminal has aroused the secret admiration of the people," on account of the always latent "sympathy of the masses against law."[21] Benjamin's words recall Rosenzweig's comparison of a people to a stream of water and the state that encases it to a dam that unnaturally stops it. The dammed water cannot but sympathize with that bit of it that breaches the walls of the dam.

Between Rosenzweig and Benjamin, the state suffers from analogous contradictions. Whether it promises a peace it cannot keep (Benjamin) or an eternity it cannot offer (Rosenzweig), it is lying. Both thinkers illuminate the violence of states by the contrast the genuinely peaceable makes with them. For Rosenzweig, this is the stateless Jewish people. For Benjamin, it is a confluence of agencies and acts that stand outside the purview of states, characterized by "heartfelt courtesy, affection, peaceableness, trust."[22] This "culture of the heart"[23] informs private, extra-legal resolution of conflict between individuals and, by implication, the aspirations of the class best positioned (for one as sympathetic to Marxist thought as Benjamin was) to contest the violence on which law is founded: the proletariat.[24] Loosely speaking, the proletariat works for Benjamin, for whom Marxist thinking was politically alive in a way it has not been for most Americans, the way the Jewish people does for Rosenzweig to mark sites that expose and contest the violence of states.

Toward the end of his essay, Benjamin identifies an agency that not only exposes the violence of states, but actually dismantles it. This is "divine violence." Here, Benjamin practices a Buberian ploy, to extract from biblical story a life-informing orientation. For he invokes the biblical story of Korah, the Israelite prince and his associates who suffered divine violence for rebelling against Moses—"the earth opened her

21. Benjamin, *Toward the Critique of Violence*, 42, 43.
22. Benjamin, *Toward the Critique of Violence*, 50.
23. Benjamin, *Toward the Critique of Violence*, 50.
24. Here is where Benjamin is most indebted to Sorel, who identified the proletarian or revolutionary general strike as the singular site within a state where the foundational violence of the law is exposed. Benjamin explicitly credits Sorel for this idea. See Toscano, "George Sorel, From *Reflections on Violence*: Translator's Preface," in Benjamin, *Toward the Critique of Violence*, 194–200.

mouth and swallowed them up" (Num 16:32)—to illustrate a visitation of bloodless violence that contests violence. "It is annihilating only in a relative sense," Benjamin suggests, "never absolutely with regard to the soul of the living."[25] He writes of this violence that it strikes "through the absence, in the end, of all positing of law."[26] A distinctive mark of the violence visited upon Korah, that the earth heals completely after it has thus opened up (Num 16:33) and leaves no sign of any disturbance to it, is the picture of peace that appears to result from it. Benjamin notes that the absence of any such sign entails the absence of any boundary (as between the divine and the human) that might have connoted room for yet more sway of law, by warning against violation of itself. As Peter Fenves puts it, the end of Korah and his supporters "represents . . . a paradigmatic countermovement to the encroachment of law [and so of its violence] over the surface of the earth,"[27] where Korah in his princely dignity, even in his act of protest, signified the claims of law. Not all violence yields law. And whatever does not yield law has a good chance, within the framework of this discussion, to be non-violent in itself and/or its implications.[28] Judith Butler suggests that what we have in divine violence is "the paradoxical possibility of a nonviolent violence,"[29] a violence that vacates its content of violence.

A notion of God is no more essential to this "divine" violence than it is to Buber's concept of the I-Thou relation. By *divine*, Benjamin means to indicate an extraordinary kind of violence that rids us of the need of state-founding law. He suggests the proletariat has a handle on this kind of violence. It is a violence-ridding violence that evokes the notion of a double negative, which yields a positive. Butler suggests we analogize it to Rosenzweig's non-legal understanding of divine commandment, which is, as Benjamin might say, also an immediate manifestation (not a means)—though of love, not law, a topic for us later under the rubrics of revelation (ch. 6) and ritual (ch. 8).[30] However we understand Benjamin's

25. Benjamin, *Toward the Critique of Violence*, 58.
26. Benjamin, *Toward the Critique of Violence*, 58.
27. Benjamin, *Toward the Critique of Violence*, 34.
28. "A fully nonviolent resolution of conflicts can never amount to a legal contract" (Benjamin, *Toward the Critique of Violence*, 49). We could rephrase: Nonviolence never precipitates law. That does not quite entail that whatever does not lead to law is nonviolent.
29. Butler, *Parting Ways*, 71.
30. Rosenzweig's important distinction between commandment and law might be set in analogy with Benjamin's between manifestation and means. The commandment,

divine violence, it fits a pattern we have been exploring of concepts that move to vacate their own content, such as Jew, God, I-Thou relation. Perhaps what we reference here are agencies, presences, locations—it is hard to know what to call them—that make sense to us only in the grammar of the first and second person, never the third, so they cannot be described. We can only address or be addressed by them, as we might be within a "culture of the heart." Now we have contentless violence, which resembles the claw-retracted swat of a cat at play.

What hope could Benjamin have that a Jewish state could bypass the violence of statehood? Despite his own reservations about it, Scholem strove heartily to enroll Benjamin in the Zionist cause. Benjamin was noncommittal. He never learned Hebrew or visited Palestine. Perhaps the other-regarding self-retractions Jews and Palestinians would practice toward each other in what Buber hoped would be their covenantal relationship could be understood in Benjamin's terms as a response to divine violence—a violence that founds covenants instead of law.

But then, the State of Israel, founded in 1948, supplies a reality-based test case for Benjamin's theory of state-founding law grounded in violence. Israeli law would deflect this interpretation of itself, if on no other grounds than that until 1984 it perpetuated its Ottoman, Muslim predecessor, the Majallah. The Majallah was the name for a codification of Islamic law the nineteenth-century Ottomans developed in imitation of western models of law. Parts of it persisted in Israeli law until 1984,[31] as though to underscore how continuous with the Islamic past—and averse to violent break with it—Israeli law understood itself to be. How different, after all, are Islamic and Jewish law? Americans are sometimes surprised to learn that sharia law functions peaceably in Israel today to govern matters of family life among Muslim Israelis. Indeed, multiple religious courts corresponding to Judaism, Islam, and several varieties of Christianity supply the family, or personal, law for those practicing these faiths. The modern state of Israel in that way illustrates an idea strange to most Americans, of legal pluralism. There is not one law for the land. There are many.

Israel lacks a constitution because the founders could not agree on the balance between religion and state in the new nation. Was Israel

---

for Rosenzweig, is not a means to enacted obedience, but an expression of divine love, as we shall see. Likewise, divine violence is not a means to lawlessness but a manifestation of law-dismantling agency.

31. See Eisenman, *Islamic Law in Palestine and Israel*.

to be a Jewish state, or a democratic state of safe haven for Jews? The cultural Zionist Ahad Ha'am (1856–1927), reflecting on the Balfour Declaration of 1917, which pledged British support for a Jewish home in Palestine, emphasized the wording: "to facilitate the establishment in Palestine of a national home for the Jewish people," *not* to facilitate "the reconstitution of Palestine as the national home of the Jewish people," as some Zionist leaders claimed. The point of the difference? Britain would not endorse any violent claim on the land exercised "by armed force, under the cover of various 'rights' invented for the occasion," so as to "override the right of the other inhabitants, which is the tangible right based on generation after generation of life and work in the country"[32]—but more shortly on Ahad Ha'am.

Where we find these two ideals of government in tension, between a democratic and Jewish state, is in the document that comes as close as anything Israeli to being the founding document of the state, the Declaration of Independence, promulgated on May 14, 1948. Let us leave aside the war that attended this Declaration, and all the violence between Jews and Arabs that preceded and followed it. For all of that could be in defiance of a peace Israeli law intended to foster simply by maintaining for so long so much of the Islamic state law that preceded. The law, like the languages of Hebrew and Arabic, so intimately inter-related, seemed to promise peace between Islam and Judaism and, by extension, between Jews and Palestinians. The violence need not be, as over against what Rosenzweig and Benjamin might insist, in any necessary relation to the founding of the state; except that the wording of the Declaration lends itself to just the critique of states that Rosenzweig and Benjamin advance.

The Declaration does this by reading new law on top of old law as though the two were of one piece. Rosenzweig suggests this is one way the state promises continuity for a people over the course of changes that affect it. By way of absorbing for a people the shock of change, the law assumes a continuity it actually lacks and an assurance of stability it cannot lastingly supply. The old law of the Declaration is the Bible's, given by God—the "Rock of Israel," in the Declaration's words—who assures the people a home in the promised land, "the birthplace of the Jewish people." The new law is modernity's, which guarantees "the natural right of the Jewish people to be masters of their own fate, like all other nations, in their own sovereign state." The old law is theistic, the new law is secular.

---

32. "After the Balfour Declaration," in Ha'am, *Nationalism*, 157–58, 160.

If either of the laws really holds, the other is otiose. They do not harmonize but conflict. But the Declaration invokes them together as though to jointly underwrite "a natural and historic right" to the land, though even that historic right is more properly mythic. It would be as though simultaneously to explain an eclipse of the sun on grounds of natural law and of conflict between the gods—Artemis blocking Apollo.

But even the myth is pushed beyond its borders when the Declaration claims, by way of founding the state just then, in May 1948, that "Jews strove in every successive generation to re-establish themselves in their ancient homeland." They did not. They merely longed for a homeland that God would restore in God's own time. Do these stretches of truth on the surface of the Declaration register a violence that boils within it? Certainly for Gershom Scholem so flagrant a mixing in Hebrew of ancient religious and modern secular notions would seem a doom-filled violation of the Third Commandment. Shlomo Sand would tell us the very notion of a historically continuous "Jewish people," finally come to claim its rightful home, is fictitious. It is "Zionism's principal imaginary,"[33] to deny which "might lead to a broad challenge against the State of Israel's right to exist."[34] Readers of the Declaration, today, can only wince at the words of promise within it, to "promote the development of the country for the benefit of all its inhabitants" and "to uphold the full social and political equality of all its citizens." Historian David Myers admits about this document that "there are of course disturbing aspects, even insoluble tensions, in that narrative framing, particularly revolving around the place of non-Jews in a Jewish state."[35] Perhaps the legal demoting of Arabic in Israel from its prior station as an official language of the country, a consequence of the Basic Law passed in 2018, "Israel as the Nation-State of the Jewish People," is more of the violence of the Declaration against the non-Jewish other, within and around the land, declaring itself.

To the extent the Israeli Declaration of Independence conceals an interplay of lies and incipient violence, it illustrates Rosenzweig's and Benjamin's critique of nation-states in general. But then the State of Israel is no different from any other state in which the same intertwining of lies and violence would show. And now, far from holding Israel to a higher standard than we do other states, we understand it to exemplify the same low standard that applies to all states. We might adjust our

33. Sand, *Invention*, 239.
34. Sand, *Invention*, 236.
35. Myers, "Response to Jay Harris."

expectations of it accordingly. Or we might reiterate the prime negation of this chapter—of political Zionism.

What comes into view as a result?—What else but its chief competitor within the larger landscape of Zionisms that Buber introduced to us awhile back: cultural or spiritual Zionism. We are primed to receive whatever illuminations we can from it, buried in history as it has been. Perhaps it can reawaken within us a view of the State of Israel less burdened by *realpolitik*, more open to the revisioning Buberian idealism might bring to it without holding it to an impossible standard. Let us pick up where we left off with Martin Buber, waxing eloquent over the Jewish homeland he envisioned of expansive I-Thou relations.

For Buber, the people of the I-Thou relation—for that is what Jews are—move naturally toward a homeland. For the I-Thou relation is never merely a self-enclosure of two. It is always a threesome, by virtue of the third reflected in that three-way mirror of meaningful indefinability: God. "In every You we address the Eternal You."[36] God may be characterized as the One who never leaves the I-Thou relation, unlike every other Thou we might encounter, who invariably subsides into an It for us. For, while it "is the sublime melancholy of our lot"[37] not to continuously inhabit I-Thou relations, "only one You never ceases in accordance with its nature to be You for us."[38] Otherwise put, God is always and only for us a subject of address, never an object of description. That's another way to state the indescribability of God, a topic for chapter 9 we here anticipate.

The role of God here is to stretch the partnership of I-Thou relations toward community. But Buber does not need God to introduce the I-Thou relation. As Walter Kaufmann observes in the introduction to his own translation of *I and Thou*, "God actually does not appear much before the third part, . . . [since] the book deals centrally with man's relationships to other men."[39] The I-Thou relations are alive, in Buber's book, before God enters the picture. They have a life of their own; and, like the charge to humanity itself, to be fruitful (Gen 1:26), they naturally multiply from one to many. They call each other into being. Unlike romantic relations, they are not exclusive or self-enclosed, but expand toward "the community built of relation."[40]

36. Buber, *I and Thou*, 150.
37. Buber, *I and Thou*, 68.
38. Buber, *I and Thou*, 147.
39. Buber, *I and Thou*, 31, 38.
40. Buber, *I and Thou*, 155.

"The isolated moments of relationships join for a world life of association"[41]—in German, *Verbundenheit*, a word for community founded on *Bund*, or covenant. And indeed, a communal matrix of I-Thou relations exhibits, for Buber, just those more generalized features of covenant: "functional autonomy, mutual recognition and responsibility,"[42] a "process of differentiation and . . . integration,"[43] a paradox of "bound and free."[44] Just now, key for us is the "functional autonomy." A matrix of I-Thou relations needs a space of its own to self-nurture and grow. It cannot be confined or restricted by narrow political ambitions or lusts for power. This becomes the foundation of Buber's Zionism. "Zionism," he says, "is actually a movement dedicated to realizing the theopolitical covenant between the people of Israel and their God, which centers on the reformation of the worldly kingdom by the heavenly one."[45] Otherwise put, the Jewish people need a space of their own, a "worldly kingdom," to optimally manifest their special gift for the I-Thou relationship (which *is* the covenant in action). For one as steeped in the Bible as Buber was, there was one place only for this kingdom to be: the promised land of biblical provenance.

Buber did not read the Bible fundamentalistically. But he did read in mythically, in the grandest sense of that term, as a text that supplied life-determining stories. The story of the exodus determined the Jewish people to be a *people*, defined according to his own philosophy as bearers of the ideal of the I-Thou relation. But they were also a *nation*. Their national identity, given by the story of Sinai, determines them not simply to carry the ideal of the I-Thou relation but to manifest it within the framework of a functioning, worldly society, the kind of society mandated by the books of Leviticus and Exodus. The Bible located that society in the promised land. Buber makes much of the fact that the Zionist movement is named after a specific place, not an idea, person, or people. Zion was a hill in Jerusalem that served as "the old stronghold of the Jebusites, which David made his residence, and whose name was applied by poets and prophets to the whole city of Jerusalem . . . as the place of the sanctuary, . . . that is, of God."[46]

41. Buber, *I and Thou*, 149.
42. "In the Midst of Crisis," in Buber, *Writings of Martin Buber*, 125.
43. "Experiment That Did Not Fail," in Buber, *Writings of Martin Buber*, 138.
44. "Question to the Single One," in Buber, *Writings of Martin Buber*, 84.
45. Buber quoted in Hever, "Buber versus Scholem," 234.
46. "Zion and Other National Concepts," in Buber, *Writings of Martin Buber*, 300.

At the same time, just as Buber can bypass God in his presentation of the I-Thou relation, so can he skirt the Bible in his understanding of the foundations of Zionism. That strip of land variously called Canaan, Palestine, Judah, and Israel speaks in the Jewish people to "deep inner forces and energies, whose roots lie in the very beginning of time,"[47] back further than Sinai, to just that primordial Jewish identity, perhaps, we had such a struggle to articulate in the previous chapter. Buber suggests that the identity of the Jewish people "has been bound up from its beginning with this land, . . . that they might elevate it to perfection, and that it, the land, might in turn bring about their own perfection."[48] Here is yet another covenant—this time between land and people—and also another I-Thou relation, insofar as the land can be a Thou to the people who cultivates it and are in turn cultivated (spiritually) in tune with it.

Of course, the challenge to the realization of this ideal is that other people were already living in that space: "the Arabs, who have dwelt in this land for something like thirteen hundred years."[49] But this could be a blessing insofar as it provided an opportunity for an expansive covenant of Jews in I-Thou relations with each other and the land to extend outward and inclusively toward non-Jews. For "what lies hidden in the name of Zion" are implications that extend "far beyond the frontier of national problems and touching the domain of the universally human, the cosmic, and even of Being itself."[50] Jews may carry the ideal of the I-Thou relation, but all humanity and beyond, including animal, vegetable, and mineral, make the context for its full realization.

Buber envisioned an organically expansive web of covenantal communities in the promised land, for which the kibbutz was the model. What he pictured for the kibbutz was a framework for interpersonal relations in which "people . . . have mutual access to one another and are ready for one another,"[51] which is a more homey than usual description of I-Thou relationality and Buberian covenant. The general reference to "people," rather than Jews, in that vision is not casual. To picture the ever-expansiveness of covenantal community, Buber chose images from Christian history. He suggested that the historical movement within the religious orders of Christianity from hermitage to monastery to friary,

---

47. Buber, *Land of Two Peoples*, 195.
48. Buber, *Land of Two Peoples*, 196.
49. Buber, *Land of Two Peoples*, 195.
50. "Zion and Other National Concepts," in Buber, *Writings of Martin Buber*, 303.
51. "Experiment That Did Not Fail," in Buber, *Writings of Martin Buber*, 137.

over the course of a millennium, represented an ever-expanding vision of the scope of Christian community, from separate solitudes to remote collectives to urban communes.[52] Correspondingly, out of a network of kibbutzim would emerge "an order of life for future mankind, for all peoples combined into one people."[53]

Here is a vision for the State of Israel that rides on the coattails of Christianity toward a network of I-Thou relations between "all peoples combined into one people." In practice, what Buber supported locally was a binational homeland for Jews and Palestinian Arabs. Even after 1948, until his death in 1965, Buber continued to argue for what he called a "federative union" between Jews and Arabs, i.e., a covenantal union as he understood it. His last published piece appeared within the Arab-friendly Jewish organ *New Outlook*, in which Amos Oz would later also publish on Jewish and Israeli identity. There Buber wrote, "the basis on which a federative union can be established is, by necessity, so that for each of the two partners the full national autonomy is preserved; neither one should be allowed to injure in any point the national existence of the other."[54] That is as *realpolitik* as Buber gets.

Before we extract from Buber's Zionism any lights to shine on the State of Israel today, let us consider the thought of his predecessor in cultural Zionism, indeed the founder of it, Ahad Ha'am (1856–1927), "One of the People," only briefly cited above. This was the pen name of Russian-born Asher Ginzberg, who, for all the streets named after him in Israel, "in Western Europe and America . . . is practically unknown," and even in Israel, "can hardly be said to be held in official favor."[55] These words of historian Hans Kohn, written in 1962, hold true still today. Among the many paradoxes of Ahad Ha'am is that he wrote philosophically on a topic so emotionally charged, in his own time and now, as to appear to resist philosophical analysis: Zionism. But this is so much true of him that he has been called "the philosopher of Zionism."[56]

Ahad Ha'am already locates himself in the Jewish philosophical tradition by writing so appreciatively of Maimonides. On the occasion of the seven hundredth year of Maimonides's death, in 1904, Ahad Ha'am dedicated an essay on "The Supremacy of Reason" to the

52. "In the Midst of Crisis," in Buber, *Writings of Martin Buber*, 129.
53. "Hebrew Humanism," in Buber, *Writings of Martin Buber*, 298.
54. Buber, *Land of Two Peoples*, 305.
55. Ha'am, *Nationalism*, 30.
56. Harry Sacher, quoted in Ha'am, *Essays, Letters, Memoirs*, 50.

memory of the great philosopher. He unapologetically boldfaced what he took to be Maimonides's reigning goal: "to translate Judaism into pure philosophy,"[57] and in so doing to forefront the determinative role of reason in human life. "We may put the whole teaching of the *Guide* in a single sentence: Follow reason, and reason only."[58] That is certainly one read of the whole philosophical endeavor. But, to return to his paradoxical self, Ahad Ha'am also admired Maimonides's medieval philosophical counterpart, Judah Halevi, whose attachment to the Jewish people took him beyond the bounds of reason. To close one of his earliest published pieces, "Truth from Eretz Israel,"[59] from 1891, Ahad Ha'am cited one of Judah Halevi's poetic laments over the Zion for which he longed, "To Zion."[60] But Ahad Ha'am adapts the language of lamentation, which for Halevi referenced a suffering Zion, to the regrettable behavior of the colonists *in* Zion. His essay describes the physical challenges and moral failings of early Zionist colonization efforts in then Ottoman Palestine, which he had just visited. Sorrowing over these failures as he stands before the Wailing Wall, he imagines himself possessed by "the spirit of Rabbi Yehuda Halevi,"[61] who longed for the land of Israel. But for Ahad Ha'am, the longing is less for the land than for a spirit the people has lost. "My lament would not begin with Zion but with Israel,"[62] he writes—meaning, with the people Israel, who have lost their way.

Ahad Ha'am's joint philosophical descent from Maimonides and Judah Halevi lends a unique quality to his thoughts on what in his time was still a future state of Israel. Reason may be an important guide but there is also "the wisdom of experience."[63] As Jacques Kornberg writes, Ahad Ha'am's "conception of the national bond raised feeling and instinct over reason."[64] His interpretation of Halevi's poem already subordinates the land of Israel to its people. "Let the land be destroyed, and yet the people remains full of life and force—. . . they will return and rebuild it. But if the people be destroyed, who shall arise and from

---

57. "Supremacy of Reason," in Ha'am, *Essays, Letters, Memoirs*, 182.
58. "Supremacy of Reason," in Ha'am, *Essays, Letters, Memoirs*, 172.
59. Ha'am, "Truth from Eretz Israel," 160–81.
60. Rosenzweig, *Ninety-Two Poems*, 272–74.
61. Ha'am, "Truth from Eretz Israel," 179.
62. Ha'am, "Truth from Eretz Israel," 179.
63. Ha'am, "Truth from Eretz Israel," 167.
64. Kornberg, *At the Crossroads*, xix.

whence shall come its help?"[65] The land matters only for its service in the moral life of the people. According to Hans Kohn, Ahad Ha'am's "emotions often shaped his ultimate outlook."[66] He shared Halevi's intensity of feeling for the people Israel; how natural that he should channel his feeling for the people through the poetry of the medieval philosopher. At the same time, as Kohn continues, "his intellectual honesty and self-discipline, his sober and responsible realism,"[67] channeled a rationalist sensibility more akin to Maimonides, that shrank from all violence—"Jews and blood, are there two greater opposites than these?"[68]—and that deeply suspected, as Buber would after him, "that national egoism which he rightly regarded as a greater danger to mankind than individual egoism,"[69] as Kohn puts it.

Buber, whom Ahad Ha'am anticipated, brings another lens through which to read "the philosopher of Zionism." For in their respective Zionisms the two shared a vocabulary of wholes and centers; and they both appreciated the import of biblical myth, which laid the foundation for the Jewish sense of historic home in Palestine. For Buber, the I-Thou relation set the whole of persons in mutual encounter. Ahad Ha'am is less poetic, but for him too, part of the reason for Zionism is that Jews cannot be whole except in a land of their own.[70] They are otherwise divided between local and Jewish national loyalty, as in fact many diaspora Jews do indeed experience. A Jew by nature gives "his whole soul"[71] for the sake of "the whole nation,"[72] and ultimately for "the whole human race."[73] She can only do that in a land of her own.

For the whole of the Jewish people to function, though, it needed what Ahad Ha'am called a "spiritual center"—in Hebrew, *merkaz ruhani*. Ahad Ha'am's signature Zionism envisioned a center for the Jewish people in Palestine, surrounded the world over by vibrant diaspora

---

65. Ha'am, "Truth from Eretz-Israel," 179.
66. Ha'am, *Nationalism*, 9.
67. Ha'am, *Nationalism*, 8.
68. Ha'am, *Nationalism*, 26.
69. Ha'am, *Nationalism*, 24.
70. The diaspora Jew is "a stranger in a strange land in which he cannot make himself truly at home except by tearing himself in halves, with the inevitable result of a lack of wholeness" ("Zionism and Jewish Culture," in Ha'am, *Essays, Letters, Memoirs*, 86).
71. "Zionism and Jewish Culture," in Ha'am, *Essays, Letters, Memoirs*, 84.
72. "Jewish and Christian Ethics," in Ha'am, *Essays, Letters, Memoirs*, 137.
73. "Jewish and Christian Ethics," in Ha'am, *Essays, Letters, Memoirs*, 130.

communities that drew their energy from that central source, like planets from the sun. A settlement of Jews in Palestine would be "a fixed center of our national spirit and culture, which will be a new spiritual bond between the scattered sections of the people and by its spiritual significance will stimulate them all to a new national life."[74] This was a departure from what would become mainline Zionism, which pictured a return of the entire Jewish people to Palestine. It is also as good an indication as any of how practical Ahad Ha'am was in his moral idealism—he knew not all Jews would *want* to leave their diaspora homes. But this picture of an expansive circle of Jews focused on an energizing center is Buberian too. It was Buber's vision of a true community: "The real essence of community is to be found in the fact, manifest or otherwise, that it has a center";[75] and "the more earthly, the more creaturely"[76] that center, the better. No mere abstraction could exert the centripetal pull on the satellite communities. And what more earthly center for a community could there be than land? Though Buber did not focus on the relation between center and diaspora, his vision of true community superimposes neatly on Ahad Ha'am's Zionism.

Finally, the two philosophers shared a non-literalist, mythic read of the Bible. For all his departure from Orthodox Judaism, Ahad Ha'am was loath to endorse the historical-critical readings of the Bible already popular in his day that reduced it, as Spinoza did, to a pastiche of mutually contradictory accounts of a dubious past, however literally correct Spinoza might have been. It was not just that he would not "wound the susceptibilities of the believers,"[77] though it was partly that, but that the determinative impact of the Bible on Jewish national consciousness lent it the force of truth. This comes out most especially in his reading of Moses. Ahad Ha'am relied less for his Zionism on the plotline of the exodus and Sinai stories than Buber did, and more on the figure of Moses himself, the paradigmatic prophet, which for Ahad Ha'am meant (as it does for Muslims): moral exemplar. To an "erudite questioner" of biblical history that he conjures, Ahad Ha'am replies, "even if you succeeded in proving beyond all doubt that the man Moses never existed . . . that would not in the slightest degree affect the historical reality of the ideal Moses, . . . who

74. Ha'am, *Nationalism*, 127.
75. "In the Midst of Crisis," in Buber, *Writings of Martin Buber*, 129.
76. "In the Midst of Crisis," in Buber, *Writings of Martin Buber*, 129.
77. Ahad Ha'am to Dr. S. Bernfeld, June 9, 1902, in Ha'am, *Essays, Letters, Memoirs*, 259.

... has led us for thousands of years in all the wildernesses in which we have wandered since the Exodus."[78] The ideal Moses was as good if not better than the historical one. Why?—because as "a creation of the Jewish spirit," he embodied the moral ideals of the Jewish prophetic consciousness, which for the individual Jew at his best "fills his whole heart and mind [and] . . . is the whole purpose of life."[79] The triad of wholeness, center, and Bible begins and ends in wholeness.

Unlike some Orthodox Zionists, Ahad Ha'am was not messianic in his beliefs. He predicted a disastrous unfolding for any messianically motivated Zionism.[80] But he was prophetic. As Leon Simon writes, "he saw the Jewish people as essentially the people of the prophets"[81]—in secular terms, an ethical people. To the extent he accepted the doctrine of chosenness, it was on those terms, of a people whose "inherent characteristics make it better fitted than the others for moral development. . . . The Jewish people is preeminent in its genius for morality."[82] Moral fitness plays the role for Ahad Ha'am that exceptional attunement to I-Thou relationality played for Buber and begins to mark the central divide between the two thinkers. For unlike Buber, who, having called attention to the I-Thou relation, gives it a theistic framework, Ahad Ha'am needs no God to sustain Jewish ethics, which belongs to the people's national character too fundamentally to need any outward warrant or creator. This is also where Ahad Ha'am loses the link Buber maintained, through the sublimity of the I-Thou relation, to our postulate of Jewish indescribability. For ethics is indeed describable, as Ahad Ha'am does succinctly and without fuss, by way of the biblical precept "thou shalt love thy neighbor as thyself," adding only that, beyond the level of the individual, "it can be carried out by a whole nation in its dealings with other nations."[83] He confessed outright, "the branch of Jewish study which attracts me most is Jewish ethics."[84]

---

78. "Moses," in Ha'am, *Essays, Letters, Memoirs*, 104.

79. "Moses," in Ha'am, *Essays, Letters, Memoirs*, 104, 105.

80. Hans Kohn writes, "Ahad Ha'am firmly believed that to confound messianic hopes and political potentialities could lead only to moral and physical disaster." Ha'am, *Nationalism*, 20.

81. Ha'am, *Essays, Letters, Memoirs*, 42.

82. "Judaism and Nietzsche," in Ha'am, *Essays, Letters, Memoirs*, 80.

83. "Jewish and Christian Ethics," in Ha'am, *Essays, Letters, Memoirs*, 137.

84. Ahad Ha'am to E. Lubarski, April 30, 1906, in Ha'am, *Essays, Letters, Memoirs*, 308.

This is also Ahad Ha'am's secularism. We are apt to be misled by Ahad Ha'am's choice of term for his vision of Jewish destiny: *spiritual* Zionism. His Zionism was not spiritual for any theistic or even broadly religious connotation, but only in contrast to the political Zionism that competed with it. By "spiritual" Ahad Ha'am meant, as Germans do by *geistlich*, that which is of the mind, and its products in culture. By his notion that the Jewish people carry a special gift for ethics, Ahad Ha'am already lays ground for another of his signature terms: "national spirit." The notion that nations carried a spirit distinct to them was much in play in Ahad Ha'am's day, a heritage of eighteenth- and nineteenth-century secular philosophies of nationality.[85] For Ahad Ha'am, nations birthed the ideas that bound them and shaped them into a whole of parts. The spirit of a nation, as its sustainer, even enjoyed a primacy over its body of individuals. "The body should not be given empire over the spirit."[86] Otherwise put, no nation's bodily existence is ever an end in itself, or even self-sufficient enough to exist on its own.

As Ahad Ha'am saw it, the national spirit of the Jewish people had given rise to three cultural products that effectively defined it: the Hebrew language (as spoken chiefly in the liturgy), Hebrew literature (as present in the Bible), and Jewish religion (as given first by temple priests, and then by the rabbis). Though all three of these had been in decline within Jewish life and consciousness for some time by Ahad Ha'am's day, at least Hebrew language and literature were undergoing a visible revival. Ahad Ha'am himself wrote all his works in Hebrew. Hebrew language and literature were taking new shape outside the framework of the Bible and the liturgy, but in continuity with those former expressions. No one illustrates this better than Ahad Ha'am's admirer Chaim Nahman Bialik (1873–1934), who edited a compendium of rabbinic lore,[87] even as he composed his own original Hebrew verse. More problematic was the decline of religion among the Jewish people: "Religion is a mass of irksome duties,"[88] Ahad Ha'am wrote, speaking for many East European

---

85. The notion was indebted to "ideas of philosophers such as J. G. Herder and J. G. Fichte, who argued that humanity was fundamentally divided into distinct 'nations,' each of which had a unique history, culture, and 'national spirit'" (Stanislawski, *Zionism*, 4). We will encounter this idea again under the topic of history, in the work of Nachman Krochmal.

86. "Judaism and Asceticism," in Ha'am, *Essays, Letters, Memoirs*, 124.

87. Bialik and Ravnitzky, *Book of Legends/Sefer Ha-Aggadah*, was first published in Hebrew in Odessa by the firm the two founded, Dvir, between 1908 and 1911.

88. "Diaspora Nationalism," in Ha'am, *Essays, Letters, Memoirs*, 224.

Jews. Here is where Zionism enters the picture. Zionism was an idea that stood to perform the same unifying function for the Jewish people that rabbinic religion once did. It does indeed emerge from rabbinic Judaism as fulfillment of a longing encoded in prayer for a lost land; but now, with the decline of rabbinical religion, Zionism "is not merely a part of Judaism, ... it is the whole of Judaism, but with a different focal point"[89]—return to the promised land. Zionism was, as Leon Simon puts it for Ahad Ha'am, "the outcome and fulfillment of Judaism."[90]

Ahad Ha'am effectively invented, or at least adroitly packaged, a kind of secular Judaism. As Jehuda Reinharz writes, "Ahad Ha'am contended that secular Judaism need not be a radical break in Jewish life because [it] could be grounded in cultural forms that are more fundamental than the religious practices of traditional Jewish life."[91] The new Judaism would comprise a Hebraic culture evolving from a Hebrew-speaking people in a land of their own, inspiring Jews everywhere and, ultimately, all humanity.

But the sense of belonging to the land would not come from ruling it, but from tending it, which would nurture a further flourishing of culture. Ahad Ha'am envisioned for Palestine a "rural proletariat" of Jewish agricultural laborers, for each of whom "the inherited link between himself and the land is so strong and deep that he can never sever it."[92] Though he saw little promise of such a proletariat arising among Jewish colonists when he visited Palestine again in 1912, he saw signs of a class of "independent farmers" who would unite something of that love of land with an appreciation for "the fruits of contemporary culture."[93] Out of this foundation a "Hebrew national atmosphere" would grow within "the whole social order

---

89. "People of the Book," in Ha'am, *Essays, Letters, Memoirs*, 63.

90. Ha'am, *Essays, Letters, Memoirs*, 51. Or, as Jacques Kornberg puts it, Ahad Ha'am "interpreted the whole of the Jewish past form a nationalist perspective, displacing God and placing the nation at the center of Jewish history" (Kornberg, *At the Crossroads*, xv–xvi).

91. Reinharz, "Ahad Ha-am," 147.

92. Ha'am, *Nationalism*, 139.

93. Ha'am, *Nationalism*, 137, 143. On this point, hear the commentary of Adi Ophir, "Zionism was supposed to transform Jewish economy and turn Jews into productive workers. In the Jewish state, Jews have abandoned most kinds of manual and traditional industrial labor to others. A system of labor relations has formed in which Jews control capital and the means of production while non-Jews work in their fields and factories, sometimes in inhuman conditions, underpaid and exploited" (Ophir, "Identity of the Victims," 97).

[and] all the communal institutions"[94] of the renewed Jewish homeland. A confirmation of this process successfully in play was, for Ahad Ha'am, the founding of Hebrew University in 1918—"a great historical event," whose culmination in the opening of the university, in 1925, he lived to see. The foundation stones of the university would also be those of "our future national life,"[95] he wrote, as if a Jewish professoriate might at least partially compensate for the lack of a Jewish proletariat.

In fact, the faculties of Hebrew University, among those of other Israeli universities, have spoken, as we will soon see, to what from Ahad Ha'am's point of view, were he alive today, could not but proclaim itself the great Zionist failing: the suffering of Palestinians under Jewish Israeli hegemony. He saw the seeds of this already in his own day, as he reported of the Jewish settlers on his 1891 trip to Palestine: "They walk with the Arabs in hostility and cruelty, unjustly encroaching on them, shamefully beating them for no good reason and even bragging about what they do."[96] He feared this was a case of the license the persecuted practice when empowered, and warned the colonists, "in our conduct toward a foreign people among whom we live once again, to walk together in love and respect."[97] He had enough confidence in this possibility to advocate in 1920 that the Jewish home in Palestine rise up "without overthrowing the national home of the other inhabitants,"[98] and to imply, as Buber would later, that the only viable state for two different peoples claiming the same land was a bi-national one in which neither held sway. But this was entirely consistent with spiritual Zionism, which subordinated life on the land to growth of spirit there. Ahad Ha'am trusted that the political arrangement appropriate to two peoples sharing in amity the same land would emerge organically over time, "so that they may together administer their joint affairs fairly and justly, in accordance with the needs of each of them,"[99]

---

94. Ha'am, *Nationalism*, 148.

95. Ahad Ha'am to Chaim Weizmann, August 12, 1918, in Ha'am, *Essays, Letters, Memoirs*, 294.

96. Ha'am, "Truth from Eretz Israel," 175. Ahad Ha'am saw the personhood of the native inhabitants of Palestine. As Alan Dowry puts it in his introduction to "Truth from Eretz Israel," "in 1891 Ahad Ha'am did see beyond what others saw. He saw the Arabs not simply as passive objects of manipulation by others, but as actors with their own desires and aims" (Ha'am, "Truth from Eretz Israel," 157).

97. Ha'am, "Truth from Eretz Israel," 175.

98. Ha'am, *Nationalism*, 161.

99. Ha'am, *Nationalism*, 161. Dmitry Shumsky makes the point plainly: In the wake of the Balfour Declaration, of 1917, "Ahad Ha'am sketches out a distinctly binational

without the diplomatic stratagems, coercions, and heroics of violence that would come to characterize political Zionism.

Had he miraculously lived to see the founding of the State of Israel, Ahad Ha'am might have sensed, with Gershom Scholem and other cultural Zionists, that the exigencies of the Holocaust and its aftermath pushed the state into existence prematurely, before a requisite base in spirit was firmly established among the people. For the Holocaust figures in the rationale for the founding of the state, as even the Declaration of Independence attests. This of course defies our own negation of any instrumentality to be extracted from suffering in general or the Holocaust in particular. But it does raise the question of at what point the ideals of Buber and Ahad Ha'am for a Jewish homeland—at what point a vision of pervasive amity between Palestinian Jews and Arabs—became so seemingly unrealizable. If a time can be pinpointed before which the ideals of cultural Zionism might indeed have been realized, then perhaps some measure of that time can be purposively and intentionally recovered even now.

Various candidates for that time are on offer. The notion of such a time turns on the history and memory of relatively easy coexistence between Jewish and Arab inhabitants of the Ottoman Empire, both within and outside Palestine. On those grounds, journalist Amy Dockser Marcus suggests 1913, the eve of World War I and the fall of the Ottomans, as the *terminus ad quem* for prospects of peace in Palestine.[100] For historian Hillel Cohen, the year 1929 marks that time, when over a hundred Jews died in Palestinian attacks on them, the most—fifty-nine—in Hebron.[101] But recently, in an online webinar, director of the Alliance for Middle East Peace Huda Abuarquob found the latest turning point against peaceful coexistence in the 1995 assassination of Israeli Prime Minister Itzhak Rabin:

> The message after Rabin's assassination in 1995 was clear to the Palestinians and to the world: The Israeli people are going to be ruled and are now ruled by the most extreme among them. . . .

---

political vision for the relations between the Jews and Arabs of Palestine" (Shumsky, *Beyond the Nation-State*, 18). One of Ahad Ha'am's critiques of political Zionism was that in its impetuous desire for immediate victory, it moved too fast and so blocked the organic emergence of a conflict-averse coexistence in Palestine. The tortoise had the wisdom over the hare.

100. Marcus, *Jerusalem 1913*.
101. Cohen, *Year Zero of the Arab-Israeli Conflict*.

In 1995 the message was, there is no two-state solution, no peace, and we [Israeli leadership] will continue to practice our right to exist and to defend ourselves even if this is going to be at the expense of suppressing an entire nation.[102]

Of course, the fact of three proposed closures suggests that none of them are really that, and an opening to peace can reappear. Politicians and diplomats have not given up on the prospect. But the whole point of cultural Zionism is that politics is not the way to go. Our negation of political Zionism invites the input of cultural Zionism on just this point. Ahad Ha'am was very much a feet-on-the-ground kind of Zionist. On his several visits to Palestine, he *saw* the treatment of Palestinians at the hands of the *halutzim*. He *moved* to Tel Aviv toward the end of his life. He *knew* Arab-speakers in the region. Such personal engagement is even truer of Martin Buber, who lived in Jerusalem among Palestinians and cultivated relations with Arabs. The light a revived cultural Zionism sheds on Israel today spotlights the many grassroots organizations within Israel and the West Bank that nurture personal interaction between Jews and Palestinians. It is no small endeavor, given all that separates the two in living out their daily lives within Israel today.

Let us consider one instance of personal interaction between a Jewish Holocaust survivor and a Palestinian refugee. The case is significant because of the role of Holocaust remembrance at the foundation of Israeli statehood. Israeli historian Ilan Pappé goes so far as to say that "everything in Israel is measured vis-à-vis the Holocaust."[103] But a Palestinian refugee from Israel puts a question mark on what the memory of the Holocaust can justify and possibly opens an irenic communication between Jews and Arabs on displacement, death, and suffering. Or as Amnon Raz-Krakotzkin puts it more dramatically: "the Palestinian memories of dispossession are the Israelis' suppressed nightmares."[104] Can they be helpfully un-suppressed?

In 2016, Menachem Daum and Oren Rudavsky released their film, *Ruins of Lifta: Where the Holocaust and Nakba Meet*. It is a documentary of meeting between a Jewish Holocaust survivor, Dasha Rittenberg, and a Palestinian refugee from the 1948 war, Yacoub Odeh. As reported in the

---

102. Abuarquob et al., "Jerusalem Crisis."

103. Pappé, *Out of the Frame*, 140. He adds that "worst of all was the Zionist and later Israeli abuse of the Holocaust memory to justify the dispossession of Palestine" (179).

104. Raz-Krakotzkin, "'On the Right Side of the Barricades,'" 375.

film, "Lifta is the only Arab village abandoned in 1948 which has not been completely destroyed or repopulated by Jews."[105] The film takes viewers into the abandoned town and reports on a movement to halt plans to raze it to make way for a new development that would erase the memory of its past. The filmmakers communicate a hope that Lifta could be a site of reconciliation between Israeli Jews and refugee Palestinians.

One of the film's commentators on this project is Hillel Cohen, cited briefly above, who teaches in the Department of Islam and Middle East Studies of Hebrew University. Professor Cohen explains of his book, *Year Zero of the Arab Israeli Conflict, 1929*, that he intended, as a Jewish Israeli historian, to give voice in it to the Palestinian side of the conflict, and to represent the emotional impact on Palestinians of Jewish encroachments on the land.[106] To exist simultaneously on opposing sides of a boundary is no easy task, and one of the questions *Ruins of Lifta* asks is whether Israeli Jews in sufficient numbers can practice this in any consequential way.

In the midst of his sensitivity to the good intentions of the filmmaker, Menachem Daum, himself a child of Holocaust survivors, Professor Cohen raises a caution. He admits that, "I see all your good intentions and again am your partner in these good intentions,"[107] but frames these with the "place of privilege, of power" that Daum occupies as a visiting American Jew. From that place, Daum can assume a stance of magnanimity toward the refugees, Cohen says, "letting the people back to there, to establish a Jewish-Arab Center for Reconciliation," but adds, "this is a Jewish chutzpah." It comes from a noble place, "the beginning of seeing the other," but "this is yet you, not you and him [i.e., the refugee]." The viewer can read this as a reproof of the American Jew extending an olive branch he does not really have to give. Daum has only *begun* to see the other—the refugee—but not his wholeness, as Buber might say. At this first encounter with the refugee, Daum's view of him is too slanted by the use he wishes to make of him to assuage an American Jewish conscience that has begun to suffer over the shadow side of Israeli independence, the Naqba. So "this is yet you, not you and him."

---

105. Daum and Rudavsky, *Ruins of Lifta*. For a more recent documentary on the lasting impact of the Naqba on a Palestinian city within Israel, see Younis and Friedland, *Lyd*.

106. Cohen, "Writing *Year Zero*."

107. Hillel Cohen, interview by Menachem Daum, in Daum and Radevsky, *Ruins of Lifta*. Subsequent quotations from the film come from this interview.

Cohen is suggesting that what Ahad Ha'am might have called the national spirit of the Jewish people is not yet at the point of fruitful dialogue with Palestinians. More work needs to be done if there is to be any hope of recovering the time before the overt conflict. Menachem Daum's reconciliation efforts are "better than Israeli bulldozers," Cohen concedes. But perhaps the interpersonal approach of cultural Zionism needs a deeper probe to uncover the good it still might do. Something within it, itself, may be blocking our way.

A helpful critic most specifically of Buber's Zionism is Judith Butler. Butler observes of Buber that he did not see that the very effort to wrest the land away from its former inhabitants was relation-destroying.[108] He did not see the magnitude of that consequence of the settlements. Perhaps within Ahad Ha'am's time, pre-1929, the Palestinian sense of land loss was not so pronounced. In any case, if a revival of cultural Zionism is to clear a space of healing for Israeli Jews and Palestinians, it needs some corrective.

This Judith Butler provides. Butler is indeed a self-identified *Jewish* philosopher, whose "schooling and early childhood formation within Jewish communities as well as an engagement with the educational programs of my synagogue . . . prompted me to study philosophy."[109] Part of what motivates Butler's book *Parting Ways: Jewishness and the Critique of Zionism* is her objection to the careless identification of Jewishness with Zionism. Not even Ahad Ha'am identified *Jewishness* with Zionism. He merely thought Judaism, the religion of the Jewish people, had formed itself anew in Zionistic terms.

Butler's help to us relates more to yet another view of Jewishness she explores in dialogue with the work of American-Palestinian philosopher Edward Said (1935–2003). Said, who was born in British-ruled Palestine, was an outspoken proponent of a Palestinian state, but in peaceable relation with the Jewish state. Butler reads Said's book *Freud and the Non-European* (2003) for still another take on Moses besides the ones we have already had from Buber (Moses as facilitator of Jewish peoplehood and nation) and from Ahad Ha'am (Moses as model prophet). Critical for Said, building off Freud, in Butler's reading is that Moses was the "*Egyptian* founder of the Jews" (31) (emphasis ours).

---

108. "He could not see the impossibility of trying to cultivate certain ideals of co-operation on conditions established by settler colonialism" (Butler, *Parting Ways*, 36).

109. Butler, *Parting Ways*, 20. Subsequent citations to pages of this text are given parenthetically.

The implication of this for Jewishness is the suggestion that this identity is from the start ineluctably bound up with non-Jewishness. Jewish identity is, by its very nature, in continuous retreat from itself before an other to it. This keeps Jewishness "from being fully incorporated into a monolithic and unified identity, singular and exclusive" (31). It is by nature an identity open to "wound" (Said's word) and to an ongoing "irresolution of identity" (31) (Butler's phrase). "It is Jewish/not Jewish, and its meaning lies precisely in that conjunctive disjunction" (6–7). The result is an identity "both ruined and vibrant" (13)—vibrant in its ruin, as though its ongoing life is in its proximity to collapse.

In Moses's day, Egypt supplied the non-Jewish identity that permeated Jewish identity. But in our day, in the vexed context of Israel/Palestine, Palestinian culture can be understood to fill that role. For Israeli Jews today, in other words, "Moses is an Arab Jew" (228n) who "moves us beyond both the nation and the binary of Jew/Palestinian" (31).[110] Butler reading Said touches base here with Rosenzweig, for whom a non-violent Jewish state would exist always on the precipice of its own demise. It would generate from within itself its own inherently self-undermining, non-identarian identity. Jewish identity reframed along Butler's lines informs a Jewish statehood that naturally accommodates the Palestinian, not so much from propensity toward I-Thou relations, as Buber might say, but from its own need to accommodate otherness within itself. Could such a state ever be?

If so, it would take its place within a line of self-undermining gestures that work in sync with our practiced negations of creation doctrine, of theodicy, of contentful Jewishness. But the self-undermining gesture is endemic to biblical Judaism, which raises the prospect of child sacrifice only to negate it (Gen 22), of battle, only to undermine it (Deut 20:8), of kingship, only to critique it (1 Sam 8:4–19), or even of law, only to ignore it (Ecclesiastes and Job). As for the rabbis, do they not confirm this line of reasoning when they limit capital punishment by so many conditions as virtually to negate it?[111]

Butler invites a recovery of cultural Zionism that absents any claim on land that dispossesses another. The land was never foundational for Ahad Ha'am to begin with; its only purpose was to provide context for the Jewish national spirit to thrive. That spirit only thrives in something

---

110. A further, Jewish development on this idea comes from Azoulay, *Jewelers of the Ummah*.

111. See Blidstein, "Capital Punishment," 159–71.

like the I-Thou relations Buber envisioned for Jewish Israelis in relation with Palestinian neighbors. A grassroots organization that realistically builds toward an ideal of mutuality between the two peoples is A Land for All: Two States, One Homeland.[112] But another picture comes to mind, of a land of two loves: a parent's for their child, and a child's for their parent. The Children of Israel in the mythic consciousness of the Bible precede the land of Israel. The land is like a child to the people who, as the Declaration of Independence boasts, "made deserts bloom" there; while for the Palestinians who lived on the land for centuries under a succession of Muslim states, it is more like a parent, which protected them under expanses of *already* blooming olive trees. It is "just" a matter of joining the two loves into one. The land is both parent and child for all who dwell there.

---

112. https://alandforall.org.

Chapter 5
History

IT IS NO DRAMATIC gesture within the historically rabbinic tradition to negate the import of history. The aggada confidently proclaims: "no strict order as to 'earlier' and 'later' is observed in the Torah,"[1] which is especially true of the great sea of rabbinical literature. As Rosenzweig opined, this is a compendium for exiting time. And until relatively recently, the philosophers agreed. Here is Maimonides on history: "Books found among the Arabs describing historical events [and] the government of kings . . . neither possess wisdom nor yield profit for the body, but are merely a waste of time."[2] The problem was not the ethnic origin of these books. Historical stories beyond the Bible's had little meaning for Maimonides. As Maimonides scholar James Arthur Diamond comments on his subject's behalf, "truth is preserved—not by history but by independent thought"[3] and "Judaism entails an overcoming of history, memory, and heredity . . . [and] all such mundane dimensions of human experience."[4] Historian Salo Baron adds, "the logical bent of

---

1. Mekhilta, 2:54 (par. Shirata, to Exod 15:9–10). Also: https://www.sefaria.org/Mekhilta_DeRabbi_Yishmael%2C_Tractate_Shirah.7.1.

2. Baron, "Historical Outlook of Maimonides," 7–8. The quotation is from Maimonides's commentary on Sanhedrin 10:1. See Maimonides, *Maimonides's Commentary on the Mishnah*, 150. Maimonides did not think critically about Jewish history. Salo Baron comments, "In point of history, he [Maimonides] leans heavily on legendary sources" (Baron, "Historical Outlook of Maimonides," 110). Kenneth Seeskin adds, "He rarely takes a critical approach to his [historical] material" (Seeskin, "Maimonides's Sense of History," 131).

3. Diamond, "Maimonides vs. Nachmanides," 111.

4. Diamond, "Maimonides vs. Nachmanides," 114–15.

his [Maimonides's] mind was frequently impatient with the accidental turns of historical events."[5]

If history is accidental, it might be either or both of two things: purposively meaningless and/or pointlessly calamitous. An accident might be either. To affirm them together, as perhaps Maimonides does, is an implicit negation of history, both of any *telos* to it—overarching project, purpose, intended culmination, or discernibly guiding hand behind it—and of any moral or religious meaning to the suffering within it. In denying that kind of meaning to it, we simply extend the negation of theodicy we already practiced in chapter 2. We here negate all historical theodicies.

These two negations provoke different ideas to view. Much of the purpose religiously ascribed to history turns on an interpretive structure drawn from the Bible, of promise and fulfillment. Later events relate to earlier ones as fulfilled promises, whether for good or ill, as the founding of the people relates to a promise made Abraham, the divinely led exodus to a promise made Moses, the Babylonian exile to the predictions the prophets prophesied for failures to obey the law. Within some circles of interpretation, the Holocaust was a punishment for Jewish assimilation to gentile ways. That would lend it a "meaning" we were at pains three chapters ago to negate. But our negation now is of the whole model of promise and fulfillment for interpreting history.

In wake of that negation another take on history comes into view, as an academic discipline of the modern university. History in this sense replaces the interpretive model of promise and fulfillment with one of cause and effect, in imitation of the natural sciences. This view of history shines a light of its own on past events we will want to explore, but it is not without challenges, as model academic historian of Jewish history Yosef Yerushalmi tells us. "As a professional academic historian, I am a new creature in Jewish history,"[6] he says. His point is that in his academic role of historian he does not necessarily endorse the Jewish people's collective memory of itself, which is much older than academic history. The issue is that the two—the historian's research, the collective's memory—stand opposite each other across a methodological divide. Academic history commits to writing history from sources that can be reliably dated and evaluated for truthfulness, rather than from

5. Baron, "Historical Outlook of Maimonides," 7.

6. Yerushalmi, *Zakhor*, 81. Subsequent citations to pages of this text are given parenthetically.

however rich the treasure trove of collective memory. Yerushalmi wrote on this in his now classic text, *Zakhor: Jewish History and Jewish Memory*. "My purpose in *Zakhor* was to make a sharp distinction between collective memory and historiography" (116). "Historiography cannot be a substitute for collective memory" (116). If anything, it "constantly challenges even those memories that have survived intact" (94). And this may be either reassuring or troubling.

The other branch of the accidental nature of history is the calamitous one. It is true that for some time much of post-biblical Jewish history was unfairly interpreted as calamitous—*lachrymose*, according to the memorable phrasing of Salo Baron.[7] Reflecting again on Maimonides, Baron observed, "The general course of Jewish history appears to Maimonides as to all medieval writers as an uninterrupted series of persecutions."[8] Baron critiqued this view and aimed at a more balanced presentation of the Jewish past. But the sufferings within history, as those within nature, can deeply impress the philosopher. Simone Weil called history "a tissue of base and cruel facts in the midst of which a few drops of purity sparkle at long intervals."[9] Franz Rosenzweig references the "murder and manslaughter"[10] within "the curse of historicity."[11] More subtly, novelist Rachel Cusk sights (outside the Jewish context but applicable to it) "the problem of history itself, as it insidiously bequeathed its dark inheritance to each unsuspecting new generation."[12] If we have negated any meaning that might accrue to this darkness from the promise-fulfillment model, what else might come into view, in the wake of that negation, to help "structure"—to borrow Rosenzweig's verb—this suffering for us? We are not seeking a theodicy or justification of historical suffering, but more practically, a psychic healing from the burdens of it on both us and the deceased ancestors. Let us address this difficult challenge first; and then return to the mixed blessing of what shows through our negation of purposive history, which is history as told by academic historians.

One of the most interesting if puzzling efforts to structure historic suffering is Walter Benjamin's "Theses on the Philosophy of History,"

---

7. Baron, "Newer Emphases in Jewish History."
8. Baron, "Historical Outlook of Maimonides," 103.
9. Weil, *Need for Roots*, 226.
10. Rosenzweig to Hans Ehrenberg, October/November 1908, in Rosenzweig, *Briefe*, 40. Translated in Rosenzweig, *Franz Rosenzweig: His Life and Thought*, 17.
11. Rosenzweig, "Atheistic Theology," 24.
12. Cusk, *Parade*, 19.

from 1940. Benjamin broadens our sights on the sufferings of the past by uncovering just those we are primed to miss by way of any privileged place we occupy. There is a massive untold history of subjection to conquest. "All rulers are the heirs of those who conquered before them. . . . Whoever has emerged victorious participates to this day in the triumphal procession in which the rulers step over those who are lying prostrate."[13] But then, this applies as much to the cultural treasures from the past that claim (conquer?) our attention today. We cannot "contemplate [them] without horror" once we acknowledge the collateral suffering of victimized others that helped to pave their way (256).

Benjamin was targeting a particular view of history according to which it advances progressively from worse to better states. For many twentieth-century thinkers, World War I already laid that view to rest. Benjamin called history viewed that way "homogeneous, empty time" (261), as though it were a continuous blank canvas on which events were successively painted in increasingly bright and vivid color. But sadly, history advances the causes of death as much as those of life. Benjamin's image for that takes off from a painting by Paul Klee, called *Angelus Novus*, which once belonged to Benjamin himself, but which now hangs in the Israel Museum and is much reproduced. It is the winsome portrait of a heavenly being in distress. For Benjamin, Klee's angel is "the Angel of History" (257), to which he devotes a paragraph in his "Theses on the Philosophy of History." He sees in the angel's face a look of startled defeat, as it contemplates the unfolding of history before it. For history does not unfurl according to a visibly beneficent plan, as believers in progress might hope, but as "one single catastrophe which keeps piling wreckage upon wreckage . . . in front of his feet" (257). And yet he is powerless to arrest or mitigate the gusts of destruction, which actually blow him backward before it. What we call progress is actually the massive accumulation of debris that piles up before the angel as he is blown backward into the future (258).

So-called progress is really catastrophe. The angel who sees this has exited homogeneous time and regards it from outside it (257). As though we on our own are incapable of such a feat of extraction from our customary view of time, Benjamin gives us an angel through whose eyes to see it. The homogeneity translates into a single catastrophic event, rather than a chain of disparate events progressing by means of cause and effect

13. Benjamin, "Theses," 256. Subsequent citations to pages of this text are given parenthetically.

to a greater goal. The emptiness translates as destruction devoid of meaning. If that were the end of history's story, our predicament within it would be bleak indeed. But just by suggesting a stance outside empty homogeneity, Benjamin implies another view of history: heterogeneous and full. Presumably, this is how the angel would prefer to view history. But by some untold decree, the angel is made to witness what empty, homogeneous history looks like bare and naked, without benefit of the fuller, heterogeneous view. The angel is made to witness the true face of "progress" (258): an unassimilable, insupportable, despair-inducing accumulation of loss and debris.

One of the reasons there is so much debris (it grows skyward) is that the angel is witnessing *all* that is lost or forgotten on the homogeneous and progressive view of the past. The appearance of progress rests on obscuring all "those who are lying prostrate" (256) in subjection or defeat. To quote just one example outside Benjamin's context from the popular press: "In New York City . . . vestiges of slavery are everywhere present yet scarcely marked. . . . Enslaved workers helped to clear land for the construction of Broadway."[14] On the heterogeneous and full view of history, none of these folk are forgotten. "Nothing that has ever happened should be regarded as lost for history" (254), as indeed many things must be, to create the illusion of progress. Benjamin attunes us to a view of history that allows for what has been lost to be recovered. That is what the angel would like to do but cannot. But *we* can. It depends on rethinking the past not as a progressive continuum but as a disjunction of moments each of which Benjamin calls a "presence of the now" (261). To restore a lost moment of the now it must be "blasted out of the continuum of history" by a "secret agreement" (254) with the present that effaces the inbetween. In that agreement between a present and past "now," "time stands still and has come to a stop" (262). The time that carried that past moment of the now into oblivion has been arrested. What was lost in that moment "flares up" (256) out of the oblivion that held it. It is almost as though the present and past moment of presence enter into a kind of I-Thou relation. By its regard for a past now, the present awakens the past to a relation with itself that is vivifying. Benjamin implies by the secrecy of this synergy between present and past that it does not come about intentionally but takes them both by surprise, with the shock of "emergency" (257). It is as though the present, wakened to its own volatility, confronts

---

14. Lucas, review of *How the Word Is Passed*, 13.

its own looming oblivion. What saves it in that moment of emergency is a recollection from the past, recalled from *its* oblivion. That moment of synergy between past and present mounts a defense against oblivion. But that synergy failing, both present and past are truly lost or, as Benjamin puts it, "even the dead will not be safe from the enemy" (255), as though oblivion were a malevolent agent that first targets the living, and only afterward, to slack its insatiable hunger, the dead.

Benjamin borrows from Jewish theology to name a time so restorative as to recover the past: "Messianic time" (263). It is a time "referred to redemption" (254). Messianic time reverses hope from its customary look to the future back toward the past (255). Benjamin suggests that Jewish practice has known this for a long time. The Passover seder rightly directs the celebrants' attention to "the image of enslaved ancestors rather than that of liberated grandchildren" (260). If the liturgy works as it should, whoever slaved to build the pyramids joins virtually in the joy of reciting the Haggadah. But this only if the liturgy works as it should. That is the problem. Messianic time is not subject to human control. We may find ourselves caught up in it in tandem with an urgency that suddenly claims us over some impending loss, under a sense of emergency. But, like Abraham's sacrifice of his son, however we experience the sense of emergency, it is not something we would ever choose. It chooses us. We just have to be at the ready. Perhaps the only Passover celebrants who actually experience the redemption on offer through the liturgy are those who, able to suspend memory of the redemptive outcome, recover for themselves the terror of the Israelite plight in Egypt.

Over the course of Benjamin's essay, an unexpected illustration of his thesis occurs. The French Revolution, he suggests, succeeded in part by way of its synergistic recall of ancient Rome. In the moment of recall, the present does not simply vivify the past—the past energizes the present. The redemption works both ways. The past is redeemed from oblivion and the present from the meaninglessness of empty, homogenous time. But then, a startling comparison: The French Revolution "evoked ancient Rome the way fashion evokes costumes of the past" (261). How many readers, holding out their hands to receive from the often elusive Benjamin whatever insights they can glean from him, expect to receive the French Revolution in one hand and fashion in the other?[15] Surely in

---

15. Benjamin may have had in mind a passage from Proust, a writer he admired and interpreted, that does indeed indirectly associate fashion with the French Revolution. In the final volume of *In Search of Lost Time*, the narrator analogizes the revival of

the balance of significance, the one far outweighs the other. In the stress of the comparison, it is tempting to drop the world of fashion. But for any museumgoer in the recent past of New York City, that will not happen. For the Metropolitan Museum of Art mounted between October 2020 and February 2021 an exhibit titled *About Time: Fashion and Duration*, which, startlingly, makes just Benjamin's point.

The exhibit designer, Andrew Bolton, explains that the array of gowns shows one hundred and fifty years of fashion, from 1870 to 2020, according to two parallel timelines, one that is "forward-moving and progress-oriented"[16] and the other that features "interruptions that pre- or postdate the first timeline." By the parallel between the timelines, garments arrayed along the first appear in front of the pre- or postdating garments visible behind them. In each pairing, some feature connects the two pieces across time, whether "shape, motif, material, technique, or decoration." The point is that "each pairing achieves a kind of temporal autonomy through its union of past and present, a view of time that's free from the confines of chronology."

The exhibit credits the philosopher Henri Bergson for the ideas on time it explores, but it might just as easily have cited Benjamin.[17] In Bolton's words we hear echoes of Benjamin on the two kinds of time, the one continuous and falsely progressive, the other discontinuous (interruptive) and truly redemptive. We recognize from Benjamin the notion of an occurrence in the present that vivifies a bit of the otherwise forgotten past by way of some commonality between them that surfaces unexpectedly. For the exhibit intends to startle the viewer into amazement over the juxtapositions across time it makes. The exhibit designer may have planned the juxtapositions, but they take the viewer by surprise. And the result is an experience for the viewer of both present and past redeemed from empty, homogeneous time, "free from the confines of chronology."

But the exhibit does more than just channel Benjamin's view of redemptive history. It *performs* it, in a way, by being a present occurrence, for the viewer of it in the then present 2021, that vivifies from the past the few words in Benjamin's own 1940 essay on the import of fashion,

---

fashion in wartime France (during World War I) with the improbable flourishing of art during the French Revolution (Proust, *In Search of Lost Time*, 6:48–49).

16. Bolton, "Exhibition Tour." Subsequent quotations from Bolton are from this video.

17. The catalog to the exhibit does briefly cite Benjamin for his concept of empty, homogeneous time. Bolton et al., *About Time*, xxiii.

otherwise so easy to forget on account of the overshadowing French Revolution. Suddenly what might have seemed the folly of fashion's juxtapose with the French Revolution on the import of history does not seem so ignorable. Fashion is a serious business after all, revolutionary even, for the insights it can supply about time, as Benjamin opined and the Metropolitan Museum hoped to demonstrate.

We could call what Benjamin has given us, after Rosenzweig's phrasing, a structure for the suffering peculiar to history of transience, oppression, death, and oblivion. By way of "messianic time," these do not have the last word. The only trouble is that time such as that does not come at our bidding. It takes us by surprise, like the recovery of the past that unintentional memory accomplishes in Marcel Proust's *In Search of Lost Time*. The title alone connotes a conflation of times. Proust is so close to Benjamin on this point, and translates his thought so effectively into narrative, that it is worth quoting him on what he (or his protagonist, Marcel) experiences in what Benjamin would call messianic time: "the past was made to encroach upon the present and I was made to doubt whether I was in the one or the other."[18] That sounds a little like an experience outside time, of eternity. It is more than a way of structuring the suffering implicit to time; it is a way out of time and of history. For Proust it is ecstatic.

An exit ramp from history, if only momentarily, constitutes another way of negating it. It has an ancient history among the Jewish philosophers, dating back to Philo. Philo is only to a minor extent an historian. (Curiously, Philo appears among the historians Cecile B. De Mille credits at the end of his *Ten Commandments*.) But he did write two treatises that can count for history by ancient Greek lights: *On the Embassy to Gaius* and *Against Flaccus*. They both recount the history of the ancient Alexandrian Jews' troubles with their non-Jewish neighbors and rulers: the local governor of Egypt, Flaccus, and the then emperor of Rome, Gaius Caligula. And so they both address the problem of suffering in time.

In the long and painful history of anti-Semitism, the year 38 CE figures for marking, in Alexandria, "the first pogrom against Jews in Western history."[19] Philo describes the events of the pogrom in harrowing detail: The mob "broke open the workshops of the Jews, . . . [who were] stabbed, dragged through the whole city, and trampled on, . . .

---

18. Proust, *In Search of Lost Time*, 6:262.
19. Sanders, "Causes of the Alexandrian Pogrom," 29.

[and] burnt in the heart of the city" (Flacc. 65–68)—stimulated by the malevolent Flaccus, who hoped by permitting these acts to gain favor with the anti-Semitic emperor. *Against Flaccus* relates this tale up to the later fall and execution of Flaccus. *On the Embassy to Gaius* tells the story of the delegation, headed by Philo, that the Alexandrian Jewish community sent to Caligula to protest the pogrom.

Historians do not doubt the pogrom occurred, that Roman rule—as over against the more benevolent Ptolemies—played a role in the decline of Jewish fortunes generally, or that a delegation including Philo made its way to Caligula. Caligula, who proposed erecting a statue of himself in the Jerusalem temple, was truly a threat to Jewish well-being. And the Jews' neighbors in Alexandria—the native Egyptians and the Greeks— were in competition with them for Roman favor.[20] But our interest is less in these actual historical events than in how Philo's telling of them reflects a philosophical disposition toward history itself.

The two histories evince, respectively, two different philosophical understandings of how events unfold. Within *Against Flaccus* the historical events demonstrate that "the hopes of the wicked are without foundation" (Flacc. 109) and that "justice . . . watches over human affairs" (Flacc. 146). The demonstration occurs in the imperial punishment, culminating in death, visited on Flaccus for enabling the pogrom against the Jews. Philo even puts these words in Flaccus's mouth, in a prayer he utters as he suffers in exile before his death: "King of gods and men, . . . Thou dost not disregard the nation of the Jews . . . but all who say that they do not find in Thee a Champion and Defender go astray. . . . I am clear proof of this, for all the acts which I committed against the Jews I have suffered myself" (Flacc. 170). Philo suggests that the significance of history is in the justice that God metes out over the course of it. He goes so far as to suggest that the state executioners inflicted on Flaccus "butcheries . . . as numerous as the number of Jews whom he unlawfully put to death," which is "proof that the help which God can give was not withdrawn from the nation of the Jews" (Flacc. 190–91).

Of course, this represents just the kind of retributive history we are negating. We include it for the contrast it makes with the history Philo

---

20. For an historical account of the pogrom, based on more sources than just Philo's, see Safrai and Stern, *Jewish People in the First Century*, 1:124–28. The editors note that "the Roman takeover [of Egypt] led to some deterioration in Jewish-Greek relations in Egypt as a whole" (124), due to tensions between the two ethnic groups over their comparative social standing under the Romans.

tells in the companion treatise, *On the Embassy to Gaius*. For Philo could tell history in several keys. Gaius Caligula is as much a bad actor as Flaccus was—more so, in light of the power he wielded. Jews had cause to fear him for the resentment they knew he would have for their refusal to worship him (for the god he took himself to be) and for the anguish he would cause if he fulfilled his threat to erect a statue of himself in the temple. But Philo's treatise on Caligula stops short of the "punishment" history had in store for him: his assassination. In fact, by the end of the treatise, Philo remains worried that Caligula will "decide in favor of our enemies" (Legat. 371) after all. So this treatise has less scope than its companion to tribute the workings of justice in history. Instead, Philo leaves a picture of his own probity in light of the grief he anticipates from this emperor. At their very first meeting, where Caligula makes a show of welcome, Philo alone of the delegation, on account of "my age and my good education" (Legat. 182), suspects the emperor of insincerity. "What was his object?" if not to indulge the "short-sighted fancies" (Legat. 182) of the naïve delegation, unwise to the ways of the world. In this case, Philo's hopes are not in outward redress but an inward resolve "to bear misfortunes with a resolution that is fortified by reason (*logismos*)" (Legat. 196), wherever this might lead. Here is another exit ramp from history, less into eternity than an inner sanctum of reason, beyond history's sway. Already at the start of this treatise, Philo enjoins us to prefer to the lures of "erratic sense-perception," the "reason [that] reaches to the unseen" (Legat. 2). On the one hand, this is Stoicism. But on the other, it is a nod to allegory, Philo's stock in trade and his answer to Benjamin's messianic time.

Philo's *Allegory of the Law* comprises a sequence of treatises that interpret verses from the book of Genesis in creative conversation with other verses from the Bible. But the "horizontal" interplay between the verses is meant to spark a vertical ascent to visions of utter otherness to the prosaic and often brutal reality we know. That is the dynamic of the allegory, which is literally other-speaking. The words of the allegory reference earthly events such as happened in history, while simultaneously drawing attention away from them. As Maren Niehoff puts it, "Philo provides a rich cluster of verses, reading several biblical stories in light of each other and creating an overall tapestry that depicts the soul's ascent from the material realm."[21] We need not trouble with the nature of the

---

21. Niehoff, *Philo of Alexandria*, 182.

TOWARD A NEGATIVE THEOLOGY OF JUDAISM

non-material realm, except to acknowledge its status as a sanctuary from the brutalities of history. Maren Niehoff again: Philo "creates via allegory a creative space of contemplation that lies outside the field of rigorous investigation into historical truths."[22] In other words, philosophy in Philo the allegorist's hands sidelines the burdens of history.

We might select any of the allegorical treatises to illustrate, but one that practices allegory already in its title is *On the Migration of Abraham*, for this event, announced in Gen 12:1–3, where God commands Abraham to "Get thee out of thy country," turns out to reference in truth a command "to quit the objects of sense-perception and go after those of Mind" (Migr. 20), which here names the history-transcending sanctum Philo wants us to know, and which he gestures toward in *Embassy to Gaius*. Philo capitalizes on an association between the words Hebrew and Apiru—a name in currency among ancient nations for the wanderers among them who seemed to have no home[23]—to suggest that *all* of Israel is Abraham, the migrant whose ultimate home is outside of history. Philo assembles an array of stories that share the theme of exit, whether from homeland (Abraham), oppression (the exodus), sexual pleasure (circumcision), or even from life itself (Abel) that in tandem, he hopes, project us beyond their narration of earthly, historical events to a realm of transcendence better experienced than described. Little may many of us have known that the Passover story is really about our "passing away from the passions without turning back" (Migr. 25). What drowns in the sea is our sensuality.

Abraham himself has another meaning. His very journey, from fatherland to promised land, indicates the life of progressive learning (Migr. 223), which is itself one of the exits from history. Philo suggests that Abraham's movement from Chaldea, the land of his fathers, to Haran, was really one from the godless astrology of the ancient Middle East to a more sensible appreciation of God's creation. But Abraham culminates in the kind of soul that is effortlessly attuned to the Mindful world beyond the senses, which Isaac represents. Isaac—the middle patriarch miraculously born to elderly parents, nearly sacrificed by his father, deceived by his son Jacob—seems always to fill the passive role. And yet this primes him for an activity he alone of the patriarchs is said to perform: contemplation (Gen 24:63), as he wanders the fields

---

22. Niehoff, *Philo of Alexandria*, 178.
23. Anderson, *Understanding the Old Testament*, 39–40.

without express purpose. Isaac is "the kind [of soul] that is taught without a teacher, is nourished by no one, but is a source of nourishment to others, being capable of teaching and not needing to learn" (Migr. 140). What need of the action-filled life of an Abraham or a Jacob when you are already at life's highest goal? Philo suggests that the story of the sacrifice of Isaac tributes a life so naturally (not effortfully, as Abraham's and Jacob's) good that it gives way spontaneously before the better world it channels. Allegory, it turns out, can invert the valence of the plain meaning. Isaac who on a literal read of the patriarchal narratives is perhaps the forgettable patriarch is on the allegorical read the most memorable. Insofar as this is the work of allegory—to recover to memory what might otherwise be forgotten—it plays perfectly to the task Benjamin's Angel of History hopes but fails to accomplish.

As though on cue, Benjamin himself picks up on this conversive feature of allegory. For if history is indeed a tissue of base and cruel facts, as Simone Weil opined, then the allegorical read of them may somehow redeem those who suffered them. Allegory is Benjamin's Angel of History empowered to redeem. Benjamin develops this thought over the course of a difficult book he wrote early in his career, in pursuit of an academic post, and long before his late-in-life tribute to the Angel of History. *The Origin of German Tragic Drama*, from 1924 and 1925, plumbs the role of allegory in seventeenth-century German plays. History is implicated in these dramas for the horrors of it: the typical plot exhibits the decline and fall of a ruler and the collateral damage in other lives lost. The results of beheadings and fateful accidents litter the stage. Part of Benjamin's point is that these plots mirror the violence of seventeenth-century Germany, the time of the horrific Thirty Years War. These baroque playwrights had "a clear vision of the misery of mankind in its creaturely estate"[24] and sought by their plays to ease it. But their method was counterintuitive. The characters and plots were representations, just as the biblical patriarchs and their stories were for Philo. But what they represented to the audience was the sheer meaninglessness of history, its ceaseless enactment of pointless violence. History is a succession of deaths. That was what the plays *meant*: the "hopelessness of the earthly condition" (81). And that was the allegory. It was "a just verdict . . . passed on the profane world" (175). But by what standard could that justice hold except by reference to a more perfect world we do not inhabit? The plays do not show that world. But a

---

24. Benjamin, *Origin of German Tragic Drama*, 146. Subsequent citations to pages of this text are given parenthetically.

vision, however contentless, of that more perfect world cannot but dawn in the very passing of verdict on this one. "Ultimately in the death-signs of the baroque the direction of allegorical reflection is reversed; on the second part of its wide arc it returns, to redeem" (232). By implication, all that the plays showed lost was, beyond our notice or reach, recovered. What motivated allegory was "an appreciation of the transience of things and the concern to rescue them for eternity" (223).

Benjamin prompts an alternative (to Philo's) read of the terrible pogrom of 38 CE, which resembles, in violence, the horrors of the Thirty Years War that he took the German baroque playwrights to have dramatized. Philo could not have predicted how disastrously Alexandrian Jewish history would unfold a hundred years from his time. Not long after the defeat of the Jerusalemite Jews, in 70 CE, Rome effectively destroyed Alexandrian Jewry, too, in response to their rebellion of 115. Philo's time was shaping up to be rather like that of the German baroque dramatists. And his vivid description of the sufferings of the pogrom may work better to engage the sympathy of post-Holocaust Jewish readers, today, than the downfall of Flaccus, and so to indicate, along the lines of Benjamin's notion of allegory, a redemption beyond the confines of history.

From the history of Jewish philosophy, Philo and Walter Benjamin have risen up in the wake of history's negation to "structure" the sufferings within it allegorically. The use of allegory is both for those who have painfully died under the march of history—to restore them to memory—and for us, now, seeking a posthumous "redemption" for them; all the better if Benjamin's Angel of History turns out to be Allegory. Allegory itself has a checkered history in the annals of literary, philosophical, and theological criticism. It has risen and fallen from grace, and risen yet again, like the very movement it itself narrates from here (below)—*ici bas*, as Simone Weil likes to put it—to better (and higher) realms. Let our last word on this topic come from the French philosopher and Erasmus scholar Jean-Claude Margolin, who commends to us "the delicate pleasure of allegory, comprising a sense of estrangement and of the unknown . . . and of the inducement to reverie."[25]

And now for what appears in the wake of purposive-history denied, and the "accidental" (unintentional) quality of it affirmed, for all the distress this may have caused Maimonides: academic history. Yosef

---

25. Margolin, "Aspects du surréalisme," 520.

Yerushalmi has already warned us to be on our toes. Academic history is simultaneously friend and foe to Jewish cultural memory.

Yerushalmi reminded us that, as an academic historian himself, he has only relatively recently come on the scene of Jewish historiography. Historical studies rose to eminence within Jewish orbits in the nineteenth century, under the rubric of *Wissenschaft des Judentums*: the Science of Judaism. We would better say in English: the academic study of Judaism. German Jewish rationalist Immanuel Wolf (1799–1847) led the way when in 1822 he published a call for a new science of Judaism that would "depict Judaism . . . from a historical standpoint" by way of "first, the textual study of Judaism; second, a history of Judaism; third, a philosophy of Judaism."[26]

The scholars who would take up Wolf's call hoped to vivify a love for the religion they felt flagging among many educated Jews, influenced by the Enlightenment, by plumbing the breadth and depths of its history. In practice this meant at the very least: writing history from sources that could be reliably dated and trusted. Up to that time, even those as keen on reason as Maimonides took Talmudic and midrashic accounts of the Jewish past as reliable history. The Wissenschaft scholars varied in their focus. Some of them, like Leopold Zunz (1794–1886), edited newfound manuscripts;[27] others, like Heinrich Graetz (1817–1891) composed substantive histories based on source material they trusted.[28] Together they celebrated history as such, almost as a substitute for religion. As Yerushalmi writes, "History becomes what it had never been before—the faith of fallen Jews. For the first time history, not a sacred text, becomes the arbiter of Judaism."[29]

If not the faith of fallen Jews, history as an academic discipline and set of methodologies still commands a very high position within the broad framework of academic Jewish studies today. New York City boasts a Center for Jewish History that combines the resources of several history-focused organizations, including the Leo Baeck Institute, YIVO, the American Sephardi Federation, and the American Jewish History Society. (There is no such amalgamating Center for Jewish Philosophy,

---

26. Wolf, "On the Concept of a Science of Judaism," 202.

27. "The personal correspondence of Wissenschaft scholars with each other is replete with inquires, reports, and discussions on the discovery and nature of unknown manuscripts" (Schorsch, *From Text to Context*, 180).

28. Graetz's project was his eleven-volume *History of the Jews*, published 1853–1876.

29. Yerushalmi, *Zakhor*, 86.

TOWARD A NEGATIVE THEOLOGY OF JUDAISM

at least in New York.) And as Professor Yerushalmi observes, the field is wide open to the researcher's fancy. "No subject is potentially unworthy of his interest, no document, no artifact, beneath his attention."[30] And this breadth of scope often has positive implications for those previously marginalized by collective memory, for instance, women, LGBT persons, mystics, heretics. Might academic historians be Benjamin's Angel of History? Yerushalmi almost sounds like Benjamin when he writes of the historian who "reaches back into an often distant past to recover forgotten or neglected elements with which there is a sudden sympathetic vibration, a sense of empathy, of recognition."[31]

An instance of this comes readily to mind, not so much of a forgotten past as of one all too painfully recalled to devotional readers of Torah: the commanded extermination of the ancient Canaanites. By divine decree, the Canaanites fell under the rubric of the biblical ban, or *herem*. Whatever is declared herem is beyond the pale and must be destroyed.[32] Accordingly the Israelite tribes in exodus from Egypt and en route to Canaan (the promised land) are commanded of the dwellers there, "Thou shalt utterly destroy [*hahareim taharim*] them" (Deut 7:2).

The Bible supplies a rationale for this, that the native peoples' own false religion will tempt the Israelites away from their divinely given true one. In biblical retrospect, that is an irony, since for all the destruction that ostensibly occurred in Canaan, the native religions continued to lure the Israelites into them right up till the time of their own divinely sanctioned destruction at the hands of the Assyrians and Babylonians and precisely for their idol-worship (among other things). But for some Jewish philosophers, the story has been not so much an irony as an embarrassment over what we today would call a command to commit nothing short of genocide.

A case in point is the ancient Jewish author of the Alexandrian text *The Wisdom of Solomon*, one of the so-called apocrypha, or "hidden books" of Hebrew Scripture that failed to make their way into the Jewish canon, but that are still bound with Catholic and some Protestant

---

30. Yerushalmi, *Zakhor*, 94.
31. Yerushalmi, *Zakhor*, 113.
32. *Herem* comes from a Hebrew root with a seeming range of opposite meanings: to ban, to exterminate, to devote, to prohibit from common use, to consecrate to God (Brown et al., *Hebrew and English Lexicon*, 355). When we think of extermination we might think of ridding ourselves of a pollution or vileness; while consecrating something to God connotes offering up the best of something (not the worst): the "first fruits" as the Bible puts it. The word almost seems a contranym.

Bibles. Composed, scholars judge, sometime in the first century BCE, the Greek text reflects a deep impact of Greek philosophy on the writer, and so admits him into our guild of philosophical Jews. The book includes a retelling of the exodus story up through the presumed conquest of Canaan that greatly exaggerates the evils of the Canaanites. According to the writer, the Canaanites not only sacrificed their children in religious rites, but then consumed their flesh (Wis 12:5–6). The Torah, which would have been the writer's key source, may indeed accuse the Canaanites of child sacrifice, most especially at Deut 12:31,[33] but not of cannibalism. There are several ways to interpret this exaggeration. Perhaps the Greek-educated writer was mixing the apparent reference to Canaanite child sacrifice in Deuteronomy with Greek myths that do indeed horrifically link the sacrifice of children to consumption of their flesh.[34] But a reading that better fits our train of thought here is that the author was so disturbed by God's command of the Israelites to exterminate whole Canaanite peoples that he supplied further "explanation" for that charge. These people by their abominable practices had forfeited the right to live. Possibly confirming this interpretation is the worry the writer shows over judgments hearers of this story might make on so seemingly cruel a deity. "Who will accuse thee," he wonders, "for the destruction of nations which thou did make?" (Wis 12:12 RSV); who indeed if not the distressed author himself?

It is easy to imagine that the writer, who took the conquest story for truth, was embarrassed by it. Schooled as he was in Greek philosophy, he would have been familiar with Plato's embarrassment over Homer's stories of badly behaving gods and heroes. Simone Weil has suggested that the Greek conquest of Troy as told in the *Iliad* haunted the Greek conscience for centuries after the presumed event itself.[35] And so Pseudo-Solomon was just as apt to be troubled by the story of the conquest of Canaan; hence, his graphic and distorted retelling of it, to justify the destruction of the Canaanites. David Winston lends some support for this reading by suggesting that the writer shows "a clear intent in this section to justify the Israelite conquest of Canaan." Winston locates this

---

33. Scholarship is not resolved on whether Deut 12:31 actually connotes sacrifice of children, or an application to them of some non-lethal, fire-related rite. Compare *New Oxford Annotated Bible*, 232, 238, and Tigay, *Deuteronomy*, 464–65.

34. Gill, "Greek Sources of Wisdom," 383–86.

35. Weil, *Intimations of Christianity*, 74–75.

TOWARD A NEGATIVE THEOLOGY OF JUDAISM

justification within a framework of "Jewish-Hellenistic apologetics,"[36] among efforts by Jewish writers to justify to non-Jewish readers the violence of the conquest. But perhaps the writer is trying to persuade himself of both God's and Israel's goodness. He is practicing what we negated three chapters back: theodicy.

Here is a case where academic history, if only it had existed then, might have saved the author all that guilt over the presumed violence of his ancestors and spared posterity his crudely concocted theodicy. For archaeology suggests the Israelites never conquered Canaan, but only gradually mingled with Canaanite peoples, if indeed they ever left the land of Canaan at all.[37] A theory widely accepted among biblical archeologists and now historians is that there never was an Exodus at all. There was rather a kind of civil war between barely differentiable ethnic groups among the peoples of ancient Canaan who only in hindsight, and within the Bible's memory, divided between Canaanite and Israelite.[38] The problem is, as archaeologist Eric Cline explains, that "most of the sites described [in the Bible] as being destroyed [by the invading Israelites] do not show any archaeological evidence of destruction."[39] Of course, this cuts another way, to undermine the ritual celebration of the Passover seder, as Rabbi David Wolpe discovered when he preached this theory from his rabbinical pulpit.[40]

Philo found his own way to ease what was perhaps his own guilt over the conquest story—and more in keeping with his own allegorical way of negating history. He denies there was a conquest at all. What strength for conquest could the wandering Israelites have had after forty years in the desert?[41] Instead, Philo suggests that once the native inhabitants discerned in the physically weakened Israelites "their respect for law, . . . their religion and justice and piety," they "voluntarily surrendered"

---

36. Winston, *Wisdom of Solomon*, 238.

37. "This ruthless myth of settlement [of Canaan], described in the book of Joshua in colorful detail as one of the earliest genocides, never actually happened." See Sand, *Invention*, 119. See also Cline, *Biblical Archaeology*, 76–79, for a summary of the arguments on this point.

38. The distinction between Israelite and Canaanite may have been fabricated by the ancient biblical writers to differentiate between those among them who followed Yahweh and those who did not (Niehr, "'Israelite' Religion and 'Canaanite' Religion," 23–36).

39. Cline, *Biblical Archaeology*, 77.

40. Niebuhr, "Rabbi's Look at Archaeology," A11.

41. Philo sloughs over the detail that the older Israelites had by this time died out.

(Hypoth. 6:5–8), as the less virtuous might to the more so. Philo's retelling of the story fits with his philosophy, according to which sensuality and goodness are in inverse relation with each other (Somn. 1 72). The Canaanites were effectively blinded into submission by the shining light of the emaciated Israelites. Philo knows this is not how the story is told in the Bible. But no matter. For, "in discussing the probable facts of this occupation I think it better to go not so much by the historical narrative as by what our [allegorizing] reason tells us about them" (Hypoth. 6:5). Allegorizing reason was to ancient Philo what historical method is to modern academic historians. By happy accident, the two explanatory models agree in negating the conquest story entirely.

Of course, even if the conquest never happened, a problem remains: the *command* to eliminate a people still sounds in the Torah. Has academic history anything to say about that? It does. Now the history that applies is to the book of Deuteronomy itself, where the genocidal command occurs.[42] Biblical historians date Deuteronomy to the seventh century BCE. This was not long after the northern kingdom of Israel had fallen to the Assyrian empire, in 722 BCE. The people needed a morale boost in the face of Israel's fall, and the telling of the conquest story, relegated unverifiably to many centuries before, provided just that boost, if only for those remaining in the southern kingdom of Judah (soon to face their own fall to the Babylonians). Deuteronomy passes down the conquest story as a consolation for the fall of Israel. As biblical interpreter John Collins puts it of the biblical conquest story, "The texts [of it] are not naïve reflections of primitive practice, but programmatic ideological statements from the late seventh century BCE. . . . Most of the biblical endorsements of violent human action are set in the context of early Israel, even if they were written later."[43] Robert Eisen elaborates: "the violence of the Assyrian Empire in the eighth century BCE inspired the story of the Canaanite genocide that was purported to have occurred centuries earlier. . . . The need on the part of the Israelites and Judeans to engage in violence for defensive reasons ended up spinning off fantasies of violence that was aggressive in nature both in the

---

42. Helpfully, in the earlier book, Exodus, where God issues the command against the Canaanites, it is not so harsh: God will expel the Canaanites first from the land in preparation for the Israelites to enter and destroy all evidence of the native cult. See Exod 23:31–33 and 34:11–17.

43. Collins, "Zeal of Phineas," 1:18, 21.

imagined past and in the imagined future."[44] Thank you, professors Collins and Eisen—academic history to the rescue from biblical warrants to violence we may not, today, want to own.

But academic history is not always a friend to Jewish ethics or piety. It has muddied the waters on much of biblical history. There is not only no evidence of an exodus, but the prior stories of the patriarchs lack historical foundation, to say nothing of the presumed creation of the world in what by biblical reckoning would be 3760 or 3761 BCE. The first archaeological evidence of ancient Israel at all comes from the so-called Merneptah stele, of 1208 BCE, in which an Egyptian king boasts that "Israel is laid waste." Scholars debate the evidence for the stories told of Kings David and Solomon. But all this is reconcilable with a Jewish piety that rests more on the mythic status of the biblical stories, to supply life-meanings, than on their historicity.

Where the reconciliation is harder is between Jewish cultural memory and what some of academic history has to say about the founding of the State of Israel. Certainly academic history's interpretation of the biblical conquest story is no comfort to Israeli settlers, today, who resource the story to justify their settlements among and in place of native Palestinians in the West Bank.[45] But what about the very founding of the state? As Israeli historian Avi Shlaim observes of Israeli history, this matter "is not one of merely historical interest. It cuts to the very core of Israel's image of itself."[46]

Israel's early history came under new scrutiny in the 1980s, when the Israeli state archives opened to researchers, along with relevant archives in Britain and the United States, and at the UN, on the conflicts surrounding the founding of the state. Articles and books began to appear that told a more morally troubling history of the War of Independence and the years following, among them a tome provocatively titled *The Birth of Israel: Myths and Realities*, by Simha Flapan, who edited the Arab-sympathetic *New Outlook* magazine. Flapan's book, which appeared in 1987, was the first of several pieces to follow by more academic historians, such as Benny Morris, whose seminal essay, "The New Historiography: Israel Confronts Its Past," first appeared in the American magazine *Tikkun* in 1988. Morris there recounts the history of this new telling of Israel's history, which he called the New History. Salient points

44. Eisen, *Judaism and Violence*, 18.
45. Greenberg, "On the Political Use of the Bible," 461–71.
46. Shlaim, "Debate About 1948," 143.

in this retelling of the 1948 war, based on primary resources and state documents, rather than participant memory, include that many Arab inhabitants were forcibly expelled from Palestine or fled under duress, were killed in massacres by Jewish forces, or died in virtual death marches; that the neighboring Arab states were less interested in destroying Israel than plundering the lands the UN had assigned to a Palestinian state; that Israeli authorities were happy to postpone peace negotiations once they tasted the pleasures of conquest. Historians writing in this vein became known as the New Historians or, by their detractors, as Postzionists. Postzionism is a misnomer to the extent it suggests that Zionist ideals do not inspire these new historians. The ideals do—of a state that strives "to uphold the full social and political equality of all its citizens," as the Declaration of Independence puts it—but not what they judge to be false, face-saving accounts of Zionist history. When Benny Morris comments on the half-truths or outright falsehoods of the Old History—its heroic tales of valor, moral rectitude, willingness to compromise, and commitment to peace—that "raison d'état often took precedence over telling the truth,"[47] he reminds us of Benjamin and Rosenzweig on the lies that attend the violence of states. For Rosenzweig, history is in effect a product of states telling lies about their own significance. As Morris puts it: "If Israel, the haven of a much-persecuted people, was born pure and innocent, then it was worthy of grace, material assistance, and political support. . . . If, on the other hand, Israel was born tarnished, besmirched by original sin, then it was no more deserving of that grace and assistance than were its neighbors."[48]

If that is the last word of academic history's assessment of the founding of Israel, it is not so bad. It is only to restate what defenders of Israel say when it seems to them unfairly critiqued by being held to a higher standard than any other polity. Benny Morris leaves us with the reasonable thought that, morally speaking, Israel is no more deserving than its neighbors; but then, also, at least, no *less* deserving. Still, there seems an implicit fall from grace at academic history's hand.

If our contemporary historians of the Jewish past descend from Isaac Wolf and his calls for a Jewish historiography more attentive to the recovery and study of texts, as indeed the Postzionist historians have been toward texts documenting the founding of Israel, his additional

47. Morris, "New Historiography," 14.
48. Morris, "New Historiography," 15.

call for a new *philosophy* of Judaism is harder to meet through historical studies. Academic history is limited in the larger meanings it can pull from history. Some of the Wissenschaft scholars did attempt to extract from their studies an essence of Judaism that showed through the historical facts. Heinrich Graetz opined that "the totality of Judaism is discernible only in its history. Its complete nature . . . becomes clear only in the light of history."[49] Abraham Geiger (1810–1874), a leading light of early Reform Judaism, identified that nature as love of God and neighbor, which he felt constituted "the essence of the faith of Judaism,"[50] and that the Prophets, rather than the legislative Torah, best represented it. "It was not the outward, rigid laws which made Israel indestructible; it was the . . . prophets."[51] We can hear an ideological bias in these words. Scholars of Jewish history today would be wary of them. Yosef Yerushalmi doubts "there must be an essential 'idea' of Judaism behind the shifting norms that history casts up to our view . . . [or that] the very notion of a 'normative Judaism'" is credible.[52] Academic historical studies build whatever larger pictures they can piecemeal.

But it is possible to deploy the tools of academic history toward a read of history that, working within the explanatory model of cause-and-effect, rather than of promise-fulfillment, or of any other theodicy-enabling method, suggests a meaningful structure to it. Such a read would respect our negations of both purposive and theodicean history. And it could constitute a philosophy of Jewish history, such as Wolf desired.

Let us close this chapter with reflection on a thinker who essayed just such a project, Nachman Krochmal (1785–1840), whom Jewish Theological Seminary president Solomon Schechter (1847–1915) memorialized so fondly for his "fascinating charm, . . . which made him irresistible to all who came into contact with him,"[53] and whom historian of ideas Elias Sacks has encouraged us to rescue from what has been his relative obscurity.[54] Krochmal lived during the rise of the Wissenschaft movement, but in Eastern Europe (Galicia), not Germany. For that reason, Amos Bitzan suggests we distinguish Krochmal, who wrote in Hebrew, from his German counterparts by a term for his writing

49. Graetz, *Structure of Jewish History*, 65.
50. Geiger, *Abraham Geiger and Liberal Judaism*, 288.
51. Geiger, *Abraham Geiger and Liberal Judaism*, 263.
52. Yerushalmi, *Zakhor*, 92.
53. Schechter, "Nachman Krochmal," 326–27, 344.
54. Sacks, "Law, Ethics," 352–77.

that better captures that difference: *hokhmat Yisrael*,[55] Wisdom of Israel, rather than Science of Judaism. Still, Krochmal knew of developments in Germany and read widely in both German and Jewish philosophy. His *Guide for the Perplexed of the Time* was by its very title a nod to Maimonides, whom he much admired.[56]

His own guide for the perplexed is an unfinished potpourri of reflections on philosophy, history, and sacred literature, designed, like Maimonides's *Guide*, to reconcile Judaism with the learning of his day. His historical reflections include both the critical evaluation of source materials that the new science of history demanded and a more comprehensive structuring of history that could issue in a larger meaning of it. If his Jewish inspiration was Maimonides, his German one was Hegel, who simultaneously opined on the history of philosophy and the philosophy of history. In that way, Krochmal hoped to fulfill those two framing goals of Immanuel Wolf's historical program, at the micro level to critically evaluate historic texts, and at the macro level to infer a larger meaning from them.

The two goals interrelated. For instance, at the level of textual analysis, it would be obvious to students of the Psalms that, contrary to received tradition, David could not have written all of them, since he wasn't alive to witness the historical events to which some of them allude, e.g., the exile to Babylon.[57] The "traditional" response to that problem, that David foresaw the exile, no longer persuades. Better simply to admit that the traditional dating of all the Psalms to David's time was chronologically mistaken. Assigning some of the Psalms a later date, in sync with the history they reference, would not lower but raise the esteem of their authorship, for showing how the spiritual ability to compose Psalms in the first place perdured through time among the whole people as one of their gifts, rather than being limited to a single, exceptional poet.

That reflection opens onto Krochmal's second goal (and Wolf's third), to extract from the history of Israel in proper chronology a *meaning* of the people that could sustain them through time. A proper

---

55. Bitzan, "Wissenschaft des Judentums."

56. As he did Philo, to whom he devoted a chapter of his book. On this point, Steven Schwarzschild comments (tendentiously) that "the almost unbounded admiration which Krochmal expresses for Hellenistic Judaism sometimes goes beyond all proper limits" (Schwarzschild, "Two Modern Jewish Philosophies," 45). We might ask: who sets the proper limits?

57. Krochmal, "Philosophy of Jewish History," 191–92.

chronology, even and perhaps most especially one that defies tradition, will provoke to clearer view the deeper, philosophical meaning of Jewish history (as the German Wissenschaft scholars also thought), which the broad Jewish public, steeped in fanciful rabbinic lore, was previously unready to receive.

The chronology that Krochmal offers Jewish history is a periodization. Periodizations of Jewish history are not new. Even Maimonides had his schema of Jewish time.[58] All the same, Yosef Yerushalmi, quoting Jewish historian Gerson Cohen (1924–1991), warns us of historical "schematology," that it "always betrays a very superficial interest in the events themselves, but a deep desire to unravel their meaning and their place in the plan of history as a whole."[59] Krochmal might plead guilty to this, if "plan" is taken for pattern, while nonetheless citing his care with his source material. He identified three grand periods preceding his own of the nineteenth century: from Abraham to the end of the First Temple (586 BCE); from the Babylonian Exile to the defeat of Bar Kochba (135 CE); from the rise of rabbinism to the Khmelnitski pogroms in Poland (1648–1649).

What the periods reveal is a pattern of destruction and renewal. The tragedy that ends one period relates causally to whatever flourishes in the following one. For example, the heights of Second Isaiah's prophecy follow on the disaster of the temple's destruction;[60] and the oral law of the rabbinical period follows as effect to cause on the failure of Bar Kochba's rebellion, rather than simply perduring from an original revelation at Sinai, as the rabbis themselves taught.

Krochmal himself inhabits a new period of growth, on which he does not elaborate;[61] but he need not. His point is that tragedies in Jewish history mark a nadir that issues causally in the peaks that follow. This works

---

58. But his periodizing did not extend beyond biblical times. See Baron, "Historical Outlook of Maimonides," 103. For a periodization of much broader scope, Yerushalmi cites the sixteenth-century work of Samuel Usque for its sensitivity to the "larger rhythms of Jewish history" (Yerushalmi, *Zakhor*, 62).

59. Yerushalmi, *Zakhor*, 39.

60. Steven Schwarzschild comments on behalf of Krochmal, "In the Babylonian Exile and due to its dispersion, Israel reached a height of religion never before attained," as though statehood and land blocked the spiritual growth of the people. Schwarzschild, "Two Modern Jewish Philosophies," 44.

61. Except to imply by the need for his book that it is a time of perplexity among Jews, who want to reconcile the rise of the new historical science with received rabbinic wisdom on the past.

as a law of nations. All nations rise up from nothing, flourish, decline and die; only Israel perennially rises again. What can explain it?—only another cause-effect relation, in this case one that holds between Israel and the sustainer of nations, which Krochmal calls, after Hegel, Absolute Spirit. This is God, but renamed to connote a particular work of "spirit" as traditionally conceived, to impart and sustain life: to *enliven.*

That is the essence of Israel's nationality, to be enlivened by its sustained focus on Spirit. Krochmal reads that meaning off of Israel's perduring history, as the logical effect—perdurance—of its cause: spirituality. The notion has roots in Maimonides, who will restate it for us later on as it applies to individuals, rather than nations, and under the rubric of spiritual life (in ch. 10). But it also recalls Judah Halevi, as Steven Schwarzschild makes plain for us: "Yehudah Halevi actually does claim, even as does Krochmal, that the peculiarity of Israel is due to its attachment to Absolute Spirit,"[62] which he only differently names, as (in Arabic) *amr ilahi*, the divine entity or influence.

This national essence of Israel can define it only because no other nation shares it. What defines the other nations are lesser manifestations of Absolute Spirit that they take for their collective focus, such as strength, beauty, governance, or some other such definite quality. These make for what Jay Harris calls an "incomplete spirituality."[63] For instance, Egypt, otherwise unloved in Jewish collective memory, was for ecumenical Krochmal "rich in buildings, crafts, useful and decorative arts, as well as sciences."[64] But these lesser manifestations of Spirit do not without qualification sustain nations that cling to them. A gift for governance naturally decays into tyranny, for war into cruelty, for art into decadence. And so nations that hold to anything but *Absolute* Spirit die out. As Jay Harris puts it of Israel's life-sustaining Spirit, "it is absolute and thus secures for the Jews an eternal existence."[65]

We have invoked Krochmal in support of our negation of purposive history. Whatever meaning history yields derives not from purposes it fulfills but from patterns discernible within it of cause and effect. That is how academic history works. But Krochmal's eternal people of Israel lends support as well to our negation of theodicean history. Krochmal can concede all that is lachrymose in Jewish history. But all national

62. Schwarzschild, "Two Modern Jewish Philosophies," 33.
63. Harris, *Nachman Krochmal*, 127.
64. Krochmal, "Philosophy of Jewish History," 206.
65. Harris, *Nachman Krochmal*, 315.

histories suffer from the same feature. Nations are organisms rather like plants that, once seeded, grow, flourish, and die. This is no more a theodicy than is plant biology. What Krochmal gives Israel is a read of its past that buffers it against the sufferings of its past, in that nothing that lays it low will ever destroy it. He has not invoked either an Angel of History or a practice of allegory. Jewish history on its own, thoughtfully considered, is its own bulwark against the burdens of itself.

Krochmal's uniquely eternal people might seem to have revived an idea we were at pains in chapter 3 to radically qualify if not wholly negate, that Israel is the chosen people. But Krochmal obliges our qualification of that idea by negating any definable content to Absolute Spirit, just as Judah Halevi had done of his God. Absolute Spirit "cannot at all be grasped by the imagination or by common thought and understanding . . . [for it is] supreme over all rational thought."[66] As historian of Jewish philosophy Julius Guttmann puts it on Krochmal's behalf, "'Nothingness' was the only name predicable to God, to whom it is forbidden even to attribute existence and, therefore, he appears to human thought as nothingness."[67] The Jewish national ethos stakes its all on Nothing. But this accords perfectly with our theme of impactful concepts that, for all their import, lack definable content, which already subsumes under it Jewishness, God, I-Thou relations, and useless suffering. One more shortly joins the list: Revelation.

---

66. Krochmal, "Philosophy of Jewish History," 201.
67. Guttmann, *Philosophies of Judaism*, 379.

Chapter 6
Revelation

THE FIGURE DEEMED THE first of the medieval Jewish philosophers, Saadia Gaon (882–942), posed the problem of revelation this way: "I have heard that there are people who contend that men do not need prophets [who deliver revelation], and that their Reason is sufficient to guide them."[1] The problem for Saadia Gaon, who venerated reason, was that it seemed to obviate any need of revelation. Reason was revelatory in its own right. His task became to show that we do indeed need revelation because our reason may not be up to finding what revelation so clearly supplies, or else might be too slow in its workings for our needs, or else, in its penchant for generalities, might leave unspecified the specifics necessary to guide our behavior. Maimonides's concern was slightly different; he worried over any seeming conflicts between reason and revelation, and undertook rationally to justify all the commandments, both ethical and ritual, or as many as he could.

But these medieval thinkers would take us down a path we do not wish to follow. For our intent in this chapter is to negate just the notion of revelation they presuppose, that it comprises definitive commandments recorded in Scripture revealed on Mount Sinai. In fact, the negation of purposive history we already practiced in the preceding chapter might seem to have negated revelation so understood along with it; at least insofar as revelation so understood establishes a purpose for history, to be the context in which its prescriptions are fulfilled. But that is just the meaning of revelation we mean to negate in this chapter, that it comprises prescriptions,

1. Saadia Gaon, *Book of Doctrines*, 103.

predictions, or discursive linguistic content of any kind. Sinai is a paradigm of what we negate: a determinable moment in historic time (1250 BCE?) when directive contents of some kind (613?) are given.

Insofar as those commandments fall under a rubric of law, they are already in tension with philosophy. Any non-lawyer who has ever served on a jury trial will sense a tension between philosophy and law: the framework of lawyerly antagonisms, the restrictions on question and answer, the silencing of nuance, the discounting of context, the attack on witnesses, the very ritual of the courtroom proceedings. George Eliot (a great friend of the Jewish people) had a phrase for those who exhibit a certain species of self-confidence, that it shows "like a lawyer's flourish, forbidding exceptions or additions."[2] The words often inscribed over the judge's bench, "In God We Trust," suggest that within the confined precincts of the court, trust is in doubt, and if to be directed anywhere, somewhere *outside* the courtroom. As Leo Strauss comments in his introduction to Hermann Cohen's *Religion of Reason Out of the Sources of Judaism*, the problem with law is that "it leaves no room for man's theoretical and aesthetic interests,"[3] or not enough. Even that paradigm of simultaneous expertise in both law and philosophy, Moses Maimonides, pointedly distinguishes between "the men of the law" and "the philosophers" (GP138). And as Chaim Saiman puts it, "whereas law seeks to close options and strive for unambiguous conclusions, literature and philosophy are designed to open discussion and enable further reflection."[4] It really only makes matter worse that, as Saiman continues, "the rabbis use concepts forged in the regulatory framework to do the work other societies assign to philosophy,"[5] since this implies philosophy can never fully flower on its own within a rabbinical framework.

And so: *No* to revelation conceived as law. And then our question becomes: In the wake of this negation, what other meanings of revelation come into view? The notion of coming-into-view is already a clue. In his correspondence with Walter Benjamin, Gershom Scholem suggested that revelation was a "process of appearing,"[6] by implication of something previously hidden, noteworthy, and surprising. That covers a lot of territory. In that sense it may well be that the sudden confluence of past

---

2. Eliot, *Felix Holt*, 66.
3. Strauss, "Introduction," xxxv.
4. Saiman, *Halakhah*, 126.
5. Saiman, *Halakhah*, 8.
6. Scholem and Benjamin, *Correspondence*, 142.

and present, which so intrigued Benjamin and Proust, and that dawns on us without our having intentionally provoked it, is revelatory. It takes us by surprise. The agency is with that which appears, not with us.

Scholem's own explorations of revelation, as the kabbalists understood it, led him to a view of it that nicely introduces our own approach to the topic. As he wrote to Benjamin:

> You ask what I understand by the "nothingness of revelation"? I understand by it a state in which revelation appears to be without meaning, in which it still asserts itself, in which it has *validity* but *no significance*. A state in which the wealth of meaning is lost and what is in the process of appearing . . . still does not disappear, even though it is reduced to the zero point of its own content.[7]

Our modern philosophers are less devotees of reason than their medieval counterparts were. As Levinas opines, speaking for many modern philosophers, "we put into question the rationality of reason."[8] And Scholem opens up here another way than by way of reason for understanding revelation. But the medieval thinkers, too, knew something of the "nothingness of revelation," and not just the kabbalists, who built on their philosophical predecessors, but Maimonides too. We begin with him, segue to the kabbalists, as Scholem interprets them for us, and then move on to the moderns.

We might wonder why Maimonides could devote so much of his *Guide of the Perplexed* to rationalizing the commandments. It comprises "the largest self-contained bloc of the *Guide* dedicated to a single theme."[9] Does not such an effort threaten to do just what Saadia feared: render the commandments dispensable in light of reason's powers? Maimonides, whom we have already seen subject creation doctrine to doubt, might well be open to doubting any need for revealed commandments at all. Or, he might have another understanding of revelation in mind, for which the commandments are largely irrelevant. What if reason was itself revelatory and so broad in scope in what it reveals as to subsume the commandments within its purview and something else besides?

Maimonides was not only an Aristotelian. Like other medieval philosophers and theologians who absorbed the wisdom of the ancient

---

7. Scholem and Benjamin, *Correspondence*, 142.
8. Levinas, "Revelation," 209.
9. Stern, *Problems and Parables*, 2.

Greeks, he was also up to a point a Platonist. Within the framework of Platonic philosophy, which carried into the Middle Ages, reason glowed with the warmth of the sun and with the Goodness that held its attention and guided the acts it motivated. Reason at its highest was more an agency of contemplation than of discursive or dialectical (as Plato would put it) analysis. Goodness itself was above definition (Rep. 509) and our reason once captivated by it surpasses itself in what it beholds.

That is a poor précis of Platonic mysticism, but it lays a foundation for reading those sections of the *Guide* that frame for us what the prophets, and especially Moses, actually beheld.

Maimonides of course knew the biblical account of revelation at Sinai, which he understood many of his fellow Jews to accept, that God expressly chose Moses for a prophetic mission (GP360). Such a view presupposes a God who interrupts the flow of natural events with a revelation. But this is the last account of revelation Maimonides would accept. Moses was rather a very acute philosopher and the revelation vouchsafed him an advanced form of knowing accomplished by his own reason.

What Moses experienced was more a vision than an audition. With the other medieval philosophers, Maimonides inhabited an Aristotelian cosmos of revolving spheres, each governed by an immaterial intellect that doubled in the Bible, said Maimonides, for an angel. Our own sphere, the lowest, was governed by the moon. God governed the outermost sphere. Fixed in the inner spheres were most of the planets, up to Saturn, that we know much better today for their purely mineral and gaseous being. But, as Israeli writer Micah Goodman puts it, "The medieval cosmos was alive. When man looked up at the night sky he saw beings that were suffused with intelligence."[10]

The prophetic experience was in effect a heavenly ascent.[11] A prophet within that rise might look down on the spheres he has surpassed and behold all of the causal interplay within our own sublunar sphere, the lowest in the system. Such a vision was, by medieval lights, a scientific one of the causal workings of our world and a perfect instance of Maimonides's conviction that religion and science allied. In the case of Moses, the knowledge attained was particularly comprehensive, involving for all worldly things, "their nature and the way they

---

10. Goodman, *Maimonides*, 214.

11. This is not a metaphor Maimonides employs, but it fits so well his understanding of the relation between the Aristotelian cosmos and prophetic knowledge, I take the liberty of applying it on his behalf.

are mutually connected, ... in general and in detail" (GP125). Within Maimonides's schema of esoteric knowledge, inherited from the rabbis, this would constitute *Ma'aseh Bereshit*, the "work of creation," or rather, knowledge of the created order.[12]

But a prophet might also look upward toward the God of the outmost sphere. And there he beheld what surpassed his reason: the God of negative theology who, as we shall see in chapter 9, offers itself to ecstatic contemplation, not causal analysis or definition of any kind. Such a vision is the highest prophetic revelation. It is a matter of *Ma'aseh Merkavah*, the "work of the Chariot," which references the prophet Ezekiel's mystical vision of a divine chariot (Ezek 1:4–28) and which sparked an early form of Jewish mysticism. Like the Platonic Good, it is above any definition, and in that sense a Nothing to our reason. In beholding it, reason surpasses itself.

Maimonides's *Guide* opens with an extended introduction to this, his negative theology. He wants to disabuse us of any pretensions to positively contentful understandings of God. No positive predicates apply to God, only negative and active ones. We can say what God is *not* and what God *does* (for instance, create), but not what God *is*. If the Bible is broadly anthropomorphic in its descriptions of God, that is because in its address of human intelligence it employs *amphibolous* terms.[13] Those are, loosely speaking, ambiguous words that, with reference to God, pull in two directions at once, toward positive descriptions of God and away from them.

The Bible itself cues us to this by the range of ways it speaks of God. On the one hand, God exhibits anger, jealousy, and love. On the other, God is above all such terminology, for "Who is like unto Thee, O Lord?" (Exod 15:11). The question is rhetorical and does not expect a positive answer. No one or thing is like God. Any positive description of God implies just such a likeness to other beings, and so cannot apply. Maimonides puts this in another more strictly philosophical way. It is exclusively true of God that "His existence is identical with His essence" (GP132). As later philosophers, e.g., Kant, would tell us, existence is not a contentful

12. Maimonides, *Book of Knowledge*, 11–12.
13. This is the term Shlomo Pines uses to translate the Arabic word *mushakkak*, which connotes double-meaning. It is a technical term in medieval Islamic philosophy. It connotes not a flaw in a word but a power of connecting disparate things. While "ambiguous" carries a negative connotation, "amphibolous" suggests a connective power in words to mean more than one thing. For more on *mushakkak*, see Harvey, "Key Terms," 310–14.

predicate of things. It follows that a being whose essence *is* its existence is an essentially contentless being, at least to the human mind.

A lesser intelligence receives only the positive turn of the predicates the Bible applies to God; a higher one receives it for the sheer purpose of negating it, toward a contemplative, non-discursive awareness of God; arguably, the goal of the book. One interpretation of Maimonides's *Guide* is that the extended exercise at the start of it in negating positive predicates of God culminates at the end in a mystical apprehension of God. If so, Maimonides illustrates, paradigmatically, the operations of our negative theology of Judaism.

Unlike the biblical account of the Sinaitic revelation, Maimonidean revelation in these two senses, of the scientific and the apophatic, are both attainable by humans educated and gifted enough for the ascent. Micah Goodman again: Revelatory knowledge "is a human spiritual achievement rather than an act of God."[14] Revelatory knowledge comes *naturally* to one who has beforehand applied his "strength of mind"[15] to the sequence of the sciences in "proper order," from logic to mathematics to natural science to astronomy (GP75). This is itself a causal chain that naturally, indeed "necessarily" (GP362), culminates in revelatory knowledge. That links up handily with our negation of purposive history. Revelation in this esoteric sense is not a set of prescriptions that position history to be the purposive context for their realization, toward some messianic future. It is something gifted individuals, such as Moses, attain in the here and now by following the proper program in natural causal sequence.

It is no surprise that a negation of discursive revelation should allow to show in its wake a non-discursive and mystical counterpart. The direction of descent in the one view of revelation, from God to human, finds its mirror image in the reverse ascent of the other view, from the human to God. But then Maimonides was a rabbi enough concerned with his community not to disparage revelation in the exoteric sense of disclosed commands. After all, that is the point of his *Mishneh Torah*, to re-present those commands in a handy, assimilable way. And when called for pastorally, he could invoke and express traditional theodicies of comfort based in exoteric revelation.[16] He is far from abandoning

14. Goodman, *Maimonides*, 19.

15. Maimonides, *Book of Knowledge*, 20.

16. For Maimonides's pastoral voice, see his "Epistle to Yemen" (Iggeret Teiman). The Yemenite Jews wrote Maimonides beseeching him for guidance in their distress

exoteric revelation. He even takes pains to ingeniously connect esoteric and exoteric revelation: the exoteric revelation of Mosaic commandments is a translation from the declarative voice of scientific vision, which only a prophet or philosopher "hears" (really, *sees*) into the imperative voice of commandments for the benefit of ancient Israelite polity. As Micah Goodman puts it, here was an attempt "to translate the wisdom of nature into wisdom for leadership."[17]

This way, with Maimonides, we have our cake and eat it too. Sinaitic revelation holds up as both a charge and comfort to the majority of Jews *and* as a translation of Mosaic visions for the very few: the philosophers. Both versions of revelation are rational, the first for its accord with reason, the second for mounting on reason to visions above it. Maimonides is, as Alvin Reines opines, "a constant inspiration to contemporary Jewish rationalism."[18] For us today, it is perhaps our spiritually affectable scientists who update the Maimonidean vision of esoteric revelation into words more suitable for our age. Revelation understood as surprise appearances of note applies most aptly here. For scientists report on the religious impact on them of what their effortful experiments and theorizing have caused to appear to them. An instance is Einstein, who wrote of the "cosmic religious feeling" born of an acute awareness of "the universal operation of the law of causation," culminating in a "rapturous amazement at the harmony of natural law." In words that recall Heschel, Einstein retraces the prophetic movement we suggest Maimonides limns from scientific to apophatic revelation. Einstein opines that this is a common experience of scientists, to such an extent that "in this materialistic age of ours, the serious scientific workers are the only profoundly religious people."[19]

And now come the mystics, for whom Maimonides has paved a way. With Gershom Scholem's help, we read them for the intensifications they make of apophatic vision, doubling as revelation. Paradoxically, this comes by way of the very language that apophasis transcends.

---

under an unusually harsh Muslim ruler. He acknowledges their grief: "This news has broken our backs and has astounded and dumbfounded the whole of our community" (Maimonides, "Epistle," 438) and consoles them with traditional theodicies.

17. Goodman, *Maimonides*, 101.

18. Reines, *Maimonides*, xiii.

19. Einstein, *World as I See It*, under "Religion and Science," and "The Religiousness of Science."

If Maimonides negated discursive revelation by limiting language, the mystics did so by stretching it to breaking points.

The letters of the Hebrew alphabet were animated with life prior to and beyond the words they formed. They did not have to cohere into discursive sentences. Whence, after all, did language originate? Within the creation story of Gen 1 God simply begins speaking. And creation happens through it. The mystics believed that the twenty-two letters of the Hebrew alphabet pre-existed in God's being. According to Scholem, these were "the organs which God availed himself of" to create the world. "In the process of the Creation, God manipulated these letters in accordance with determined procedures" such "that every created thing has a linguistic essence which consists in any conceivable combination of these fundamental letters."[20] The notion of a means by which God creates is not new with the mystics, as personified Wisdom already filled a role like that in the book of Proverbs (Prov 8:30). But language as an instrument of creation hints at an unexpected relation between it and the world around us. If letters in certain combinations "spell" things into being, as it were, then words *for* things are really words *of* things. The words animatingly inhabit things. When Adam named the things around him he simply read the words off of the things they inherently carried. Words so understood were more a presence to Adam than an instrument of his naming agency. And this pushes language into its own agency of presence rather than of discursive description. The names things carry *are* those things, and vice-versa. As Scholem puts it, speaking for a mystical instinct across the religions,

> A close and substantial relation exists between the name and the name's bearer. The name is a real, non-fictitious quantity. It contains a declaration about the nature of its bearer or at least something of the potency attaching to it; it is, further, identified with the nature and essence of what is named by it.[21]

Insofar as the name of a thing presents it, it bears the thing to its hearer. For mystics longing for the presence of God, this invested God's name with special significance. It was *this* name that invoked, studied, and contemplated drew the mystic near to God. They were especially drawn to those two mysterious and interrelated divine names of Exodus: *Ehyeh-Asher-Ehyeh* of Exod 3:14, in context of the story of the burning

---

20. Scholem, "Name of God," 74, 75.
21. Scholem, "Name of God," 65.

bush, and the Tetragrammaton, YHWH, of Exod 6:3. Neither indicated any definable content of the divine. They were negations of describable content. They were presentations of God.

But then, to push the non-discursiveness further: the whole of the Torah was itself "the one and only great name of God, ... whose purpose, in the first analysis, does not consist in conveying a specific message, but rather in giving expression to the power and almightiness of God."[22] "God reveals nothing but Himself as He becomes speech and voice."[23] What matters for us here is that this name is not a communicative message, commanding any variety of behavior or speech, but an expression of the divine being beyond our ken, as indeed we might expect a name as long as the entire Torah to be. As Scholem exclaims, "this communication is incomprehensible!"[24] We cannot fathom it. But the point of it is not to be fathomed but to arrest and hold our attention. To our understanding, the divine name is contentless, meaningless.[25] The mystics proffer a helpful metaphor: just as the divine name, *Ehyeh* (Exod 3:14), begins with the first letter of the Hebrew alphabet, the soundless aleph, so revelation originates with the meaningless divine name.[26]

When Scholem writes on behalf of the mystics that "the name of God ... is accordingly nothing more than a revelation of the divine being, which in itself, is directed at nothing else outside it,"[27] he suggests that, for the mystics, there is no more expectation that revelation should register meaningfully with our understanding than that God should. For revelation is simply the divine being externalized. It is what shows of God when God no longer directs at "nothing outside it," to something outside: the world and humanity, rather like the externalization Rosenzweig's protocosmic God performs to produce creation. Language functions here to *express*, rather than to describe.

The medieval and early modern mystics foretell how several of our modern philosophers press language into the service of an expressive, non-discursive revelation. They stretch language, rather than negate it. We have three such philosophers on offer: Walter Benjamin, Rosenzweig, and Levinas. For Benjamin, revelation is indeed a kind of naming; for

22. Scholem, "Name of God," 78, 79.
23. Scholem, "Revelation," 293.
24. Scholem, "Revelation," 294.
25. Scholem, "Name of God, pt. 2," 194.
26. Scholem, "Name of God, pt. 2," 170.
27. Scholem, "Name of God, pt. 2," 175.

Rosenzweig, a kind of love; for Levinas, a solicitous cry. None of these revelations are expressly Sinaitic; but all are linguistic. As Benjamin's views most readily recall the mystics, we begin with him.

Benjamin had some awareness of kabbalistic thought through his friendship with Gershom Scholem. And some of his ideas on revelation have clear precedent there. He certainly understands their sense of the intimacy between revelation and language. For Benjamin, language exists, in Susan Handelman's words, "as mediation and medium of revelation through time."[28] Benjamin was as intrigued as the mystics were by the origin of language, which the Bible never fully discloses. God is shown creating many things, but not language. Benjamin did not have recourse to Hebrew letters pre-existing within the divine. (He never learned Hebrew.) But he did opine that language was less a means of creating, prior to creation and in need of its own explanation, than something simultaneous with and endemic to creation itself. "Language is . . . both creative and the finished creation, it is word and name."[29] Creation was a speech-act which all of reality echoes. "There is no event or thing in either animate or inanimate nature that does not in some way partake of language. . . . We cannot imagine a total absence of language in anything."[30] Everything speaks, though not necessarily in words.

We are bordering here on the creation doctrine we negated in chapter 1. But it is not as though Benjamin needs the creator God for language to function creatively. The early German romantics, on whom Benjamin wrote a doctoral thesis, had already claimed an agency implicit to language, to speak for itself.[31] And Spinoza implied something like it when he suggested that the worlds of mind and matter, though radically distinct, superimpose on each other in parallel sequence (E2p7). If language can substitute for ideas in that Spinozistic claim, then it seems words and things exist in parallel, perhaps superimposed, realities. Even non-organic things speak, as Proust invited us to consider, when he wrote in his novel of "some inanimate object[s]" that harbor "the souls of those whom we have lost," and which "call us by our name" when we pass them,[32] such as "windows [that] appeared conscious of being pro-

---

28. Handelman, *Fragments*, 20.

29. Benjamin, "On Language," 323.

30. Benjamin, "On Language," 314–15.

31. A point for which Novalis argues in his short piece "Monolog" (Novalis, "Monolog," 83–84).

32. Proust, *In Search of Lost Time*, 1:59.

tectingly closed,"[33] or, at an historic church, "a flagstone almost endowed with thought, which is made of the ashes of Arnauld or Pascal,"[34] or at a brothel, pieces of furniture that "seemed to me to be alive and to be appealing to me" for some redemption from their condition.[35]

Benjamin, with some help from Proust, has primed us for an experience of revelation in the language voiced or unvoiced all around us. It would be a revelation if the silent speech of inanimate things or the vocal speech of animals underwent translation into the word-language of humans. For then those non-human languages would undergo a process of appearing to us more forcefully. But this is just what Benjamin, commenting on the biblical creation stories, suggests Adam did when he named the animals, and by implication everything else around him. Adam spoke revelatory language. There is a "communicating muteness of things (animals) toward the word language of man," who receives "the unspoken nameless language of things and convert[s] it by name into sounds."[36] It is not so much that this happened in some primal time, but that the biblical story captures an intuition about inanimate and animal language that writers like Proust express for us. If the language things speak are actually their inherent names, as the mystics taught, then what they speak is a language of names that doubles for themselves. The language of names does not describe the things that bear the names. It presents them, the way onomatopoeic words sound the very things they name. It is no surprise for us to be surprised by the notion of such a language, we have so lost the capacity to hear or speak it. (It is the Bible that mythically preserves the idea of it, in Adam.) We have only remnants of such a language in personal names like Verity, which in our "fallen" world may well attach to untruthful persons. It is as though our recognizable language is the ruin of a perfect language that seamlessly matched word to thing.[37] That would be a revelation in two senses: of our language as a ruin and of the lost language of which it is the ruin.

But now the surprise of language extends further to an additional match Benjamin makes between the notion of that ideal language, which

33. Proust, *In Search of Lost Time*, 1:591–92.
34. Proust, *In Search of Lost Time*, 5:919.
35. Proust, *In Search of Lost Time*, 2:208.
36. Benjamin, "On Language," 325–26.

37. This is a thought the fictional Gustave Aschenbach expresses when, within Thomas Mann's *Death in Venice*, he experiences with "its own pang, that language could but extol, not reproduce, the beauties of the sense" (Mann, *Death in Venice*, 50).

we do not speak and of which we have only a ruin, and the fact of translation between the languages we do speak. Between the language of things and of human beings, we were already dealing with translation "of the mute into the sonic."[38] Translation between languages, even those we recognize, is itself a mystery. For if languages define worlds, as is sometimes said, how can anyone really be bilingual?—that would be to inhabit two worlds at once. We must rather successively, not simultaneously, speak several languages we fluently know. Furthermore, the very translatability of texts is a puzzle, as there is no neutral medium between two texts in different languages to monitor the conversion of one to the other. Or is there? If there were, it would have to be a language so adaptable that, sandwiched between the two in translation, it would simultaneously conform to both when the translation worked; or so transparent, that the differently encoded texts on either side of it would espy through its clarity their semantic equivalent on the other side. So transparent a language would have no substantive content of its own. It would be contentless, a language of sheer transmissibility: a "pure language" that instances the form of language, to express, but without any content to be expressed apart from express-ability itself. "This pure language . . . no longer means or expresses anything [of its own], but is, as expressionless . . . word, that which is meant in all languages,"[39] or that which allows meaning to occur across languages. In Susan Handelman's words, so pure a language is a "contentless transparency,"[40] the "contentless . . . source of all meaning."[41]

Benjamin matches the ideal language of the creation stories, in which names fit the named, to the pure language of translatability. For what they share is a reduction of distance between the expressing function of language and what it expresses. Names that fit the named express the named with a minimum of distance between the two, or with no distance at all. We sometimes say our clothes express who we are. It would be as though a particularly well-fitting suit of clothes was to merge with our skin.[42] The expressed and the expressing merge. Per-

38. Benjamin, "On Language," 325.
39. Benjamin, "Task of the Translator," 80.
40. Handelman, *Fragments*, 91.
41. Handelman, *Fragments*, 76.

42. Under the heading of Intimacy, by implication between a garment and its wearer, the Metropolitan Museum of Art, in an exhibit of recent American fashion, described a piece by designer Jean Yu this way: "Delicate silk georgette is suspended from grosgrain ribbon, forming an intimate connection between body and cloth"; we'd like to say, forming an *identity* between them. Metropolitan Museum of Art, *In America*.

haps this is more evident in the case of birds whose brilliant plumage is designed to attract a mate. The "clothes" *are* the bird. By the same token, the pure language that enables translation between other languages expresses only express-ability itself. In the languages we speak, we sometimes mistake or misinterpret what we hear. What a person meant to say is not what they actually said. But the pure language of translatability lacks any content of its own to interfere with the transitions it enables between other languages. There is no distance between what it means to say and what it says, which is always the equivalent in one language of what has been said in another.

We have lost the ideal language of words for things. Our own language is a ruin of it. But we have not completely lost the pure language of translatability. We engage with it unknowingly each time we translate from one language to another. "To regain pure language fully formed in the linguistic flux, is the tremendous and only capacity of translation."[43] Susan Handelman again: "Human language is imperfect and fragmentary on account of the breakdown of the original correspondence of word and thing, but translation is a function within language that can help redeem it."[44] It is the translator's unknowing engagement with pure language that makes the awareness of it, when it comes into view, a revelation. For the translator does not force pure language into view. And it itself does not really appear, except hiddenly, behind the veil of the two spoken languages in translation. "Revelation," Benjamin says, has thus "elevated itself to the center of linguistic philosophy."[45] That is good news for humankind. For if pure language is also the ideal language that Adam spoke, then our translators effectively transport us back to Eden, or at least enliven the biblical idea of it to a place of sustaining presence in our lives.[46] But it is also good news for us, for it enlists Benjamin in support of our effort to negate a discursive idea of revelation in favor of a descriptively contentless but expressive one.

Let us pick up now that thread linking Scholem and the mystics to Rosenzweig, over the notion of externalization, which we dropped to make room for Benjamin. Scholem had led us from the revelation of divine names to the self-externalizing God of Rosenzweig, who

43. Benjamin, "Task of the Translator," 80.
44. Handelman, *Fragments*, 87.
45. Benjamin, "On Language," 320.
46. Benjamin comments that "the life of man in pure language-mind [where names matched the named] was blissful" ("On Language," 329).

partners with the world in creation. What we now want is the partnership that yields up *revelation*. We already know from chapter 3, on Israel the people, what that is in Rosenzweig's schema: the meeting between self-externalized God and humanity. Rosenzweig is explicit on its link to creation, which partners God and world. "The created death of the creature is at the same time the sign that announces the revelation of life which transcends that of the simple creature" (SR168). Within the middle part of Rosenzweig's *Star of Redemption*, this sentence occurs just at the end of a chapter on "Creation," immediately succeeded by one on "Revelation." It is our bridge out of creation into revelation. Revelation echoes creation by being a self-externalization, but this time of God and humanity, toward an expression of love between the two. Revelation is not a description of love or even, really, a command to it, for love cannot be commanded. It is the actual phenomenon of love, itself, but carried on the back of a linguistic command.

How does it work?—by way of a time-honored association between death and love that Rosenzweig newly interprets. Under the rubric of creation, we know that for Rosenzweig a key service of death is to identify each of us as a singularity. We each die our own death. Death forefronts our singularity in all its gravity, apart from any consolation we might find in larger causes or projects we may have furthered and that might preserve the memory of us for a time. The problem with the world is that it cares only for its genera and species. To sustain those, it has programmed into all living things a drive to self-perpetuate. That creatures bear offspring is evidence of nature's care for the species, which channels that drive (more or less successfully) into each of its living individuals. But the perpetuation is at best only of the family, tribe, group, or species, not the individual. Reproduction is the biological means of species-preservation at the cost of the individual. Even the garden of Eden story hints that death and (the pains of) childbirth are the (punishing) substitute for the immortality Adam and Eve might otherwise have had as individuals. Indeed, some organisms die at giving birth, as though at that point their reason for being at all is accomplished. The individual within the species is always imperiled. This was the problem of creation for Rosenzweig.

But there is another reality, apart from death, that also addresses itself solely to the individual, not the group; and, says Rosenzweig, that is love. Love—for a spouse, child, parent, friend—always extends to individuals as singularities, not "through the bias of a multiplicity" (SR201). We are talking now about the "individual without a genus" or as "its own genus unto itself" (SR201), not as "a representative of a category" (SR188), which is just how individuals figure in nature. So now death has an adversary that meets it on the same grounds it itself claims: the singularity of the individual. And in that contest, love proves to be "as strong as death" as Song 8:6 maintains. Love appears—self-reveals—to address the singular life of the individual and lift it above the station assigned it by nature (SR168) to be mere "representative of a category."

The Song of Songs is the biblical book Rosenzweig enlists to detail the work of love. He highlights Song 8:6 for the limit it puts on death (SR217), that "love is strong as death." But that verse stands out for another reason, that it "is the only passage that is not spoken, but simply told" (SR217). That is, it is the one purely descriptive, rather than expressive, verse in the poem. Among the books of the Bible, one of the several distinguishing features of the Song of Songs is that it is almost entirely in dialogue form, from "Thy love is better than wine" in the opening verses (Song 1:2) to "Make haste, my beloved" of the end (Song 8:14). Those two verses are representative for the second person singular of their grammar, which Rosenzweig takes for the grammar of love. Rosenzweig invites us to read the partners in dialogue, the lover and the beloved, as conduits of love itself, who speaks through them both, rather like language speaking itself, as some of German romantics thought it did. Only at Song 8:6, Rosenzweig suggests, a claim *about* love intrudes on its speaking voice, to assert its equality of strength with death; as though the rest of the verses exist to demonstrate that fact, that as long as love is speaking through us, whether as lover or beloved, it enlivens us to a point beyond death. If only all of reality could be absorbed by the words of this biblical book and we remain forever within its scope of address, whether as lover or beloved within it, we could not die. And perhaps those of us who are currently "in love," or remember what it is like, will best understand.

But that is in effect Rosenzweig's claim: the promise of love is the end of death. And because, he implies, the voice of love speaks all the time, for those who have ears to hear, we need never fall out of its embrace. If and when we hear love's voice, we experience revelation, for that is what revelation is for Rosenzweig. As in the case of Scholem and Benjamin, revelation is not a communication of doable or instructive content. It is pure *expression*. Anyone in the grip of revelation is overwhelmed by the voice of love. Rosenzweig, whose account of language is cheerier than Benjamin's, might insist that, after all, one bit of Eden's perfect language is with us still in full flower, without having fallen into ruin: the matching of the words Love me! to the expression of love itself.

But then, how is this seeming commandment an expression of love rather than the command to love it appears to be? The grammar of the case inverts that of the first of the Ten Commandments, which by Jewish reckoning is simply a declaration, not a command—yet it *is* a command, the first of the ten: "I am the Lord thy God who brought thee out of the land of Egypt" (Exod 20:2). Now, with the utterance of Love me! we have the grammar of command in expressive or presentative mode, for all its look of the imperative. The problem with Song 8:6, for all its memorability, is that by its very claim *for* love, it distances love. Descriptions always distance; whereas what Rosenzweig wants is a grammatical form that presents love in its immediacy. Rosenzweig wants the linguistic equivalent of a kiss. And his venture is that the imperative can do it.

It cannot do so as a general rule. "Surely love cannot be commanded" (as in Lev 19:18) in that way. "Love your neighbor as yourself" (SR190) awaits its fulfillment by my acts, does not itself bear my love to my neighbor. But "Love me!" is immediately realized if it comes "from the mouth of the lover" (SR190); only not in the way we might expect. It happens by way of a precise match between the form of the command (its grammar) and its content (to love). But looks deceive. What the command realizes and projects is not toward the lover, as it seems, but the beloved. It *expresses* the lover's love. For the imperative taking the object it does ("me") dislodges the speaker from the grammatical position of subject to object and elevates the addressee to the station of subject. It converts what within a description, such as "I love you," would be object to the subject of the imperative. And that grammar of the imperative in this case matches perfectly the workings of love, as Rosenzweig understands it, which is always to self-negate in face of an other. Love, says Rosenzweig, is a "perpetually new self-negation" (SR173). The form of the imperative, Love me!, so matches its content as to realize the content in the form, in imitation of the workings of onomatopoeia, or even of the ontological argument, which "proves" the existence of God by the singular identity it realizes between the form (existence) and content (essence) of God.

The Song of Songs lends itself to illustrate. For within the pervasive grammar of the second person singular are many commands, and some specifically in the Love me! form: "Give me!" (Song 1:2), "Draw me!" (Song 1:4), "Tell me!" (Song 1:7), as though to provide the framework for

Love me! to sound. If those words never appear as such, it is because the whole of the poem cries them out. Only once does the spoken command cease, as though to reflect on the import of it, when the "narrator" comments on what we need to realize, that love is strong as death.

The paradox of love's expression within language, that it commands without commanding, matches the stress on our understanding of Benjamin's wholly transparent language of translation or Scholem's stupefyingly long name of God. All three of these linguistic expressions of revelation absent descriptive content in favor of expressive presence. A transparent language cannot be spoken, an infinitely long name cannot be pronounced, a command that is not a command is not subject to mere obeisance.

Revelation unfolds from this account another feature of itself: it is all about relationship. It has that in common with creation. For what sustains the externalizations of God and world in their now vulnerable stations is their relation with each other. But it is only the categories of the world that God sustains in creation, not the individuals who fill them. This is why for us, as individuals, rather than instances of a category, death is so terrifying. The world provides no succor for it. It cares only about its species and classes of things, that they perdure. But the death we are subject to secures the very singularity we need to enter into relationship with another. And now revelation comes to be that relationship. It is the love we receive over separating distance. For Rosenzweig, that love is ever-present, waiting only to be received. It is what supports us over the death that isolates us. Its ever-present quality assures it a strength as great as death's.

For Rosenzweig, this love comes from God. We have negated the creator God, but not the loving one. But we can part even with that. For Rosenzweig has invested love with a voice of its own. It speaks in the Song of Songs, but for that one verse. Rosenzweig's friend Martin Buber helps us here with a picture of what it might be like to receive revelatory love even apart from any notions of a creator God.

> Sometimes we have a personal experience related to those recorded as revelations. . . . We may unexpectedly grow aware of a certain apperception within ourselves, which was lacking but a moment ago, and whose origin we are unable to discover. . . . What occurred to me was "otherness," was the touch of the other. Nietzsche says it more honestly: "You take, you do not

ask who gives." . . . When we . . . experience the giving, we find out that revelation exists.[47]

It is only each of us who can answer whether we have ever received such a revelation, or it took the form of love. Proust gave us a literary expression of Benjamin's transparent language of names, which speaks to us even from inanimate things. Love is too checkered a thing in Proust's novel for it to oblige us here, except for one curious passage that, as Rosenzweig would have it, links to death. After one of the characters has died, the narrator speculates on a

> world entirely different from this one and which we leave in order to be born on this earth, before perhaps returning there to live once again beneath the sway of those unknown laws which we obeyed because we bore their precepts in our hearts, not knowing who traced them there . . . [toward] kindness, scrupulousness, self-sacrifice. . . .[48]

If those unknown laws from we know not where were bearing kindness toward us in our very hearing of them, then Proust has given us a bit of Rosenzweig and Buber combined.

Levinas, who took inspiration from Rosenzweig, understands as much as Buber did that for "modern Jews, [who] . . . are the majority,"[49] revelation is a problem. He allows that for all the presence the sacred literature of Judaism may have in a life, it is still possible to ask of it, as Buber did: "from where?" (191), which presses forward all the more forcefully once Sinai is discounted. For an aura of "mystery" (194) hangs over these texts, if we include the broad expanse of the rabbinical literature, on account of a coherence with each other they exhibit despite the "innumerable meanings" (194) at work within them. At the same time that a centripetal force works toward their convergence, a centrifugal one explodes them outward and away from each other. They both cohere and self-contradict. The tradition itself authorizes a language at odds with itself, as in this Talmudic aphorism: "These and those are the words of the living God."[50] But what might just as much result from such tolerance of contradiction is a negation of discursive content.

---

47. "Man of Today," in Buber, *Writings of Martin Buber*, 246–47.

48. Proust, *In Search of Lost Time*, 5:246.

49. Levinas, "Revelation," 192. Subsequent citations to pages of this text are given parenthetically.

50. b. Eruvin 13b, and other places. See http://www.sefaria.org/Eruvin.13b.11?lang=bi.

Levinas does not draw that inference. Instead, he asks us simply to grant of revelation that "its word comes from elsewhere, . . . from outside" (194). He turns our attention to the impact on the prophets of the revelations they receive, as recorded in the Bible, for instance, on Moses, a stammering "disability" (197); and on the rest of the prophets generally, "a traumatic upheaval in experience which confronts intelligence with something far beyond its capacity" (205). This sounds quite different from the gift Buber implies revelation makes us, or the love that Rosenzweig says it extends to us; and it is. For Levinas darkens the impact on our experience of revelatory encounters. Revelation does not so much vacate descriptive content as undermine it. He has in mind the content of the self.

For Levinas, what the self undergoes within an experience of revelation is a "fracture" and "breach" of itself (194). That traumatic upheaval to which the prophets attest is an "irruption" (202) and "bursting" (202) open of the self. This sounds less like the extraversion Rosenzweig associates with revelation than a massive deconstruction. Up to a point Levinas's account follows Rosenzweig's. Just as Rosenzweig presumes an isolated, or isolatable, humanity prior to the revelation of love it receives, so for Levinas, "the uniqueness of the 'self' is the necessary condition of the breach and the manifestation which enter from outside" (194). There cannot be a breach without a wall for it to occur in. The walls of the self that lie broken around us witness to a revelation received. But Rosenzweig's self, in emerging from its broken walls of self-enclosure, encounters love. There is barely a moment for Rosenzweig's self to suffer the loss of its walls before it is cradled by love. Levinas will not go so far. We will see in the next chapter what a recipient of revelation encounters "from outside" (194), as Levinas puts it. For now, Levinas implies that if we have received revelatory books, such as the Bible, then their impact on us must be to devastate the self, as they did the prophets who first received them, if we are to experience those books *as* revelation.

Levinas has returned us to a topic from several chapters ago: suffering. For suffering is a consequence of revelation's receipt. Among the prophets, Ezekiel and Jeremiah are prime examples. Part of what revelation reveals is how little confidence we can have in our own self-sufficiency. And this offers itself another lens on our perduring theme of contentless identity, in ourselves, the covenant, even God. The deconstructed self is virtually contentless. But Levinas will not leave us here. Under the rubric of ethics (next chapter) it will emerge anew. "Is there not a certain way of 'losing one's soul' which comes from deference to something greater or better or 'higher' than the soul?" (209). The self (or soul) must pass through a liminal state of shorn identity over that transition. As Susan Handelman puts it, speaking for Levinas, "Vulnerability . . . itself becomes the foundation of the self."[51] In a culture of self-assertion this may indeed come as revelation, as much as the many exhortations that fill our public rhetoric toward leading passionate lives might reveal themselves a contradiction when an older meaning of the term, as in "the Passion of Christ," shows itself. And maybe that is enough to expect of revelation. Levinas will not leave us in these doldrums. Ethics will revive us.

---

51. Handelman, *Fragments*, 275.

Chapter 7
Ethics

WE WOULD NEVER PRESUME to negate ethics itself, especially when it figures so centrally in American Jewish self-understanding. According to the 2020 Pew Research Center survey of Jewish beliefs, 72 percent identify "leading a moral and ethical life" as central to their Jewishness.[1] Insofar as Judaism is the *moral* monotheism it is often presented as being in textbooks of comparative religion, this is no surprise.

But then, what *is* Jewish ethics? Those same textbooks of comparative religion may advise those seeking to defend the view that "all religions are the same" to look to ethics to support their claim. The Golden Rule, for example, is found in pretty much all major world religions, from Buddhism to Zoroastrianism. Variations occur: It may be framed positively or negatively, in terms of what we should or should not do to others; it may limit its reach to inter-human behavior, or expand to include all life forms; it may promote empathy for the other or actual identification with her. But the general gist of it is the same.

The best-known version of the Golden Rule in Judaism, attributed to Rabbi Hillel, reads in the negative: "What is hateful to you do not do to others." The negative formulation sets the stage for the conclusion to this advice: "the rest is commentary, go and learn it."[2] If we want to know what positively to do toward others, no general command can suffice. We must study Jewish law, or halacha, for the specifics. For instance, loving our neighbor as ourself means returning to them any lost

---

1. Pew Research Center, *Jewish Americans in 2020*.
2. b. Shabbat 31a. See https://www.sefaria.org/Shabbat.31a.10?lang=bi.

thing of theirs we find (Deut 22:1–3). This was one of Saadia's defenses of the need of law in the first place, to supply the specifics that reason in its generality cannot generate.

This seems a very moderate approach to the moral life. Surely it is, on the whole, less demanding *not* to do something, such as murder someone, than do it. And what the law prescribes when we consult it will not overwhelm. Moses, speaking for God, proclaims for it, "It is not too hard for thee, neither is it far off . . . [but] is very nigh unto thee . . . that thou mayst do it" (Deut 30:11, 14). Maimonides praises the law precisely for its "equibalance and wisdom," its freedom from "burden and excess" (GP380). As Isadore Twersky puts it, speaking for Maimonides, "the Torah [law] is a delicately constructed instrument, designed to produce perfect spirituality through moderation."[3]

Sometimes in apologetic contexts of contrast between Judaism and Christianity, a Jewish ethics of moderation finds favor over against a New Testament ethic of extremes to, for example, "turn the other cheek" in response to injury (Matt 5:38), forgive excessively (Matt 18:22), or extravagantly disregard our daily needs (Matt 6:25–33). The apocalyptic context of Jesus' teaching may then be summoned to explain this difference—if the world we know is shortly to end, in a great overturning of accustomed procedures and relations ("the last will be first," Matt 20:16 RSV) then an ethic of extremes may sensibly apply. But Judaism is not typically apocalyptic. And so it is not typically extreme. That is an implication of its denial the messiah has come. The accustomed normalities prevail. We still await the end.

But then, in places, Jewish tradition does indulge the ethical extreme. There is martyrdom and self-denial. Within the Torah an instance of self-denial is the Nazirite (Num 6:1–21), and within Isaiah a case of the martyr is the Suffering Servant.[4] Even the law for all of Israel is not so consistently modest about itself. When the Talmud claims that it takes only two correctly observed Sabbaths for the messiah to come,[5] it implies

---

3. Twersky, *Introduction to the Code of Maimonides*, 463.

4. The Suffering Servant, from the Second Isaiah, e.g., Isa 42:1–4, was never admitted into the haftarah readings of the Jewish liturgy, according to some scholars, from a sense that this figure had been irrevocably claimed by Christianity. That the prescribed readings from the prophets stop just a verse short of referencing the Suffering Servant may confirm that. An Orthodox Jewish friend once wondered if the Suffering Servant was even a Jewish idea, so different was he from anything she had been taught in her Jewish education.

5. b. Shabbat 118b. See https://sefaria.org/Shabbat.118b.4?lang=bi&with=all&lang2=en.

this is easier said than done. A source that by its English title proclaims its relevance to Jewish ethics, *The Ethics of the Fathers*, from the Mishnah, sets up a range of ethical options, including these two:

> He who says what is mine is mine and what is yours is yours: that's the mean between the extremes; he who says what is mine is yours and what is yours is yours: that's the *hasid*.[6]

This adage erects for us a contrast between the just person and the saintly person. For *hasid* here connotes a person who excels in charitable love. The one is moderate, the other extreme. We are not told which is better. On behalf of tradition, Gershom Scholem raises a caution about the hasid, that by his extremity he distinguishes himself from the community, which draws from it toward him "some noticeable reservation . . . or even a certain mistrust."[7] And yet, for Maimonides, this is only to be expected of the law-observant community, which fails to accommodate the exceptional person, for the ever-moderate law does not address exceptionality (GP534).

Perhaps no one lays out the distinction between a moderate and extreme ethics more starkly than Maimonides. He does not strictly follow the terms of the contrast that we find in the Mishnah. For him, the distinction is between the hasid and the *hakham*, the one wise and learned in the law. He elaborates on the hasid, who specializes in displays of altruism, even at expense to himself. He is in his regard for others "excessively critical of himself," and exhibits an "extreme of humility," as opposed to the hakham who, learned in the law, "keeps in the middle path" in the practice of self-critique.[8] Insofar as the biblical Moses is a moral model, and also one of "very lowly spirit,"[9] i.e., a hasid, Maimonides might be expected to commend saintly over sage behavior. But at the same time, Moses is the very giver of the law and so by implication a model of moderation. The moderate's rule of thumb, after Aristotle, is "to aim at the . . . proper mean" and to avoid "going to one extreme or the other,"[10] the practice of the sage. Maimonides appears to harmonize the two by suggesting that extreme humility is warranted

---

6. m. Avot 5:10. This is my translation. For original Hebrew and alternative translation, see https://www.sefaria.org/Pirkei_Avot.5.10?lang=bi.

7. Scholem, "Three Types," 19–20.

8. Maimonides, *Book of Knowledge*, 29.

9. Maimonides, *Book of Knowledge*, 31.

10. Maimonides, "Eight Chapters," 374.

in persons prone to pride, as a kind of therapy that results in moderate self-regard. It is as though humility applied to pride moderates it toward something half-way between them: the golden mean. And yet, even a little pride is so extreme that "one must go from [this] extreme to the opposite."[11] And in the end, as Maimonides reminds us, the Torah notes in Moses not moderate self-regard, but the state of being "a very humble man, more so than any other man on earth" (Num 12:3).[12] The reader is left wondering how humble he should aspire to be, if indeed it is not an oxymoron to *aspire* to humility.

One way to reconcile this tension in Maimonides is to assign each of the two halves of it—the extreme hasid, the moderate sage—to the Maimonidean text where he is most at home: the sage to the *Mishneh Torah*, which interprets the law for common use, and the hasid to the *Guide of the Perplexed*, which subsumes the law under a higher philosophy intended for the exception, which the law does not cover—indeed for the philosopher attuned to the higher reaches of revelation such as we explored in the last chapter. The hasid of the *Guide* is a philosopher. His "excess in beneficence" (GP630) flows naturally from his visionary knowledge, without explicit guidance of the prescriptive law (GP441). The consequence is remarkable in the extreme. His mind so "rejoices in what it apprehends" (GP627) that it becomes virtually immune to harm—"all evils are prevented from befalling [it]" (GP626)—and it looks forward in death to being "separated from the body" (GP627). An extreme of providence hovers over an extreme of knowledge that overflows into an extreme of charity.

Maimonides writes here in striking consonance with Judah Halevi's description of the philosopher in his *Kuzari*. For Halevi, a cosmopolitan inhabitant of medieval Spain, knew the appeal of philosophy as a worldview that promised a highly ethical life of its own, apart from what the religions had on offer. He invests his philosopher, in dialogue with the Kuzari king, with persuasive praise of the philosophical life. Having

> grasped the inward truths of all branches of science, . . . the limbs of such a person [the philosopher] only serve the most perfect purposes in the most appropriate time and in the best condition, . . . [resulting in] contentment, humility, meekness,

---

11. Maimonides, *Book of Knowledge*, 31.
12. Maimonides, *Book of Knowledge*, 31.

and every other praiseworthy inclination, . . . without concern for the decay of his body or his organs.[13]

Halevi's philosopher, like Maimonides's hasid, lives ecstatically beyond the sufferings of the body, which his mind also seems to have exited. Halevi's philosopher, who is not the hero of his book, sounds a lot like Maimonides, which is only to underscore a resolution of the tension in Maimonides between the hasid and the sage by implying that, under the aegis of philosophy, the two merge into one: a highly knowledgeable being exhibits the highest reaches of ethical behavior under a warmly protective guardianship.

Maimonides implies that if we negate the moderate ethics of his *Mishneh Torah*, which condenses centuries of legal thought within rabbinic Judaism, what will remain for our attention is the more extreme ethics of his *Guide of the Perplexed*, which culminates centuries of thought within philosophical Judaism. Let us follow that lead. He will draw our attention to precedents of his thought among the philosophers who preceded him, and extensions of it within those who succeeded him. We need not fall in with the Platonic disembodiment of either Halevi's or Maimonides's philosopher. Other more amenable expressions of the ethical extreme will show. Some of them may inspire us. Among the precedents, we will look at Philo's Therapeutae and Bahya ibn Paquda's duties of the heart; among the successors, the ethical paradigms embedded in the thought of Spinoza, Hermann Cohen, and Levinas.

Maimonides would not have known of Philo, who died in Jewish consciousness when his Alexandrian community did, under a punishing Roman attack in 115 CE. (He was only reborn to Jewish awareness long after Maimonides, during the Renaissance.) But Maimonides suspected there was a heritage of philosophical Judaism, lost over the course of so many expulsions and migrations (GP175–76), and he would have recognized in Philo a part of that. But Philo was much more Platonic than Maimonides, especially in what we might call his body negativity. He explicitly disparaged all physical pleasure as bad (Leg. 3 68). For example, the exodus story serves as much more than prelude to Sinaitic revelation. At a higher level, it describes the passage of the soul from passion to virtue (Sacr. 63). The matzoh that figures so prominently in the story symbolizes "the opposite of over boastful arrogance through meditation on humility" (QE 2, 1:15), as though to foretell Maimonides's own tribute to that virtue.

---

13. Halevi, *Kuzari*, 37–38.

But by its very flatness of taste, not only of appearance, it also rebukes delight in pleasures (Congr. 168–70) and passions of any worldly kind (Sacr. 16). This tendency in Philo moved him to either describe or envision—scholars are not sure which—in glowing terms an ascetic Jewish monastery, that of the so called Therapeutae, who lived in communal solitude by a lake outside Alexandria, Egypt. His tribute to the Therapeutae is a singular defense within Jewish cultural memory of a monastic ideal, often thought off bounds to Jewish sensibility (having been claimed by Christianity). It also witnesses to the appeal an extreme ethic of behavior can have within a Jewish (philosophical) framework.

According to Philo, the Therapeutae spent their days in solitary study, taking only occasional bread and water for nourishment, and gathering for sober communal celebrations every seventh day and once every fifty days for a more festive but still frugal meal and vigil observance. We already hear the note of the extreme in their lives, so akin to later Christian monasticism that they were taken for monks by some of the early church fathers who read Philo. Their asceticism, as we might expect if we approach them with Maimonides in mind, follows on the sublimity of their study of what revelation has disclosed to them in Torah: "the verities of nature, following the truly sacred instructions of the prophet Moses" (Contempl. 64). They "have taken to their hearts the contemplation of nature" (Contempl. 90), on grounds of what Maimonides would also teach, that the seeming laws of Torah are actually descriptions of the workings of the cosmos. That deeper meaning, as Maimonides would also say, must be plumbed beneath the merely surface meaning. They "discern the inward and hidden through the outward and visible" (Contempl. 78). It is just their attunement to the deeper meaning referencing the cosmos that makes them "philosophers" (Contempl. 2) which, according to Philo, is another apt name for them. They are those among "our people who embrace the contemplative life" (Contempl. 58).

Though we are informed largely of their ritual life, which turns on weekly Sabbath observance, but does not expressly involve any other Torah-based practice, we get an inkling of their ethics too. Before entering the community, they give away all their worldly goods to family and friends, which Philo deems an act of magnanimity (*megalonoia*)—an English word that in Greek translation also connotes elevated thought, as befits the connection between high-mindedness and ethics that Philo (and Maimonides) discerned. Their ethics shows in another way: Philo suggests that all the service that one member of the community performs for another comes "not under compulsion nor yet awaiting for orders, but with deliberate goodwill" (Contempl. 71). We have here a foretelling of the spiritual life, our topic for chapter 10. For now, the behavior of the Therapeutae implies an ethics so transformative of human nature that altruistic behavior flows effortlessly from character, in the spirit of what professional ethicists call virtue ethics.[14] Such magnanimous and effortless virtue may not seem extreme, but it would be more aspirational than real for many of us.

Of course, that these ethical behaviors occurred within the framework of what was effectively a monastery is already extreme from a rabbinical perspective. Philo even terms each of the rooms "consecrated" to the private worship life of each member a *monasterion* (Contempl. 25). The Therapeutae were celibate. Lest we think they thus violated the commandment to "be fruitful and multiply" (Gen 1:28), Philo can respond that they *do* bear fruit, only not in the form of children but of virtues (Congr. 56). Maimonides's own endorsement of extreme virtue did not go so far as to sanction monasteries.[15] But the Therapeutae were unusual—extreme—even by Christian monastic standards as they embraced both men and women in a common life.[16] Nor were their lives always separated. At festive banquets, they would sing in combined choir: "they mix and both together become a single choir" (Contempl. 85). The rabbis, if not the Platonically inspired Jewish philosophers, would raise an eyebrow, or two, at that. But Plato had allowed for both men and women to become philosophical rulers of the state. So why should they not sing together?

Maimonides was not alone among medieval Jewish philosophers prone to an extreme ethic. Bahya ibn Paquda, who preceded him, devoted a whole chapter in his magnum opus, *The Duties of the Heart*, to the importance of abstinence, or asceticism (*prishut*). Like Maimonides, he admired the hasid, or saint, who in all his extremity "used to abstain from seventy kinds of things permitted."[17] Bahya

14. See for example the popular treatment of this idea in Sullivan and Blaschko, *Good Life Method*.

15. As Isadore Twersky notes, speaking for Maimonides: "Ascetic behavior or monastic life-style are only tolerable for limited purposes and restricted periods of time, but should never be adopted permanently or imitated indiscriminately." Twersky, *Introduction to the Code of Maimonides*, 464.

16. Within the history of Christian monasticism, so-called double monasteries did occur. See Johnson, "Double Houses"; and Peyroux, "Abbess and Cloister."

17. Bahya, *Duties*, 2:147. Subsequent citations to pages of this text are given parenthetically.

carries over from the Platonic tradition, as did Philo, that the body is fundamentally a burden. It is the soul's "bad neighbor" (1:237), working always to corrupt the moral life. Such a view of our humanity shifts Bahya's focus of attention away from any "external activity of the bodily limbs" (1:201), including those commanded by Jewish law, toward what he understands to be the equally obligatory "duties of the heart," also commanded but less obviously so. "The chief aim and purpose of the precepts performed physically with our bodies and limbs, is to arouse our attention to the precepts that are fulfilled with the heart and the mind" (2:249). Bahya founds these commandments of heart and mind on such biblical locutions as "Know this" (Deut 4:39) (1:33) and "Love ye" (Deut 10:19) (1:23). Indeed, knowing and loving will prove to go hand in hand. For the duties of the heart, which by implication ally with love, "are all rooted in rational principles" (1:19).

Bahya discusses the duties of the heart under ten principal headings in his book, including such ethically resonant ones as Humility and Spiritual Accounting. Part of the extremity of his ethics owes to his exclusive focus on the purity of our intentions. He understands our reason to direct our intentions toward utter selflessness, without concern for our "own interests in mind" (1:187). And as intention presumably operates continually in our lives, the heart-commands multiply accordingly to cover all its twists and turns. The overt biblical commandments may be many, but at least reach an upper limit of 613; while the duties of the heart are "exceedingly numerous" (1:27), "almost infinite" (1:201), and constitute "a perpetual duty to be fulfilled continually at every moment . . . with every breath" (2:283). It is as though the commands over our intentions individually customize themselves to the conditions reigning at each moment of our lives.[18]

If we doubt there really are so many biblical commandments over our intentions—of the ethical imperatives within the Ten Commandments, only the last (against coveting) appears to direct our psychology—Bahya repeats what Philo and Maimonides have already told us, that the words of Torah speak at two levels: of "plain sense . . . as well as [of] their inner meaning" (1:221). It is the inner meaning of the commands that is resolutely ethical. But he is less concerned than Philo and Maimonides

---

18. Bahya says of the inward commands that "their derivative obligations cannot be enumerated" (*Duties*, 1:27).

were with hidden cosmological meanings. He is more concerned with ethics, is "essentially ethical," as Moses Hyamson puts it.[19]

Bahya's focus on our intentions sets the ethical life at a very high bar if only because, as the Torah itself seemed to understand, at least outwardly, our inner lives are much less subject to our control than our bodies. Bahya allows, with Maimonides, that the surface meaning of the commandments favors a moderate moral life of "the middle road" (1:203). But in their inward sense, the commandments address a soul plagued by self-division, calling for stern measures. In our inner lives we are complex beings, "made up of diverse entities, natures conflicting and mutually antagonistic" (1:195)—chiefly a virtue-loving intellect and a bubbling cauldron of bodily desire (ta'avah), which carries a connotation of (disgusting) lust. The physicality of the body in itself is not the problem; Bahya admires the organicity of its internal systems. The problem of the body is the way it shapes our psychology toward irrational, short-term satisfactions of desire. The charge to the intellect is to wean us away from bodily pleasure. For "the intellect is a spiritual entity, originating in the higher, spiritual world. It is a stranger in this world of gross material bodies" (1:195) and their pleasures.

This is where the ethic turns from a rabbinical perspective even more extreme, away from communal commitments. Inevitably the intellect inclines us toward solitude. For "the majority of transgressions require for their commission at least two" (2:239).[20] That is, the social body as much as the individual body lures us to sin. And so our intellect inclines us away from "this world" (of social temptation) toward "love of solitude and its acceptance" (2:239). And even if we cannot contrive to live as Philo's Therapeutae, we can be as those saints (hasids) who "labored in secular affairs and yet in thought and feeling were apart from them" (2:317). We can withdraw even from the chief culprits of bodily desire, our own five senses, as though to "see without physical eyes, hear without physical ears, speak without the tongue, sense things without their special organ" (1:217).[21] As Howard Kreisel observes, Bahya

19. Bahya, *Duties*, 1:9.

20. Bahya cites, in particular, "fornication, commercial fraud, perjury, false testimony, and all transgressions in speech" (*Duties*, 2:239).

21. Bahya's wording here recalls a Muslim hadith (saying attributed to or about the Prophet Muhammad) according to which God becomes, in the life of the spiritual adept, "his sense of hearing with which he hears, his sense of sight with which he sees, his hand with which he grips, his leg with which he walks" (Sahih al-Bukhari 6502). See also Lobel, *Sufi-Jewish Dialogue*, 48. Bahya drew from Sufi, mystical thought. Another

would like to "see all of Israel become a nation of ascetics, thereby attaining *hasidut*."[22]

As in the case of Philo, so for Bahya, these ascetic extremes of self-diminution ally with a correspondingly elevated altruism. Maximally humble persons are "exceedingly magnanimous" (2:309) toward others, speaking "gentle speech . . . showing mercy, graciousness and compassion" (2:313). They receive others "with a cheerful countenance . . . [come] to their assistance . . . [and] patiently bear their rough speech" (2:313). They "keep at peace with all human beings and act beneficently toward them" (1:233). Bahya would not likely have known Saint Paul's hymn to love in 1 Cor 13:4–7, but he certainly writes here in its spirit.

Bahya suggests that these outwardly observable acts of love follow of necessity, in cause-effect sequence, on an inner life of self-diminution; and that this depth of inward humility, "to which all [other] moral qualities are secondary" (2:111), in turn follows in cause-effect sequence on a program of intellectual development he commends to the reader. Knowledge culminates in love. Bahya reasons here in sync with a rationalist ethics as old as Plato that, in the words of Jonathan Jacobs, "the instinct that . . . leads to wrong action is bad reasoning."[23] Knowledge is so important to Bahya that he risks exiting the rabbinic Judaism that held him when he likens the sin of Adam and Eve, to reach for knowledge, to an admirable effort to escape from blindness (2:255). Surely God would not discourage us from taking to heart the basic truths of ourselves and the world. Knowledge of ourselves: that we are a chaos of conflicting drives, which makes us, of all animals, "the most defective and weakest of them all" (1:187), insignificant in our lowliness (2:241). Knowledge of the world: that it inspires awe in its complexity and grandeur. Bahya devotes a whole chapter, "On the Examination of Created Things," to the awesomeness of nature, which he encourages us to study,[24] and though his point is to infer from that the existence of a Creator, an inference we have doubted since chapter 1, we need not follow him so far. We can stop, with Heschel and Einstein, at the wonder of nature itself, whatever its origins. Our intellect directed

---

image Bahya may have from the Sufis is of the holy soul as polished plate that reflects the divine: "The steel plate is the human soul. The polishing of the plate represents the training of the soul in sciences and moral instruction" so that God's wisdom is reflected there (2:281).

22. Kreisel, "Asceticism," 11.

23. Jacobs, *Law, Reason, and Morality*, 33.

24. "Investigate everything in the universe from the smallest creatures to the largest" (*Duties*, 2:253).

outwardly to ongoing study of the grandeur of the world, and inwardly to sustained awareness of our own fragility, results in the humility that issues in turn in the ethics of love Bahya commends.

So, oxymoronic as it may sound, we *can* aspire to humility. It "is one of the qualities of the soul that can be acquired" (2:73). It is the fruit of what Bahya understands his book to limn: "a science of the inward life" (1:17), with all the overtones of repeatability, predictability, and necessary connection that our modern understanding of "science" connotes. Like revelation within Maimonides, moral goodness within Bahya accrues almost of necessity on a program of intellectual training. "It is impossible that you should not attain what you are fit for" (1:251). As Maimonides would later teach, our inner life improves in tandem with our intellectual one. And so, as in the case of Maimonides, the philosophical intellect here also allies with an ethic of ascetical and affective extremes.

Even apart from the specifics of Bahya's thought, the title alone of his book might give us pause. The *heart* connotes the whole domain of the inner life, for Bahya, but for us today it can also signify something we have by memory, like a poem. "What we know by heart," comments George Steiner, "becomes an agency in our consciousness, a 'pace-maker' in the growth and vital complication of our identity."[25] A heartful appropriation of the biblical commandments invests them with transformative agency inside ourselves, incorporates them into our very selves, so that duty is less obedience than outward flowering of interior life. This is how Philo understood the biblical patriarchs, who predated Sinai: they from within their own nature fulfilled what would later be commanded by letter. And we have a suggestion here of how Franz Rosenzweig would understand observance of the Torah's ritual commands. But this is to anticipate the next chapter.

Bahya may be too ascetic for our modern tastes. Haym Soloveitchik has suggested that the days of religiously inspired asceticism among Jews are largely over.[26] But before we dismiss Bahya as too hopelessly medieval in sensibility, we might take in hand a recent (as of this writing) book by Zena Hitz entitled *Lost in Thought: The Hidden Pleasures of the Intellectual Life* (2020). Hitz, a scholarly classicist who knew and

---

25. Steiner, *Real Presences*, 9.

26. Reflecting on the long-term impact of assimilation on Jewish spirituality, Soloveitchik comments on the "gradual disappearance of the ascetic ideal that had held sway over Jewish spirituality for close to a millennium" (Soloveitchik, "Rupture," 80). Soloveitchik credits Bahya with inaugurating the ascetic tradition.

grew disillusioned with the worldly side of academic life, restates for us in more familiar terms what Bahya has been preaching from his location in the Middle Ages. When a subsection of a chapter appears in her book titled "Intellectual Life and the Human Heart," we wonder if she has just come from reading Bahya. Part of the problem with academic life is an aspect of its social body, as Hitz sees it, with its orientations toward status and privilege; in the case of academe, toward tenure and the increasingly few full professorships. This "locus of competition and struggle for wealth, power, prestige, and status"[27] is "something that needs to be escaped" (53). These are the modern translations of the body-induced lusts Bahya targeted. And of course they occur in many social contexts outside academe.

As Bahya opined, Hitz writes that our desires are dual and opposed: on the one hand toward efforts "to know, learn, and understand" (57) and, on the other, to engage with "the surfaces" (196) of life, and worse: "the selfish, the banal, the superficial, and even the cruel," which we "drift toward . . . by default" (98). This "human fragility" that Hitz uncovers for us corresponds to the weakness and deficiency within us that Bahya called to our attention. To pull back from these requires a relatively ascetic lifestyle, to which Hitz devotes a short section of her book.

Intellectual life turns out to be a sort of asceticism, a turning away from things within ourselves. Our desires for truth, for understanding, for insight are in constant conflict with other desires: our desires for social acceptance or an easy life, a particular personal goal, or a desirable political outcome (85).

Alongside Bahya, Hitz commends a constriction of the senses. "To be dominated by the senses is to be helpless in the face of whatever they present, to be drawn haplessly from one thing to another" (91). It is painful to rein in the sensual life that comes so naturally to us. But the reward is larger scope for the exercise of intellect, which sets its sights on realities beyond what we immediately see, hear, or touch. "The intellect has no limit to its subject matter" (187). With Bahya, Hitz encourages us to know the natural world around us, which is "a proper object of contemplation" (81). We return to the senses, but now for the knowledge we can glean from them, not the immediate pleasures we can indulge with them. And in so doing, we lose preoccupation with ourselves.

---

27. Hitz, *Lost in Thought*, 54. Subsequent citations to pages of this text are given parenthetically.

The same connection Bahya explored between knowledge and love now reappears in Hitz's book. The ascetic intellect extends outwardly toward others. At the start of her book, Hitz cites the relevance to her project of Somerset Maugham's novel *The Razor's Edge*, which traces a pilgrim path from self-absorption to other-concern. As the protagonist Larry Darrell observes, "in nothing are the wise men of India more dead right than in their contention that chastity intensely enhances the power of the spirit."[28] The ascetic life of the intellect "nurtures genuine forms of community" (105). In our "freedom from the self-interested conclusion and the agenda-driven hope" (188) our capacity for connection with others expands. "It is as if love overflows from understanding, or as if understanding were intrinsically generous" (112). "We learn in order to love" (111). Hitz, a convert to Catholicism, is Jewish by descent. Could she be here any closer to a Jewish root in Bahya?

The triadic link between knowledge, asceticism, and *hasidut*, which structures at least some of medieval Jewish philosophical ethics, finds its culmination in Spinoza. Given Spinoza's own location on one of the far extremities of Jewish tradition, hovering between pantheism and atheism, it should come as no surprise that he climax a medieval Jewish ethic of extremes. And that, with Spinoza, we are indeed in the domain of ethics he reminds us with the very title of his magnum opus, *Ethica*, or *The Ethics*. Its subtitle, *Ordine Geometrico Demonstrata*, or *Demonstrated in Geometrical Order*, recalls Bahya's "science of the inward life." For Spinoza is as much preoccupied as Bahya was with the cause-effect relations between knowledge and emotion, toward paving for us a path to well-being. But Spinoza goes further than Bahya by framing his work geometrically, with definitions, axioms, and proofs, after Euclid, as though to claim for the science of the inward life all the tightness of logic that characterizes that queen of the sciences, mathematics.

Under the rubric of suffering, in chapter 2, we have already encountered Spinoza's analysis of human emotion in all its vagaries. And we already know the trust he has in reason, arch-rationalist that he is, to guide our emotions toward our own well-being. The "precepts of reason," "the dictates of reason," (E4p18s), "the guidance of reason" (E4p24), all work in our favor. They do so at the very least by making our emotions an object of study. Like a Buddhist master, Spinoza frees us from what he calls our bondage to emotion simply by understanding the causal sequences

---

28. Maugham, *Razor's Edge*, 280.

that govern them. Spinoza is never far in spirit from the Buddhist image of the pig (ignorance), snake (hate), and rooster (greed) caught in a cycle of mutual predation. Ignorance yields lust (so Bahya might call it), which in turn yields hate when we do not get what we want. Spinoza recalls Bahya when he comments on the explosive spawning of emotion into "variations that . . . cannot be numbered" (E3p59s), as though, so Bahya might say, to generate for each a duty of the heart to govern it. And he recalls Zena Hitz's sense that we too easily and naturally follow our least attractive instincts when he writes how much we are "motivated by uncritical belief" (E4I7s) toward a host of negative emotions that require some discipline to be curtailed. These tendencies in us are so powerful that, as Bahya and Hitz prescribed, we need to enact some measure of ascetic discipline to curtail them.

But not as much as Bahya thought necessary. Spinoza departs in a crucial way from the Platonic tradition that Bahya had absorbed: the body and mind are not enemies. On the contrary, they are two versions of the same thing. Our emotions, which straddle the two, manifest in both mental and physical form, just as a contemporary neuroscientist might say. So the body cannot be blamed for them. And of course the pleasurable emotions that reason generates by way of our self-understanding are desirable. Still, Spinoza advises caution in all matter of emotion, and even took for his life motto, *caute* (caution).[29] By all accounts, he lived in accord with his autobiographical reflections at the start of his *Treatise on the Emendation of the Intellect*, in disciplined detachment from "love of perishable things."[30] Spinoza biographer Steven Nadler comments, "He made an effort all his life to keep his material needs to a minimum."[31] Spinoza allowed for the modest enjoyments of life. But even so tolerant an asceticism in the service of our highest well-being was, he understood, difficult and rarely undertaken. That is part of the import of the last sentence of the *Ethics*: "all things excellent are as difficult as they are rare" (E5p42s).[32]

Spinoza's cultivated pleasures center on things that everyone can share, for example, detached observation of our own emotional lives, in modern terms: meditation. Reasoning people tend to agree in valuing

29. Nadler, *Spinoza*, 244.
30. Spinoza, *Ethics*, 235.
31. Nadler, *Spinoza*, 183.
32. For an insightful exploration of this phrase, see Mock, "Reading of the Last Sentence of the *Ethics*."

simple goods available to all (E4p35, E4p36). We can imagine that in today's world Spinoza would rank planetary health among the highest of the common goods. But another noteworthy instance is the recently launched Webb Telescope, now orbiting the sun for visions of the beginnings of the cosmos, and celebrated within *The New York Times* under the headline "The James Webb Space Telescope and a Quest Every Human Shares."[33] "Building it required the best of humans," writes science columnist Dennis Overbye: "cooperation and devotion to knowledge, daring and humility, respect for nature and [for] our own ignorance." This and the fact that the project was a "collaboration of NASA, the Canadian Space Agency, and European Space Agency"[34] tributes not only science at its collaborative best, but the nexus of ideas our ethicists have been exploring between knowledge, humility, and love. We can imagine Spinoza, a lens-grinder by trade and maker of lenses for microscopes and telescopes, reading this news with pleasure. He might approvingly comment, "He who lives by the guidance of reason desires for another, too, the good that he seeks for himself" (E4p51), in this case knowledge of cosmic origins. He "tries to establish friendship with others" (E4p70), in this case with scientists across national boundaries. The reason-guided virtually merge into one harmonious mind and body (E4p18s), toward realization of so great a common good as the Webb telescope. Spinoza deems so reason-inspired a cooperative spirit, which combines intellect and altruism, "intellectual love" (E5p36), to which we will return at the end of our study, under the rubric of spiritual life.

This may not seem an extreme ethical vision today. But even in Spinoza's estimation, the entirely reasonable life he envisioned for philosophers was difficult and rare or, as Ian Buruma puts it, speaking for Spinoza, "extremely hard to achieve,"[35] our irrational emotions pull so forcefully on us. But the note of the extreme sounds another way for Spinoza, within the context of his times. He reasoned his way to a good life without much help from the Bible, on which clergy of all kinds based much of their claim to authority. As Buruma wryly opines, "like the Marquis de Sade, . . . Spinoza didn't believe that man was bound by morals dictated by God."[36] If so, there was scarcely the need for a clergy

33. Overbye, "James Webb Space Telescope."
34. Overbye, "Webb Telescope."
35. Buruma, *Spinoza*, 128.
36. Buruma, *Spinoza*, 157.

class to expound those morals. This was an extreme view indeed for seventeenth-century Europe.

Spinoza shared Maimonides's interest in the laws of nature. But he rejected the effort to read these off of biblical law, as Maimonides understood a philosopher could do. There was no call to read "the notions of a Plato or Aristotle"[37] into the Bible, and so inaugurate a dual reading of it, one for philosophers and the other for the common people. Philosophers do not need the Bible at all. The laws that mattered most to Spinoza took the form of declaratives, not imperatives. They were descriptions of nature, not commands. The Bible itself he understood to be a humanly composed collection of documents written by different hands across vast stretches of time. It was riddled with errors and contradictions, reflecting the prejudices of its mostly unenlightened authors. Its laws and stories did indeed serve as the foundation for the ancient Jewish state. But with the passing of the state, little of the Bible remained relevant. For philosophical readers, there was some benefit in the Wisdom books credited to King Solomon, "who possessed the natural light of reason beyond all men of his time."[38] Otherwise, the prophets could be mined for ethical teachings to be commended to the populace who, under state pressure to observe them, would remain in their behavior within the bounds of civility. While the ethical behavior of the (rare) philosophers emerges from their exercise of intellect, the populace receives its ethics "not as eternal truths [as the philosophers do] but as instructions and precepts"[39] enshrined in the Bible they are motivated by fear to obey.

In seventeenth-century Europe, openly expressing such views could land their exponents in jail. Apart from the Catholic-sponsored Inquisition, the Calvinist leadership of Holland kept a sharp eye out for such heresies. Spinoza only aired his historical-critical read of the Bible, which is now quite standard in academic settings, anonymously, within his *Theological-Political Treatise*, published over his lifetime in 1670. There, he argued for the state to guarantee freedom of thought, especially for philosophers, against the theologians (and rabbis) who would censor them. That included a vigorous take-down of the Bible. A consensus of opinion at the time on Spinoza's book was that it was a work "forged in Hell," as Steven Nadler underscores by titling his study of it after this

---

37. Spinoza, *Theological-Political Treatise*, 153.
38. Spinoza, *Theological-Political Treatise*, 31.
39. Spinoza, *Theological-Political Treatise*, 53.

phrase.⁴⁰ Maimonides had covertly implied what Spinoza openly stated, that an altruistic ethic of kindness and regard for others followed naturally on advanced states of knowledge, without any need of biblical revelation. Spinoza's open, if anonymous, defense of this view was extreme enough in his time, even within relatively tolerant Holland, for historian Jonathan Israel to deem it part of a *radical* Enlightenment that prepared the way for the more moderate one of the eighteenth century,⁴¹ which in some of its voices at least nodded courteously to religion. But if ethics can be widely understood, today, to flourish independently of the Bible, we have Spinoza in some measure to thank for that.

Spinoza marks a culmination of the medieval nexus of intellect, asceticism, and altruism because of the release he secures for it from the hold of the Bible. Jewish philosophers post-Spinoza must recover the Bible for philosophical Jews if it is to continue to inform their thought. And several, such as Buber and Rosenzweig, who newly translated it, have done so. But if we are looking for continuations of the extremity theme, one place this shows is in the stature of ethics itself, which for some modern Jewish philosophers moves to center stage within the Jewish mindset. It becomes the heart of Jewish identity, over all other contenders for that position, including belief in God or observance of law. And with that, we find ourselves within easy reach of the 2020 Pew survey of Jewish belief cited at the start of this chapter. Even *within* ethics, extremity themes continue for at least two modern Jewish philosophers who prioritize it: Hermann Cohen (1842–1918) and Levinas, who has already offered us philosophical takes on suffering and revelation.

Cohen inherited from a secular philosopher he much admired, Immanuel Kant (1724–1804), a view characteristic of the eighteenth-century Enlightenment that what chiefly mattered about religion was its ethics, which is quite in tune with majority Jewish belief about Judaism today. Kant went so far as to reduce religion *to* ethics. He famously wrote that what religion amounted to, insofar as it was admirable or desirable, was "the recognition of all duties as divine commands,"⁴² by which he meant: the recognition that what our reason tells us to do God also happens to approve. But that approval is irrelevant to the claim on us of what our reason dictates. In fact, "morality does not need religion at all,"⁴³ not

40. Nadler, *Book Forged in Hell*.
41. This is a central theme of Israel, *Spinoza: His Life and Legacy*.
42. Kant, *Critique of Practical Reason*, 136.
43. Kant, *Religion*, 3.

its God, dogmas, stories, rituals, communal structures, or even whatever spin on ethics it might happen to have.

With this view, Kant bequeathed to Cohen a rejection of Spinoza, who had suggested that reason always properly operates in the declarative voice: it declares cause-effect relations in all their necessity. It does not issue commands. Not even the medieval philosophers invested reason with an imperative voice. Reason could recognize the reasonableness of a command; it did not *issue* commands. For Maimonides, the biblical commands Moses spoke were really cosmic truths repurposed in imperative form for the unenlightened. But for the philosopher who rose to visions of the truth, ethical behavior followed naturally without having to be commanded. It was Kant who with his notion of practical reason invested reason with the power to command. And as he elaborates in his *Critique of Practical Reason*, what reason commands is that whatever we do be done in accord with universal law.[44] It is the universalizability of our behavior that makes it moral, lawful, and desired by reason. What Kant envisions here is behavior freed entirely of self-seeking desire, in sync with such visions of selflessness as saints or hasids might illustrate, but motivated not by love but by law. "It is a very sublime thing in human nature to be determined to actions directly by a pure law of reason."[45] Surely we have here another ethic that counts for extreme in its ascetic discounting of desire. We can imagine a Kantian equivalent of the hasid.

Up to a point, Cohen accepted these views. Ethics was certainly a product of reason beyond the need of any religion to supply it. Cohen thought we could infer ethics from the reality of being, or existence, itself. He believed, as he put it, in an "ethics on the basis of logic."[46] He stimulates a line of thought that might be stated most simply this way, though very distant from his own language: We know existence to be meaningful. It could not be meaningful without purpose. And it could not have purpose without ethics, which takes its bearing from the purpose it identifies and serves.[47] The boldness (extremity?) of the argument

---

44. According to Kant's famous categorical imperative, you (we) should "so act that the maxim of your will could always hold at the same time as the principle giving universal law." Kant, *Critique of Practical Reason*, 30.

45. Kant, *Critique of Practical Reason*, 123.

46. Cohen, *Religion of Reason*, 114. Subsequent citations to pages of this text are given parenthetically.

47. This is a loose and simplifying paraphrase of Cohen's much more complex argument involving being and becoming, God and creation (*Religion of Reason*, 59–70). A more intuitive derivation of ethics from being might go like this: Suffering exists and

is in the presumption that we can infer what ought to be from what is, which many a philosopher would contest. But the persuasiveness or not of the argument is less important here than the evidence it supplies of Cohen's heartfelt rationalism, more profound than Kant's and very in sync with the medieval philosophers he admired. But where Cohen departed most markedly from Kant, who disparaged religion as such, was in his appreciation of Judaism. What mattered for him most about Judaism was its ethics. As Robert Gibbs writes, "the primacy of ethics for Judaism, received one of its greatest and most philosophically rigorous treatments in Cohen's work."[48] And now Eva Jospe: "Judaism . . . for Cohen is the ethical religion par excellence."[49] Cohen thought of Judaism as a kind of hearing aid: it magnified the sound of the commands reason issued. This was so much true that he thought we could extract reason's commands from the sacred texts of Judaism, which he called its sources: the Bible, the Talmud and Midrash, even the philosophers. Reason may authorize the ethical commands it issues, but tradition sharpens our receptivity to them. This explains the title of Cohen's book on the philosophy of Judaism: *Religion of Reason Out of the Sources of Judaism*. As Cohen puts it, "the sources of Judaism unveil the religion of reason" (34).

This is a little like what the medieval philosophers opined about the relation between reason and Judaism. The implied difference is that, for Cohen, reason is complex enough in how it works and what it says to need some interpretive aids for us to receive its teachings. It had taken Kant three difficult books to reason about reason, *The Critique of Pure Reason*, *The Critique of Practical Reason*, and *The Critique of Judgment*. The first laid a foundation for the natural sciences, the second for ethics, the third for aesthetics. Student of Kant that he was, Cohen also needed three key works, roughly analogous to Kant's, to explain his version of reason's workings and teachings, *The Logic of Pure Cognition* (1902), *The Ethics of Pure Will* (1904), and the *Aesthetics of Pure Feeling* (1914). Written in "sometimes forbidding prose," as Samuel Moyn tells us, these texts "are [so] difficult," so *extremely* difficult, we might say, that they defied the comprehension even of some of his professional philosophical colleagues.[50] If reason is so complex, we may well need amplifying aids to hear clearly what it commands us. Kant himself was so obsessed with the *form* of reason's

---

asks not to; ethics exists in response to that plea.

48. Gibbs, *Hermann Cohen's* Ethics, xi.
49. Cohen, *Reason and Hope*, 20.
50. Cohen, *Hermann Cohen: Writings*, xi, xii.

commands, as universalizable rules of conduct, that he told us little about their actual content. In *Religion of Reason Out of the Sources of Judaism* (1918), Cohen fills in that content abundantly.

Cohen answers Spinoza in another way, by recovering the Bible for Jews who have lost touch with it. For the Bible is the key "source" Cohen plumbs to unveil Judaism as a religion of reason. Reason's teachings are just easier to see in the Bible's plain statements of law. True, the Bible presents the law as divinely commanded. But our reason, on encountering biblical law, recognizes it as its own. As Cohen puts it, "reason is ... the root of the content of revelation" (82). Or as Franz Rosenzweig, Cohen's student, put it speaking for Cohen, "reason was itself for him a miracle."[51] So the biblical commands were not, as Maimonides implied, cosmic truths repurposed for lesser minds. They were the commands of reason itself, or something like them, made plain to us. Part of what extends the length of Cohen's book are the many, heavily quoted Bible passages. He cannot presume, as medieval writers might, a familiarity with the texts. But any secularist who reads the book will be brought back to the very Bible Spinoza disdained.

For Cohen, the Bible is inherently philosophical without need of any special reading of it. Insofar as it sources reasoned religion, it cannot help but be. For instance, Cohen comments on the mysterious name of God revealed at Exod 3:14, *Ehyeh-Asher-Ehyeh*, which for Cohen and many readers translates, I Am That I Am, that "here, a primeval language, emerging without any philosophical concepts, stammers the most profound word of any philosophy."[52] What Cohen sees in the divine name is a reference to a being so self-identified that it cannot be equated with any other thing but is, in itself, separate. That this is a name for God need not detain us here; more important for us just now to Cohen's ethics is the foundation laid here for the idea of separation between beings. For it is just the fact that I am not the same as my neighbor, or cannot be subsumed with her under any category that equates us, which is "the supposition of the separation of both elements" (105), that for Cohen motivates ethics in the first place. If by way, say, of a pantheism or monism, there was no "other" to me, the command to love my neighbor (Lev 19:18) could get no traction, as there would not really be a neighbor in the first place.

---

51. Rosenzweig, "Introduction to the Jewish Writings of Hermann Cohen," 192.
52. Cohen, *Reason and Hope*, 93.

Bahya, who alongside Maimonides was one of Cohen's favorite Jewish philosophers[53] made this point in another way: "If human beings commit wrongs against each other, [one] must not conduct himself as is his custom in forgiving them when they wrong him. He must on the contrary come to the rescue of the person wronged."[54] Otherwise put, just because my neighbor is different from me, I cannot presume for him what I assume for myself, which makes an interesting correction to the Golden Rule. But Bahya anticipates Cohen in another way when he comments that "anyone who bestows benefits on others has first his own interests in mind."[55] Bahya's point in context is that even a self-interested benefit bestowed on another obligates gratitude in the receiver. But read another way, Bahya's seemingly skeptical insight into human behavior suggests a certain reciprocity in the most generous ethical acts. Generosity is not one-sided. The other in need helps to satisfy my own need to be needed. If this notion sounds familiar it may be because it has already operated for us at high pitch in Rosenzweig, who had it from Cohen, his teacher. For the elements of reality Rosenzweig posited—God, human, world—in their extraversion exchange the need they satisfied in themselves for that of another, which in turn renders them needful in their own right. Each of them becomes a needy supplier of another's need. In their giving, they must also receive.

For Cohen, reciprocity was the keystone of ethics. He called it *correlation*, which is "the term for all concepts of reciprocal relation" (86).[56] Leo Strauss helpfully adds that, for Cohen, two in correlation "are equally, if in different ways, active toward one another."[57] Correlation presupposes the very separation between beings that Cohen took the divine name to indicate: without two, no reciprocity. The interplay between two separables is so important to Cohen he borrows an august term from the language of theology to name it: holy spirit. Holy spirit is

---

53. Rosenzweig, "Introduction to the Jewish Writings of Hermann Cohen," 194. Cohen references both Bahya and Maimonides several times in his *Religion of Reason*.

54. Bahya, *Duties*, 2:103. Cohen agrees: "Even if the individual were able ... to train himself successfully ... to disregard his own wellbeing and woe, he is not permitted to disregard the woe of the other fellow" (132).

55. Bahya, *Duties*, 1:187.

56. Cohen sounds very much like Rosenzweig when he writes that "the creation itself is only a kind of correlation" (104); or more properly, when Rosenzweig writes about creation, he sounds like Cohen! However, Rosenzweig would omit any reference to creation as *only* a correlation.

57. Strauss, "Introduction," xxviii.

not a thing or agency, but reciprocity itself in action. It comes as close to holiness as anything else Cohen might name by that phrase. And its implications for inter-human relations are profound. For the condition of humans apart from reciprocity between them is dismal. "Man's life as a whole is regarded as suffering. . . . [There is a] suffering that comes from being a man, from the essential humanity of man" (225). This is true of both our individual and social lives. Cohen sounds like Bahya when he laments that our hearts are filled with "contradictions" (188), "envy and violence" (179), "discordant opinions and passions" (280), "wavering and vacillation" (200). But his response to this is not for us to adopt ascetic disciplines. Cohen moves beyond Bahya and closer to our own sensibilities when he focuses, at the social level of suffering, on poverty. "Poverty represents the greatest suffering of mankind" (135). And we are all implicated in it. "In poverty . . . woe becomes the suffering of the human race. . . . This is the profound meaning of social suffering: that the entire consciousness of culture is implicated in it" (136). The answer to our inner discordance is to focus our attention on the suffering, especially the poverty, outside us.

It is within this context of social suffering that Cohen pushes toward the extreme. For it does not matter where poverty occurs, whether near us or distant, for it to command our compassion. Cohen was a socialist, but within *Religion of Reason* he is less concerned with economic programs than with the transformative effects of compassion on both us and those we feel with and for. Compassion is itself a correlation, as its Latinate base implies, and as the German *Mitleid* mirrors: a feeling-with another, which presupposes two in relation. Cohen suggests that in my compassion for another, a transformation occurs in both the other and me. The other emerges from mere otherness into my fellow human, or *Mitmensch*. The German more pointedly links compassion to fellowship by way of the preposition *mit* (with) that figures in both words. Compassion "is the fundamental power of the moral universe, which unlocks the fellowman [and] . . . constitutes the key to the fellowman" (141). Cohen recalls Bahya when he insists the compassion come "from the heart" (138).[58] And he anticipates Martin Buber when he writes that by way of my compassion for "the other man's suffering . . . the other is changed from a He to a Thou" (17). I, in turn, emerge from the

---

58. Rosenzweig suggests that for Cohen, Bahya represented the "unity of heart" he (Cohen) only attained in his final work, on Judaism. Rosenzweig, "Introduction to the Writings of Hermann Cohen," 240.

compassion I feel into an awareness of reason's (and the Bible's) command to me, in my actions, to alleviate poverty.[59] Since "poverty is the universal suffering of the human race" (143), the alleviation of it qualifies for what Kant would call a universalizable law of ethics.[60] Reason dictates that participants in a common humanity leave none out of the basic well-being any one of us enjoys. And if our inner ear is deaf to this reasoned command, the Bible spells it plainly for us in the text: Love your neighbor as yourself (Lev 19:18).

Cohen pushes further toward the extreme when he insists our compassion extend beyond the poor to the stranger. He suggests that prior to our experience of compassion, the neighbor (*re'a*) referenced in Lev 19:18 is really the stranger (*nokri*), the non-Jew with whom I fail to be in correlation.[61] In that way, Cohen stretches the distance my compassion for the other must cross to reach him. For the stranger, as opposed to the neighbor, is always a problem bordering on threat. As Jonathan Jacobs suggests, a crucial issue within ethics is "how we are to relate to strangers, both individuals and communities, and in such a way as to regard them as being in a common world with us."[62] Elie Wiesel, in an essay on the stranger, is more dramatic: "The stranger . . . suggests the unknown, the prohibited, the beyond . . . [and provokes] suspicion, terror, or repulsion. The stranger is the other."[63] The command to love the stranger asks more of us than to love the neighbor. And Cohen can cite the Bible's heightened concern for strangers—"for you were strangers (*gerim*) in the land of Egypt" (Exod 22:21)—to justify this interpretation of *re'a*. As Adam Sutcliffe puts it, speaking for Cohen,

> Critiquing the Christian interpretive tradition of the biblical exhortation to "love your neighbor as yourself" (Lev 19:17–18),

---

59. In the commands, for example, to leave of the harvest for the poor (Lev 19:9–10), return a garment taken in pledge (Exod 22:26–27), forgive debts in the Jubilee year (Lev 25:8–13), among others.

60. In a sense, we are all poor: "the poor man typifies man in general" (137).

61. On a traditional interpretation, the neighbor referenced in Lev 19:18 is the fellow Israelite. Cohen rejects that view categorically, commenting, "We can understand how the acknowledgment of the other as the fellow countrymen only arose from a biased misinterpretation" (119). Eva Jospe notes in Cohen his "deep-seated and abiding abhorrence of any 'nationalistic' interpretation of Judaism" (Cohen, *Reason and Hope*, 17).

62. Jacobs, *Law, Reason, and Morality*, 200. In context, Jacobs is paraphrasing an argument in Novak, *Natural Law in Judaism*.

63. Wiesel, *Inside a Library*, 32.

he argued that the translation of the Hebrew word *reʿa* as "neighbor" introduced a privileging of proximity that was not only incorrect but also undermined the ethical imperative of love being outwardly directed toward "the other," whether near and familiar or alien and distant. Cohen reframed love of the neighbor as love of the stranger.[64]

Cohen builds on two of the biblical words for stranger, *nokri* and *ger*, to make his case. As Wiesel puts it,

> A *ger* is the stranger who lives in your midst, . . . has not adopted the Jewish faith but he has acquired Jewish customs, values, and friends. . . . A *nokri* . . . wishes to remain aloof or separated, . . . different, an outsider.[65]

Strikingly, both Elie Wiesel and Adam Sutcliffe characterize the stranger as "other." That would be the stranger as *nokri*, from a Hebrew root connoting the foreign or alien. What Cohen finds in the Bible is a means by which the *nokri* becomes a *ger*, a non-Jewish friend of Jews, a fellowman, or *Mitmensch*. He suggests this happens by way of "the wonderful concept . . . of the Noahide" (118), according to which all humanity were united in descent from Noah and, said the rabbis, bound together by seven key laws, not to commit idolatry, blasphemy, murder, adultery, theft, or cruelty to animals and, on the positive side, to establish courts of justice.[66] We recall this notion from chapter 3, in context of the covenant idea. "According to the covenant with Noah, every man is already the brother of every other" (118). It just took the several biblical laws mandating care for strangers to make that plain. Reason also commands kindness to strangers on grounds that in one way or another we all share the "status [of] a stranger in this world" (271)[67] and so, as Kant might say, cognize the universality of the rule to ease the burden on strangers. It is just another case of the Bible serving as a source (or confirmation) for a moral dictate of reason.

The stranger was not an abstraction for Cohen, as Franz Rosenzweig relates in a story he tells about his mentor. Once, another student of Cohen's witnessed him drop a coin into the hand of a begging vagrant

---

64. Sutcliffe, "Stranger," 302.

65. Wiesel, *Inside a Library*, 28.

66. Cohen suggests the Noahide laws are ethical laws prefiguring the fuller revelation of the Torah. Like the Torah in full, they "have a strictly moral character" (122).

67. A sentiment that echoes Bahya, who wrote, "you clearly realize that you are a stranger here and will soon depart hence" (Bahya, *Duties*, 1:267).

(*ein Stromer*, in Rosenzweig's German) presumably unknown to him. As Rosenzweig tells the tale, the student asked, "'Doctor, why did you give that fellow anything at all? He'll just waste it on drink.' And [Cohen] said: 'Silly boy, don't you ever like a little treat?!'"[68] The seeming lightness of that response is misleading. Cohen's response in German, as Rosenzweig gives it, *naschst du nicht?* might be more broadly rendered: Are you so above indulgence?—which may refer as much to Cohen's need to indulge a stranger, as the stranger's need for indulgence. Later, as a mature adult, the former student on a visit to Cohen confessed the deep impression this indulgence toward the stranger made on him. Rosenzweig, for his part, took it to instance what Cohen meant by socialism. But for us the story serves another purpose, to foretell the ethics of Emmanuel Levinas, for whom the approach of a destitute stranger inaugurates ethics as "first philosophy."

For that is the title of one of Levinas's signature essays: "Ethics as First Philosophy." Here is where Levinas returns to us from that dire place he left us in the previous chapter, under the rubric of revelation, stranded with our suffering and catastrophized self. This might seem the tragedy of the self. But it is not. It is the beginning of ethics. For, as for Rosenzweig love begins in the diminution of the self, so for Levinas ethics begins in the devastation of the self. He takes aim at a quality of human being often passing for a virtue: self-possession (which is a kind of self-sufficiency) and indeed at *possessing* as such. Insofar as the outward face of self-possession is dispossession of the other, it allies with the violence implied by grasping, gripping, seizing, insisting against, and mastering the other.[69] Levinas suggests that these verbal states characterize the act of *knowing*.[70] We do after all claim to know something after we have *grasped* it. We *under*stand it, as though to under*mine* or dislodge it from itself. So knowing, too, falls under his critique. In that way, he departs sharply from Hermann Cohen and takes his place with the other modern philosophers suspicious of reason's powers. But in another way he is very close to Cohen, in their shared esteem for the stranger and her

68. Rosenzweig, "Introduction to the Jewish Writings of Hermann Cohen," 198. For the German, see Rosenzweig, *Kleinere Schriften*, 310.

69. All these verbs occur in Levinas's essay "Ethics as First Philosophy," subsequent citations to pages of which are given parenthetically. Levinas suggests that by my self-possession I am implicated in all the "acts of repulsing, excluding, exiling, stripping, killing" that threaten the other (82).

70. "Knowledge as perception . . . refers back to an act of grasping . . . of seizure . . . [and] gripping" (76).

import for ethics. Levinas, writing in French of the stranger, *l'inconnu*, has before him in the language itself a perfect foil to anything we can knowingly grip, grasp, or master: the Unknown, which, as in a good sci-fi thriller, is more likely to master *us*.

Levinas, like Rosenzweig, wants to undo a false image of ourselves as self-standing beings. For Rosenzweig, we do not stand on our own but in our receipt of love. For Levinas, we do not stand at all. Rather my selfdom is "backed up against . . . a wall" of itself; indeed, is over the wall, "on the hither side of consciousness," "in itself already outside of itself," "an exile in oneself."[71] More: I am not a *being* at all. That helps to explain the title of one of Levinas's major works: *Otherwise Than Being*. If I can wean myself from self-images of self-possession and self-assurance (that so much in American culture promotes), what I find myself to be is, in the words of Edith Wyschogrod, speaking for Levinas, a "lambency before the appearance of [any] identifiable entities"[72] that I can recognize either inside or outside myself. I am a "self without a concept."[73] I am a location without content or substance, with "no intentions or aims" or "insistence" on itself (81). "I" am beginning to sound like those other contentless contents we have already seen associated with Jewish identity, revelation, and God. Levinas calls it "pre-reflective consciousness" (80), which he likens to what we "do" when we age. We are not the active agents of our own aging. Aging is something that happens to us. Like suffering (as Levinas discussed it for us in ch. 2), both aging and pre-reflective consciousness are "less an act than a pure passivity" (80).

Accustomed to ideals of self-possession, we may receive this view of ourselves with the force of a revelation. But if we do, we need to remember what Levinas (and Buber) taught about revelation, that it comes "from outside." The passivity of the pre-reflective consciousness, hanging back from any kind of self-instatement, coordinates with what it receives from outside, which is not love, as Rosenzweig would have it, but accusation. This is indeed the very reason for its suffering, as though under question in the courtroom for its very being, like Job before the God who accuses *him*: "Who is this that darkeneth counsel?" says God, ". . . I will demand of thee and declare thou unto Me" (Job 38:2–3). "One comes not into the world," says Levinas, "but into question" (81). We have an inkling of that, Levinas suggests, on those occasions when we

71. Levinas, "Substitution," 92, 93, 96.
72. Wyschogrod, "Profligacy," 172.
73. Levinas, "Substitution," 105.

ask after the meaning of our life. Language lends Levinas a helpful way to put this. Pre-reflective consciousness stands always in the accusative case, as object of a verb, never in the nominative case, as agent of an act. "The accusative [is] in some way its 'first case'" (82).[74] And who is the subject or agent of the accusation? It is whoever is standing by, whoever occupies a space outside me that I register, "the first individual to come along" (83), like that destitute man who confronted Hermann Cohen. It is what Levinas calls the Other.

The Other corresponds to what Cohen called the stranger, with all the connotations of imposing, even threatening, distance implied by that word. But Levinas extends the distance of the Other beyond that of Cohen's stranger when he insists I receive her as one who "did not have anything [in] common with me."[75] It is almost as though Levinas would appropriate for the Other what Cohen recognized in God's name, I Am That I Am, an utter "singularity."[76] And indeed, for Levinas, the Other approaches me imperiously, though paradoxically. Exceeding even the stranger in his poverty, Levinas's Other comes to me in "nakedness and destitution," in "extreme exposure, defenselessness, vulnerability itself" (83). The Other "presents to me the destitution of the poor one and the stranger."[77] This is surely the look of many a refugee who has turned up on America's borders. The Other in her destitution incarnates death for us in a way our own self rarely can for ourselves, and by that very asymmetry over the looming of death (applicable to the Other, but not to me), I become responsible for the Other's death, "as if I had to answer for the Other's death even before *being*" (83), that is, even before I muster myself into a self-conscious self that positions myself in relation to others, even before I could ever presume to say, I Am That I Am.

Even the being I muster for myself cannot remain mine but must offer itself in what Levinas calls *substitution* for the Other. "It is the responsibility of a hostage which can be carried to the point of being substituted for the other person and demands an infinite subjection" of myself (84). Language again obliges to make a point: the only way in which I function

74. "Everything from the start is in the accusative" (Levinas, "Substitution," 102).
75. Levinas, *Otherwise Than Being*, 86.
76. Levinas, *Otherwise Than Being*, 86.
77. Levinas, *Totality and Infinity*, 213. Dana Hollander comments, "*Totality and Infinity* is punctuated throughout by the refrain of 'the stranger, the widow, the orphan,' sometimes also accompanied by 'the poor one,' biblical figures for the obligation that issues from a condition of absolute poverty, destitution, and need" (Hollander, "Is The Other My Neighbor," 97).

TOWARD A NEGATIVE THEOLOGY OF JUDAISM

as subject, in relation to the Other, is as *subject to* her, in my extreme responsibility for her. I can and should go to the death that looms for her, in her stead. And so like the prophet Isaiah, in response to God's call, all I can say to answer the Other's accusation of me is, "Here am I" (Isa 6:8). It is almost as though the subject of this sentence is the contentless location of my pre-reflective self—"here"—which offers for the Other a self that has not yet even come to be: "I." Let me not dare to ask whether the Other bears the same responsibility toward me. Responsibility does not operate so symmetrically. Rather, for whatever ethical failings the Other bears toward me or anyone else I am *also* responsible. I bear "the responsibility for the responsibility of the Other."[78]

This is surely the most extreme ethic we have yet to encounter among the philosophers. Edith Wyschogrod puts it this way: "The ethics of Emmanuel Levinas is one of radical self-giving, of boundless expenditure in the interest of the other."[79] It is no wonder a collection of essays on Levinas's ethics is entitled *The Exorbitant*.[80] But Levinas is not done. For at the same time that the Other approaches me in destitution, she also does from a height beyond my grasping, i.e., beyond my capacity to register her as an object of knowledge. The quotation from Isa 6:8, but also from Job 38:2–3 just cited, quite rightly assimilates the Other to God, who commands from on high. Levinas heightens that impression when he suggests "the privileged manifestation of the Other" is a "revelation,"[81] which correlates (as Cohen might say) with the fracturing of the self that Levinas had associated with revelation in the previous chapter. It is as though the height from which the destitute Other approaches me invests her with the authority to command me and disabuse me of any claims to self-possession I might make. Levinas calls it transcendence and intends by that another rebuke to my grasp for knowledge. Just as I, stripped of my presumptions to selfdom, am thoroughly unknowing, so the Other in her approach of me defies my claim to know her, insofar as that implies grasping, gripping, seizing,

---

78. Levinas, "Substitution," 107.

79. Wyschogrod, "Profligacy," 171.

80. Hart, *Exorbitant*. In his introduction, Hart explicitly likens the practitioner of Levinasian ethics to a hasid: "One might say that the whole of Levinas's philosophy is supported by the word exorbitant.... In content and form, Levinas invites us to practice what in Hebrew is called *hesed*, unrestrained and generous charity, given without thought of return" (Hart, *Exorbitant*, 12).

81. Levinas, *Totality and Infinity*, 66.

subjecting. My unknowing self meets the unknowable Other in my responsibility for her.

Levinas's exorbitant ethics calls to mind that most extreme figure from Second Isaiah, the Suffering Servant, who extends his life unto death for the healing of others. We need not enter Christianity to be moved by this figure. But nor is the call necessarily for us to *imitate* him. Kierkegaard opined that the one who scaled the heights of extremity within his own worldview, the Knight of Faith, which Abraham instanced, is not an imitable model. If a person is not a knight of faith, and most of us are not, our best charge is to admire him, as Johannes de Silentio does, and to draw inspiration from him. This may be the role of extremity in Jewish philosophical ethics. Susan Sontag is a helpful guide on this point. The extreme figure who draws her admiration is Simone Weil, whom we briefly encountered in chapter 3. Weil did indeed deny herself unto death in sympathy with the sufferings of others. Sontag does not expect us to follow this model. But she grants leave to moderate lives to be moved and bettered by this extreme example of self-disposal toward others. As she writes of Weil, one Jewish philosopher of another:

> No one who loves life would wish to imitate her dedication to martyrdom or would wish it for his children or for anyone else whom he loves. Yet so far as we love seriousness, as well as life, we are moved by it, nourished by it. In the respect we pay such lives, we acknowledge the presence of mystery in the world. . . . Some (but not all) denials of life are truth-giving, sanity-producing, health-creating, and life enhancing.[82]

To the extent that Levinas climaxes a tradition of extremes within Jewish philosophical ethics, he also partners that tradition with the apophatic one we have been tracing all along within other contexts. The Other who commands me is not subject to description. My response is rather a declaration: "Here am I," which serves Levinas in lieu of description, just as the "Love me!" command does in Rosenzweig. Both are locutions that enact what they express in the very speaking. Just by uttering "Here am I," I put myself at the other's disposal. Levinas calls it an "effusion of oneself, 'extraditing' of the self to the neighbor."[83] This sounds a lot like Rosenzweig's love, which externalizes toward others a self-diminishment. But unlike Levinas, Rosenzweig did not characterize

---

82. Sontag, "Simone Weil," 93.
83. Levinas, *Otherwise Than Being*, 149.

loving self-diminishment under a rubric of ethics. Rosenzweig understood Nietzsche to have overturned the whole rationalist tradition of philosophy which, for Rosenzweig, subsumed ethics (SR17). The love that focused so much of Rosenzweig's thought was less bound to ethics, in his vision of Judaism, than to ritual. If ritual holds the promise of love, it is surely worth a philosophical look. Let us see.

Chapter 8
Ritual

Our negation in this chapter is not of Jewish ritual itself, but of any dependence of it on heteronomous, apodictic law. We take *apodictic* to imply brooking no dissent, and *heteronomous*, a term we take from Kant, to connote law imposed from without, whether by a presumed God or by religious functionaries. In effect, we simply repeat here the negation we practiced with regard to revelation, in chapter 6, but now with specific reference to ritual. The ritual laws of Judaism ally with the apodictic in a way the ethical ones do not. For it is just the ritual ones that are more likely than the ethical ones to rely on heteronomous law exclusively for their authorization. The Bible underscores the apodictic of law as such by having the Israelites so readily accept it: All that God has commanded "will we do and obey" (Exod 24:7). By traditional interpretation, they have submitted to "subjection to an order before understanding the order,"[1] as Emmanuel Levinas puts it. It is enough that it is law and comes from God. But the rabbis nuanced a distinction between the ethical and ritual laws, by distinguishing between "laws that would have been valid even without having been 'written' in the Torah," and those to which "'the evil inclination' and the Gentiles object."[2] Those "objectionable" laws were largely the ones mandating ritual practices, such as circumcision, kashrut, and the Sabbath. And they enact that tension in dialogues they imagine between rabbis and pagan philosophers,

---

1. Levinas, "God," 184.
2. Altmann, "Commandments, Reasons For," 5:85. This version of the distinction comes from b. Yoma 67b.

who always come out the losers.³ From an ancient rabbinical perspective, a *Jewish* philosopher is at best an oxymoron, at worst an *apikoros*, or heretic⁴—which is only to suggest that the philosophical strain within Judaism constitutes a style of Judaism all its own.

A minority voice among the Jewish philosophers would dispense with halachic ritual entirely. Of course, Spinoza did so in the seventeenth century, but at the price of exclusion from the Jewish community of his day. And that was just a small part of Spinoza's rejection of rabbinic Judaism entirely. Thanks to the early days of Reform Judaism in Germany, the renunciation of halachic ritual no longer has such dire consequences. The *Wissenschaft des Judentums* movement, which briefly crossed our path under the heading of History, prepared the way for the Reform thinkers. For a desideratum of that movement was an essence of Judaism to be summoned into view from a broad take on the Jewish past. We have already heard from Abraham Geiger (1810–1874), a leading light of early Reform Judaism, who believed the prophets better captured the essence of Judaism than the pentateuchal law. He wrote of "an eternal and solid core" of the religion that "outer religious practice[s] . . . have had an injurious effect upon."⁵ By "outer religious practice" he means the "ceremonial law[s]," which "are of no further use to piety once they no longer bear the spirit within them," when, in accord with reason, they "would gradually cease to exist."⁶

But it was Samuel Holdheim (1806–1860), rabbi of the Jewish Reform Congregation in Berlin, who took this thought to its logical conclusion. That congregation met in a grand synagogue building on Berlin's Johannisstrasse until its destruction during Kristallnacht in 1938. Jakob Petuchowski has called him "Germany's most radical and revolutionary Reform rabbi."⁷ Holdheim took a cue from the Haskalah thinker Moses Mendelssohn (1729–1786) who, committed as he was to the ritual laws, believed they endured "as long as God does not

---

3. For instance, by asking why Adam was not circumcised; how the *tohu v-vohu* of Gen 1:2 could precede an all-creating God; or why idolatry exists under an all-powerful God. For these examples, see Bialik and Ravnitzky, *Book of Legends*, 6, 456, 514–15.

4. In his novel *As a Driven Leaf*, Milton Steinberg projects a philosophical sensibility onto the ancient heretical rabbi Elisha ben Abuya, who reflects admiringly on Aristotle and Euclid (183, 296–97). There is no record of that in the rabbinical memory of him.

5. Geiger, *Abraham Geiger and Liberal Judaism*, 276.

6. Geiger, *Abraham Geiger and Liberal Judaism*, 288, 248, 287.

7. Petuchowski, "Abraham Geiger," 148.

explicitly revoke them with the same public solemnity with which he bestowed them."[8] Holdheim believed that very revocation had publicly and solemnly occurred when the temple was destroyed in 70 CE. With that event, Holdheim understood God to have effectively rescinded the ritual laws.[9] Of course, the ethical laws, which were independent of the temple (and authorized by reason) remained.

But the destruction of the temple also taught that the Jewish people no longer held a "chosen" place apart from other peoples. The ceremonial law and the doctrine of Israel's election were coincident. As Holdheim put it,

> A large part of the ceremonial law exists . . . [to ensure] the separation and election of this people from all other peoples. . . . Should the rest of mankind . . . be converted to pure monotheism, in that very moment the ceremonial law would cease to have binding force for Israel also. For then . . . the law would sink into complete insignificance.[10]

Holdheim believed that time had come in his own, nineteenth-century Germany. Accordingly, he taught that the Jews no longer constituted a separate people but, as Michael Meyer puts it for him, "all human beings who acknowledged and loved God, and not the Jews alone, were to be counted among the chosen."[11] Consequently, there was no more need for Hebrew prayers, separate seating in synagogues, circumcision, kashrut, or marriage exclusively within the Jewish fold. Holdheim expressly endorsed and performed interfaith marriages.[12] In accord with majority social practice—for there was no need to distinguish from it—Sunday became the weekly day of communal worship, devoted not to rest but to "ethical sanctification."[13] In allegiance to a Western musical aesthetic, services featured choir performances of sacred pieces by Handel, Beethoven, Mozart, and Schubert alongside those by Lewis Lewandowski (1821–1894), the noted cantor and composer of Jewish liturgical music. The German classical music on display made such an

8. "From 'Counter-Reflections to Bonnet's *Palingenesis*,'" in Mendelssohn, *Moses Mendelssohn: Writings*, 22.

9. Petuchowski, "Abraham Geiger," 144.

10. Holdheim, "Ceremonial Law," [141–42].

11. Meyer, "'Most of My Brethren,'" 11.

12. Meyer, "'Most of My Brethren,'" 11. But Meyer suggests that Holdheim's radicalism ebbed as he aged.

13. Holdheim, "New Concept," [201].

impression that a young person reared in Holdheim's synagogue could, decades later, on first attending a concert hall performance in Berlin, wonder over hearing "synagogue music" in secular spaces.[14] There was no longer need for emphatic cultural distinctions between Jews and gentiles when a single monotheism now effectively reigned, thanks to worldwide spread of Jewish ideas.

The Reform Congregation of Berlin was admittedly an exception to the rule of Jewish congregational life in nineteenth-century Germany. "The majority of Berlin Jews . . . felt that the Reformers far exceeded acceptable limits of religious freedom. . . . The Jewish Reform Community [Congregation] was not large and was looked upon purely as an elitist social group."[15] In light of the succeeding history of Jews in Germany, the Johannisstrasse synagogue now seems a fragile bubble that was soon to burst. Within the larger annals of Reform Judaism, it represents a radicality now largely abandoned by the communal structures of the denomination, which has intentionally recovered more of traditional ritual practice. In a 2022 interview, Andrew Rehfeld, president of Hebrew Union College, the seminary that trains Reform rabbis, reflected that from Modern Orthodoxy to Reform Judaism, there is more continuum than separation between the mainline Jewish branches, who might reasonably cooperate more.[16] The rejection of inherited ritual practice, as preached by Samuel Holdheim, is an inheritance of so-called Classical Reform, a minority redoubt within the living practice of Reform Judaism today.

But a major thinker within philosophical Judaism based his critique of ritual on a philosophical worldview he evolved outside the framework of the mainline denominations, and hence independent of changing courses in their own institutional lives. This is Martin Buber, who has already spoken to us on Israel, both the people and the state. We might already suspect from the status of the I-Thou relation in his

---

14. For this memory I credit former Stephen Wise Free Synagogue (New York, NY) member Ann Neubauer, z"l.

15. Alexander et al., *Musical Tradition*, 12. This booklet accompanies a two-disc recording of the music sung in the synagogue, produced between 1928 and 1930, and intended to advertise the appeal of the congregation's liturgy to German Jews. In his memory of the services, George Mosse comments especially on the importance of music to the congregation (6–7). As it turned out, the recorded music, recovered and reissued by Beth Hatefusoth, wound up serving another purpose entirely, to memorialize, in Gabriel Alexander's words, "that specific Jewish culture which perished in the Holocaust" (13).

16. Rehfeld, "Great American Rabbi Shortage."

thinking that ritual practices will play a very small, if any, role in his understanding of Jewish life. Buber may have God in mind when he writes within *I and Thou* that "no prescription can lead us to the encounter and none leads from it,"[17] but this is as much true of the rule-defiant I-Thou relation generally. Over many of his works, over many years, we read the same sentiment, variously stated: "we . . . consider life as more divine than law and rules,"[18] "no command can tell me how . . . I decide"[19] to respond to a given situation of ultimacy; "no ceremony can cope"[20] with what matters most to human beings. Buber wrote to Rosenzweig that, having been raised by his grandparents in an observant household, he "stopped putting on tefillin," already at age fourteen.[21] Later, living in what would become the state of Israel, even Yom Kippur could not draw him into the synagogue except at the insistence of his close friend, the writer S. Y. Agnon.[22] This attitude toward ritual would of course not endear him to Israel's Orthodox rabbinical establishment, against which we can only cite this trenchant observation, from Buber to Rosenzweig: "I hope I would be prepared to die for this postulate [that 'revelation is not legislation'] if I were faced with a Jewish universal church that had inquisitorial powers."[23]

It is no accident that much of Buber's thought on ritual observance evolved in dialogue with Rosenzweig, who, on this point, stood on the other side of the ledger, as we will shortly see. The two were friends from their first meeting, in 1914, on until Rosenzweig's death in 1929, and over that time authorial collaborators as well. They sparred collegially over the import of ritual. In that debate, Rosenzweig wittily and insightfully cast Buber as the "reverential *apikoros* [heretic]" and himself as the "homecomer"[24] who, on the brink of becoming Christian, returned

17. Buber, *I and Thou*, 159.

18. Buber, *On Judaism*, 152. The quote is from Buber's address, "Herut: On Youth and Religion," delivered in German in 1919.

19. Buber, *Between Man and Man*, 68. The quote is from a talk Buber gave in 1936, in German, entitled "Die Frage an den Einzelnen" [The Question to the Single One].

20. Buber, *Prophetic Faith*, 90.

21. Buber to Rosenzweig, October 1, 1922, in *Letters of Martin Buber*, 290. Buber's assertion is interesting in light of the role tefillin play in the efforts Lubavitcher Jews make to win over (male) secular Jews toward observance; an invitation to "lay tefillin" is among the first overtures extended.

22. Mendes-Flohr, *Martin Buber*, 235.

23. Buber to Rosenzweig, June 3, 1925, in *Letters of Martin Buber*, 327.

24. Rosenzweig to Buber, August 19, 1922, in *Letters of Martin Buber*, 271.

toward an increasingly observant Judaism. We might say they met at the middle of a road they were walking in opposite directions. Over their exchanges, they found points of agreement. For Buber could countenance the language of *commandment*, as opposed to law, so long as "it takes place in conformity with the full capacity of the person."[25] He opines that, whether we have "filled the law or broke[n] the law—both are required on occasion."[26] What matters is, as Bahya ibn Paquda might say, "the direction of the heart,"[27] according to which "every deed is hallowed if it radiates the spirit of unity,"[28] including, presumably, the commanded deed. But then, the commanded deed need not hail from tradition. "Every man, by living authentically, shall himself become a Torah, a law."[29]

Rosenzweig, for his part, was not so far from this. He did suggest that with just a "gentle push"[30] toward receptivity, all Jews could be brought back without coercion into a ritually observant life. At the same time, he allowed for integrity in failing to hear any call to observance at all; "maybe nothing at all"[31] of the law reached even a Jew whose ears were open to its call, and instead some other spiritual path stood open for him. At just this crossroads of observing the ritual law or not Buber and Rosenzweig could find common ground.

But then, the problem of law as Rosenzweig understood it was, for Buber, "the rubble with which rabbinism and rationalism have covered it."[32] Buber took the ritual law to serve a purpose beyond it, which he variously characterized as unity, religiosity, or relationship. But for him, it was not so much that other regimens emerged to compete with that office, and perform it better, as that the law ceased to work that way at all, if indeed it ever did. It was a demotion from the start when the "living communion with the unconditioned"[33] morphed into "a formulation of

---

25. Buber, *Two Types of Faith*, 56.
26. Buber, *I and Thou*, 92.
27. Buber, *Two Types of Faith*, 64.
28. Buber, *On Judaism*, 152.
29. Buber, *On Judaism*, 92.
30. Rosenzweig, *On Jewish Learning*, 65. In this context, the "gentle push" is toward a Jew's identification with the Jewish people, but we might say, by extension, toward hearing the Love me! command.
31. Rosenzweig, *On Jewish Learning*, 86.
32. Buber, *On Judaism*, 81.
33. Buber, *On Judaism*, 80.

law"³⁴ effected by mere humans. Early on in Buber's thought, religiosity, as opposed to religion, was the heart of Judaism and the desideratum to be recovered. He identified religiosity with a decision that united a divided self by orienting it toward "the unconditioned."³⁵ The unconditioned, in turn, was whatever could evoke such a unified response: "the unconditional affects a person when he lets his whole being be gripped by it ... and when he responds to it with his whole being."³⁶ Later, in the wake of the I-Thou relation, what the law tended to impede was the emergence of just that relation, since "I cannot admit the law transformed by man into the realm of my will, if I am to hold myself ready for the unmediated [relationship emergent upon] ... a specific hour of life."³⁷

From start to finish of his writing, Buber subsumed under notions of unity and wholeness a variety of desiderata that bypassed prescribed ritual observances. There was to be "personal unity, unity of being, unity of life, unity of action";³⁸ and we were to enter into our mutual encounters "with one's whole being."³⁹ But none of this would happen by way of ritual practices. Nothing so subject to our will as ritual observance could help—indeed, would obstruct. When Buber wrote relatively late in his career that "in moments and forms of grace, unity can arise from ... contradiction,"⁴⁰ he suggested that the high times of resolution in our lives—whether characterized in terms of ultimate decision, the Unconditional, or I-Thou encounter—occur beyond our control, even take us by surprise. It is less that we are determined or free in our acts

---

34. Buber to Rosenzweig, June 24, 1924, in *Letters of Martin Buber*, 315.

35. In his early writings, such as *On Judaism*, Buber augments his references to God with this more abstractly philosophical, less religiously freighted term. And before Buber coined the phrase "Eternal Thou," which appears frequently in *I and Thou*, he referenced "the Absolute Thou," a name more resonant of his (Hegelian) philosophical inheritance. See Horowitz, *Buber's Way*, 96. The "Eternal Thou," by contrast, would impress German readers more religiously, as "the Eternal" (*das Ewige*) was Moses Mendelssohn's rendering of the biblical Tetragrammaton (YHWH) in his translation into German of the Torah, and that usage was widespread in German Jewish circles. See Rosenzweig, "Eternal,"100.

36. Buber, *On Judaism*, 153.

37. Buber to Rosenzweig, June 24, 1924, in *Letters of Martin Buber*, 315. Here I have replaced Buber's reference to the "Word of God" with "relationship emergent," to which I hope he would not object, in light of what remains for us, until the next chapter, the abeyance of God.

38. Buber, *Between Man and Man*, 116.

39. Buber, *I and Thou*, 54.

40. Buber, *Knowledge of Man*, 64. The citation is from an essay, "Distance and Relation," first published in 1951.

than that, at high points of decision, when we decide "with [our] whole being,"[41] the very distinction between free and determined dissolves: "the unity of the contraries is [a] mystery"[42] in all its "unforeseeableness and ... irrecoverableness."[43]

Buber cautions against idolizing the law. Citing the Rabbi of Kotzk, he writes, "The Torah warns us 'not to make an idol even of the command of God.' What can I add to these words?"[44] In the end, he added quite a lot. His vision stands as one of the few within Judaism that would dispense with ritual law and behaviors. Unsurprisingly, it caught on more with Christian readers. Within a more normative Jewish framework, our negation of apodictically observed heteronomous ritual allows for other adoptions and defenses of ritual to shine. And we consider a few of them, from Maimonides, Moses Mendelssohn, Samson Raphael Hirsch, Rosenzweig, and Yeshayahu Leibowitz. Each in his own way defends ritual practices on philosophical grounds without recourse to apodictic, heteronomous law.

We already know how much effort Maimonides expended to rationalize the commandments. That attempt belongs to the larger genre of writing, *Ta'amei ha-Mitzvot* (Reasons for the Commandments), in which halachic rationalists of any kind have a particular stake. But Maimonides has a distinctive approach to the rationality of law. He subsumes the law under a broader commitment he has, partly as a medical scientist, partly as an Aristotelian, to natural processes of cause and effect. We already saw that commitment operate in his views on revelation. But it colors his entire philosophy of law in ways that ease the apodictic quality of it. Insofar as our grasp of the causal reasoning behind the law informs our practice of it, we are less dependent on the coercive imperiousness of it.

Maimonides has already told us that the law Moses delivered at Sinai had two levels of meaning, one oriented toward nature, the other toward community formation. Oriented toward nature, the law was descriptive. It disclosed the cosmic networks of cause-effect relations that held the universe together. Oriented toward community, the law was prescriptive toward human behavior within polities (GP511). Of course it took the perspicuity of the philosopher, a rare breed, to discern the natural law behind the communitarian one. One place where

41. Buber, *Eclipse of God*, 103.
42. "The Faith of Judaism," in Buber, *Writings of Martin Buber*, 256.
43. Buber, *Eclipse of God*, 35.
44. Buber, *For the Sake of Heaven*, xii.

the communitarian law opens a window onto the natural one is by way of the Jewish calendar, which takes its cues from the operations of the sun and moon. Jews can tell where they are in one of the Jewish months by the look of the moon, which may awaken appropriate awe over the heavens themselves. And this view of the law is perhaps a bridge to what we heard awhile back from Heschel and Einstein, that there is no better gateway to feelings of awe and reverence than nature writ large. But ritual in sync with nature also improves it, by inflecting it with higher purpose than nature itself can bestow (GP571), as in the case of the menorah, based on the natural form of plants, but humanly crafted more explicitly toward beauty, so that God may be worshiped "in the beauty of holiness" (Ps 96:9).

Maimonides's own reverence for the natural workings of cause and effect (GP504) motivates his interpretation of the law according to pure principles of utility. Every law operates as a cause toward some desired effect, whether to instill in us a correct opinion, e.g., that God is One, as the Shema teaches; an admirable character trait, e.g., humility, as modeled by the paradigmatic lawgiver, Moses; or a cooperatively communal disposition, e.g., by way of the ethical laws. The Shabbat has special significance for Maimonides in context of his worry, from Aristotle, that the world might be eternal, which would effectively falsify the whole of Judaism. Against that danger, the Shabbat command at Exod 20:11 authorizes rest on the very grounds of creation, which ceased on the seventh day (GP570). Reason itself may withhold assent to creation doctrine; but the practicing Jew reasonably cannot. That there is so much practical, rational utility in the structure of Jewish law is good news for the rationalists among us.

Maimonides underscores his commitment to the sheer utility of ritual law by mildly disdaining all metaphorical (poetic) interpretations of it, such as the Midrash promotes. An interpretation might be "excellent in the manner of the midrashim" (GP578) he concedes, but these "poetic conceits" (GP573), charm as they might the imagination, do not illuminate the text (GP573). For example, he has no use for the lovely midrash on the ritual lulav, the gathering of four species of plant waved ritually at Sukkot, that it represents the four types of Jews: those with learning and deeds, with learning but no deeds, with deeds but no learning, and with neither deeds nor learning, that they all together constitute the variegated people of Israel.[45] No, he drily comments, the point of the particular plants gathered to make the lulav (leaves from the date palm, myrtle, and willow trees, plus fruit of the citrus, or etrog) is no such symbolic meaning they might carry, but that they maintain their freshness longer than other flora (GP574). Maimonides keeps a tight leash on the imagination, lest it overwhelm our reason with distracting and misleading fantasies.

We may not buy some of his explanations. For instance, he does not offer the reason we often hear for the prohibition on pork, that it threatens us with disease (trichinosis, we would say today), as Maimonides the medical doctor and advisor on diet might well have done within a framework of medieval medicine. Instead, he simply comments that the pig is "very dirty" (GP598). And we might have hoped he would somehow dismiss the manifestly irrational, to say nothing of misogynistic, trial mandated for women suspected of adultery (Num 5:11–31), but instead he excuses it on grounds that the very prescription itself—"the horror of the waters" (GP603) involved—would itself discourage sexual improprieties.

But more strikingly, Maimonides openly admits to being confounded by some of the laws. With regard to the "table bread" (*chalot*) prescribed for the tabernacle (Lev 24:5), he writes, "I do not know the reason for this" (GP578); likewise, any use of ritual wine stymies him (GP591). Several factors might account for this incomprehension, which could result from: "the incapacity of our intellects" to understand (GP507); our tendency to more greatly respect what we *cannot* understand (GP508); or the insignificance of such particulars to the heights of reason's purview (GP509). But why should these commandments in particular, relating to bread and wine, stand out for their seeming inutility? Might this be a sly sweep at the eucharistic rite of the church, which he surely knew about, but cannot openly disparage? Or is Maimonides hinting that the exceptions to the comprehensibility of the law undermine his claims for its utility *tout court* and leave it to stand shakily without defense, rather like creation doctrine?

Maimonides opens a path to such a critique of ritual practice in his discussion of animal sacrifice. This clearly disgusts him. The utility of the command to burn incense within the tabernacle, he suggests, is "to improve its smell" which otherwise "would have been like that of a

---

45. Leviticus Rabbah 30:12. See *Vayikra Rabbah*, Sefaria, https://www.sefaria.org/Vayikra_Rabbah.

slaughterhouse" (GP579). He rehearses a rabbinic thought that at Exod 15:25, where the Israelites are said to stop on their way to Sinai, they receive a foretaste of the law—but, adds Maimonides, one that mandates no animal sacrifice (GP531), as though to exclude this from the primal base of the mitzvot. But then, by the "wily graciousness" (GP525) or "gracious ruse" of God (GP532), the very prescription of animal sacrifice comes to gradually wean the Israelites away from it toward a regimen of spoken prayer. For like all ancient peoples, the Israelites labored under the illusion that the divine somehow fed off of hapless animals offered up to it. And now the radical thought: Maimonides implies that at some future time, at the culmination of the ruse, "your worship should consist solely in meditation without any works at all" (GP526). How can the doubt not arise that the whole regimen of ritual commandments is itself a ruse stimulating toward a purely contemplative worship that, for all its location in an ideal future, cannot but undermine commitment to ritual practices now? Might Maimonides slyly raise that doubt for the exceptional readers of his *Guide*? For let us not forget, the law does not address the rare exception (GP534).

But Maimonides reins himself in from such doubts, as he did from doubts over creation doctrine. For he has an overall explanation for all the seemingly non-rational ritual laws, that either at one time or even in his own day they combatted idolatrous thought and practice, inasmuch as "the first intention of the law as a whole is to put an end to idolatry" (GP517). So, for example, if cows were worshiped by idolaters, they became food for true monotheists; if blood featured ritually in pagan diet, it would be food forbidden to Jews. Part of the reason the provisions for wine troubled Maimonides is that it was so common for pagans to drink it, and so should have been proscribed (as it is for Muslims). Maimonides is convinced that any perduring perplexity over ritual law would evaporate in face of fuller knowledge of ancient idolatry (GP612). If idolatry itself embraced a multitude of sinful practices, a wide scope opens for laws to contest them and to find their rationale in how they do so. But then, how tempted were Maimonides's own contemporaries, to say nothing of us today, by ancient idolatries? According to the Midrash, in post-biblical times "the impulse to worship idols has already been eliminated."[46] But the charge of idolatry has continued

---

46. Song of Songs Rabbah 7:7. See Neusner, *Song of Songs Rabbah*, 190. See also Talmudic tractates b. Yoma 69b and b. Avodah Zarah 17a–b.

to sound, from Maimonides's time up through our own, so perhaps his worry over it as not as anachronistic as it seems.

Maimonides did not understand idolatry the way the biblical writers did, as in the concise words of contemporary Christian theologian Stephen Fowl, "worship of other gods by means of images."[47] We ourselves would hardly be tempted by that, at least not as, say, the ancient Egyptians or Babylonians were, from the biblical standpoint; nor were Maimonides's contemporaries. Idolatry, for Maimonides, was anthropomorphism: ascribing—in the case of it that disturbed him—human qualities to God. The biblical commands may have been directed against worshipful images of animals, trees, or astronomical bodies understood to be divine. But, Maimonides implied, they could serve just as well in his own day to discourage *any* incorrect attributions to God, including inapplicable human qualities. So it was important still to observe the idolatry-contesting ritual commands, howsoever archaic they might seem.

Of course, the Bible is full of anthropomorphic pictures of God—walking, talking, emoting. But we already know from Maimonides's account of revelation that these pictures rest on what he called *amphibolous* terms, i.e., words that straddle the divide between what Moses experienced in his revelatory visions of the cosmos and what he needed to state in the form of community-building law. All the Bible's anthropomorphisms do double duty to shape in common worshipers a reverence for God and in philosophers true understandings of the universe. In no case are they literal descriptions of deity. That is something philosophers like Maimonides can teach the common worshiper, as he did in his reframing of the law for a broad audience, his *Mishneh Torah*, written in pellucid Hebrew, when he wrote right up front in that work that God "is not comparable to the reality of any other existing thing."[48]

God is our topic for the next chapter. For now, we can restate Maimonides's understanding of idolatry as an evaluational reduction of what is most important to what is less so, or the reverse, a promotion of what is less to more important. After all, we sometimes attach the word, *God*, to the best of something, as Columbia University professor of linguistics John McWhorter did when, asked to explain why composer Scott Joplin's "Maple Leaf Rag" was so popular, he replied, "because it's God"[49]—god within the universe of ragtime compositions. And Maimonides

47. Fowl, *Idolatry*, 6.
48. Maimonides, *Book of Knowledge*, 1.
49. McWhorter, "Why Scott Joplin's Ragtime Matters," 6.

had reason to worry about idolatry so understood. For his own view of the divine was so surpassingly austere that *no* identifiably human quality could be ascribed to God. Much of the beginning of the *Guide of the Perplexed* makes just that point many times over. Without perhaps thinking that much about it, we agree with Maimonides every time we sing in the popular Yigdal hymn, based on his teachings, that God is incomparably unique, *echad v-ein yachid ke-yechudo*—God is one and there is no oneness like God's—for a being beyond comparison cannot be described. How then can believing Jews praise the justice or mercy of God? They cannot, really, if they take these to be qualities of God's own being. No wonder we hear from Moshe Halbertal and Avishai Margalit that "Maimonides was exceedingly skeptical about the possibility that finite and limited creatures like us humans could form the right notion of God's perfection."[50] We will return to this fruitful thought, which links to our theme of contentless reality, next chapter.

Halbertal and Margalit speak more to the permutations of meaning within the wide scope of this word, *idolatry*, that keep alive the worry over it, so much so that if the Jewish rituals contest it this alone may recommend them to us. As far back as biblical times, errant worship of wrong or nonexistent gods was associated with immorality. For example, the prophet Hosea famously paired it with adultery. The Wisdom of Solomon expands the list of idolatry's ill effects to include "murder, theft, and deceit, corruption, faithlessness, tumult, perjury . . . and debauchery" (Wis 14:23–24 RSV). Another medieval philosopher, who postdates Maimonides and admired him, Menahem Ha-Meiri (1249–1315), took the link between idolatry and immorality so seriously that he identified the one with the other. As Halbertal and Margalit observe,[51] this shifted the error of idolatry away from mistaken conceptions of God to immoral acts. If Jewish ritual practices lend their support to *ethical* practices, as the rabbinical tradition itself taught, all the more reason for philosophical Jews to perform them even today.[52]

---

50. Halbertal and Margalit, *Idolatry*, 111–12.

51. Halbertal and Margalit, *Idolatry*, 212–13. Part of Halbertal and Margalit's point is that by this move Ha-Meiri freed Christianity of the idolatrous associations Jews had hitherto made with it, since moral Christians were, by definition, non-idolatrous.

52. Rabbinic Judaism saw a mutual supportiveness between the ethical and ritual commandments. The rabbis posited a correspondence within the Ten Commandments between each of the first five and its partner in an adjacent column of the second five. For instance, as Hosea had taught, the idolatry proscribed by the second commandment partnered with the adultery proscribed by the seventh. See Ginzberg, *Legends*,

Maimonides might have found a gracious ruse implicit in the very fact that the ritual commandments prescribe *acts*, for the most part, rather than things. Bahya ibn Paquda subordinated outward ritual to the inner duties of the heart. But, with respect to the idolatry Maimonides feared, outward acts had the virtue of passing away. A human act, by its very ephemerality, deflects attention away from itself, unlike a persistent thing, like the sun or moon, which might (and did) draw worship to itself. Another fan of Maimonides, Moses Mendelssohn (1729–1786), expounded on this idea. Mendelssohn, too, was exercised by idolatry. He reflected on the less important things that presumed to be more important and found among that class of things the animals and astronomical bodies that ancient peoples worshiped, but also the books and writings that enlightened moderns did. Plato, who Mendelssohn also admired, had already warned against reverence for the written word, which worked to deaden the spoken one.[53] Invoking the very notion of Oral Law so critical to rabbinical Judaism, Mendelssohn regretted that so much of what was meant to be communicated orally in Judaism, from person to person, most especially the law, had been committed to writing. For what accompanied the oral communication of law from elder to younger was the living *model* of faithfulness to law the elder embodied. This the dead letter could not provide. But the further problem with the written word was that, for all its unliveliness, it was a *thing* that could draw undue reverence. And as part of the eighteenth-century European Enlightenment that Mendelssohn inhabited, it *did*. Our reverence for the written word makes of each of us "a solitary creature, poring over books and articles,"[54] rather than participants in living traditions of knowledge. The written word is *our* idolatry. Any present-day academic seeking tenure will recognize the force of this critique.

One answer to our singular idolatry are the ritual laws of Judaism, which wean our attention away from writing—on the Sabbath, it is forbidden—toward temporal acts that in their very temporality deflect reverence from themselves. As Mendelssohn puts it, "Man's actions are transitory; there is nothing permanent or enduring about them which,

---

3:104. Ginzberg draws from the original midrashic text, *Mekilta de-Rabbi Ishmael*, 2:262.

53. *Phaedrus* 274b–277a.

54. Mendelssohn, *Jerusalem and Other Writings*, 90. Subsequent citations to pages of this text are given parenthetically.

like . . . script, could lead to idolatry through misuse or misunderstanding" (90).

For Mendelssohn, the ritual laws of Judaism are actually all that distinguish it from any reasonable religion. For in its *teachings*, Judaism has nothing to say that is not universally available to human reason. And that fundamental teaching that there is a "God, the necessary autonomous Being, omnipotent and omniscient, who rewards men in a future life according to their deeds" (69) is available to reason by sheer contemplation of "creation itself in all its inter-relatedness, which is legible and intelligible to all men" (65). Mendelssohn famously inferred from this that Judaism was not "revealed religion" but rather "divine legislation—laws, commandments, statutes, rules of conduct" (61), the point of which were, with regard to the universally available religious teachings, to "remind us of them, or induce us to ponder them" (71). "The ceremonial law itself is a living kind of script, as it were, stirring heart and mind, full of meaning, stimulating man to continuous contemplation" (74).

In so writing, Mendelssohn is not above a gracious ruse himself. By way of recommending the ritual laws of Judaism, he employs a figure for the chief idolatry of his own day—*script*—toward a weaning of us away from it toward its very antithesis: the *living* of the law. So never mind Mendelssohn's theistic creationism or theory of revealed law. He reminds those of his own day and ours not to accord the written word more reverence than it deserves and to keep our eyes on the prize: eternal truths.

Of course, if the commandments performed vivify truths that contest tempting idolatries, all the more reason to practice them. Mendelssohn offers up what is in effect a symbolic way of reading ritual performances. They are less important for what they literally accomplish—a candle lit, a prayer chanted, a bow enacted—than for the truths they subtly display in their performance, that God enlightens our reason, cares for us through our prayer, dignifies the body in worship, though Mendelssohn does not draw out these particular "truths." That effort of symbolization was better executed by one of Mendelssohn's many later admirers, the Orthodox thinker Samson Raphael Hirsch (1808–1888), who deemed some of the ritual acts commanded symbolic at heart, which he called the *edoth* (literally: witnesses or testimonies, Hirsch would say, to the truth). These are "symbolic words and acts," by which "the essential principles of [Jewish] life" are stamped "indelibly upon your soul."[55] Hirsch suggests that

---

55. Hirsch, *Nineteen Letters*, 83.

truths actively performed, by way of mitzvot, give more forceful "expression to ideas, without splitting them up into words."[56] And while Hirsch's structure of symbolic interpretations may fall flat to the twenty-first-century reader, perhaps for losing a freshness it once had—Rosenzweig called it "rigid and narrow, . . . unbeautiful despite its magnificence"[57]—some of it is memorable even now, for instance the suggestion that the Sabbath envalues the kinds of "occupations without purpose"[58] that our working lives (and pragmatist cultures) tend to diminish. And we may take Hirsch, building on Mendelssohn, to invite us to rethink the mitzvot in relevantly symbolic ways that marginalize or even entirely bypass any apodictic quality with which the Bible may have invested them. They, rather, invite performance as an artwork does attention to itself.

But the master of that gracious ruse, if that is what it is, is really Rosenzweig himself, who found the symbolic read of the mitzvot forced and artificial, just as Spinoza did the interpretation of them after Plato or Aristotle. Franz Rosenzweig enjoys the singular distinction within the twentieth century of fitting Jewish ritual into a philosophical system—his own—that even without the presumption of a legislating god authorizes and virtually enacts the whole body of the ritual commandments. Under the rubrics of creation and revelation, we have begun to follow the erection of his system. There is one final building block to it that we need briefly to add before proceeding to his philosophy of ritual, and that is the relation of redemption.

For Rosenzweig, redemption is an outcome of revelation, just as revelation was of creation. For it transpires that the love we receive when we hear the Love me! command does not remain with us. That love is erotic in its intensity and exclusive in its bilateral intimacy. The soul who receives it wants to linger within it, apart from the rest of the world. It is the erotic/exclusive love of the Song of Songs. But the world still suffers outside this love for its death-prone individuals. For creation assures only its species and genera. The beloved soul cannot but hear the cry of the individuals within the world. And so what seemed a private love follows the pattern Rosenzweig has been augmenting all along, of externalization. What was private becomes public. A self-contained love between two expands toward three or more, to whom- or whatever stands near. The Love me! command effectively echoes beyond the confines of the soul

---

56. Hirsch, *Nineteen Letters*, 85.
57. Rosenzweig, *On Jewish Learning*, 80.
58. Hirsch, *Nineteen Letters*, 86.

who receives it, toward the nearest neighbor. Christians would say that the love Rosenzweig describes combines the intensity of eros with the inclusiveness of agape: love as desire with love as care.

From this transferal of love, a hope the world has had for its death-prone individuals is fulfilled, or begins to be. Now, thanks to humanity, love has very wide scope to meet and defeat death. The world presses forward all its death-enshrouded life—the "branches, twigs, leaves, flowers and fruits of [all its forms of] life"—for the love that comes to it from the beloved human, toward what needs affirmed in each: "a soul, eternity" (SR258). Any individual within the cosmos of creation is ripe for receipt of death-defying love, from the human who receives it first. It need merely be standing next to the beloved human, whose receipt of love cannot but overflow. Neighbor by neighbor, love wends its animating way through the world (SR177). An accumulation of such overflow points to a time of the universally enlivened and beloved (SR241). Everything will have found its place in the "covenant of a supra-natural community" (SR2190). Rosenzweig, who is at his most idealistic and lyrical here, takes whatever visions of the messianic age rabbinic Judaism may have imagined to an absolute extreme. It is not just lions lying down with lambs. It is all of nature flourishing under human hands in Edenic fullness. A ritual practice within Judaism proleptically lives that fullness if only for a day. It is Yom Kippur, an observance which is itself commanded. We will need all three of the stellar relations—creation, revelation, and redemption—to locate ritual within Rosenzweig's system.

To fathom Rosenzweig on the commandments we must begin with his philosophy of revelation. For Rosenzweig, the grammatical form of the command to "Love me!" already carried love to the human who received it. It was "the absolutely perfect expression, the perfectly pure language of love" (SR191). A paradoxical feature of this love is that it extended by contraction of its agent. By that self-withdrawal, space for the other expanded. But here is another feature of it: it is "an absolutely pure present" (SR191). What intensifies the force of the language of love is its constriction of focus to the present moment. The love the commandment bears does not persist through time. Instead, it continually renews or rebirths in the unceasing issuance of the command. "The commandment knows only the moment" (SR191). It is always fresh and new. "It is the today in which the love of the lover lives" (SR192), what Rosenzweig calls in German *Heutigkeit*,[59] literally today-ness or contemporaneity, translated elsewhere as "living reality."[60]

It is on just this point that what Rosenzweig calls mere law differs from commandment. Law is time-bound (SR191). It lends itself to perduring inscription. It is not alive with anything it expresses. It relies for its accomplishment on obeisance. It appeals to our will, which agrees or not to obey. The commandment differs on each of these points. It can only be heard, not read off a page. Once heard, it is irresistible. It appeals not to our will but to our ability to respond to it, which we do because we can, not because we must. It does not constrain but empowers. What we do in response to a commandment "is not choosing but listening and therefore only accepting."[61] Like Plato's Reason, which always chooses the Good whenever it encounters it, spontaneously and without coercion, so we who receive the love command always respond positively to it. Both are cases of like attracted to like, whether Reason to the Good or humanity to God. Only the law stands in need of the utilitarian explanations Maimonides and the rationalists supplied, or the symbolic ones Mendelssohn and Hirsch did. The commandment is as self-explanatory as love itself.

God is a commander, not a lawgiver. "Revelation," Rosenzweig says, "is certainly not law giving."[62] Law and commandment are effectively opposites but they can convert back and forth between them. The Ten Commandments inscribed on sculpted tablets that decorate a synagogue have the form of law. But at any moment they can reach whoever regards them there as address. When Rosenzweig writes that "the voice of the commandment causes the spark to leap from 'I must' to 'I can,'"[63] he implies that the authoritarian face of the law can convert to love. It is all in the listening. Only one commandment, he suggests, can never be law and that is the Love me! command itself. Because it only exists in the hearing, never the writing, it is always alive. "All other commandments can pour their content into the form of law" (SR191); but by the same token, all of them can recover at their heart the voice of "the one pure commandment, . . . the highest of all commandments" (SR191), which is the love command. Rosenzweig suggests that the love command can

59. "Die Bauleute," in Rosenzweig, *Kleinere Schriften*, 116.
60. Rosenzweig, *On Jewish Learning*, 85.
61. Rosenzweig, *On Jewish Learning*, 91.
62. Rosenzweig, *On Jewish Learning*, 118.
63. Rosenzweig, *On Jewish Learning*, 86.

"take the lead" (SR191) of all the laws so that each in turn "becomes a commandment" (SR191) in its own right. That is, each mandated ritual can render itself an envelope for enclosing the love command. In that case, the ritual performed attests to the call of love. Indeed, "law must again become commandment,"[64] if Jews who have lost their link to Judaism are ever to recover its living reality.

Rather than provide a reason for the commandments, Rosenzweig has recast them as a path back into Judaism for those who have lost it. In his middle-class, Jewish Germany of the 1920s, he was indeed addressing for the most part assimilated Jews. On those grounds, too, he collaborated with Martin Buber on a then new translation of the Bible into German, but a German that, sometimes tortuously, imitated the structure of the Hebrew it translated, as though to supply those ignorant of Hebrew access back into it. And he headed a center for adult education in all matters Jewish, called the Freies Jüdisches Lehrhaus,[65] where he and the teachers practiced "learning in reverse order . . . from the periphery back to the center,"[66] that is, from the assimilated periphery of Jewish life to what he understood to be its commandment-rich core. He adjured his readers to listen for the commands that empowered, not compelled. As we have already seen, these might be many from the tradition, or few. "Whether much is done or little or maybe nothing at all is immaterial in the face of the one and unavoidable demand; that whatever is being done, shall come from that inner power"[67] of the love command.

So experiential and open-ended an approach to Jewish observance had wide appeal among American rabbis who first heard of it via the

64. Rosenzweig, *On Jewish Learning*, 85.

65. The German word *Lehrhaus* means literally "teaching house," rather than the more expected "learning house." It helpfully connotes a feature of the enterprise, that most of the instructors were not professional Jewish educators, but rather learners sharing what they knew. It was as though to elevate everyone who had learning to share to the status of teacher, regardless of professional training, somewhat as happens today in the Osher Lifelong Learning Institute. It was not "free" of charges, in fact the classes were relatively costly, but of presupposing any particular stance toward Jewish belief and practice among the participants. It was a place of exploration, even experimentation, with various aspects of the tradition. It lasted six years (1920–1926) in the city of Frankfurt, where at its height it enrolled eleven hundred students, about 4 percent of the city's Jewish population. See Brenner, *Renaissance*, especially the chapter "A New Learning: The Lehrhaus Movement," 69–100.

66. Rosenzweig, *On Jewish Learning*, 98. The instructors were themselves "learners" in the Jewish enterprise and included, as Rosenzweig announced in his opening address, "a chemist, a physician, a historian, an artist, a politician" (99).

67. Rosenzweig, *On Jewish Learning*, 86.

translation of Rosenzweig's works into English, largely under the guidance of Rosenzweig's student, friend, and colleague Nahum Glatzer. *Commentary* magazine attests to this when in its issue for August 1966 it reported on results of a survey it conducted among a cross section of American rabbis on their beliefs. The editors announced their surprise over one of their gleanings, that Rosenzweig proved to be "the single greatest influence on the religious thought of North American Jewry," adding, "we have not given Nahum Glatzer and Schocken Books anything like the thanks we owe them for telling us about Rosenzweig in English."[68] But this is not all. Rosenzweig is cited in one of the classics of youthful, popular Judaism of the 1970s: *The Jewish Catalog*. There, the editors assembled on one page, in chart form, a variety of interpretations of the three festive meals prescribed for Shabbat. Among them is Rosenzweig's, according to which each meal highlights one of the key relations of his system: creation, revelation, or redemption. In natural sequence, the meal of Friday night, when Shabbat begins, takes for its theme creation; the Saturday morning meal, revelation; and the third meal, redemption.[69] The editors drew from a section of Rosenzweig's *Star* that interprets the whole of the Jewish ritual calendar according to those same structural categories. It is a marvel of systematic embeddings and expansions of these ideas across the ritual calendar.

So, at the broadest level, the Sabbath, the pilgrimage festivals, and the High Holy Days divide between them a focus, respectively, on creation, revelation, and redemption. But then, within the pilgrimage festivals, for example, the same categories distribute, respectively, over Passover, which celebrates the creation of the people Israel; Shavuot, the revelation of the law; and Sukkot, the anticipation of redemptive rest in the promised land. And now, microcosmically, the same categories repeat again within each of the pilgrimage festivals. For instance, in the case of Passover, creation sets the theme of the seder at the start of the holiday, when the community of family, friends, and even strangers forms at the table; revelation, the theme of the Song of Songs, ritually read over the course of this eight-day festival; and redemption, that of the prophetic reading prescribed for the last day, from Isaiah, on the wolf at peace with the lamb (Isa 11:6), which shows nature redeemed after Rosenzweig's picture of love-suffused nature. Rosenzweig's liturgical vision of the three

---

68. Himmelfarb, "Symposium," 71.
69. Siegel and Strassfeld, *First Jewish Catalog*, 115.

primal categories caught on: Reform Judaism's *Gates of Prayer* labels the two blessings that precede the Shema, Creation and Revelation, and the blessing that immediately follows, Redemption.[70]

None of this is child's play for Rosenzweig. Creation, revelation, and redemption are not only theological categories, though they are that. They are also *philosophical* categories—Rosenzweig expressly calls his book "a system of philosophy"[71]—in the sense that what they name actually constitutes reality. The world as we know it, and we ourselves, would not exist without them. Creation, revelation, and redemption name the relations that structure the reality we inhabit, between ourselves and the world, and, so Rosenzweig surmises, between the world, us, and God. The fact that one of these relations, redemption, is chiefly between us and the world gives Rosenzweig room to account for the secularists, atheists, and agnostics among us. We can inhabit that relation without expressly acknowledging the divine presence. But then, for Rosenzweig, all of us, of whatever religion or belief structure, inhabit the real world. It is just that, for Rosenzweig, only Judaism (and Christianity) offer up liturgical structures that expressly and pointedly, over and over, on microcosmic and macrocosmic levels, *model* for us the relations that constitute reality. Otherwise put, reality held up to a mirror comes back to us fully and accurately reflected only in the liturgical structures of Judaism and Christianity, and in no other religion or philosophy—a bold claim indeed; and a hint at the appeal and danger of such systematizing philosophy as Rosenzweig practices.

For the philosophical system, whether Plato's, Aristotle's, Spinoza's, Kant's, or Hegel's, has always appealed by way of its claims to accurately mirror reality. The philosophical system is like the blueprints of a building that, unearthed after its completion, reveal the underlying physics and geometry of its construction. The philosophical system has surprises in store as it repositions common elements of reality within its structure. Kant's system does this, famously, for the artwork, which shows itself within his system as nature curiously repurposed. While science uncovers for us the diverse purposes the varied elements of nature serve in their causal relations with each other, the artwork shows itself an organism whose purpose is its own self. But it is the scientific structures of cause and effect that underlie the appearance of

---

70. *Gates of Prayer*, 129–31.
71. Rosenzweig, *Franz Rosenzweig's "The New Thinking,"* 69.

the artwork and allow for it to be at all. Kant's analysis may uncover for us features of art we previously missed. For instance, it makes sense on Kant's grounds to frame a picture. The picture frame cues the viewer that what's inside is free of relations to everything outside and has for its purpose nothing but itself. Art is for art's sake.

The problem with the philosophical system, its danger even, is when it locates an element of reality in a place that, in our judgment, distorts its nature. For most Jews, this happens in Kant's case over the location of Judaism within his moral system. Since for Kant the worth of a religion is in its ethics, and the worth of an ethics is in the autonomy of its agents, Judaism in his view fails as a religion on account of the heteronomy of its ethics, which is imposed by God. We can read part of Rosenzweig's own system as an answer to this charge. True, the commandments come from God but not by way of constricting our agency, rather by empowering it. The constriction is all on God's part. We, by contrast, expand in our empowerment to *do* the chief commandment, which is to receive the divine love.

Many features of the Jewish festivals may well be newly and attractively framed for us by Rosenzweig's analysis and shed a new light on at least the liturgical commandments. For example, the succession of Sabbaths do not just recall creation, they enact it by laying the foundation for (creating) the liturgical year (SR330). We might appreciate there the matching of form and content. The Sabbaths, in effect, walk their talk; though paradoxically, they "work" in sum to build the liturgical year. Rosenzweig may also waken us to a purpose the Sabbath rest serves beyond itself, to heighten our capacity for "silence and listening" (SR333)—for the love command, we may presume. A learned and ecumenical imam once repunctuated the Shema this way: Hear, O Israel, the Lord! Our God the Lord is one.[72] That is, O Israel, now is the time for you to *hear* God—the claim *about* God (that God is one) is more an afterthought. I think Rosenzweig would delight in this interpretation of the Shema, which fits so well his understanding of the Sabbath as a day for accentuated listening. This punctuation makes of the command to hear a frame for the command to love. It is as though the Sabbath is appointed, under a rubric of creation, as the time for ever renewed hearing of the love command,

---

72. Thanks to Imam Feisal Abdul Rauf for sharing with me his creative and insightful alternative punctuating of the Shema. It might well have taken a Muslim, accustomed to the public call to prayer, to do it!

which inaugurates both revelation and a ritually Jewish life, which in turn incorporates within it visions of redemption.

Passover and Yom Kippur, which mark the two festivals within the cycle of sacred times that even many secular Jews observe, may also appear in a new light. They build on the accentuated listening of the Shabbats toward an increasingly expansive community, as though the love received at Shabbats extends broadly outward. At the seder table, Passover opens the Jewish community to its widest limit by spotlighting the youngest child present, who traditionally asks the Four Questions. He "stands ... on the outermost edge of the circle" (SR337) of the community, which might hold within it the "wicked" child the Haggadah cites, or anyone who has struggled on the margins of Jewish community, whether women, unmarried adults, childless adults, LGBTQ+ individuals, or philosophers (though Rosenzweig does not himself itemize these). Then, this inclusiveness broadens still further at Yom Kippur, the high festival of redemption, when, according to Rosenzweig's radical interpretation, the Jewishness of the confessing people pales before their simple humanity; they stand "in the sin of man simply" (SR344) and so by implication in the forgiveness for all. The Yom Kippur gathering implicitly includes all humanity (SR344–45). Rosenzweig's visions of the Sabbath, Passover, and Yom Kippur cohere into a picture of love-transmissive listening so actively inclusive it expands to embrace all that lives and breathes.

Rosenzweig has one more approach to ritual that we may wrest from him, though against his wishes, since within his own system it applies only to Christianity, and that is to regard it as applied art. Under the rubric of suffering, in chapter 2, we already heard Rosenzweig reflect that art has a healing, not explanatory, role in our lives. Art structured suffering without explaining it. It eased suffering by externalizing it for us in an art object we could appreciate. Art was not for its own sake but for ours. But art serves another end beyond itself: at its best it is *for* religion (SR375). This was against a backdrop of German philosophizing about art that elevated it to the status of revelation itself. According to that tradition of thinking, the depth of reality disclosed itself best through art.[73] Rosenzweig would have known this view of art as itself religion within

---

73. This was a tenet of early German romanticism, to be found in the works of Novalis, the Schlegel brothers, and Schelling. See for example Schelling, *Philosophy of Art*. Hegel, for his part, titled a section of his highly influential *Phenomenology of Spirit* "Religion in the Form of Art" (424–53). One of the most sustained and culminating arguments for this view is Schopenhauer's.

his framework of assimilated, bourgeois German Jewry. For many Jews, Judaism was best experienced through visits to Jewish museums, which put ritual objects such as menorahs, tallits, Torah scrolls, binders, and finials on display for their aesthetic appeal, to say nothing of works by the few overtly German Jewish painters of note, such as Moritz Oppenheim (1800–1882).[74] But for Rosenzweig this was not living religion, and art on its own presumed to deeper insights than it actually supplied. It was fundamentally self-enclosed, as Kant had implied, divorced from the reality outside it, *not* revelatory. It was at worst "a dreamland of egoism" (SR376), filled by concert performances and museum exhibits that afforded no real escape from the harshness of reality outside them (SR360).

And yet, Rosenzweig knew the glories of Christian art all around him. Christianity, he opined, had made a bargain with the arts, to supply the steps by which the faithful approach the heart of Christian ritual experience. A key difference of Christians from Jews is that they are not born into their Christianity, as Jews are into their Jewishness. And so they must always and again, even after baptism, be led into it. The arts can and do serve this purpose for the church. They may begin in the human imagination, but they end as handmaids to the Christian take on creation, revelation, and redemption, which the Christian liturgical calendar, just like the Jewish one, images forth. If Jews had the commandments to guide them, step by step, into a Judaism they had lost, Christians of all stripes had the arts to escort them routinely into the heights of worship that they must always effortfully re-enter. Rosenzweig focused on three: architecture, which set the space for liturgical experience; music, which gathered the community for worship; and dance, understood to subsume gesture, which realized the community in fullness. These, too, follow the pattern of working in the service, respectively, of creation, revelation, and redemption. And so we read of architecture that it "creates a united space" (SR378) of gathering (SR377); of music, that it reveals the succession of time-points in which revelation occurs (SR381); and of dance that it redeems individuals from their isolation by uniting them in common gestures of greeting, bowing, processing (SR394). Anyone who has witnessed a solemn procession of the cross on Easter day or the choreography of priestly movement during mass at the altar of, say, an Episcopal or Catholic church, toward the cross,

---

74. Michael Brenner notes that in Weimar Germany, among many non-observant Jews, "places of memory, such as archives and monuments . . . had replaced . . . spontaneous collective memory" (Brenner, *Renaissance*, 4–5).

the congregation, and the elements of the Eucharist—the turning, the bowing, the lifting, the motions of the hands—knows what Rosenzweig means by the role of dance in the Christian liturgy.

Rosenzweig did not think of Judaism in artistic terms. He had every reason not to. There is no commandment addressed to the whole people to be artistic or fashion artworks. If anything, the second of the Ten Commandments discourages creative artistry. Significantly, the one figure in the Torah who might hold the place of Artist, because he produces the objects of the sanctuary commanded by God, is Bezalel, whose very name means "In the Shadow of God." Artworks are sanctioned in the Bible only to the extent that God directs them. And so the Jewish museums have every right to fill their exhibit cases with Torah binders and finials, for these derive some divine warrant from the biblical prescriptions for worship in the ancient tabernacle. This is as far as Jewish art, under the aegis of the commandments, can go. Nonetheless, as philosophers of the very viability of commandments, we are not bound by their restrictions. Rosenzweig himself would have known of gorgeous synagogue buildings in Frankfurt, where he lived, and beyond. But he would have said of them that their artistry, unlike that of the church building, was inessential, perhaps even pointlessly diverting from the Jew's true escort into ritual life, which was the primal love command and all of the 613 brethren designed to bear it. But we need not agree with him. If the artistry of the synagogue building and its appointments attract us, let them work their magic on us. The same holds true for what Rosenzweig deems the other key Christian arts: music and dance. Even one reared in the aesthetic of western European music can hear in non-Orthodox services the strains of Handel and of Schubert, who, commissioned by the Viennese cantor Salomon Sulzer, set to music the Hebrew of Psalm 92, to say nothing of works composed by Solomon de Rossi and Leonard Bernstein. As for dance, the procession with the Torah, the *hakafah*, may stir as much unitive feeling of hopefulness in a Jew as that with the cross, within a church service, does in a Christian.[75]

But in the end, the appeal of Rosenzweig will be to a certain kind of philosopher: the systematizer, who longs for structures in which to locate the objects and energies of the surrounding world. Rosenzweig's system is a marvel of ingenuity. Manfred Vogel calls it a "philosophical/

---

75. Rosenzweig associates processions, especially ones that exit the church or synagogue, with the work of redemption, in that they move the work of worship and of the love command out into the wider world.

theological edifice."[76] Our last philosopher takes an almost opposite approach. He will not locate ritual practices in a larger system, or rationalize them, aestheticize them, or subordinate them to any end beyond themselves, even toward a closer relation with the deity. He invests them with a solicitous voice of their own. After the model of art for art's sake, they are commandments for their own sake. It is as though prescribed words of prayer issue their own command to be spoken. Those of us who speak them are simply conduits of their self-expression. This is Yeshayahu Leibowitz (1903–1994), an Orthodox thinker who carried the epithet "the conscience of Israel," for his outspoken critiques of Israeli government policy.

Leibowitz, a chemist by trade, revered Maimonides, "the greatest of Jewish believers since the biblical age."[77] They shared an esteem for the science of their respective eras, which prioritized explanations in terms of cause and effect. But Leibowitz departs markedly from Maimonides in his view of the law. His signature thought is that the mitzvot demand observance for their own sake and not for any desirable consequence that may accrue from practicing them. "Halacha . . . cannot admit of utilitarian justification" (19) or warrant as "psychological phenomenon" (17). As over against Maimonides, they are not "expressions of philosophic cognition" (17), or indeed of anything we might identify with "philosophy, literature, [or] art" (7). The practice of them is for many likely to be "cheerless" (71) in that they "constitute constraints upon human nature" (20), not fulfillments of it. This is the marvel of the commandments, that they invite a ritual life that is "contrary to nature, both nature in general and human nature" (22), and in so doing lift us above them both. And yet they operate with full regard for "the world as it is" (70), not as we wish it would be, and subject to "the bondage of raw nature" (21).

Leibowitz is here responding, in part, to a worry that hovers over all those rationalistic defenses of the commandments, from Maimonides to Mendelssohn, that the very subordination of the mitzvot to an end beyond them "runs the danger of allowing, if not encouraging, the substitution of other regimens that appear to be more conducive to the attaining of that end,"[78] as Howard Kreisel neatly puts it. If wordless contemplation was the desired end of mitzvot observance, as Maimonides hints, or

---

76. Vogel, *Rosenzweig*, 2.

77. Leibowitz, *Judaism*, 39. Subsequent citations to pages of this text are given parenthetically. See also Leibowitz, *Faith of Maimonides*.

78. Kreisel, "Asceticism," 13.

awareness of reasoned truths, as Mendelssohn suggests, then the point of them seems to evaporate if better means to the same ends arise. Leibowitz is so concerned to block those possible outcomes that he withholds from the law any end beyond itself it might serve. We might say it is to be without *means*, even to the point of meaninglessness.

That is an extreme, even outrageous, way to state the case, though Leibowitz might like it better for that. Nonetheless, his view has precedents in both the rabbinic and philosophical traditions, which join forces to make his point. The rabbinic thought is that we should indeed observe the commandments without any anticipation of reward. "Whoever occupies himself with the Torah for its own sake, his learning becomes an elixir of life to him,"[79] says the Talmudic passage that Leibowitz cites (61) in support of his position. The philosophic thought comes from Immanuel Kant, "the greatest of ethical theorists" (63), according to whom our free conformity to the moral law within us lifts us above the natural world we inhabit, determined in all its doings by morally indifferent cause-effect relationships, including our own animal nature. To agree with Kant, Leibowitz would have only to replace "a pure law of reason" with "the mitzvot" in this encomium from the German philosopher we already read in the previous chapter: "it is a very sublime thing in human nature to be determined to actions directly by a pure law of reason,"[80] and not consideration of our own interests.

The Kantian precedent is especially germane to our purpose as it suggests the imperative of the law does not descend on us, restrictively, from the outside but rises up from within ourselves. Whatever apodictic quality it has for humans, or more specifically for Jews, is self-imposed. That accords with one version of Kant's categorical imperative: that the moral laws we obey be ones we self-issue. Leibowitz does not assimilate himself that tightly to Kant, but he comes close when he insists that the voice of the mitzvot precedes "recognition of the Giver of the Torah" (5). This is so much true that Leibowitz can invite us to question that "the world was created by the will of God, and that he liberated our forefathers from Egypt and that he revealed himself to them on Mount Sinai and that the Torah was given from heaven" (75). We can let all of that go for it is all story that contextualizes the law, and presumes to authorize it, when

---

79. b. Ta'anith 7a. The passage continues, "But whoever occupies himself with the Torah not for its own sake, it becomes to him a deadly poison," as cited by Leibowitz, *Judaism*, 61. See also https://www.sefaria.org/Taanit.7a.5?lang=bi.

80. Kant, *Critique of Practical Reason*, 123.

the law is self-authorizing. If we hear its voice address us, it can only be because we have so internalized it that we address ourselves through it, as Kant would have it. The mitzvot function effectively as Kant's practical reason, commanding us from within us.

Of course, once we internalize the law, the contextualization of it within Torah comes along with it. And so we admit the stories of creation and revelation to our inner life, too; but only *after* having taken the autonomous law upon ourselves. Since Jews are not born with the law inside them—so natural an internalization of law happens only in the end time, or so implies Jer 31:33—Leibowitz needs to *commend* it to his possibly skeptical and secular readers. And so he does, by arguing that the only thing that has not divided Jews "over a period of three thousand years," and preserved for them "a constant identity ... was embodied solely in the mitzvot" (6)—a prioritization of the religion that oddly recalls that self-described renegade from Judaism and Jewishness, Shlomo Sand. Leibowitz seems to say: Observing the law is a choice Jews have autonomously to internalize the autonomous law, and here is a good reason to make it, that the law is so very anciently unifying. This accords with our own negation of ritual authorized by *heteronomous* law imposed upon us. (Of course, it also invests the law with something Leibowitz is at pains to deny it: a purpose beyond itself.) We self-impose the law. And then it commands without regard for any of our interests or goals, just as the categorical imperative does within the Kantian framework.

Leibowitz does not say it, but the logic of his stance seems to require the kind of self-division between good will and desire that informs Kantian ethics. Leibowitz lauds the will that in obedience to law disregards desire. This affront to desire is the face of law that remains in view once any effort to ground it in factors or agencies beyond it, such as a creator God or Sinaitic revelation, are negated. Here Leibowitz evokes that asceticism we encountered in Jewish philosophical ethics, especially Bahya and Maimonides. But it is quite a different law from the one Maimonides defended on account of its utility, or Mendelssohn, for its witness to truths, or Rosenzweig, for its encasement of love. But it is exalting, even without having that for a goal. The law exalts by way of the translation it effects between the observance of itself and love of God. The one is not a means to or expression of the other. The law never sublimates itself to any end beyond itself. Mitzvot observance *is* the love of God.

"Love of God is but the observance of the mitzvot" (73). The "but" is key, for it implies that whatever more than mitzvot observance the love of God pretends to be, it is not. Meantime, the mitzvot rise to the station of God—the replacement of God?—by the love for God their observance constitutes. Leibowitz's departure here from Rosenzweig on the relation between commandment, love, and God, will further illuminate his position. For Rosenzweig, the point of the *law* to love God with all our heart, mind, and soul, given at Deut 6:5 is to waken us to the *command* that comes from God to Love me! Deut 6:5 is the legal transcription of the love command, which can only be *heard*, not read. But for Leibowitz, the law as it stands is effectively "unintelligible" (44) since, as Rosenzweig himself concedes, love cannot be commanded. So Deuteronomy continues with the actual meaning of the law to love God, which is to enact "these words which I command thee this day" (Deut 6:6), that is, to do the mitzvot that follow in the text. Unlike Rosenzweig's God, Leibowitz's is not so personal as to speak at all. But no matter, since the mitzvot themselves tell us what it means to love God. All the more sublime is our service of God if we do not even hear the God that commands it, since all the more impossible is it then for us to anticipate any divine reward for our service. But we will return to this God in the next chapter.

Helpfully in sync with our own negations, Leibowitz here uncovers yet another application of the contentless content. He goes so far as to attach the word *meaningless* to the commandments.[81] They are meaningless in the same way liturgical Hebrew was, in Rosenzweig's view, for interpersonal communication among Jews at prayer, since the addressee of prayer is God. Their emptiness of inter-human communicative meaning allies with the absence of descriptive content we suggested informs Jewish identity and God's, useless suffering, and revelation. Indefinable Jews observing meaningless mitzvot in worship of a contentless God make a coherent if Kafkaesque picture.

That picture is not as remote from practice as it seems. Insofar as what makes a Jew observant are the *ritual* laws she follows, not the ethical ones, Leibowitz's take on the law for Jews positions ritual front and center. If, as Leibowitz claims, the law has sustained the cohesiveness of Jewish community for centuries, it is not the ethics (shared with many others) that has done so but the distinctive ritual, as Mendelssohn opined. For Buber, Leibowitz's approach to ritual would seem itself idolatrous by the God-supplanting commitment it draws. Leibowitz would respond that, on the contrary, his own approach to ritual witnesses to the highest

---

81. "Most of the mitzvot are meaningless except as expressions of worship" (Leibowitz, *Judaism*, 6).

worship of God, practiced without hope of reward, even of the vaunted (by Buber) encounter with God. The hope of relation with God can be so absent for Leibowitz and so seemingly supplanted by mitzvot observance that he begins to sound atheistic. No wonder Yeshiva University philosophy professor Daniel Rynhold could title a lecture he delivered on Leibowitz's thought "Orthodox Atheism."[82]

The coinage is not far-fetched. In a now classic article on the tenor of modern Orthodox Judaism, Haym Soloveitchik explores the diminution within the community of any live or lived sense of God behind the ritual observances. Ritual has indeed taken on a life of its own. This, he suggests, is because the penumbra of inherited custom and spirituality that had once surrounded and infused the community, and rendered more flexible its approach to law, has attenuated. Transplantings from traditional European societies to secular pluralist ones in America took their toll. Science also made its claims: "Modern science ... had reduced nature to ... an immutable nexus of cause and effect which suffices on its own to explain the workings of the world."[83] (Leibowitz, a scientist himself, would agree.) In addition, bureaucratic modernity could not but inflect religious practice. "The world now experienced by religious Jews ... is rule-oriented and in the broadest sense of the term rational," understood as "governed by regulations, mostly written, and interpreted by experts."[84] Under these conditions, a soft observance of ritual grew hard. The quest was for authorized accuracy in keeping the rituals. There arose "a flood of [written] works on ... correct ritual performance ... of what had previously been routine acts"[85] executed by heart, in both senses of that term: by memory and out of loving attachment. But now, the ritual law served to fill the breach left by the

82. Rynhold, "Orthodox Atheism."

83. Soloveitchik, "Rupture," 102.

84. Soloveitchik, "Rupture," 87. Soloveitchik concludes, revealing his sense of loss, "The perception of God as a daily, natural force is no longer present to a significant degree in any sector of modern Jewry [and] ... individual Divine providence ... is no longer experienced as a simple reality. With the shrinkage of God's palpable hand in human affairs has come a marked loss of His immediate presence, with its primal fear and nurturing comfort.... Religious Jews seek to ground their new emerging spirituality less on a now unavailable intimacy with Him than on an intimacy with His will, avidly eliciting Its intricate demands and saturating their daily lives with Its exactions. Having lost the touch of His presence, they seek now solace in the pressure of His yoke" ("Rupture," 103).

85. Soloveitchik, "Rupture," 71.

departed divine Presence and normalize for Jewish practice the ideal reigning in the secular society of written regulation.

Perhaps Orthodox atheism, if less provocatively named, has itself become accepted practice within modern Jewish Orthodoxy. Twenty years after Soloveitchik's article appeared in the Orthodox journal *Tradition*, *Commentary* magazine ran a piece titled "The Rise of Social Orthodoxy," which celebrated what Soloveitchik had appeared to regret. "Social Orthodox Jews are observant . . . in service of Jewish culture and Jewish community . . . and the survival of the Jewish people . . . and not because they are trembling before God," but for "the powerful feeling of belonging.[86] The tone of the writing is both prideful and exultant. The writer practices the advice already implied by the title of a book by Orthodox thinker Donniel Hartman, *Putting God Second: How to Save Religion from Itself*. As Daniel Korobkin neatly summarizes, "Being Orthodox can mean observance devoid of God, and for some [many?], that's just fine."[87]

Whether we call it Orthodox Atheism or Social Orthodoxy, the phenomenon so named certainly evokes the philosophy of Yeshayahu Leibowitz. University of Haifa philosophy professor Daniel Statman explicitly links Soloveitchik to Leibowitz. "How interesting it is that the philosopher [Leibowitz] and the social historian [Soloveitchik] have come up here with more or less the same picture [of modern Orthodoxy]."[88] The agreement is so striking to Statman that he suggests Leibowitz, "far from being an eccentric philosopher with radical views . . . seems to express . . . the true *zeitgeist* of contemporary Orthodoxy."[89]

If so, these cannot be glad tidings for Haym Soloveitchik, who wrote ruefully of this trend in 1994. He could certainly draw backing from the tradition. We can imagine Mendelssohn also regretting what would seem to him embedded in this turn of events: an idolatry of the written word, invested with too much guiding authority. Joining this emergent chorus of regret might be the historian of Jewish philosophy Julius Guttmann (1880–1950), who, as Paul Mendes-Flohr tells us, "was deeply vexed by . . .

---

86. Lefkowitz, "Rise," 40, 42.

87. Korobkin, "Rupture," 66. This observation applies even more readily to Reform and Conservative Jews, to the extent they practice the ritual mitzvot. Rabbi Arnold Jacob Wolf, *z"l*, a brilliant Reform rabbi and teacher, once suggested to his congregation, K.A.M. Israel in Chicago, that the point of the law was to preoccupy Jewish minds *away* from God, which/who as focus of cognitive attention could only disturb.

88. Statman, "Negative Theology," 70.

89. Statman, "Negative Theology," 70.

the tendency to divorce the mitzvot from their religious basis."[90] Perhaps Buber, for all the marginalization he suffered among Jews for his departure from ritual law, could serve, ironically, in the spiritual rejuvenation of it. A dialogue between Buber and Leibowitz is not unthinkable. Buber almost invites a conversation with Leibowitz when he writes in an early work, "One can be a rationalist, a freethinker, or an atheist in a religious sense."[91] Their understandings of the Divine in places converge. For neither, as over against Rosenzweig, does God really issue commands in the first place. And this might be the beginning of a rapprochement between God-intoxicated Buber and God-avoidant Leibowitz. But such a meeting can no longer postpone the question: Who or what is God?

---

90. Mendes-Flohr, "Law and Sacrament," 325.
91. Buber, *On Judaism*, 154.

Chapter 9
God

THE PEW RESEARCH STUDY of Jewish identity reports that a minority of American Jews, 26 percent, take seriously the idea of God.[1] So the majority of American Jews have already negated this concept, whether expressly or by inattention to it. It cannot be our place here to examine why, though we can briefly adduce a combination of four likely causes: the Enlightenment, the Emancipation, the Holocaust, and political Zionism. Of course, there has always been a preference among Jews to circumvent the naming of God. This is to take to heart the third of the Ten Commandments, against profaning God's name. Instead of expressly naming God, many Jews have preferred outside of liturgical contexts to reference simply The Name (*haShem*). Or, if a response of "*Here* am I" (Isa 6:8) to a summons from God implies a *There* that God occupies, some Jews might prefer to reference God as The Place (*haMakom*). But these circumlocutions have more to do with a surfeit of feeling for the presence of God, not a deficit.

We will not join this pervasive negation of God. On the contrary, these last chapters are an effort to resuscitate the idea. And we do so by way of the theological tradition that has inspired us all along, that of negative theology. But now we are speaking expressly of God. And we will do so by way of negation, as Maimonides models for all drawn to this tradition,[2] and in keeping with our practice of negation throughout

---

1. Pew Research Center, *Jewish Americans in 2020*.

2. For more on the import of negative theology for Jewish philosophy, see Fagenblat, *Negative Theology as Jewish Modernity*; Seeskin, "Positive Contribution of

this book. Let Buber, who ended the previous chapter, start us off. What did he have to say about God? In response to Hermann Cohen, who believed that God was an idea, Buber wrote that God "is more exalted than the ideal sphere." In response to Plato, who divinized the idea of the Good, Buber wrote that "God is not the Good [but] . . . the Super-good." And in response to all anthropomorphisms of God, especially those that would assimilate God to personhood, so that we might claim, "God 'is' a personality," Buber wrote, "the *absolute personality* we call God . . . prohibits any such statement."[3] Pressed to fix God with a qualifier, Buber came up instead with a name: the Eternal Thou. And by that he meant a partner in the I-Thou relation that never reverted to an It. So this name too was fundamentally a negation.

Buber illustrates one reason a philosopher might be driven to negative theology: that God is just too close to us to admit of discursive descriptions of any kind. We need some distance from any object we might describe and insofar as God is real to us in I-Thou relation, that distance is not available. As Michael Fagenblat puts it, "Jews cannot see God because God is too close."[4] So it is best simply not to try to speak *about* God at all. On the other hand, as though to invert that argument, it might be just because God is too far from us, or too hidden, that we cannot speak about God. It was after all Buber who authored the book *The Eclipse of God*, with its provocative subtitle: *Studies in the Relation Between Religion and Philosophy*. Finally, a motive for negative theology might be that in the transcendent unity of God, there is no space to distinguish between distinct divine qualities.

That last notion is an evocative idea that promises a rapprochement between believers and atheists. From the standpoint of negative theology, these are not so distant as they seem. The novelist Thomas Mann put it this way, thinking of being without qualities, that it "would then be divested of all but being, unqualitied [without qualities], which would be very like not-being, and perhaps not preferable to it."[5] Atheists and believers who argue may be talking at cross purposes if the atheist misreads

---

Negative Theology"; Rubinstein, "Spirituality of Philosophical Judaism"; and Wolfson, "Negative Theology."

3. Buber, *Eclipse of God*, 60.

4. Fagenblat, *Negative Theology*, 12. This recalls a line from the Quran where God proclaims with reference to humanity, "We are nearer to him than his jugular vein" (Quran 50:16). This translation is from *The Study Quran*.

5. Mann, *Doctor Faustus*, 103–4.

the believer's idea of God. As Elliot Wolfson has put it, "the proposition that God can be defined only in his indefinable nature is notionally on a par with both . . . the conviction of faith and the skepticism of doubt,"[6] and so also with a happy picture we have from Franz Rosenzweig of a space where "atheism and mysticism can shake hands"[7] (SR31).

These three approaches to negative theology divide up roughly according to three hallowed epistemologies from the history of western philosophy: rationalism, pragmatism, and empiricism. The rational negative theologians focus on the implications for reason of God's surpassing unity. Reason clearing a path to the contentless God by denying of It all It is not culminates in what philosopher David Blumenthal has called "intellectualistic spirituality."[8] The pragmatic negative theologians divert us from a God too distant from us toward a focus on our own God-inspired acts. "Pragmatic," from the Greek *pragma* for act, fits these thinkers well. The empirical negative theologians commend to us an experience of or encounter with God that, to employ the colloquial, is so much "in our face" that we lack the poise to respond in any reasoned way. We are simply transfixed and transformed. As though to connote that link, Rosenzweig coined for his philosophy the paradoxical phrase "absolute empiricism."[9] In this chapter, we select from philosophers already encountered instances of each type to illustrate it. Our rational negative theologians are Maimonides and Spinoza; our pragmatic ones, Ecclesiastes, Levinas, and Leibowitz; our empirical ones, Rosenzweig and Buber. And we start with Maimonides, who would be the patron saint, if such existed within Judaism, of negative theologians.

For Maimonides, God's unity implies a simplicity "which is extreme and ultimate" (GP145). Maimonides thinks that to ascribe *any* quality to God fractures the divine unity. A quality ascribed to God cannot but be an addition or attachment to a being—if God is "being"—already perfect. We could think of it this way: The ascribed quality appears to single out a facet of the divine that can be distinguished from other facets. But God is unfaceted. If God submits to qualities, then each quality is identical with every other, for otherwise the divine being would be faceted. God's wisdom, power, intellect, will, must all be one and the same. But then the very meaning of those distinct qualities evaporates in their identity with each

---

6. Wolfson, "Light Does Not Talk," 110.
7. Rosenzweig did not necessarily mean this approvingly, but we do!
8. Blumenthal, *Philosophic Mysticism*, 120.
9. Rosenzweig, *Franz Rosenzweig's "The New Thinking,"* 101.

TOWARD A NEGATIVE THEOLOGY OF JUDAISM

other. This applies even to the most basic "quality" of the divine oneness. God "is one [but] not through oneness" (GP132). We cannot attach even the notion of oneness to the essence of God (GP133). That is, what seems a positive attribution is actually a negation.

English supplies a convenient way to express how much qualities would demean the divine. We would have a *qualified* God, that is, a God who is not *really* God, just as, to render more believable an idealized account of some event, we might say, "let me qualify that." A qualified God is a compromised God. Maimonides thinks our common notions of God are so heavily qualified, almost infinitely so, that the sheer mental act of prying the qualities away, by way of reasoned argument, constitutes itself a way of apprehending or drawing close to God. For instance, if all physical bodies are faceted, or subject to qualities, then the divine unity cannot be embodied, since the unity already entails qualityless-ness. And so another verse from the Yigdal hymn comes to mind: *ve-eino guph*, and God has no body. There follows in the wake of this a string of attributes to be denied of God: affections, change, privation, potentiality, any similarity to other things. As Moshe Halbertal and Avishai Margalit put it, "Strict compliance with the demands of unity leads Maimonides to the exclusion of the possibility of any linguistic description of God."[10]

Lest we think that Maimonides is here clearing dubious, new theological ground, let us consider the Svetasvatara Upanishad (ca. 500 BCE), one of the sacred texts of Hinduism that precedes the medieval philosopher by some sixteen hundred years. The path Maimonides was walking was already well-paved, even if outside Judaism. According to that Upanishad, there was another qualityless being: the soul. The writer of the text struggles to understand the state of qualityless-ness. The soul "is of the measure of a thumb, of sun-like appearance, [but] . . . appears of the size of the point of an awl [or] . . . the hundredth part of the point of a hair subdivided a hundredfold, and yet it partakes of infinity."[11] We can hear the effort to employ the physical to access the non-physical, via a progression of ever-decreasing sizes. It is as though to realize, in the infinitesimally small, the infinite itself. That is where the soul resides. But according to the Upanishads, the soul *was* God in microcosm. So Maimonides is on track with the Upanishads here. We shall see in the next chapter the implications of this way of thinking for the spiritual life.

---

10. Halbertal and Margalit, *Idolatry*, 110.
11. Svetasvatara Upanishad 5:8–9, in *Thirteen Principal Upanishads*, 407.

For now, what comes to mind is Rosenzweig's picture of meeting between atheism and mysticism. The Buddhist commentary on Hinduism's qualityless soul was that, in its very qualityless-ness, it simply did not exist. For the perduring being the Hindus took for soul was actually, said the Buddhists, simply an ever-changing conglomerate of qualities that persisted through time. There was no underlying "being" that sustained it. Translated for relevance to our discussion: there *was* no God, or none to fret about, which is one of the doctrines of early Buddhism. And yet there is hardly a religion more inclined toward mysticism than Buddhism. The negative theologians might well grant that God does not exist. Only, for them, the reason is that *existence* itself is a compromising term applied to the deity. It cannot mean the same thing applied to God and to everything else (GP144). This line of argument might at least give us pause, that atheism may miss the point. The best thing to say about God is simply nothing or, Nothing, as historian Julius Guttmann, interpreting Nachman Krochmal, told us in chapter 5. The difference between belief and unbelief is the letter *n*: whether capitalized or lowercased in the word *N/nothing*.

It is striking that Maimonides believes the existence of a God so empty of predicates comprehensible to us can nonetheless be proved by us, even granting ambiguity over the predicate, *existent*, applied to God and us. He writes that it is possible for us "to come nearer to an apprehension of Him by means of investigation and research" (GP139). And one type of investigation is of arguments that purport to prove the existence of God. These are less interesting to us here for any validity they might have than for the additional contexts they provide to explore the workings of negative theology. The arguments for the existence of God have been around for a long time, at least since Aristotle, who argued that the fact of movement in the world, at all, implied a First and Unmoved Mover (Metaphysics 1072b); for, granting the impossibility of an infinite string of movers, there has to be one who started the whole string off or otherwise underlay the whole of it. Maimonides does advance that argument (GP243–46), but we are unlikely to be impressed by it. We have been doubting, since chapter 1, that any bridge logically or persuasively leads from a consideration of the world around us to God. Maimonides had other versions of what is sometimes called the cosmological argument and its cousins: from some fact of the cosmos around us to an originating God (GP246–49). Indeed he argued that no other proofs of God were possible (GP183). But if no such proofs exist for us, the Maimonidean case for God might seem closed to us.

But not entirely. Martin Buber started us off on what was, in effect, a Maimonidean argument to rethink our rejection of the God idea. The problem lay not so much in the brokenness of the presumed bridge from the existence of the world to God, as in our very notion of God itself. Buber and Maimonides in concert might argue that the argument for God's existence cannot even begin until we know what we are talking about. The problem is: we do not. And the admission of this not-knowing, deeply plumbed, can suddenly convert, they both suggest without quite saying so, into what Buber would call a relation with God, and Maimonides an *apprehension* of God, neither of which constitutes the kind of knowledge that could figure at the end of an argument. We have what is effectively a case of peripheral vision. We will never see what we are looking for if we expect it to submit to our full frontal gaze. It repels that from the start. But it might appear peripherally on the heels of a string of things we are led to believe it is *not*. So the string involved does not comprise causes and effects playing out in sequence, but rejected candidates for a content they cannot supply. Those candidates include the entirety of what is available to our five senses, which constitutes a great deal. If at the end of such a string we find ourselves either in relation with or apprehension of God, then we have traversed what Elliot Wolfson has helpfully called "an inversion of the cosmological argument."[12] He continues: "From the physical we know what cannot be true of the metaphysical, but this lack of knowledge serves to inspire" or we might even say, invoke—to borrow a term from the world of prayer—what the arguments for God fail to do.

We might call what dawns at the end of such a meditation an epiphany or, more faithfully to a previous chapter of this book: a revelation. A revelation is the opposite of an argument, to the extent the agency of it is not with ourselves. That may seem a departure from Maimonides's own view of revelation, as the necessary culmination of an intellectual ascent; except that even Maimonides allowed for the prophetic heights of that ascent to be withheld from us—withheld, he said, by God (GP361)—as though even he felt the need to preserve for revelation a transcendence of our own agency. It is as though a negative theological approach to God replaces argument as such with the dawning-upon-us somewhere along our negating course of thought of a contentless God-idea that pleads for

---

12. Wolfson, "Via Negativa," 378.

its own reality. But then, if negative theology points us back to revelation, it is not so much convincing us of God's existence, as positioning us for a relationship (Buber) or apprehension (Maimonides) it cannot itself directly supply; and may, in the end, not be supplied.

There is another kind of argument for God's existence that takes its bearing entirely from the God-idea, rather than from the world. This is the ontological argument. It is traced back to Saint Anselm (1033–1109), before Maimonides. As we already know from chapter 1, Maimonides himself did not advance it, but his express insistence on cosmological types of argument suggests he knew of it, or something like it. He may have missed an opportunity by not taking it up, to the extent it is itself a kind of negative theology, if only by way of its tortuous linguistic expression. We are to conceive a being than which we can conceive none greater, which must exist, for by its very non-existence it would fail to be that than which there was none greater. True, *existence* is here implicitly a content applied to God, a kind of predicate that is, as Maimonides says, "superadded" (GP126) to God, which he never tires of forbidding us to do. Apart from that, since the days of Maimonides, both Kant and Bertrand Russell undermined the argument by insisting *existence* is not a predicate to begin with because, according to Kant, it is a category of our understanding that underlies predication at all or, to Russell, a logical operator in predicate logic.

But even apart from those objections, to what content are we adding this presumed predicate? It is a content that seems ever to outstrip itself since it takes its measure for what it is from something always greater than itself, from something it not yet is. It may not be contentless, but it always implies a content beyond it to increase its greatness; and that, before it even receives its existence. The ontological argument recalls the Svetasvatara Upanishad, which takes us to the infinite by way of the ever-increasingly small. The ontological argument does the same, only by way of the ever-increasingly great. In both cases, we are riding on the curve of a hyperbola toward an asymptote we are formulaically defined to ever near but never reach, for that would be infinity, by definition unreachable. How could we describe the culmination of either process except in terms of a kind of mental stupefaction? But that is just where negative theology would take us in our effort to describe God.

In fact, Maimonides does tango a bit with the ontological argument, by way of the near immediacy it sights between an idea and its referent. Only in the case of God is the unity so great that "His existence is identical with His essence" (GP132), as we saw in chapter 6. That is, in effect, an abbreviated version of the ontological argument. Think of God (in essence); the existence follows instantly, for otherwise God's unity would be compromised. Good rabbi that he was, Maimonides made the argument biblically, by way of the divine names. Most of the biblical names for God are what Maimonides calls "derivative" (GP149), by which he means, names derived from an activity associated with God, such as creating and sustaining the world. For instance, the divine name Shaddai comes "from the word *day* [pronounced: *d'eye*] meaning a sufficiency," and connotes one "who is sufficient" (GP155) to the creation of reality. Part of the problem with these names is that they seem to connote (forbidden) attributes of God. Consequently, they are apt to mislead us. There is only one name that is not derivative and thereby innocent of any misleading connotations: the Tetragrammaton, YHWH. When Maimonides writes of this name that "no commonly accepted derivation of it is known and none other than He has a part in it" (GP148), he suggests that it emerges from within the very being of God, "indicative of the essence of Him" (GP148), rather like the divine names that, for the kabbalists, *expressed* God toward humans who read or pronounced them, or like *all* names in the Edenic language Walter Benjamin imagined. Benjamin interpreting Maimonides might say this name is a unique holdover from that language otherwise lost to us. But of course, for the kabbalists, the divine names are still efficacious expressions of God.

In fact, one of the derivative names can almost stand in for YHWH, for it indicates the same identification of essence with existence. This is the name *Ehyeh-Asher-Ehyeh* (Exod 3:14) from the story of the burning bush: I Am That I Am. The name is clearly derived, says Maimonides, from the Hebrew verb "to be": *hayah* (GP154). But it proclaims of God what YHWH expresses, that "the subject is identical with the predicate" instead of anything qualified by something "superadded" to it. "This makes clear that He is existent not through existence" (GP155), but through his essence, which is another formulation of the ontological argument. But then, these divine names no more prove the existence of God than either negative theology or the ontological argument do. They are rather set-ups for a revelation, that may or may not dawn. But we can hear Heschel saying on behalf of the Maimonides he so admired: why not give them a try? If nature fails to move us religiously, perhaps language can. After all, in our own exploration of the revelation-idea, language was the chief bearer of it, not nature.

There is one more religiously evocative feature for us to extract from Maimonides's arguments for the existence of God. This goes back to the oddity of the very endeavor to prove the existence of a being we cannot conceive. Maimonides's theology is not as negative as it might be. He allows for what he calls "attributes of action" (GP124) ascribed to God. These are acts God performs "resembling the actions that in us proceed from moral qualities" (GP124), but in God do not proceed from there, for God does not possess "moral qualities" in any way that resembles ours. On this basis even Maimonides can call God just and merciful, without actually attributing justice or mercy to the divine being. To repeat a phrasing we have already encountered: God is merciful but not through the attribute of mercy (for that would compromise the divine unity).

Maimonides needs the divine attributes of action, for otherwise he loses the creation doctrine we already saw in chapter 1 is so vulnerable, both for Maimonides and for us. Unless God *acts*, there is no creation. God creates, but not through the attribute of creativity. Maimonides finds wide scope for this interpretation of the biblical descriptions of God. For example, the biblical passage that underlies the rabbinic teaching of the Thirteen Attributes of God (Exod 34:6–7) is really citing divine acts that, performed by humans, would justify attributing to them those qualities cited in the passage, such as compassion, kindness, and forgiveness. For Maimonides, this passage is key to the transition Moses effects between the cosmic vision he enjoys and the practical laws he will prescribe for Israel (GP128). By way of this transition, theory becomes practice. Indeed, a stereotypical characterization of Judaism is of a religion so ritually and morally act-oriented that what it *means* to have a certain quality is to act a certain way. We shall find this line of thought among our pragmatic negative theologians. Maimonides's theory of the divine attributes of action boldly contests so flagrant a pragmatism. For in the case of God, the acts performed reflect nothing of the divine being. In that way, Maimonides introduces a startling disjunction between the inner and outer life of the divine. Even to *perform an act*, in the case of God, implies none of the things it does in the human context, that there be a conscious being intending a result of some kind within the reality we inhabit.

There is, for Maimonides, a human reflection of this divine disjunct between the inner and outer. It has to do with the very idea of *apprehension*. Maimonides is careful to deny us any *comprehension* of God, but not *apprehension*. The English word *apprehension* carries a connotation of tremor, even fear (awe), that is not inapt in the face of God. Elliot

Wolfson articulates one difference between *com*prehension and *appre*hension when he distinguishes between "discursive and intuitive forms of apprehension."[13] We comprehend something when we can discourse on it. Intuitive apprehension, however, occurs without the medium of discursive language (declarative statements). Maimonides needs this distinction if he is to allow that a path of negating the discursive opens onto an apprehension of God. But along the way he sets up a disjunct between our inner and outer lives that mirrors the one in God. For our apprehension of God can issue in no declarative statements about God. We can speak metaphorically and poetically, in hopes of evoking, or invoking, the same apprehension in an interlocutor. We cannot describe it. Maimonides confers on us a sanctum of inner life as divorced from the outward proclamations of the declarative voice as God's essence is from God's acts. "The magnification of God does not consist in . . . saying improper things but in . . . understanding [apprehending] properly" (GP142), for the language subject to error need not infect the mind (GP111). If this is one way in which we are created in the image of God, it is no wonder Maimonides considers silence the highest praise of God (GP139). This is already implied by the odd forms discursive language takes when it presumes to take God for object (GP132): to be one without the attribute of oneness, indeed! Language may be a medium of revelation, but it cannot, for Maimonides, supply the highest content of revelation. At the goal of all speaking, words fail. These notions are rich in import for the spiritual life, the topic of our next chapter.

One way to further reflect on Maimonides's views of God, and "apprehend" them in a different way, is by way of Spinoza. Scholars disagree on how much is in common between these two. We take Spinoza for a radical evolution of Maimonides. We move from the uniquely united God to Nothing but God. Let us start with the very notion of qualities, or attributes. We know that, for Maimonides, there are only two kinds of attributes predicable of God, those of negation (GP135) and those of action (GP124). And we know that the attributes of negation, in particular, culminate—or can—in the apprehension of God (GP135). What is distinctive about these attributes, though, is that they fail to qualify God in God's own being. God remains unqualified even over the "attribution" of these actions and negations to God.

---

13. Wolfson, "Via Negativa," 402.

Spinoza inherits the vocabulary of attributes and applies it, also, to God. But if Maimonides's concern was to protect the absolute uniqueness of God, Spinoza's is to protect the absolute self-sufficiency of God. Spinoza's God, like Maimonides's, uniquely enjoys an existence that follows on essence. Now the ontological argument surfaces in full force, and in all its deceptive simplicity: If God does not exist, "his essence does not involve existence. But this is absurd. Therefore God necessarily exists" (E1p11). It is absurd for God not to exist since the very idea of that than which we can conceive nothing greater involves existence. What strikes Spinoza about this God idea, though, is not the distinctive unity (between essence and existence) it asserts that God enjoys, but the distinctive independence it implies God has from everything else. Since God exists out of the very idea of God, God depends on nothing else not only for God's existence but for the very idea of God. And so we read in Spinoza this characterization of God: "that which is in itself and is conceived through itself" (E1d3)—a double self-sufficiency.

Of course, if the idea of God is dependent on no other idea, it winds up being as empty of content as Maimonides's God-idea. For if the God-idea required another idea for its formulation, it would not be as independent as Spinoza claims it is. But an idea like no other cannot be defined. It lacks describable content. It cannot appear as a defined item within a dictionary. As Spinoza characterizes his God-idea, it turns out to be very like Maimonides's in the negations it draws to itself. Apart from being self-conceived, God is also infinite and eternal (E1d6). But these are also negations: the first of finitude and the second of placement in time. Infinity itself confirms that God cannot be defined, since *definition* implicitly asserts *finitude*, as the two words in tandem suggest. And Spinoza's "definition" of God is a negation: "By God I mean an absolutely infinite being" (E1d6).

And now for the attributes of God. What manifests the infinity of God are God's "infinite attributes, each of which expresses eternal and infinite essence" (E1d6). Suddenly Spinoza appears to have departed markedly from Maimonides. Far from having just two kinds of attributes—of action, of negation—God now appears to enjoy an infinity of them. This is *how* God is infinite, or at least one way God is. We in our finitude cannot know them all. But according to Spinoza, two of them saturate our lives and experience: thought and extension (E2p1, E2p2). We can think of "extension" as the receptacle of all physicality. Spinoza is invoking a time-honored philosophical distinction between body and mind. Already we are puzzled: by their very grammar, these two are not qualities, in the shape of adjectives, but "things," or perhaps processes, in the shape of nouns. (Descartes, whom Spinoza took for a teacher, understood them to be substances.) It would never have occurred to Maimonides to attribute these to God, even to exemplify error. Indeed, if attributing extension to God implies God has a body, Maimonides would be horrified. Spinoza does indeed claim that "God is an extended thing" (E2p2), as well as a "thinking thing" (E2p1). But does that mean God has a body? Or that God "thinks"? We need to take care here. Spinoza tells us that whatever intellect may be for God, it is not the same for us (E1p17c2s); the same is true of divine "power" (E2p3s). Here Spinoza sounds like Maimonides writing on amphibolous terms. Just as the Maimonidean God is not one through oneness, the Spinozan God does not think through thinking.

Attributes are peculiar things in Spinoza. He writes, "By attribute I mean that which the intellect perceives of substance as constituting its essence" (E1d4). Substance, for its part, is "that which is in itself and is conceived through itself" (E1p3). But then substance is really a synonym for God (E1p14), highlighting the divine in its sublime self-sufficiency. So attributes are an intellectual perception of God. They do not so much qualify God as *us*, i.e., how we perceive God. They are a lens on the divine customized to our intellects. With this notion Spinoza seems back in sync with Maimonides, for whom the attributes of God were also a means for us to apprehend God, without compromising the divine unity. Negative and active attributes do not of their own supply content to the God idea. If Spinoza follows Maimonides, thought and extension would also be means for us to apprehend God, but without supplying content to the God idea.

In fact, thought and extension turn out to be formidable abstractions. To begin with, they are infinite (E1p21). This is already implied by Spinoza's definition of God, each of whose attributes expresses infinite essence (E1d6). No sum of individual thoughts we might have or imagine others to have supplies the content of thought. Perhaps we are, once again, to conceive an infinite series approaching a limit that is never reached. That is where thought comes into view. Extension is even more a challenge to our intellects. Extension is not so much the sum total of physical things as the infinite receptacle of the physical. Spinoza offers a simplified take on it through the idea of quantity. Our imagination, he says, finds quantity to be "finite, divisible, and made up of parts. But if we consider it intellectually ...—and this is very difficult—then it will be found to be infinite, one, and indivisible" (E1p15s). It is that parenthetical reference to how difficult a concept quantity is—and by implication, extension is—that must give us pause. How much content do these attributes of God actually attribute to God?

Spinoza's other characterization of the attributes supplies a possible answer: little to no positive content. According to the definition of God, each of the divine attributes "expresses infinite and eternal essence" (E1d6). The attributes are in the business of *expressing* God, not characterizing God in some contentful, declarative way. Here it helps to recall the role of *expression* in revelation, as we explored that phenomenon in chapter 6. The divine love-command in Rosenzweig carried love to the receptive soul, but it made no statement about either God or love. The divine names as Scholem taught us were a window onto the divine, not a description of it. The Edenic language Adam spoke, as Benjamin opined, presented the very things named, did not describe them. But we need go no further afield from our context just now than Maimonides himself. For even he helpfully distinguished between the derived names of God and the one, underived name, YHWH, which, like existence itself, flowed forth from God's essence. The attributes of God, as Spinoza understands them, work as YHWH does in Maimonides's world to position us for an apprehension of God. Just as YHWH within the world of divine names shares with God a uniqueness, so thought and extension, unlike any of the individual thoughts or physical things in our experience, share with God infinity, which is a negation of finitude. They are "things" distinct from God that express God but provide no more content for the God idea than does YHWH in Maimonides's biblical worldview. As Rebecca Goldstein puts it, what Spinoza gives us in his Godward orientation is "the View from Nowhere,"[14] a place of Nothing.

Spinoza is famous for coining the phrase God or Nature (E4preface), to imply a kind of equivalence between those two terms—but only a *kind* of equivalence. It is like the equivalence between God and God's unique name, YHWH. They are intimately related. But they are not the same. They inhabit different orders of reality. The one is the one necessary being (Maimonides, GP1 32) or absolutely infinite being (Spinoza, E1d6). The other is a name. The one *expresses* in the domain of names what the other *is* in the domain of being, if *being* is not already too limiting a characterization. Even the prayerbook understands their relation when,

14. Goldstein, *Betraying Spinoza*, 192.

by way of the Alenu prayer, it hopes at the end of time "God shall be One and God's Name shall be One." It is important to the prayer to indicate both God *and* God's name, implying they are not obviously identical. The two shall be One in concert across their different (and separate) orders of being. We can take a like relation to hold between God and God's attributes within Spinoza's schema. The attributes name features of nature that exhaust the whole of it; everything is either body or mind, extension or thought. Each of those is infinite in its own domain, unlike the finite things or thoughts that instance them. They express within nature the infinity of God. But they are not the same as God, who remains contentless to our reason. Otherwise put, the God of Maimonides is to YHWH what the God of Spinoza is to Nature.

Spinoza obtains for God an immanence in nature that God lacks in Maimonides. The most expressive name of God, translated from Maimonides's worldview to Spinoza's is, in effect, Nature. Nature becomes in that way an avenue of access to an apprehension of God, as Maimonides and all defenders of the cosmological argument want it to be for us, but not by way of any argument that leads from one to the other, but by way of the expressing relation. Nature is not for Spinoza the forests, oceans, and mountains—or more grandly, the planets, solar systems, and galaxies—that might inspire thoughts of a Creator. That was the door Heschel opened for us that we refused to enter. Nature for Spinoza conforms to abstractions beyond all of that, in the form of infinite thought and extension. Nature so understood transcends our senses and shows itself only to our intellects, which must strain to apprehend it in its mental and physical infinity. Such an understanding of nature brings to mind Philo's account of creation, from chapter 1: what God first creates are abstract ideas, which are the true creation, that become blueprints for the (lesser) instantiations of them in concrete things. Spinoza may recall for us the difficulty cited, also in chapter 1, of translating the mathematics of quantum mechanics into narrative. It is no wonder Spinoza was a favorite of Einstein's, who might need very little tinkering with Spinoza's nature to make it his own. How far are Spinoza's difficult abstractions of nature from Einstein's, in terms of challenge to our intellect? But then, if nature so taxes our intellect, how much harder to apprehend the God it expresses. For all the look of simple pantheism within Spinoza's system, his God is as difficult to conceive, if not more so, as Maimonides's. Both are pinnacles of contentless content accessible only to the most advanced human intellects. "All things excellent are as difficult as they are rare" (E5p42s). How true of rationalist negative theology!

Let us move on to the next category of contentless God, who lacks content by virtue of the great distance that separates us. In light of that, the pragmatist negative theologians refocus our attention on acts we perform in service of God. For a God too distant to come into any positively contentful view for us, there is a spokesman already in the Bible: Ecclesiastes, whom Bible interpreter Jack Miles has called a "protophilosopher"[15] within the generally unphilosophical Bible. If the fundamental mood of philosophy is interrogative, as the stimulus of wonder might have it, rather than declarative, then Ecclesiastes is certainly a philosopher. It is not so much that he poses questions—he does that, but they are often rhetorical—as that on so many issues he is contradictory, as though to undermine the declarative voice in that way. This already endears him to us if, by way of the kindred path of the contentless, we have been questioning the positively contentful declarative all along. Among the many things both good and bad, according to Ecclesiastes, are pleasure (Eccl 2:2 and 8:15); laughter (2:2 and 3:4); toil (5:18 and 6:7); death (4:2 and 9:4–5); and wisdom (1:18 and 2:13). Sometimes adjacent verses appear to cancel each other out as when a thought on the wicked, "to whom it happeneth according to the work of the righteous" (8:14), follows immediately on a contrary verse, that "it shall not be well with the wicked" (8:13). Perhaps 8:13 is a bit of received wisdom that 8:14 critiques.[16] Or perhaps the writer really intends the contradiction.

Intended contradiction could be a rhetorical device in the spirit of Maimonides's tack of negation. The result is the same: cancelation of any positively contentful assertion. As though to anticipate Maimonides, what Ecclesiastes mainly attributes to God are attributes of action. Among these are both providing (2:24) and withholding (6:2); both making (7:13) and destroying (5:5)—two sets of qualities in opposition. God fashions both the crooked (7:13) and the upright (7:29). God does indeed create (12:1); but in the world God has made the good suffer and the wicked prosper (7:15); plans go awry (10:8–9); labor is in

---

15. Miles, *God*, 350.

16. In his translation of the verses, R. B. Y. Scott encloses the first verse in quotation marks—a punctuation that does not appear in ancient or medieval biblical manuscripts—to suggest a received adage the writer rejects. Scott, *Proverbs, Ecclesiastes*, 242. He comments that otherwise "Qoheleth is contradicting himself." But that could also be a strategy.

vain (2:18–19). In the end, "all things come alike to all" (9:2), "time and chance happeneth to them all" (9:11). The lovely poem on the seasons for everything (3:1–8) seems to proffer hope in bad times that the good times are coming, but then that works just as well in reverse. Perhaps the poem means to soften contradiction by casting it in such "words of delight" (12:10) as Ecclesiastes, the poet, is able to summon, and Pete Seeger, much later, to set to memorable melody. But the note of contradiction still sounds.

Maimonides understood the qualities we ascribe to God based on God's acts to be metaphors derived from what we would call humans who performed like acts. This is how it is possible to pray to a merciful God, who is not merciful through mercy. But on the basis of the acts that, according to Ecclesiastes, God either performs or implicitly sanctions within the world, what qualities—in analogy with those a human would have who performed like acts—would be divine? Ecclesiastes himself offers up a likely candidate: past-finding-out. It is striking that among the various opposites Ecclesiastes lists in 3:1–8, there is "a time to seek, and a time to lose," but evidently none to find. The puzzle of that resolves in the failures to find that repeat in other chapters of the book. Ecclesiastes cannot find "that which is . . . far off and exceeding deep" (7:24); or that "which yet my soul sought" (7:28); but most importantly, he "cannot find out the work that God hath done from the beginning even to the end" (3:11); even after having "beheld all the work of God, . . . [he] cannot find out the work that is done under the sun" (8:17). In terms of both time and space, God is past finding out. "Thou knowest not the work of God" (11:5). And so, by inference from the attributes of action, we know not God. As though to translate that ignorance spatially, Ecclesiastes locates God at the top of an enormous distance from us: "higher than the high" (5:7), if that were possible.

Up to a point, Ecclesiastes anticipates Maimonides, who in his *Guide* twice repeats (GP9, GP73) the biblical writer's rhetorical question about "that which is far off and exceeding deep; who can find it out?" (7:24). Maimonides also approves Ecclesiastes's advice, in light of God's past-finding-out, to favor silence in our relation to God: "God is in heaven and thou upon earth; therefore let thy words be few" (5:1)— also twice cited in the *Guide* (GP143, GP629). But it is not on account of God's extreme unity, a topic that scarcely occurs to Ecclesiastes, that silence on God so becomes us, but because for the most part God is simply not available to us. There is no reference to the revelation at Sinai in

Ecclesiastes, or to revelation at all. There is brief mention of the temple, which operated on the basis of revelation, but not for any positive role it played in religious life; rather, for the care it was necessary to take in its precincts, not to make sacrifices foolishly (4:17). The law surfaces only at the end, in a short closing most scholars judge a later, pious addendum, to "keep [God's] commandments, for this is the whole man" (12:13). But otherwise, they are not in play whether as Rosenzweig's bearers of divine love or Leibowitz's medium of divine service.

It must have struck Maimonides that Ecclesiastes never names God by the name closest to the divine being, YHWH, and the most philosophically resonant. God is consistently, for Ecclesiastes, *Elohim*, the divine name that builds on the generic word for god (*el*), judged by the rabbis to be one of God's more impersonal designations. But then, if YHWH is the divine name most properly revealed, underived from any attributes misleadingly attached to God (so Maimonides would say), it is no wonder Ecclesiastes eschews it. God is so distant in Ecclesiastes, as barely to exist for the writer, like a star so remote its light has yet to reach us across the light years of distance from us. It is no wonder Professor Miles finds in Ecclesiastes "as thoroughly secular a worldview as can be imagined,"[17] or that the book enjoys such favor within the small movement of expressly agnostic/atheistic Humanistic Jews.[18] In this case, atheism does not so much shake hands with mysticism as—with a critique of theism so radical its God fades into the distance—clear ground for the book that immediately follows in the Hebrew Bible, Esther, which absents any mention of God at all.

In the wake of what is effectively Ecclesiastes's negation of God, what comes into view is his focus on acts, that we "eat and drink, and enjoy pleasure for all [our] labor, [for this] is the gift of God" (3:13). But as this pragmatic advice segues to the spiritual life, as understood by the writer, we postpone its consideration to our next chapter.

As much as Maimonides makes for an easy segue to Ecclesiastes, so do they both to Yeshayahu Leibowitz. We already know of Leibowitz's reverence for Maimonides. But Ecclesiastes too finds high favor with him—unexpectedly, for one as indifferent to mitzvot as Ecclesiastes seems to be. Ecclesiastes's seeming nihilism toward the world is in fact correct,

---

17. Miles, *God*, 353.

18. See for example the two essays on Ecclesiastes within the book edited by Rubinstein and Sternhell, *Contemplation*. No other biblical book receives so much attention in the volume.

according to Leibowitz: "Man as part of natural existence . . . is nought but vanity."[19] This is the natural conclusion of one who, like Ecclesiastes, has explored all worldly sources of satisfaction and found them wanting, including the expectation of self-centered rewards for leading a religious life. Ecclesiastes is the master underminer of religious observance for the sake of reward, for rewards do not routinely follow on good behavior, or punishments on bad. Therefore, Leibowitz understands Ecclesiastes to say, observance is *for its own sake*—Leibowitz's leitmotif. It is no wonder, then, the book concludes with the pious verse, "Keep [God's] commandments, for this is the whole man" (12:13). For Leibowitz, this is the other (and logical) side of the coin of the rest of the book, and not a pious addition. Contrary to much of academic opinion, Leibowitz takes that verse for the words of the original author of the book.[20]

Ecclesiastes is also right to infer from the incomprehensibility of God not so much that God transcends our powers of description as that God is infinitely distant from us. "The aim of proximity to God is unattainable. It is infinitely distant, for 'God is in heaven and you are on earth,'"[21] Leibowitz writes, quoting Eccl 5:1. With that comment, Leibowitz raises the image of asymptotic approach of God, such as we found in the Upanishads and, by extension, Maimonides, only to deny its effectiveness. We do not come nearer to God by denying of God false attributes. This is a departure from Maimonides, with whom otherwise Leibowitz largely agrees. For Leibowitz, too, God "has no body and cannot be corporeally conceived" (32); "is not given in sensation, conception, or imagination" (44); "is not conceivable in terms of any attributes and is analogous to nothing whatsoever" (44). So far so good for Maimonides. But now the tone changes. For Leibowitz allows for no super-sensual *apprehension* of God, as Maimonides does, that might transcend the capacity of language to describe it. Leibowitz is suspicious of such a goal for religious life on grounds of the reward it cannot help seeming or being for religious practice. And his much-repeated desire is for a worship *for its own sake*, unmotivated by any proffered reward, even the reward of God experienced, cleaved to, or apprehended. In his zeal to cut off any reward for halachic observance, Leibowitz cuts off God too; or identifies the worship of God, not with

---

19. Leibowitz, *Faith of Maimonides*, 38.
20. Leibowitz, *Notes and Remarks*, 201.
21. Leibowitz, *Judaism*, 16. Subsequent citations to pages of this text are given parenthetically.

supersensual apprehensions, but with "the cheerless, day-to-day practice of Torah and mitzvot" (71). "Halacha is founded in faith and yet at the same time *constitutes* this faith" (11) (emphasis ours). Leibowitz's interpretation of Maimonides veers this way too. For he comes close in places to suggesting that the Maimonidean apprehension of God *is*, after all, nothing but the practice of mitzvot: "Maimonides reveals the secret: the purpose of the mitzvot is to educate man to recognize that knowing God and cleaving to him *consist* in the practice of these very precepts" (28) (emphasis ours).

In consequence, God is emptied of content, not from transcending our powers of description but from an assurance that needs to be given, for the sake of pure worship, that God not function as reward. The placeholder for God becomes the mitzvot we perform, rather like the Judaism that Mendelssohn also identified with performance. As a result, no distinctive ideational content of any kind remains to either Judaism, for Mendelssohn, or God, for Leibowitz. As Leibowitz puts it, "In reflecting and speaking about man's standing before God, the believer . . . tries to refer minimally to God, who has no image at all, and makes an effort to direct his religious consciousness to himself as recognizing his duty to his God" (76). As Leibowitz asserted in an interview, as reported by Professor Daniel Rynhold, in response to the question of whether he believed God actually exists: "I do not understand these words if they are divorced from the obligations that derive from them. . . . Faith in God is not what I know about God but what I know about my obligations to God."[22]

It is a paradoxical position to hold. Unlike Maimonides, Leibowitz denies we have any access to belief in God by way of argument from the world around us. Faith is not "a conclusion a person may come to after pondering certain facts about the world" (37). After all, if Ecclesiastes is right, the world around us is no argument for the existence of God. But then, on what grounds do the mitzvot present themselves as God-given? Leibowitz does allow himself to characterize God in at least one way, as "the Giver of the Torah" (42). But on what basis?—on the basis of the mitzvot themselves, which, Leibowitz believes, in accord with Maimonides, *command* belief in God. As Leibowitz explains, this is how Maimonides understands the first of the Ten Commandments on the Jewish numbering: "I am the Lord thy God, who brought thee out of the

---

22. Rynhold, "Orthodox Atheism."

land of Egypt, out of the house of bondage" (Exod 20:2). This seeming declarative claim is actually, says Maimonides, an imperative to believe in God.[23] That may not be Maimonides's *argument* for theism. But it is Leibowitz's: "Why do I believe in God? Because it is a mitzvah, a commandment to believe in God."[24] Within the logic of belief, the mitzvot *precede* theistic faith. Torah and mitzvoth must be understood "as data preceding recognition of the Giver of the Torah" (5). But this was our point about Leibowitz in the preceding chapter.

There, too, we learned a reason Leibowitz gave for Jews to self-impose the law: It is what has kept the people together since ancient times. On reflection, though, the very advancing of a reason to keep the law, based on its beneficial effects, bucks the grain of Leibowitz's signature claim, that the law commands solely of itself, not for its effects. That is what makes it exalting and godly. It is hard for Leibowitz not to sound in the end like Kierkegaard, the philosopher of worldviews that have no authorization on any terms but their own. There is no neutral authority of reason to decide between them (*pace* Maimonides and Spinoza). As Kierkegaard himself might say, it comes down to choices that *precede* the workings of reason. What Leibowitz says in echo of that is: "Faith and worship are born of the resolve and decision of man to serve God, which is the whole of Judaism" (75). Prior to our observance, we have *decided* for it. But the mitzvot address us *before* God does, if we really hear anything from God at all. They command the worship of God. If asked what that means, they reply with the specifics of the other 612 commandments of the Torah. They supply no content to the idea of God, but the commandments only. Any content to the idea of God evaporates in a cycle of commitment that begins and ends with the mitzvot. No rationalism here.

The pragmatic negative theologians might find themselves improbable bedfellows with many of the modern Orthodox, at least to judge from our previous chapter, and participants in a God-distant Judaism that effectively erases the distinction between religious and secular, insofar as the religious is what keeps the commandments, and the secular what absents God. But they would not be philosophically alone. They could easily find Levinas there, too. With just a little change of vocabulary, Leibowitz and Levinas speak the same pragmatic negative theology of the absent God. We just need to substitute ethics for mitzvot.

23. See Maimonides, *Sefer HaMitzvot*, Mitzvah One.
24. Leibowitz, *Faith of Maimonides*, 49.

It is true that when Leibowitz writes that a religious person "cannot accept ethics as the overriding norm or criterion" (18), on account of reducing God to the function of guaranteeing ethics, he seems miles from Levinas. For ethics, as we learned from Levinas, was "First Philosophy." But for neither Leibowitz nor Levinas is God present except by way of human acts, whether halachic or ethical, which effectively reads God out of our affective and intellectual lives.

We begin with what Levinas calls "this distant God,"[25] in "absolute remoteness."[26] With Levinas's God-idea, we are in the familiar terrain of that which is "unlike any content" (174). Levinas echoes Ecclesiastes, whose God is "higher than the high" (Eccl 5:7), when he writes that God is "the height above all height," which "excludes God from the thinkable, as something inapprehendable" (168). And he sounds like Leibowitz when he writes that, to the extent I register the idea of God, it is "without prehension or comprehension" (176). For this is a more radical negative theology even than Maimonides's, which allowed for an apprehension of God beyond our ability to describe. In addition, Levinas enacts a vocabulary toward God that seems, with Buber and Rosenzweig in mind, pointedly to undermine the proximate God we shall shortly see them defend. As against Buber, God is not a Thou or even a partner in dialogue. God is not in the grammar of the second person to us at all, as Buber would have it, but ineluctably the third. On account of the divine "separation or holiness, it remains a third person" (178) to us. And as against Rosenzweig, for whom the divine Love me! command actually manifests God's love for me, "God . . . renounces all aids to manifestation."[27] Levinas is as wary as Leibowitz of any claims to know God via the supersensual or trans-linguistic. "The supernatural is not an obsession for Judaism,"[28] he understatedly pronounces.

The attribution of transcendent height to God—height above height—must give us pause in a Levinasian context. For we recall from chapter 7 that it was just from such a height that what Levinas called the Other approached us. "In welcoming the Other I welcome the On High," which approaches me through a "curvature of the intersubjective space in

---

25. Levinas, *Difficult Freedom*, 143.

26. Levinas, "God and Philosophy," 179. Subsequent citations to pages of this text are given parenthetically.

27. Levinas, *Difficult Freedom*, 143.

28. Levinas, *Difficult Freedom*, 49.

which exteriority is effectuated . . . as superiority."[29] We already noticed back in chapter 7 that the Other assimilates to God in Levinas. But it is more that God assimilates to the Other. God is a particularly forceful approach of the Other: "God is . . . other than the other, other otherwise, other with an alterity prior to the alterity of the other . . . transcendent to the point of absence" (179). We might say God is the Other squared. But still the Other. Levinas here recalls Kant, who characterized religion as an intensification of ethics—ethics as godly, but without needing to be. Analogously, a religious person for Levinas would receive the approach of the Other as that of God, without needing to. And this godly Other is not clearly a singularity, but rather whoever in their proximity to us commands of us an infinite responsibility toward them. And now we are clearly back in the ethical sphere, which is where Levinas wants the God-idea to take us. As he puts it, God's "absolute remoteness, his transcendence turns into my responsibility . . . for the other" (179); and "Ethics is not the corollary of the vision of God, it is that very vision."[30] That sounds a lot like Leibowitz on obedience to the mitzvot (in place of ethics).

Levinas reaches that same conclusion by way of another tack, coming courtesy another Francophone thinker, Descartes. He builds on the old idea from Descartes that the very idea of God is so extraordinary we could never have generated it ourselves, which thereby attests to the reality of what it references. It is another version of the ontological argument. Levinas reverses the direction of the argument (173–75). It is not that the idea of God argues for the reality of God, but rather for the unreality of our self-contained selves who have the idea. It is as though an idea that had seemed to exalt us actually backfires upon us. If an idea so beyond us inhabits us then we are devastated by its presence in us. "The Infinite affects thought by devastating it, . . . like a devouring fire, catastrophying its site" (176). We are back to the devastated self we first explored with Levinas in chapter 2.

But the infinite emerges from the wreckage in the form of acts of responsibility toward the other. "Infinity . . . devastates presence and awakens subjectivity to the proximity of the other" (179), but in an infinite way. For in my solicitude for the other, "I am never finished with emptying myself of myself. There is infinite increase in this exhausting of oneself" (182). Levinas thinks of this negatively as a kind of insomnia

---

29. Levinas, *Totality and Infinity*, 291, 300.
30. Levinas, *Difficult Freedom*, 17.

(140), a ceaseless blockage from rest in illusions of self-containment or aseity; positively, it is an ongoing wakefulness toward the other, without any intent toward her but to receive her command. It is a "subjection to an order before understanding the order" (184), as the ancient Israelites appeared to do when they agreed to observe the Torah before understanding what it said (Exod 24:7). And indeed, Leibowitz as though in sympathy with Levinas restates this view in terms of the mitzvot. "Performance of the mitzvot is man's path to God, an infinite path, the end of which is never attained and is in effect unattainable."[31] Here both philosophers echo a famous rabbinic adage: "It is not your duty to finish the work, but neither are you at liberty to neglect it."[32] When Levinas warmly comments on a story of obedience to Torah[33] that survives the effective "death of God,"[34] he seems to echo Leibowitz. It is as though the infinity of God has transitioned into the mitzvot (Leibowitz) and/or ethics (Levinas). In this way, both thinkers restate the classical idea of the divine infinity in terms of an infinite responsibility that beckons us on toward an end we never reach.

But now the same question that Daniel Rynhold indirectly posed to Leibowitz by titling his lecture on him "Orthodox Atheism," the philosopher Hilary Putnam puts to Levinas: "how is this not atheism?"[35] Levinas invites this question when he suggests that the idea of the infinite "requires separation, requires it unto atheism";[36] and links monotheism to atheism more closely when he writes that "true monotheism is duty bound to answer the legitimate demands of atheism."[37] His point there is that atheism serves to wean the monotheist of infantile expectations that God protect us from useless suffering (see ch. 2). This too recalls

---

31. Leibowitz, *Judaism*, 15.

32. Avot 2:16, tr. Joshua Kulp, https://www.sefaria.org/Pirkei_Avot.2.16?lang=bi.

33. See "Loving the Torah More Than God," in *Difficult Freedom* (142–45), in which the protagonist of a story of the Holocaust Levinas interprets exclaims of God, "I love him, but I love even more his Torah. . . . And even if I were deceived by him and became disillusioned [by the extent of human suffering], I should nevertheless observe the precepts of the Torah" (144).

34. "The modern world . . . attests to the death of God" (Levinas, *Difficult Freedom*, 172). Elsewhere, Levinas writes of my relation to the other who commands my responsibility for them that this is "a relation that survives the 'death of God'" (Levinas, *Otherwise Than Being*, 123).

35. Putnam, "Levinas and Judaism," 53.

36. Levinas, *Totality and Infinity*, 181.

37. Levinas, *Difficult Freedom*, 143.

Leibowitz's objections to any subordination of God to human need, or indeed to any functional expectations at all. Judaism, as a "Religion for Adults,"[38] excites the human sense of responsibility toward the Other, not dependence on it. Ultimately, the work of atheism in service of monotheism is to rebut theodicy, which we recall from chapter 2 is one of Levinas's projects. Atheism is the natural outcome of any expectation that the omnipotent and benevolent God stand guard against the suffering of the innocent. But then there is another step, for "monotheism surpasses and incorporates atheism."[39] There is a two-pronged monotheism that simultaneously exalts God beyond our reach, or even belief—"the sentence in which God gets mixed in with words is not 'I believe in God'" (184)—and translates the God-idea into human acts, whether ethical (Levinas) or halachic (Leibowitz). A God so situated occupies a borderline between theism and atheism. And this is the God both Leibowitz and Levinas, in different ways, commend to our attention.

A life so committed to either so demanding a Jewish law or so exorbitant an ethics recalls the asceticism that figured in our discussion of Jewish philosophical morality. The asceticism is in the sacrifice of any expectation that support for such a life come from a succoring God. The halachic and/or ethical acts are ends in themselves. It is a life course that will appeal to the Kantians among us. Leibowitz reverenced Kant almost as much as he did Maimonides, and Levinas, who admired Kant for his "sobriety, disinebriation, and vigilance," deemed his categorical imperative a "remarkable" application of reason to an ethics beyond the reach of theoretical knowledge.[40] For Kant, too, by his categorical imperative sacrificed on behalf of the ethical person any expectation that in foreseeable time their moral acts would coincide with personal happiness. We might hope for that coincidence at some future time, but a time so infinitely future as to justify a belief in immortality, for it would take that long, as the Psalmist put it in his own terms, for "righteousness and peace [to] have kissed each other" (Ps 85:10).

Let us pick up now with Buber and Rosenzweig, for whom God resists description for just the opposite reason God does for Levinas and Leibowitz—for being *too close* to us. Buber is most adamant on this point. A "childlike old man" once asked him if he believed in God. We

---

38. The title of one of Levinas's essays in *Difficult Freedom*.
39. Levinas, *Difficult Freedom*, 16.
40. Levinas, *Of God Who Comes to Mind*, 16.

have already seen Maimonides, Leibowitz, and Levinas undermine the assumptions of this question. So does Buber, in his own way:

> The answer came to me: . . . If believing in God means being able to speak of him in the third person, then I probably do not believe in God. For I know, when I speak of him in the third person . . . then my tongue cleaves to the roof of my mouth so quickly that one cannot even call it speech.[41]

We already know that the I-Thou relation itself resists positive description and assimilates in that way to the divine, as Levinas implied the approach of the Other does too. But unexpectedly, it is Levinas who expresses for us most succinctly the reason for this: "We do not conceive of relations, we are *in* relation."[42] Otherwise put, the fullness of meaning to relationality registers for us only in the second person, since whatever we describe is out of relation with us, a mere object of our inquiry or gaze. This explains the tinge of guilt we may feel whenever we are put in a position to talk *about* someone close to us, for how is this not gossip? Part of us wants to respond (and sometimes we do) to inquiries about our nearest and dearest: Ask *them*! Thus we find in Tolstoy's *War and Peace* a reticence on the part of Natasha even to speak of her beloved and now deceased Andrei, for fear of diminishing him by transposing him from the second to the third person.[43]

We already had at the start of this chapter Buber's name for God: the Eternal Thou. For Spinoza, too, as we saw (above), eternity is ascribable to God. But this is just another negative attribute, here connoting nontemporality. It is, in part, Buber's wish to speak of God only in the second person that commits him to negative theology, which might otherwise be characterized as the reluctance to speak of God in the third person positive. Here is Buber's negative language on God, which recalls both Ecclesiastes in its excess of negativity (more unlimited than the unlimited, as Buber puts it) and Zen Buddhism in its extreme paradox (not in or outside the world): the Eternal Thou

> cannot be placed within measure and limit, not even within the measure of the immeasurable and the limit of the unlimited, . . .

---

41. Buber quoted in Horowitz, *Buber's Way*, 104–5.
42. Levinas, *Difficult Freedom*, 140.
43. Natasha and Princess Marya (Andrei's sister) "refrained from speaking of him for fear of profaning (as it seemed to them) their exalted feelings by words" (Tolstoy, *War and Peace*, 1293).

cannot be grasped as a sum of qualities, ... is not to be found either in or outside the world, ... cannot be experienced, ... cannot be thought.... We transgress against it ... if we say, "I believe that he is"—even "he" is still a metaphor, while "you" is not.[44]

Buber even recalls Maimonides's negative theology when he writes that the Thou "can only be indicated by drawing a circle that excludes everything else" (126).

But now, as opposed to Leibowitz and Ecclesiastes, the reason for our silence on divinity is the extreme nearness of God. Insofar as we are aware of God, we are in the presence of God, whose sheer proximity erases the distance needed to issue declarative statements. God is "the mystery of the obvious that is closer to me than my own I" (127). Within the I-Thou relation of any kind, let alone with God, the "spell of separation" (125) is broken. We do not unite with God, as some of the mystics teach. By the vocabulary Buber prefers, the Eternal Thou "*confronts* us immediately, ... and legitimately it can only be addressed, not asserted" (129) (emphasis ours). Like other phenomena we have already encountered, this one "lacks all imaginable content" (137). More vernacularly, God is "in our face" before we know what is happening. Knowledge is the last thing we can claim of what confronts us here. "We have 'known' it but we have no knowledge of it that might diminish ... its mysteriousness" (160).

This theistic language may take us by surprise when we recall, as Walter Kaufmann told us in his introduction to *I and Thou* back in chapter 4, "God does not actually appear much before the third part" (31). In the first two parts, Buber already decks out the I-Thou relation in the elusively descriptive language of negative theology. We are already primed to take the I-Thou relation, *itself*, for God, just as in the worldview of Levinas, the other so easily transforms to the divinely Other. And if Paul Mendes-Flohr interprets correctly, Buber's thought "is not based on theological propositions" at all.[45] Rather, Buber presses theological words, like God, into the service of explicating what is supremely important to him: the I-Thou relation. It is not so much that God is (Eternal) Thou, as that Thou is God.[46] But the God-language is

44. Buber, *I and Thou*, 161. Subsequent citations to pages of this text are given parenthetically. Note that Kaufmann translates the *Du* of German as You, rather than Thou.

45. Mendes-Flohr, *Divided Passions*, 238.

46. Mendes-Flohr notes that Michael Theunissen makes this point (Mendes-Flohr,

not needed to divinize the I-Thou relation, as Buber himself demonstrates. Indeed, "some would deny any legitimate use of the word, 'God,' because it has been misused so much" (123).

Buber understands himself to include atheists among his addressees, and not in order to "convert" them. On the contrary, the atheist may be nearer Buber's heart than the theist, insofar as a moment of I-Thou encounter, whether with animal, vegetable, or mineral, has arrested her in her tracks and drawn her full, undivided attention, while the theists just rotely repeat prescribed prayers at prescribed times. If earlier Buber recalled a passage from Tolstoy, now one from Dostoevsky comes to mind. In *The Idiot*, the protagonist Prince Myshkin wonders if in his conversations with atheists they really have been talking past each other. He comments, "whenever I have met unbelievers . . . it always seemed to me that they were speaking . . . about something quite different [from God], although it seemed to be about that on the surface."[47] If what is really meant by God is the I-Thou encounter, then Buber and, say, Richard Dawkins in debate are not really in dispute. Insofar as each is wholly engaged with the other, beyond the limits of the debate, but extending in their interaction a mutual receipt each of the other in the fullness of themselves, then they may be in the very midst of God. Would that all debates had such a quality!

Buber does not need God to explicate the I-Thou encounter, which in any case is not understood except by inhabiting it. For it, too, resists third person descriptions. And Buber sides with Leibowitz in refusing any *argument* that might lead from our ordinary habitat of the I-It framework of reality, which for Leibowitz is the scientifically accessible natural world, to that of I-Thou. "The existence of mutuality between man and God cannot be proved any more than the existence of God" (182). Nonetheless, Buber is not beyond trying to persuade us that the I-Thou relation is godly. Let us hear him out. An I-Thou encounter is so inherently meaningful that, in wake of it, "nothing can henceforth be meaningless" (159). The trouble is, it does not last. "The sublime melancholy of our lot [is] the fated lapse into It of every single You" (146). Our lapse may not be into meaninglessness, but it is surely into a deep sense of loss. Buber even characterizes the passage from I-Thou to

---

Divided Passions, 270).

47. Dostoevsky, *Idiot*, 212.

I-It as "a betrayal, a falling away, a distancing of ourselves from the task that is inherent in us"[48] to infuse life with meaning.

It is partly in answer to this problem of transiency that Buber invites us to consider the possibility of an Eternal Thou: "the You that in accordance with its nature cannot become an It" (123). For otherwise, the transiency of I-Thou could not but work to undermine the very reality of it, to lock us into the "sublime melancholy" of inevitable loss. On consideration, Buber opines that if there is no *eternal* Thou, then "there is no presence that lasts and fulfills life."[49] It is a little like one of the transcendental arguments from Kant, such as he advanced for the rationality of hope in immortality: If there were no assurance that happiness would one day reward goodness, we would despair. But we do not despair. Therefore we do hope in that consummation, howsoever much counts against it. It is not much of an argument and it scarcely offends Buber's own conviction that no arguments for God are possible. But it may give us pause.

Buber has another tack. A feature of the I-Thou relation, as we know, is the wholeness of attention it demands of the partners in it. I who confront my Thou have eyes for nothing else but my Thou in their wholeness. Otherwise put, "every actual relationship in the world is exclusive" (148). In that way, the I-Thou encounter resembles many a romantic relation. But this would open a path to jealousy and resentment toward anyone who intruded on the exclusivity of the relation, as happens within the framework of romance. And nothing so godly as I-Thou can be the occasion for anything so ignoble as that. And so the Eternal Thou constitutes a permanent third in every I-Thou encounter to counter its exclusivity. By way of the Eternal Thou, every I-Thou encounter encounters every other one, in a radically inclusive meaningfulness. "Solely in the relation to God are unconditional exclusiveness and unconditional inclusiveness one" (148). We come then to read that, "extended, the lines of relationships intersect in the eternal You" (123) and that the relation with the Eternal Thou "includes all others" (124).

Perhaps unknowingly, Buber here recovers the argument of a medieval Christian theologian, Aelred of Rievaulx (1110–1167), on the phenomenology of friendship, that in every *spiritual* friendship a third participant, Jesus Christ, assures it of having a charitable inclusiveness.[50]

48. Horowitz, *Buber's Way*, 82.
49. Horowitz, *Buber's Way*, 83.
50. Aelred of Rievaulx, *Spiritual Friendship*, 55, 75.

Buber does not assimilate the I-Thou relation to friendship. The I-Thou relation lacks the possibility of such long-term continuity in human experience that friendship has and it occurs without the conditions laid down by the classic theorists of friendship, such as Aristotle, Cicero, Montaigne, or indeed Aelred. We generally have something in common with our friends; we need not with a thou in I-Thou relation with us. But then, neither does the I-Thou relation assimilate to traditional understandings of the God-human relation. As Mendes-Flohr helpfully summarizes, Buber is too "ambiguous [and] . . . equivocal,"[51] or else simply negative, on whether his God is supernatural, conscious, intentional, providential, authoritative, or self-revealing, as God is traditionally taken to be, to fit our preconceptions of God. But that is just the point. Buber has channeled negative theology toward a God that so undermines our expectations of God as to, perhaps, tantalize us into a spirituality we never thought open to us.

Buber does linger on one attribute he is loath totally to dissociate from God: personalness. For as much as the I-Thou encounter transcends personality, it also channels the personal. As paradoxically exclusive and inclusive as it is able to be, so is it simultaneously personal and impersonal. Buber finds a unique way to express this by reference, unexpectedly, to the God of Spinoza, otherwise so seemingly foreign to his. Spinoza's God is a divine transfiguration of Impersonality. Its infinite and eternal attributes are forms of the impersonal. But suppose one of those forms was itself the personal, stretched to the limit of its opposite—impersonality—without passing over into it? This is what Buber asks us to conceive:

> The concept of personhood is of course utterly incapable of describing the nature of God; but it is permitted and necessary to say that God is *also* a person. If for once I were to translate what I mean into the language of a philosopher, Spinoza, I should have to say that of God's infinitely many attributes we human beings know not two . . . but three: in addition to spiritlikeness . . . and naturelikeness . . . also thirdly the attribute of personlikeness (181).[52]

---

51. Mendes-Flohr, *Divided Passions*, 262–65.

52. God, says Buber, is "absolute person" (181), as though to distinguish God from all other personhood, similar to the way the Christian Nicene creed captures the distinctiveness of the divine begetting of the Son by characterizing it as an *eternal* begetting. Within the language about God, *eternal* and *absolute* are surely cousins.

Buber here borrows from the connotation of the Spinozan attributes of thought and extension, which he more metaphorically names, to be ways of perceiving the divine. This protects the incomparability and indescribability of God from compromise while granting us leave in our relation with God to compare and describe. It is just that the ultimate reference of those comparisons and descriptions is ourselves in our efforts to register the divine. Leibowitz helps Buber out here when he concedes that all our talk of God is refracted through ourselves: The religious man's knowledge [of God] is really of "himself with regard to his duty towards God,"[53] or, as Buber puts it, "the question is not about God but only about our relationship to him" (180).

For Buber, how we talk *about* God, which is always misdirected, impacts our openness or closure to relation *with* God. A mere change of name by which we address the deity may open a path previously closed to relation with him/her/it/them. Buber hopes his own preferred name for God, the Eternal Thou, will clear a theistic path for some of his readers. He wants to attune us to what has since biblical times been the evocative power of the divine names. As the kabbalists taught, and as Scholem elaborated, the divine names are words that bridge It-language *about* God to Thou-language *with* God; names "*of* God . . . also speak *to* him" (123) (emphasis ours). Like other of our philosophers, Buber is also intrigued by the seemingly tautological name of Exod 3:14, *Ehyeh-Asher-Ehyeh*. In the first edition of *I and Thou*, Buber translated this into the German equivalent of *I am that I am*,[54] which is how Ronald Gregor Smith rendered it in his translation.[55] But later, he opted for the German equivalent of *I am there as whoever I am there*, which is how Kaufmann renders the English (160). In their joint Bible translation, Buber and Rosenzweig opted for a slightly different phrase, *Ich werde dasein, als der ich dasein werde*,[56] which would become something like *I will be there as who I there will be*. In both these later versions, a reference to place—*there*—appears which is absent in the stasis of *I am that I am*, and connotes a God who not simply *is* but who encounters us at specific locations in space and time. So this divine name, translated this way, is a better launching pad to actual encounter with the Eternal Thou than the more static name.

---

53. Leibowitz, *Faith of Maimonides*, 110.

54. As Kaufmann explains (Buber, *I and Thou*, 1st ed., 160n1).

55. See Buber, *I and Thou*, 2nd ed., 112. See also Mendes-Flohr, *Divided Passions*, 265.

56. Buber and Rosenzweig, *Schrift*, 1:158.

And now Rosenzweig picks up on that theme of the divine placement toward us in ways that scramble our very understanding of the word-name, *God*. Rosenzweig has in effect *three* understandings of this name, implying three different negative theologies, depending upon the time frame in which we relate to it. This will take readers of Rosenzweig by surprise. For his very first order of business, after his treatment of death in his introduction to part 1 of the *Star*, is to expressly name—but for the purpose of refusing—"negative theology" (SR31) as a path he will follow. Insofar as Maimonides sets the tone for Judaism's negative theology, Rosenzweig had good reason to distance it. For among the predicates Maimonides disallowed of God, alongside the positive ones, were the relational ones. No relational ones? But, for Rosenzweig, for whom relationality *defined* reality, a non-relational God would be unreal. So how *could* Rosenzweig participate in the negative theological tradition of the God-idea? And yet he does, as we shall see. For he needs the *unreal* God, as much as the real one.

One of Rosenzweig's departures from Buber is to be preoccupied with the impact of time on our experience of reality. In fact, there is only one reality: the present. This is the time frame in which we receive the Love me! command, if we can but hear it. For love is always and only in the present moment. Indeed it vivifies, if not defines, the present moment (SR218). In thrall of the love me! command, we are too close to its speaker to describe our experience in any way. No third-person, declarative statements about the speaker are available to be spoken by us within the intensity of this ever-renewed, from moment-to-moment love relation. This was the reason for the relevance to Rosenzweig of the Song of Songs, which is given almost entirely in the second person. The nameable being of the speaker who commands us to love is recessed behind the love the command carries to us.[57] It would be wrong even to suggest that, in the present, we have an *understanding* of God at all. We function in the present as receptors of a love so intensively commanding, always with an exclamation point, there is no time or space for speculation on its speaker. That is the basis for the negative theology that operates in the present. We respond to the Love me! command not with declarative statements but with our own acts of love, as we saw one chapter back,

---

57. This helps explain how difficult it can be for a reader of the Song of Songs to know who is speaking at any given point in it. There is no third person narrator to identify the speakers.

directed to our nearest neighbor, whom we love, not on command, but from an overflow of the love we have received and cannot contain.

But there are two other time frames, the past and the future, within which to associate some meaning for the word *God*. We cannot directly inhabit either of those frames. All that is ever directly available to us is the present. But we can access them indirectly: the past, by way of the preconditions of the present that we can infer backward, as it were, from the present; and the future, by way of the culminations of the present we can infer forward—for the love we channel toward our neighbor points to a distinct shape for the future, however distant.

The God of the past is a god of self-enclosure. This is the God Rosenzweig pinpoints at the start of his book as one of the three distinctive elements of reality, alongside humanity and world—but only an *element* of reality, not in itself real. For its outstanding feature is its unrelatedness. It knows only itself. This was characteristic of the three originary elements of reality: each satisfied its own need. It was only when they extraverted that each took up the need of another to satisfy, leaving itself in need of another's support. It was that mutual supply of need that constituted relationship, and relationality in turn that made for the real world we inhabit in the present. But that world could never have come to be without isolatable elements at its foundation. For relation only exists between relata different from each other. Given the reality of relationality, we can infer backward to the presupposition of it, which is a pre-world (*Vorwelt*) of separate elements. And so we read of the presupposed God who inhabits a past we never directly knew, and was in fact never real, for being wholly self-enclosed (SR41), self-contained (SR42), disengaged (SR48), and unloving (SR48).

By its very unreality, this God is by its nature a negation. And so Rosenzweig's very first teaching on God is that "God is a nothing for us" (SR31), as negative theology would have it. In this case, the negation within the negative theology is less from indescribability than from unreality. Rosenzweig suggests the Greeks described it well enough in their mythologies of Olympian deities whose care was largely for themselves and for humans only as instruments of their self-satisfaction (SR42). The Greeks had no language for the Judeo-Christian God of love. That does not mean they did not *experience* that love, but only that they lacked words for it. That love is, after all, expressible, as happens in the Song of Songs. But the Greeks, Rosenzweig implied, enjoyed no such poem.

The God of the future, too, evokes the language of negation, but for different reasons. The God of the future presides over a world that has been wholly redeemed by love. We had a brief picture of this world one chapter back. It is the world that will be when love has enlivened every single individual within it, at some barely conceivable future time. But once humans have completed their own work of loving the world, both they and it mute, as though the point to both of them, as separate entities, ceases to be. Rosenzweig suggests their very separation from God ceases at that point to hold and God becomes All in All, or as Barbara Galli so ingeniously translates his German *all-ein*[58]—"al-one" (SR407), both All-One and Alone. At that point, God "frees himself from contrasting with something that he himself is not" (SR406). It is not so much that humanity and world cease to be as that they are repositioned *within* the All of God. So, no more relationship; and, in consequence, no more reality. For this God of the future inhabits a space that, from our vantage point, is as unreal as the God of the past. Still, as in the case of the past God, we can infer this future God from the present. For we know that love is, by our agency, making its way through the world. And at some point love will have completed its course. And then, "God himself is redeemed here from his own word" (SR407), including his love-bearing word of command. Love will have borne God, us, and the world into a space beyond words: into "the silence into which he [God] one day, and we with him, will sink" (SR407). And so we have once again the language of negative theology—this time in the form of silence—from the end of words.

Of course, all three of these Gods of negative theology are one; otherwise Rosenzweig's Judaism would not be a monotheism. But time functions for Rosenzweig as the attributes do for Spinoza: they are lenses through which God appears to us, or by way of which the very word-name, *God*, bears any meaning for us at all. In all three cases, the content of the God-idea is barely describable, either from surfeit or absence of reality. And so Rosenzweig too belongs to the family of negative theologians whose thought, we suggest, overlaps enough with a given skepticism to re-energize the God-idea—for it to become, as William James put it, a "live option."

But then, Rosenzweig falls on deaf ears for those who have not experienced the ever-expansive love he celebrates. For love grounds his account of God in all three tenses of time. It is part of either the history

---

58. Rosenzweig, *Stern*, 427.

or myth of Rosenzweig that he was so transformed by a Yom Kippur experience he had, on October 11, 1913, that on his way to adopting Christianity he decided to remain within Judaism.[59] What possibly supports the presumed *history* of the experience is the climactic place of Jewish ritual in Rosenzweig's *Star* and the exceptional role the Yom Kippur liturgy plays in his account of it, which could reflect back on a euphoric religious experience he had on the High Holy Day. What supports the *myth* of this account is that Rosenzweig never cited that October 1913 Yom Kippur experience as especially eventful for him, though his silence on the point could be another expression of negative theology. However we interpret his descriptions of Yom Kippur, Rosenzweig's God is likely to reach first those who have ears attuned to the liturgy of the Jewish High Holidays, even and especially those, as we explored in the last chapter, who approach them godlessly. What rises up on the ruins of what has been lost to negation is the very thing lost.

Collectively, our negative theologians suggest that the best way to think of the word-name, *God*, is as part of a family of terms that defy all the descriptive content we try to give them. Any description we might give falls flat. This includes, to recover parts of earlier chapters, quite an assembly alongside God: useless suffering, the devastated self, the Jewish people, the divine covenant, divine violence, the I-Thou relation, revelation, the divine name, the Other, pure (Edenic) language, the Infinite, the Absolute, the Eternal. It may be that God comes back to us in some vivified way only within the framework of this family of terms, and never on God's own—to part company here with Spinoza. This would accord with Rosenzweig's view that we know God for real only as *related*, in this case not to humanity and world, as in Rosenzweig's account, but to a group of religiously resonant but contentless terms that draw meaning from their context of use and in communion with each other. At the point they enroll us in the same communion, we have begun to live a spiritual life.

---

59. For an account of the purported history, according to Nahum Glatzer, see Rosenzweig, *Franz Rosenzweig: His Life and Thought*, xvi–xx. For an alternative account, of the myth, see Pollock, *Franz Rosenzweig's Conversions*, 1–11.

Chapter 10
Spiritual Life

WE HAVE MINED FOR something very old in Jewish inheritance, submerged down deep below the people and history of Israel, all the sufferings of the past, all the ethical and ritual ideals, and which—like the law in Kafka's famous parable of the law—glimmers and possibly beckons: the God of negative theology. This is a God so remote from descriptiveness that, as Ilse Bulhof has put it, those of us who aspire to hold it in contemplation come "close to denying that there [is] an object to be contemplated"[1] there at all. It is like standing on the American shore of the Atlantic Ocean and straining eastward to see the European shore from there with only the naked eye. So far as the eye is concerned, there *is* no answering shore. But that is just the appeal of this God-idea. It neighbors so closely on atheism that it seems a small step to it from our accustomed secularity. As Michael Fagenblat opines, "The intensity of Jewish negative theology in recent decades has modified the very topography of Jewish thought, . . . enabling it to grow on secular, even atheist ground."[2]

The negation of this chapter extends that of the previous one. We have negated a personal god. There is no additional negation to perform here, except perhaps of any objection (which will arise) to *Jewish* use of the term "spiritual." We define spirituality simply as the quality of a life that focuses centrally on the idea/reality of God, understood for our purposes as the God of negative theology. We affirm that a manner of spiritual life rises up within Judaism on the basis of negating the personal

1. Bulhof, "Negative Theology," 428.
2. Fagenblat, *Negative Theology*, 1.

God. The philosophers address us here in the same groupings they did in the previous chapter: Maimonides and Spinoza, representing a rationalistic approach to spiritual life; Ecclesiastes, Leibowitz, and Levinas, the pragmatic approach; Buber and Rosenzweig the experiential one.

For the Maimonidean spiritual life, the best place to turn is the end of the *Guide of the Perplexed*. There, Maimonides denies that he has anything new to say over what has come before (GP618). He can (rightly?) presume that anyone who has borne with his book thus far, to the end, is already in the frame of mind he is about to describe, which is one of contemplative and ever-intensifying preoccupation with the idea of the contentless God. In that, Maimonides is in line with the old rabbinic prayer of thanksgiving over Torah study, where the blessing is on a God who has commanded us to *be preoccupied with* the words of Torah (*la'asok b'divrei Torah*), but not necessarily to understand them. Maimonides has brought us to the point of apprehending God. Now he wants us to linger where he has brought us. It turns out that the whole of the commandments, each one of which Maimonides was at pains individually to rationalize, have for their overarching purpose only one, to wean us from preoccupation "with matters pertaining to this world" (GP622). The commandments work in the service of a self-denial toward the world that recalls the extremist, ascetical trend in Jewish philosophical ethics.

But in addition, Maimonides offers steps to follow to both reach and sustain the lingering he commends. Maimonides presumes in his reader a life of prayer, which lays a foundation for what he has on offer. One of the perplexities of his reader is doubtless over the point of prayer to a contentless God. As though to concede the problem, Maimonides suggests the first step toward discerning the usefulness of prayer is to "empty your mind of everything" (GP622) in the pronouncing of it. It is as though to match the contentlessness of God to an albeit spoken but contentless prayer. Over time, by the very direction of prayerful thought, the contentless God comes to occupy the mind of the seeker even while engaged in everyday activities (GP623). It is as though to ride on the language of prayer which, of its own agency, leads us up a spiritual ladder. At the higher reaches of this process, perhaps only available fully to Moses, bodily functions attenuate, most especially "the various kinds of the sense of touch" (GP620); or at least, more accessibly, at a lesser degree of intensity a separation sets in between our senses and ourselves so that bodily behavior is performed by those at this stage "with their limbs only, while their intellects were constantly in His [God's] presence" (GP624).³ Here we may recall Bahya's words from chapter 7, inspired by the Sufis, on a divinely guided, senseless apperception. Maimonides suggests, in wonder, "a most extraordinary speculation has occurred to me" (GP624), that at such a stage we cease to experience all physical harm (GP624–27).

In the previous chapter, we already noticed an affinity between Maimonides and the Hindu Upanishads. They are bound by a shared preference for negative theology. Only now, the affinities broaden to include the practice of spiritual life. No one familiar with Mahayana Buddhist texts can read Maimonides's advice to "empty your mind of everything," without thinking of them. But the Hindu philosopher Sankara (eighth century) also advised a contemplative practice of distancing the data of the senses. Most in sync with Maimonides, the meditation includes the thought that touch "does not produce for me any change of gain and loss . . . since I am devoid of touch."⁴ And Maimonides shares with Hindu practice a high estimation for advanced age, when spiritual adepts within the Hindu framework are freed from the obligations of family and ritual practice to become wandering *sannyasins*, while Maimonidean sages who "in solitude and isolation" (GP621) have been advancing in spiritual life are empowered to anticipate that death will come to them as a kiss (GP628).

We have already seen that the Maimonidean life looks for its best moments to happen in solitude. Now we learn that in a solitude preoccupied with God our whole being transforms toward warmth and light. We are "like one who is in the pure light of the sun" (GP625). Maimonides has prepared for this image by emphasizing how much what he wants us to do is properly *see*. By a happy accident of English, the *seeking* we do of God by way of our minds embraces *seeing* (GP618) that very God. And if we see from very nearby, available to only a few, we do indeed receive our death when it finally comes as a kiss (GP628). There is the warmth. Indeed, for Maimonides the lingering preoccupation with God that follows on the apprehension of God, by way of negative theology, constitutes *love* of God (GP624).

But then the Platonic tradition of spirituality, in which Maimonides partially participates, has already prepared the way for this kind of life. And we saw glimmers of it in Philo's account of the first-century Jewish

3. For a helpful outline of the Maimonidean stages of spiritual growth, see Blumenthal, *Philosophic Mysticism*, 122–25.
4. See the Parisamkhyana meditation in Sankara, *Thousand Teachings*, 251–53.

monastics, the Therapeutae. Plato's reason both illumines and warms, in explicit analogy with the sun, which the Therapeutae reverenced at the climax of their services (Contempl. 89). Reason transports to the highest regions of the Platonic worldview, where the idea of the Good resides, just as the Psalmist's "songs of ascent" (Pss 120–134) do in the Bible, toward the elevated dwelling of the biblical God. There, too, the point is *seeing*: "I will lift up mine eyes unto the mountains" (Ps 121:1); "Unto Thee I lift up mine eyes" (Ps 123:1); "I will not give sleep to mine eyes" (Ps 132:4). Following the lead of Maimonides, our mental efforts soften rather than harden us and assimilate us to the active attributes of God, especially lovingkindness (*hesed*), judgment (*mishpat*), and righteousness (*tzedakah*). Lovingkindness most especially recalls the ethics of Maimonides as it inclines to the extreme, for "*hesed* is excess . . . in beneficence" (GP630). And so it seems that within a Maimonidean spirituality we emerge from our solitude after all, on the heels of a warmth and light we may have solitarily encountered but that move us beyond ourselves, toward others.

Ilse Bulhof notes that the path of negative theology is actually bifocal. There are "on the one hand negations concerning the *object* of the search—. . . the Divine [and] . . . on the other hand negations concerning the *subject* of the search, longing for wisdom."[5] The self-negations are less about descriptiveness than self-centrality. Maimonides is explicit about this. The whole of reality vastly outweighs in value mere human being (GP442), which does not—Gen 1 to the contrary—climax creation (GP452). Rather, all beings exist by divine right in their own right. Bulhof suggests that the impact of negative theology on the spiritual life is to inculcate "states in which the talk about I and me does no longer make sense."[6] It is as if "I" am evacuated of content, like the God of negative theology itself, and as though to be in that way in the image of God. In the contemplation of contentlessness, I become free of content too. Here Maimonides recalls a Buddhist adage from the Dhammapada (verse 1): "All that we are is the result of what we have thought." We may cease to speak in such a state, for fear of supplying content when it is not wanted, but we already know that silence is golden to Maimonides (GP139) and to the whole negative theological stance.

A Maimonidean spiritual life might begin with the pull of the *Guide* itself. Its hints of meaning other than what it seems to say draw

---

5. Bulhof, "Negative Theology," 423.
6. Bulhof, "Negative Theology," 441.

the reader inside. To the extent it appears to value the perplexity it aims to dispel, it intrigues.[7] Its push to the very edges of Judaism itself up to and almost beyond creation doctrine carries the thrill of all borderlands, as between earth and water at the beach, or air and earth at a precipice, or life and death itself—the inescapable borderland of all organic finitude. Perhaps we need to be shaken from our false securities, our investments in the inferior "perfections" of property, bodily health, even intellectually unilluminated moral virtue (GP634–35), all of which Maimonides disdains as ultimate life goals, and plunged into a borderland before we can even be open to receiving Maimonides's spiritual seductions. But how far from borderlands of one kind or another are any of us at any given moment of life? The borderland appears to be where Maimonides's successor, Spinoza, began.

Spinoza inhabited a number of borderlands: between Jews and Christians, merchants and philosophers, scientists and religionists, activists and contemplatives. In an early text, his *Treatise on the Emendation of the Intellect* (1659?), he writes from a borderland between the rare good life and the common unenlightened one. At the beginning of the text, he wonders whether he can move from a life motivated by the lesser values of sensual pleasure, wealth, and honor[8] to one that centers on "love towards a thing eternal and infinite . . . [that] would afford me a continuous and supreme joy to all eternity" (233, 235). Suspended within the question of this choice,

> I saw that my situation was one of great peril and that I was obliged to seek a remedy with all my might, . . . like a sick man suffering from a fatal malady who, foreseeing certain death unless a remedy is forthcoming, is forced to seek it . . . with all his might, for therein lies all hope. (234)

This is one of the few autobiographical passages in his published works and presages his magnum opus, *The Ethics*, which does indeed trace a passage from those lesser goods—if they were goods at all, and not Dantesque obsessions that fed off their own failures to fulfill—to blessedness, which his own given name connotes.

---

7. This is Micah Goodman's interpretation of the *Guide*, that it advances a "therapeutic perplexity" that is "especially relevant to skeptical questioning readers today" (Goodman, *Maimonides*, 235).

8. Spinoza, *Ethics, Treatise on the Emendation of the Intellect*, 233–34. Subsequent citations to the *Treatise* are given, parenthetically, as page numbers within this book.

The passage reflects some debt to Maimonides, who also disdained those same false values of pleasure, wealth, and empty honor. Like Maimonides, Spinoza takes the "highest human perfection" (236) to be an achievement of intellectual vision. "I perceived... quite clearly in my mind" (235) the prospect of a good that could happily occupy it to the exclusion, or at least subordination, of all else. Spinoza shares Maimonides's notion that the ideas we entertain bear on the welfare of our souls: we become what we think. But Spinoza lacked a key component of Maimonides's worldview: Ptolemaic astronomy. Spinoza postdated Copernicus and overlapped in time with Galileo and Newton. He could not believe that the earth occupied the center of surrounding concentric spheres of planets and stars, moved by divine intellects. So he is closer to us in worldview than Maimonides is. The question for him was whether ideas all on their own, without the support of the Aristotelian/Ptolemaic cosmos, could be as reassuring for him and his contemporaries in their own day as they were in Maimonides's—or, we might add, could be for us in ours.

We have already seen how, for Spinoza, our ideas could be mustered to discipline our emotions. If we could locate a painful emotion of ours in the sequence of psychosomatic causes that occasioned it we would both understand it and obtain our release from the pain of it. This was already to link ideas to therapy. But there was more to the power of ideas. They were not static but rather active elements of consciousness. An idea implicitly asserted its truthfulness until another idea showed it false. "An idea... involves affirmation or negation" (E2p49cs). It is as though those cosmic intellects that guided the planets, in Aristotle's world, ceded their activity to the ideas in Spinoza's. What Spinoza needed to know was whether some ideas were so powerful as to guarantee their own truthfulness, so that from them other reliable ideas could be inferred. Part of the reason Spinoza modeled his *Ethics* on Euclid's *Elements* was that he took the ideas of geometry—points, lines, planes, circles, triangles—for self-authenticating ideas, or at least ones deducible from those that self-authenticate. But geometry was propaedeutic to something much higher: philosophical theology. We already know from the previous chapter that one self-authenticating idea stands out for its enormous import: the idea of God. Spinoza's twist on the ontological argument was to infer the reality of God from the utter independence of the God-idea: "that which is in itself and... conceived through itself" (E1d3). For so independent an idea could suffer nothing to block its self-realization. And so of necessity it must self-realize. God must exist.

But the idea of God embraces still more. "By God I mean an absolutely infinite being" (E1d6). We have already seen how that quality does nothing to compromise Spinoza's negative theology. But it does move Spinoza's God-idea to self-realize in infinite ways. Spinoza deems each of those ways an attribute, as we saw in the previous chapter, which in turn, in totality, realize infinity by occurring in infinite number, of which we know two: thought and extension. But now each of those, as expressions of infinity, must further self-express in infinite terms, which they do by embracing within them infinite sequences of finite instances of themselves. The infinite attribute of thought embraces an infinite sequence of finite thoughts, and that of extension, an infinite sequence of finite, spatial entities. All this (in effect, the cosmos) unfolds from the sheer idea of God. God is like a sea-creature that secretes several levels of its own shell, if we may press such a homely image into service of what Spinoza deems beyond imagination.

Spinoza's worldview comes into clearer focus if understood by way of the idea of expression. Within chapter 6, under the rubric of revelation, we encountered within Scholem's and Rosenzweig's thought, especially, the notion that what we receive in revelation is less a content expressible in words than a manifestation. For Benjamin, too, Edenic language did not so much describe as present what it referred to. Those manifestations and presentations were expressions of the being behind them. The divine-love command in Rosenzweig may take the form of the grammatical imperative but its actual function is to carry love—express it—to the hearer. If it overflows to the neighbor, that too is an expression and only seemingly the realization of a *command* to love. The expression rides on the back of the command-form, which only exists in this case to carry the love.

For Spinoza, steps of a cosmic ladder express downward from God, at the top, to the individual thoughts and things of our everyday experience, at the bottom. The import of that for spiritual life, or Godward orientation, is that the direction of the steps is as much upward as downward. We can retrace the downward movement of expression, toward everyday reality, back upward toward the originating God. Of course, since God is beyond space, we can only take these directional pointers as metaphors. We can locate our own mentality and physicality (mind and body) as one among the infinite expressions of God. We are part of God (E1p36). Since, for Spinoza, ideas are self-expressive powers, he can also say that "whatever exists expresses God's power" (E1p36), since the idea of God is powerful enough to self-realize from within itself. The power is so great that the results of its exercise echo over grades of being, from the absolutely infinite God to the relatively infinite attributes to the finite thoughts and things in infinite number, which Spinoza calls modes—like the overflows of a tiered fountain, cascading from the concentrated sprouts at the top to the multiple wavelets of the lowest tier.

Spinoza's worldview is, like Maimonides's, a hierarchy that locates God at the top and us at the bottom. As much as Maimonides did, Spinoza contests the view that "God has made everything for man's sake" (E1p36appendix). We are fragile beings, prey to many forces we cannot control. We may nonetheless rest assured that whatever happens to us does so within the framework of divine being. The difference from Maimonides is that not only our minds but also our bodies express the divine. Recall Spinoza's wonder over why "matter should be unworthy of the divine nature" (E1p15s), a thought that would scandalize Maimonides. If we are to be preoccupied with God, Spinoza supplies a readier means of that than Maimonides does. For everything ultimately redounds back to God. For a God-attuned mind, the idea of God "springs to life" (E5p11) with every thought and thing we encounter. Even material things virtually speak to us, if we have ears to hear, as for Walter Benjamin they did to Adam. All that clutter of being, which was so obstructive for Maimonides, fuels the spiritual life for Spinoza. If painful emotions in particular are our concern, we need only remember that they are instances of the divine in psychosomatic form (E5p39).

But in all this relatedness to God, we need to not lose sight of Spinoza's negative theology. The God everything recalls, if we let it, is beyond description, except in negative terms, even if what *expresses* that same God at the lowest level of the modes admits of positive description. Spinoza allows us "an adequate knowledge of the eternal and infinite essence of God" (E2p47), but these divine qualities are negations—of time, of finitude. Spinoza is with Maimonides on the character of this knowledge, that it constitutes an apprehension—not a comprehension—in Maimonides's language, or an intuition, in Spinoza's (E2p40s2). In both cases, our knowledge of God transposes to positive declarations only on the acts of God (Maimonides) or expressions of God (Spinoza).

Lest we be seduced into thinking that the expressions of God in nature are unqualified divinity, as Spinoza's most famous expression of equivalence, "God or Nature," might lead us to believe, and incline us to take him for a simple pantheist, we need to hear his comment on nature as we behold it, full of "many imperfections, such as rottenness to the point of putridity, nauseating ugliness, confusion, evil, sin, and so on" (E1p36appendix).[9] Spinoza is no romanticist of nature. The individual elements of nature, though subsumed by God, are twice removed expressions of God. Christians have a ready means to comprehend Spinoza, since the figure of the Son of God relates to the Father in a similar way: he is a human being, with all the nausea and confusion that accompanies embodied life, and yet still God, on account of the eternal begetting, Father of Son, as the Nicene Creed would have it, that relates the two. The Son is to the Father in the Nicene Creed as the attributes of God are to God in Spinoza. Individual thoughts and things are one step further removed from God, the grandchildren of God, as it were. But then a Jewish understanding of Spinoza can go by way of the names of God, which *are* God but in the lesser order of being of language, just as the Son of God *is* God, but in the lesser order of being of humanity.[10]

What is the result of locating ourselves within the framework of something "in itself and conceived through itself," such as God is? The key result is immunity to harm since as modes of God, twice removed from the contentless being of God, we still participate in that same consummation of self-containment.[11] It is the same as what Maimonides claimed for the state of contemplative worship. Insofar as love is "pleasure accompanied by the idea of an external cause" (E3definition of emotions 6), the more our pleasure increases in God, the more we fall in love with God. That love intensifies the more of our being we locate within the divine frame—for *all* of it resides there, both body and soul—to such a point that "we clearly understand in what our salvation or blessedness or freedom consists, namely in the constant and eternal love towards God" (E5p36cs). And there is our Spinozan spiritual life, *sub specie aeternitatis*.

---

9. Spinoza speaks loosely here, from our human perspective, since "all things in Nature proceed from an eternal necessity and with supreme perfection" (E1Appendix). He means that nature in the raw is not designed to serve us and from a purely human perspective is not our friend, as Heschel also warned us in chapter 1.

10. For a carefully reasoned and also gracefully empathic reading of Spinoza's spirituality against a backdrop of Christian thought, see Carlisle, *Spinoza's Religion*.

11. Clare Carlisle puts it beautifully when she suggests that a person who takes up fully her habitation in God undergoes "a transformation, at once ethical and ontological, that softens the distinction, perhaps even to the vanishing point, between a human being's finite life and the eternal life of God" (Carlisle, *Spinoza's Religion*, 163).

TOWARD A NEGATIVE THEOLOGY OF JUDAISM

It is not as self-contained a life as we might suppose, given that we appear to lose ourselves in a state of "in-itself and conceived-through-itself." We already saw in chapter 7, on ethics, how Spinoza's therapy of the emotions implied also an ethics of concern for the neighbor. Spinoza enjoyed a lively correspondence with friends. He participated in the politics of his day. As it was for Maimonides, so for Spinoza, the God-intoxicated life was also a highly moral and other-regarding one, serene in its freedom from all the negative emotions (E2p49cs). This was especially important in times of violence, such as the Thirty Years War (1618–1648), which raged in Spinoza's day. For the cause of war was often desire to wholly possess what otherwise might be shared, such as wealth, land, or power. Ideas are inherently shareable. In a world where ideas surpass all other realities and are valued more for themselves than for their practical instrumentality, occasions for violence diminish. Apart from self-authenticating ideas, reasoned ideas that were widely shared, such as the axioms within Spinoza's system, e.g., "Man thinks" (E2a2), drew Spinoza's special favor (E2p38c), in part for the community they made among those who shared them. And it was easier to live toward the most consequentially shareable of reasoned ideas—that of God—within a community of like-minded souls.[12] Insofar as the good is the useful (E4d1), God-oriented souls are best of all for their aid to the God-centered life. All who know God want others to also, for the reasoned and shareable happiness there is in knowledge of God (E4p73s). Insofar as the reasoned life culminates in the Godward one, every reasonable person must rejoice in every other who takes to heart and allows herself to be shaped by the self-realization of the God-idea.

Spinoza's demonstration of his worldview according to the formulations of Euclidean geometry (definitions, axioms, proofs, corollaries) adds another dimension to the spirituality he inspires, that of necessity. There are no possibilities in Spinoza's worldview, only necessities and impossibilities. This may comfort those of us tortured by what "might have been," which is a non-thought for Spinoza. Everything that happens does so with the force of a conclusion of a valid proof in geometry (E1appendix, E2p44). Spinoza extracts the comfort of that: "to expect and to

---

12. Of course, Spinoza intends here the philosophically conceived God, which he takes to be the one reasoned view of God, not the falsely conceived and idolatrous god(s) of the revealed religions, who do indeed serve to occasion war. Spinoza hoped that the bulk of humanity, which was unphilosophical and idolatrously religious, would under guidance of the state take to heart only those aspects of (idolatrous) religion that promoted tolerance and kindness.

endure with patience both faces of fortune" (E2p49s): the smile and the frown. Spinoza may be anti-Platonic in his highly utilitarian account of the good—that it is what is most useful to us—but when the most useful things turn out to be ideas we contemplate, Plato has the final word after all. In the end, for all his endorsement of matter as expressively divine, Spinoza is an idealist, a kind of Platonist for whom ideas are the chief reality, from which, to misapply the verse from a famous Christian doxology, "all blessings flow"[13]—but in keeping with the thought of one named after the very idea of blessing: Baruch/Bento/Benedict Spinoza.

Spinoza's tripartite model of reality of God/Attribute/Mode may not persuade us. Lewis Feuer suggests that "no one recorded in the history of ideas seems ever to have accepted all of Spinoza's major tenets."[14] But it is possible to appropriate the spirit of Spinoza without the letter. Rebecca Goldstein does so when she substitutes for Spinoza's God an "infinite explanatory system, . . . the details of which cannot . . . be exhaustibly grasped in their inexhaustible entirety but can nevertheless be holistically intuited."[15] Our ascent from ourselves to what contains us takes us to an intuition of the causal inter-relationality of all reality. This is a departure from negative theology toward a more scientific view of the divine, as the link, say, between relativity and quantum theory—to the extent those are two positively describable theories that approach an infinite explanatory system. So scientific an interpretation of Spinoza is in his spirit, but it sacrifices his use to us as part of a Jewish tradition of negative theology. The entrée to Spinoza within that tradition will go by way of his idealism: his faith of the kind Plato had in the power of ideas, to, if not self-realize as Spinoza would have it, impress themselves in determining ways on our lives. A Spinozan spirituality locates us within a God-idea that simultaneously and paradoxically transcends us in its infinity, as negative theology would teach, and embraces us, body and soul, in its capaciousness. If we read the *Ethics* sympathetically, exercising some of our capacity to suspend disbelief, we may find ourselves in just that place—what Jewish tradition might name, after God, *haMakom*, The [best] Place.

---

13. The verses of a common Christian doxology, "Praise God from whom all blessings flow, praise him all creatures here below," culminate in an affirmation of the Christian trinity. See https://www.hymnal.net/en/hymn/h/8. Spinoza wrote sympathetically of Jesus in his *Theological-Political Treatise*, but he did not convert to Christianity.

14. Feuer, "Spinoza's Thought," 36.

15. Goldstein, *Betraying Spinoza*, 187.

Spinoza has not fared especially well in the estimation of his Jewish philosophical successors. Hermann Cohen vented an exceptionally harsh animus toward him. He blamed the "orgies" of anti-Semitism he observed in his own time on "the demonic spirit of Spinoza, still poisoning the atmosphere from within and without."[16] Cohen had especially in mind Spinoza's critiques of Judaism and the Jewish people in his *Theological-Political Treatise*, which he took for a major feeder of Christian anti-Semitism, though scholars since have judged that evaluation overwrought.[17] But Rosenzweig, Cohen's student, broadened the critique when, with regard to Spinoza's thought in general, he referenced "the pseudo-profundity of this great tempter"[18]—a judgment that implicitly faults *The Ethics*, too, even as it backhandedly acknowledges its appeal.

Levinas joins this emergent chorus—switching now to our pragmatically negative theologians. We already encountered, in chapter 2, his charge against Spinoza that in his rejection of Judaism he was too sympathetic to Christianity. In his *Theological-Political Treatise*, Spinoza did indeed write warmly of Jesus, who, he suggested, "communed with God mind to mind."[19] Spinoza's praise for Jesus (which was not unqualified) coheres with Cohen's own critique, only to the extent that Christianity is itself judged a motivating cause of anti-Semitism—a fair judgment, though one that needs to be nuanced. But Levinas had another complaint against Spinoza, that in the harshness of his historical-critical reading of the Bible, he missed the degree to which the succeeding "Talmud and rabbinic literature . . . sum up the efforts made over thousands of years to go beyond the letter of the text and even its apparent dogmatism and to restore a wholly spiritual truth even to those passages of the scriptures called historical or ritual or ceremonial or thaumaturgical."[20] Levinas reveals there his fondness for the rabbinic literature. Elsewhere, he writes, "It is the Talmud which allows us to distinguish the Jewish reading of the Bible from . . . [that of] historians or philosophers,"[21] a thought that subtly disowns the Jewish philosophers. But for us just now, the key word in this passage is *spiritual*.

16. Cohen, "Spinoza," 212.
17. See for example Nauen, "Hermann Cohen's Perceptions of Spinoza."
18. Rosenzweig, *Franz Rosenzweig: His Life and Thought*, 270.
19. Spinoza, *Theological-Political Treatise*, 14.
20. Levinas, *Difficult Freedom*, 116. Subsequent citations to pages of this text are given parenthetically.
21. Levinas, "Revelation," 197.

The very word itself disturbs. "Nothing is more ambiguous than the term 'spiritual life'" (6). The notion of spirituality does not figure large in traditional Jewish vocabulary.[22] It does not help a Jewish reading of this term that it enjoys so much prestige in the history of the Roman Catholic religious orders.[23] If spirituality is weighted with heavy Christian provenance, no wonder Levinas, who has already noted, for him, disturbingly Christian sympathies in Spinoza, is uncomfortable with it. But then, if spirituality is incipiently Christian, Levinas has another reason to be wary of this term, just because of his own encounters with Christianity, its people and literature. Guy Stroumsa has lectured on "the very strong impact Christianity had on Levinas from his youth onward," so much as to be "what Levinas himself has called 'the temptation of Christianity.'"[24] Stroumsa avers that Levinas had, before the Holocaust, understood the sufferings of the Jewish people after a Christian model of vicarious, expiatory atonement for the world. The Second Isaiah may have framed this doctrine in a Jewish biblical context, in the person of the Suffering Servant, e.g., Isa 42:1–4, but Christianity had clearly appropriated it beyond easy Jewish reach. So if the Jewish people lived the Passion of Christ, as the early Levinas thought, they were modeling what was in effect a Christian ideal. It was only the Holocaust that, for Levinas, exploded the temptation to read the Jewish people that way, and with it, any efforts at all to "explain" suffering. (We know from ch. 2 that Levinas opposed all theodicy.)

But Christianity continued to serve Levinas as a foil against which to set a definitively *ethical* Judaism. For example, when he writes that "justice is the term that Judaism prefers to terms more evocative of sentiment" (18), it is difficult not to believe he has New Testament (especially Johannine) ideals of love in mind. Let us not miss the pathos here. Stroumsa notes that one of the writers who sustained Levinas over his internment in Germany as a prisoner of war was Teresa of Ávila (a descendant of *converso* Jews), whose works he happened to chance upon. As Stroumsa notes, "in captivity one reads what one finds." Teresa nurtured him in his distress. As Stroumsa puts it, "a Christian saint had touched the heart of a Jewish *Untermensch*." In addition, Levinas in captivity during World

---

22. "'Spirituality' is a word for which there is no counterpart in classical Hebrew" (Kellner, "Spiritual Life," 273).

23. See, for example, the multi-volume Viller et al., *Dictionnaire de spiritualité ascétique et mystique*.

24. Stroumsa, "Christianity and the God of Israel."

War II took heart from the fact that his wife and daughter were safe in a Christian convent. So it is not from any visceral dislike of Christianity that Levinas writes, but from the intuition that in its very spirituality—its preoccupation with knowing God, such as the term *theology* already implicitly connotes—it represented a path distinct from Judaism; which, ipso facto, was *not* spiritual, at least not in the same way.

Levinas's Christian pathos comes home to us when in critique of Jewish longings in his own day for a revival of Judaism he suggests the would-be reformers of the ancient religion are implicitly calling out: "We need a Saint Teresa of our own!" (6), as if the ardor and ecstasy of Christian saintliness, which had helped sustain his own spirits in the German stalag, was the answer to Jewish torpor. It was not. Let us not, he advises, think "a Jewish revival [can] operate under the sign of the Irrational, the Numinous, or the Sacramental" (6). Levinas is articulating his discomfort with the very notion of a God-obsessed spirituality. He might just as easily have discouraged his readers from seeking Jewish revival in Maimonides or Spinoza or any rationally theological version of the religion that inclined Godward. No, the place to go was back to the classic *rabbinical* sources. The Talmud was the "work of interiorization that reveals the inner meaning" of Scripture (117). It is the "talmudic texts which try to present the nature of Israel's spirituality" (15). Levinas the philosopher always wants our return to the rabbis: "The Judaism with historic reality—Judaism, neither more nor less—is rabbinic" (13).

If modern Jewish life was torpid in places, that was not because it was not spiritual enough, but rather not *talmudic* enough. Levinas helped to revive the Talmud, even in non-Jewish settings, with his talmudic readings.[25] In places, Levinas implies a contrast between the ethics of Judaism proper and spirituality of any kind. Insofar as my spirituality inclines to private exultations with God, it enables, even causes, violence to my own freedom (14) and to my neighbor's need (6–7). Levinas allows that a deflection of spiritual life *from* God risks a rise of atheism (15). But we already know (from ch. 9) that, for Levinas, atheism constitutes a stage of religious life in any case. Atheism purifies religion of all its theodicies. When Levinas titles one of his essays within *A Difficult Freedom* "A Religion for Adults," he implicitly consigns the spiritual to a time of religious childhood.

---

25. For example: Levinas, *Nine Talmudic Readings*.

It should not surprise us by now that Levinas's religion for adults is simply ethics. If we must have the vocabulary of spirituality, let us force fit it into ethical molds. And Levinas does. "For a long time Jews thought that every situation in which humanity recognizes its religious progress finds in ethical relations its spiritual meaning" (4). We must recover this thought, and not be misled by any notion that (mere) ethics constitutes "an earthly propaedeutic" (4) to a higher spirituality. "The way that leads to God... leads ipso facto—and not in addition—to man" (18). "Through my relation to the Other, I am in touch with God" (17). Now we are on familiar Levinasian ground. We know this thought from three chapters back, on ethics. We know that God and the neighboring Other, in Levinas, morph into each other. "The justice rendered to the Other, my neighbor, gives me an unsurpassable proximity to God" (18).

For some of us, Levinas protests too much against any distinction between spirituality and ethics. He seems to know at heart (with Kierkegaard) that these are not the same. But he has begun to illustrate for us the kind of anti-spiritual spirituality, in sync with his anti-philosophical philosophical Judaism, that works to support what we have called the pragmatic version of negative theology. Levinas's point is simple. Let God be "otherwise than being," after the title of one of his books, and beyond description. There is the negative theology. What matters is what we *do*. And now comes the deflection from God: the theological pragmatism. "To know God is to know what must be done" (17). What must be done is ethics. And for Jews the way is already paved toward that. "The ritual law of Judaism constitutes the austere discipline that strives to achieve... justice" (18). We are back to the rabbis. And at just this juncture Yeshayahu Leibowitz issues his *amicus brief* in support of Levinas's suit against the spiritual.

We already know that Leibowitz is not entirely on the same page with Levinas. Leibowitz is adamant that Judaism is *not* ethics, that "ethics is an atheistic category par excellence."[26] That can be taken as a backhanded appreciation of the extent to which Levinas borders on atheism, as Leibowitz himself does. But Leibowitz's point is that the mitzvot command without any further good they intend to fulfill—including ethics—beyond devotion to God. Where Leibowitz and Levinas dovetail is on the issue of spirituality itself and its affiliation with Christianity, which for these thinkers is likely the loser in any comparison with Judaism.

---

26. Leibowitz, *Judaism*, 18. Subsequent citations to pages in this text are given parenthetically.

In lieu of Levinas's euphemisms for Christian spirituality, such as *sentiment*, we find a host of terms and expressions in Leibowitz: "abstract principles," which "tend to petrify" (4); "the personal, private, subjective, and individual," which cannot produce "religious community" (11); the "interior of a man's soul" (17) which threatens to obstruct "the orientation to practice" (17); "ecstatic enthusiasm and fervor," which fail to sustain us in "life's prose" (13); "the incidence of religious experience" (13), which is by nature fleeting; "a means of satisfying man's spiritual needs" (14), which fails to stimulate his "sense of duty" (16), and raises a false hope of "extricating man from the human condition" (15). For Leibowitz, spirituality reduces to a kind of pathos, a suffering over the constraints of reality, that is diametrically opposed to the spirit of halachic life. "Most characteristic of the halacha is its lack of pathos" (13).

But before we would turn this critique against Levinas, too, whose pathos we expressly called out, we need bend toward Leibowitz a more attentive ear, which hears him say: "Precisely this nonpathic attitude hides a depth of intense pathos" (13). Of course it does. If what we want is intimate proximity to God, and if that is spirituality, this is the very thing we cannot have. For at no point have we ever "fulfilled" our halachic observance. The mitzvot never cease to command; they are never satisfied. "Performance of the mitzvot is man's path to God, an infinite path, the end of which is ... in effect unattainable" (15). And so, "the aim of proximity to God is unattainable" (16). This is precisely the theological pragmatism that deflects attention away from God toward our own acts which, in the practice and "prose" of life, effectively substitute for God. The dovetailing with Levinas intensifies, insofar as the pathic non-pathos of Leibowitz resembles the spiritual non-spirituality of Levinas. And so the word *spiritual* finds its way positively into Leibowitz's vocabulary after all, as it did into Levinas's, Christianity notwithstanding. There is, after all, "a spiritual and mental world of the Jewish religion" (4), but it must be understood as "a superstructure rising above a basis of religious practice" (5), rather than the other way round.

Leibowitz might draw support from that light of early modern Orthodoxy, Samson Raphael Hirsch, whom we briefly encountered back in chapter 8, and who wrote of any particular halachic ruling that, while what mattered most about it was its "practical execution and fulfillment," nonetheless "the universal, the spirit ... [within it was] for direct individual instruction or personal effort to attain."[27] With that, Hirsch implies that, for all the particularity of the law, by way of both its detail and the chosen people it commands, there are still within it features that address solitary individuals in their perplexity (as Maimonides might say) and communicate universal ideals to those who pine for them. It is just that these, like aspects of mystical insight reserved for mature, private audience, require to be approached under cover, as it were, for misinterpreted they mislead. That combination of terms Hirsch used to describe hidden aspects of the law—the universal, the individual, the spirit—connote just those features of spirituality that Leibowitz called into question: the abstract, the private, the interior. Leibowitz might rephrase Hirsch in this way: beneath the pathos of the law lies a spirituality that, just because it does not serve the community, addresses itself solely to private individuals in their longing to hear that "still small voice" Elijah the prophet heard (1 Kgs 19:12). It is not the point of the law to communicate that voice. The law has no point beyond itself. But perhaps Leibowitz, inspired by Hirsch, might grant to spirituality the status of epiphenomenon to the practice of the law, which is more than Maimonides (or certainly Spinoza) would have conceded it supplied.

Still, there is no escaping that both Levinas and Leibowitz give us—the one by way of ethics, the other by way of law—an "austere discipline."[28] We are to surrender ourselves extravagantly to the demands of either the Other or the law. There is no horizon here on which the God of negative theology might appear to us, but just the stern logic of exorbitant regard for what transcends ourselves. Perhaps the borderline atheism of these views will appeal; or the very austerity itself of them. The latch onto these pragmatic versions of negative theology is something like the latch onto Kant for those moved by the pathos of that philosopher's ethic, which offers up so little overt or easy comfort. When Kant toward the end of his *Critique of Pure Reason* asks: "What can I know, What ought I to do, What may I hope,"[29] the answers implied are bleak indeed. What I can know are not the most important things, what I can do falls short of the ideal, and what I may hope for is infinitely distant. If Plato inspires Maimonides and Spinoza at their most visionary, Kant does Levinas and Leibowitz at their most demanding of us.

27. Hirsch, *Nineteen Letters*, 74.
28. Levinas, *Difficult Freedom*, 18.
29. Kant, *Critique of Pure Reason*, 635.

Let us not leave the pragmatists on our roster without another version of negative theology—some would say the Epicurean version—we get from the biblical Ecclesiastes. Of course, for Leibowitz, Ecclesiastes is a proto-halachist on grounds of those closing words of his that most scholars judge a later (pious) addition: "Fear God and keep His commandments" (Eccl 12:13). Levinas for his part briefly cites Eccl 1:18—"He that increaseth knowledge increaseth sorrow"—for the implicit argument it makes, in reverse, for the use of suffering in quest of knowledge, "where suffering appears at the very least as the price of reason and of spiritual refinement";[30] when we know that, for Levinas, suffering is best understood as useless. But what undermines both these interpretations of Ecclesiastes, Leibowitz's and Levinas's, is the radical skepticism the biblical author brings toward all ostensibly reliable logics of cause and effect. We can hear Ecclesiastes respond to these modern interlocutors: Anyone who expects suffering to yield knowledge will find only ignorance; she who observes the law in expectation of serving God will serve instead the satan.[31] For that is how causality works in Ecclesiastes's universe. Ecclesiastes offers up more than what R. B. Y. Scott has called a "philosophy of negation."[32] It is a philosophy of frustrated expectation, overturning a treasured assumption of nearly all the other biblical writers, most especially the prophets, that fulfillments follow on promises, and expected effects on causes.

But more importantly for us now, Ecclesiastes shares with Leibowitz and Levinas the deflection of attention they practice away from God and toward our own acts. Ecclesiastes puts it this way in a familiar refrain:

> There is nothing better for a man than that he should eat and drink, and make his soul enjoy pleasure for his labor. This also I saw, that it is from the hand of God. (Eccl 2:24)

It is not so much that Ecclesiastes values eating, drinking, and the pleasure of work (independent of its results). It is that, in context of his skepticism toward the cause-and-effect bond, he understands these acts to be doable in and for themselves, without regard for their status as cause or effect; for the pleasure, even joy (Eccl 3:12), in them is so immediate. If I get sick from eating, drunk from drinking, or exhausted

---

30. Levinas, "Useless Suffering," 160.

31. If we can put Ecclesiastes in dialogue with Job, who introduces the satan figure (Job 1:6).

32. Scott, *Proverbs, Ecclesiastes*, 206.

SPIRITUAL LIFE

from working—no matter, for these acts can just as easily result in pleasant satiety of hunger, thirst, or of the need to achieve. Since we cannot count on any causes to have their predicted effects, let us savor the tastes and acts of the single moment.

On this read of Ecclesiastes, eating, drinking, and the pleasure of work stand in for every moment of self-contained satisfaction in our lives. More than an Epicurean, Ecclesiastes is a proto-practitioner of mindfulness, drawing our attention to the exact present moment, freed of causal or effective bonds.[33] There is one connection Ecclesiastes permits himself to claim obtains, which is between that moment of focus and God. For "it is from the hand of God." A theistic practitioner of mindfulness meditation might agree. Such a read of Ecclesiastes reflects back on "vanity" too—*hevel* in Hebrew, which converts from sorrow to good when the fleetingness of it focuses our attention on the moment. *Hevel* is also Hebrew for Abel, that primordial figure of theistic devotion who was himself fleeting and good in contrast to his earthy and enduring brother Cain. It is easy to see emerging here a very different kind of spirituality from what Levinas and Leibowitz commend to us, though based on the same idea, that the unknowable God deflects attention away from itself toward our own acts.[34]

And now for the third category of negative theologian on our roster: the "absolute empiricists" Buber and Rosenzweig. Anyone who reads or browses Buber's *I and Thou* will have at hand an instance of what Leibowitz might call a celebration of life's poetry (over its prose). Buber himself calls the I-Thou moments "queer, lyric-dramatic episodes."[35] This owes not just to the poetic tenor of the text itself, especially its first part, but to the very nature of the I-Thou relation itself. Like the theme of a Japanese haiku poem, it will not be grasped or defined (as we saw in ch. 3) but only savored on appearance. More, as Buber has described it, it supplies the very *meaning* of life, as poetry might for the poetically inclined. But it is no more a life program than is poetry itself—it is anti-programmatic. It is one of the *folds* of this twofold reality we inhabit characterized alternatively by the "basic words" (53) I-Thou and I-It. We

33. In all of Torah, only Isaac seems to come close to understanding this practice. See Gen 24:63.

34. For more on the spirituality of Ecclesiastes, see Rubinstein, *From Ecclesiastes to Simone Weil*.

35. Buber, *I and Thou*, 84. Subsequent citations to pages of this text are given parenthetically.

move back and forth between the folds, never inhabit both simultaneously, though the one (I-Thou) can shade the other. Of the two folds, I-Thou is explicitly spiritual by our use of that term, for it orients us toward God: Buber's quasi-personal version of the God of negative theology. For we read, "In every relational act [of I-You] . . . we gaze toward the train of the eternal You" (150). Conversely, "the absolute relationship [with God] includes all relative relationships" (129).

Though it is only in part 3 of the book that God becomes central, we already know by the second page of part 1 that we are in the domain of the spiritual. For we read there that "Being I and saying I are the same" (54). Buber is talking about the role of the respective I's in I-Thou and I-It configurations. When we say Thou to someone or thing, we generate the I that so speaks; when we say It, we generate a different I. Where language produces what it says in the very speaking it approximates what Benjamin understood Edenic language to do. And so Buber evokes our sense for the primally good when he ascribes to *our* language a power so like that of the *divine* language in Gen 1, to *be* what it says, since almost everything the divine language speaks in Gen 1 is good.

But the book *I and Thou* is not only about I-Thou relations. The shadow book it subsumes is *I and It*, a central theme of the text's part 2. The I-It fold within our world is a necessary but stressed one. The I of I-It does not produce what it speaks. It *describes* it. What is described is by that very description distanced and dis-related to the speaker. I-It language is always *about* something in the way I-Thou language never is. I-It language is voluble; I-Thou language speaks largely through silence (83). In what Buber calls the It-world, we size each other up for mutual use and abuse. It is the world of our jobs, professions, and resumes, as well to some extent of our loyalty-demanding, pride-inducing, and emotionally constricting families, tribes, and nations. What happens within it is highly describable and categorizable. "Without It a human being cannot live. But whoever lives only with that is not human" (85). That is a problem. For, as we already know, "it is the sublime melancholy of our lot that every You must become an It in our world" (68).

Already in this contrast between I-Thou and I-It a feature of Buber's spirituality begins to emerge: its dualism. Dualisms are frequent within Buber's writing. It is as though to see reality under the sign of the number 2, as opposed, say, to the Christian (or Hegelian) preference for the number 3. There are dualities of "truth and reality, idea and fact, morals and politics" that are "inherent to some degree in all men but especially in Jews."[36] There is the duality of the "true public and true personal life" (95); of the domain of "God's command . . . [and] the laws of economics and politics";[37] of "a truth known to man [that God is good] and of a reality sent by God [of inexplicable suffering]."[38] For Buber, these variously intersecting dualities draw a string of disturbing adjectives to them: "absurd,"[39] "ominous,"[40] "tortuous" (69). As though in sync with Levinas, they indicate the dark side without any attempt at excuse or explanation—no theodicy. This was the stark comfort of our chapter 2, to begin our conversation with the philosophers with our eyes wide open on the issue of suffering.

But Buber will not leave us in that dubious comfort. In fact, the chief duality, between the I-Thou and I-It folds of reality, is not *really* a dualism. There is only one reality. Reality draws the I-Thou and I-It folds of itself precipitously toward unity, like the lines of an optical illusion that spin off of themselves two opposing interpretations, as appear in some textbooks of cognitive psychology. That might seem to ease the prospects for transition from I-It to I-Thou. But it does not, any more than within Mahayana Buddhism the relative identity of samsara and nirvana opens an easy route from the burden of the former to the peace of the latter. For, sadly, the I-It fold of reality has dominated in modern times almost to the exclusion of I-Thou. As Buber laments, in sync with Heschel's own critique of modernity we encountered in chapter 1, "modern developments have expunged almost every trace of life in which humans . . . have meaningful relationships" (97). Buber wants very much for his readers, grown deaf and blind to the I-Thou fold of reality, to find it, for it "has become so unfamiliar, in fact so sunk in oblivion."[41] Like a kabbalist seeking to free the divine sparks from their bodily prisons, Buber addresses his burdened reader:

> I am concerned with the turbid, the repressed, the pedestrian, with toil and dull contrariness, . . . [with] the dully-tempered disagreeableness, obstinacy and contrariness in which the man, whom I pluck at random out of the tumult, is living.[42]

36. Buber, *On Judaism*, 126–27.
37. Buber, *Israel and the World*, 235–36.
38. Buber, *Prophetic Faith*, 240.
39. Buber, *Prophetic Faith*, 240.
40. Buber, *Israel and the World*, 236.
41. Buber, *Between Man and Man*, 36.
42. Buber, *Between Man and Man*, 36.

Buber's aim to free his readers from "the slavery of the It world" (107) makes of him what Laurence Silberstein, borrowing from Richard Rorty, has called an *edifying* philosopher: one who works to question "conventional ways of thinking and speaking [that] alienate the individual from the authentic self, other persons, and the natural world."[43] Buber would surely accept that aim for his own. Buber denies, with Leibowitz, that there is any convincing *argument* from some other thing, like nature, to God (129), but not that there could be a convincing *evocation* of God, which is just what he tries to supply via his account of the I-Thou relation. This is what makes him a *spiritual* philosopher.

But Buber himself is no more comfortable with that word, *spiritual*, than Levinas was. The word surfaces in *I and Thou* as "mere spirituality" (115, 152), to connote an interiority of feeling or attitude divorced from reciprocal relations with others or the world, when the whole point of his work is to reawaken his readers to just those reciprocal relations. Drawing from his earlier work, Buber might prefer we speak of *religiosity*, which connotes "man's wonder and adoration, an ever anew becoming . . . [and] longing to establish a living communion with the unconditioned,"[44] that is, with God. But let us not quibble over these words. We know that for Buber, the "inmost Judaism"[45] is deeper than its laws and ethnicity but touches on the primacy of I-Thou relations in the living of life, which in turn open onto God. And so a Buberian spirituality will lay out, to the extent possible, a life program toward this anti-programmatic ideal. But this is easier said than done.

The problem is that the I-Thou relation cannot be located as the effect of a cause. It is not just that within the I-Thou fold of reality, cause and effect relations cease to register. It is that the relation itself defies cause-and-effect analysis. Buber, who found use for Spinoza's attributes in his own effort to justify reference to a personal God, might invoke him again here. For how else could Spinoza, for whom causal reality was exhaustive, read the I-Thou relation except as self-caused, that is, as divine? Buber would welcome so easy a segue from the I-Thou relation to God; but not the means of it, by way of causation, even self-causation. The Thou never appears "as if it had been fitted into a causal chain" (81). "Can one say what is needed [for I-Thou]? Not by way of a prescription" (125). By what way, then?

43. Silberstein, "Renewal," 407.
44. Buber, *On Judaism*, 80.
45. Buber, *On Judaism*, 108.

One starting point in answer to this question is Buber's analysis of the primal history of I-Thou. He writes that in the early life of both humankind and the individual human, relationality precedes objectification. "In the beginning is the [I-Thou] relation" (78). There is not even an understanding of a separate I. But at some point there is a "bursting point" for the I of I-Thou. It recognizes its own separability and elementarity. It is just then that the fold of I-It comes into view, and a way of seeing other people and things as categorizable, manipulable objects. Buber lays this out toward the end of part 1 of his book (73–81), in sync with what anthropologists study under the heading of "ontogeny recapitulates phylogeny." The programmatic use of this is to suggest that at some primal, forgotten level, we all once inhabited the I-Thou fold of reality exclusively. Accessing the relation is not something new for us, but rather, in the language of the High Holiday liturgy, a matter of Return. Perhaps that very characterization, of Return, is already an evocation of I-Thou.

The very language of return, or turning, must evoke for Jewish readers the liturgy of the High Holidays. And Buber might be speaking for serious participants in that liturgy when he says of that turning that it "comes upon the whole person, is carried out by the whole person."[46] Once again we are not in the domain of cause-and-effect. Buber writes elliptically of the turning as something "come upon" me, we know not how. We are not to think in terms of "consequences and effects."[47] We recognize this language of wholeness (from ch. 3) as endemic to the I-Thou fold of reality. When I say Thou to someone or something, I receive them as a whole, not as an "aggregate of qualities" (69). But correspondingly, I too have become whole in this relation that now embraces all of me. That suggests my habitual modus operandi within the I-It world is as a fragmented being, who portions myself out in segments as contexts demand, whether of family, work, play, vocation, avocation, or indeed religion. But Buber invites the thought that the reciprocity of wholeness within the I-Thou relation also works in reverse. If I become whole when I say Thou, then conversely, perhaps my own wholeness awakens a Thou to me. And Buber does indeed write, "It is the whole being, closed in its wholeness, at rest in its wholeness that is . . . able to venture forth toward

---

46. Buber, *Israel and the World*, 20.
47. Buber, *Israel and the World*, 20.

the supreme encounter" (125). So, can I effect my own wholeness, in anticipation of I-Thou relation with another?

A distinct line of thought in Buber suggests I can. It has to do with my capacity to make decisions of what we might call centripetal force, i.e., a decision that by its forcefully attracting nature draws all aspects of myself toward it as their center. A decision to life-partner with someone or accept a job abroad might qualify. We have typically a "polyphony" of voices within us[48] which, if they do not harmonize, so chaotically rend us that, as that tortured Jew Saint Paul said of his own soul, in Buber's rendering, "it does what it wills not to do, what is preposterous to it, the alien, the 'evil.'"[49] The alternative to this is "the audacious work of self-unification,"[50] involving "personal unity, unity of being, unity of life, unity of action."[51] Buber suggests that such work can happen within us even before we are attuned to the I-Thou fold of being, and even if it is not entirely subject to our will to "cause" it. If the work is audacious, it is daring and likely difficult. Nonetheless, it makes a place for us to start and the culmination is momentous, since "he who decides with his whole soul decides for God."[52]

The notions of unity and unification are central to Buber. He expressly does not intend by these terms any ideal of what scholar of mysticism Evelyn Underhill called "the art of union with reality."[53] What he intends is a resolution of the tension within the many dualisms that course through life. For Buber, this is a highly Jewish matter:

> The fundamental attitude of the Jews is characterized by the idea of the *yichud*, the unification ... [which] involves the continually renewed confirmation of the unity of the divine in the manifold nature of its manifestations ... [especially] in the face of the monstrous contradictions of life.[54]

We might grant Buber that this is one explication of Judaism's central prayer, the Shema. But Buber, with his emphasis on ideals of wholeness, whether of the Thou or the I in I-Thou relation, slants the

---

48. Buber, *Between Man and Man*, 86.
49. Buber, *Good and Evil*, 127. Cf. Rom 7:15.
50. Buber, *Good and Evil*, 127.
51. Buber, *Between Man and Man*, 116.
52. Buber, *On Judaism*, 66.
53. Underhill, *Practical Mysticism*, 3.
54. Buber, *Israel and the World*, 15.

unification ideal in a particular way. Unification does not erase oppositions, it reconciles them in harmonious balance. This is really the work of the Jew. "Israel's charge is to serve the cause of unity in the world"[55] or, more accurately, the cause of harmony. When Buber writes in one of his Hasidic texts that "this is the secret of the unity of God; no matter where I take hold of a shred of it, I hold the whole of it,"[56] he articulates the dual poles of any model of wholeness: the whole and the part (or shred). Though the whole contains the part, there is a sense in which the part contains the whole. Each illuminates the other. This is really what Buber understands to happen in I-Thou relation. Whoever is Thou to me "fills the firmament, . . . everything else lives in his light" (59). The part even becomes the whole, and the whole the part.

The import of this for spiritual life stands out especially in contrast to the alternative we find in Spinoza, for whom a causal understanding of the world is exhaustive. Even God is in a sense "caused"—by the idea of God, which, for Spinoza, is to be self-caused. For Buber, the model of cause-and-effect applies to the I-It fold of the world only. Within the I-Thou fold, the model of whole-and-part obtains. This is significant because with this casting of the spiritual life, Buber locates himself within a very wide swath of writing on *secular* spirituality that understands the spiritual life in just that way. As Peter Van Ness has written in his appropriately titled *Spirituality and the Secular Quest*, "Human existence is spiritual insofar as one engages reality as a maximally inclusive whole."[57] If we can take the "one" who so engages with reality as part of the whole, then Van Ness's formulation includes both poles of the whole-part model. With a switch of orientation, rather like that from I-It to I-Thou, I can receive the world around me less after the model of cause-and-effect, and more after that of part-and-whole. That would be a turn to spirituality. This is incidentally a not uncommon way to understand the quality of a fine artwork, through a dialogical coherence it shows between the whole of it and its parts. It is not surprising that within *I and Thou* Buber addresses the case of the artist (60–61) and her relation to the I-Thou encounter through her work. Buber does not follow through to a whole-hearted religion of art. But he invites us to circumvent, spiritually, the whole problem of God—that "most burdened of all human words" (123)—by way of art. And yet he

---

55. Buber, *On Judaism*, 183.

56. Buber, *Ten Rungs*, 54.

57. Van Ness, *Spirituality and the Secular Quest*, 5. Many books treat this topic. An early instance is Johnson, *Search for Transcendence*.

would likely add, "whoever abhors the name [God] and fancies that he is godless—when he addresses with his whole devoted being the You of his life . . . he addresses God" (124).

It is generally said of Buber that his influence among Jews has been less than among Christians. That same survey of American rabbis cited in chapter 8 on their beliefs, conducted by *Commentary* magazine in 1966, reports of Buber that his "influence on Jewish thought in America . . . [has been] hardly any."[58] Walter Kaufmann notes that the first English translation of *I and Thou*, from 1937, had its greatest impact "among Protestant theologians" (20). And I confess I first read the book under guidance of an Episcopal priest, who became a beloved mentor. But outside the official spokespersons of Judaism, Buber may have had more impact among Jews than we know. One example: a Jewish psychiatrist, secular and humanist in belief, reports that it was by way of Buber's book he was guided toward what became his profession.[59] But the American Jewish reception of Buber—or not—stands in contrast to the impact we have already seen Rosenzweig to have had on American Jews. The irony of that is that Rosenzweig's *Star of Redemption*, an enormously challenging book, is likely much less read among American Jews than Buber's *I and Thou*. Still, Rosenzweig's understanding of the mitzvot communicates to American Jews beyond his difficult book, especially by way of Nahum Glatzer's presentation of it in his *Franz Rosenzweig: His Life and Thought*. Non-Orthodox readers will especially warm to the role of love in Rosenzweig's understanding of the mitzvot, inviting but not forcing participation in them. A Rosenzweigian spirituality may well culminate in halachic observance, as it did for Rosenzweig himself, but need not. In dialogue with Martin Buber, Rosenzweig was open to the view that the mitzvot simply fail to reach many a modern Jew with the love they carry—in which case they fail to that extent in their mission.

We already know from chapters 6 and 8, on revelation and ritual, how great a role love plays in Rosenzweig's thought. That it works in the service of spirituality is evident immediately since the love that inaugurates the human power to love is from God. Rosenzweig is much more upfront about God than Buber is. God is inescapable in his thought. But God is inescapable as part of a philosophical system that casts a critical role for a supreme partner in creation and revelation. We could argue

---

58. Himmelfarb, "Symposium," 72.

59. Mark Wilson, "In the Beginning Is Relation," in Rubinstein and Sternhell, *Contemplation*, 94–97.

that, for Rosenzweig, God derives from the *system*, just as for Spinoza God derives from the *idea*. We enter a philosophical system as we do a novel, by suspending disbelief. If the system makes a home, we remain; if not, we depart. What might hold us to Rosenzweig's system?—the centrality of love to it, for one. Rosenzweig is at his most beautiful when writing on love (SR173–78) and most akin to the look and scent of the rose in his name, which across cultures connotes love. Perhaps the only other Jewish philosopher to locate love so centrally in his thought is the Renaissance writer Léon Hebreo (also known as Judah Leon Abravanel) (1465?–1523?), whose *Dialogues of Love* we have not even considered. Do we know this love from our experience? Seduced by Rosenzweig's system, might we know it? That is for each of us to try.

But Rosenzweig's system will pull some of us into it by another route and in tension with love, by way of the climactic vision of God that occurs at the end of the *Star*.[60] A visionary Rosenzweig brings to mind his rationalist forbears in Jewish philosophy, Maimonides and Spinoza, who empowered the eye of reason with comparable daring. But the visions are not the same. We encountered the climactic vision of the *Star* back in chapter 3, by way of illustrating a match between the contentlessness of God and of the Jewish people. But let us linger here a bit more with it. We recall from chapter 3 that we receive at the end of the *Star* a vision of God's face. It is as though Rosenzweig has taken to heart the priestly blessing of Num 6:24–26, which hopes for God's face to shine upon us, even though "man shall not see me and live" (Exod 33:20). The face is a superimposition upon the star of redemption, itself a configuration of all Rosenzweig has been saying throughout his book: that the three elements of reality—God, human, and world—yield in their partnerships creation, revelation, and redemption. God, human, and world occupy the points of the upward triangle; creation, revelation, and redemption the points of the inverted triangle. In configuration, creation appears between God and world, revelation between God and humanity, and redemption between humanity and world. The forehead, eyes, nose, and mouth of the divine face correlate with various points of the star. The star of David will always have this look to anyone who has internalized Rosenzweig's system.

But the star is expressly a configuration. It is a "configuration in the truth" (SR441). Truth has been an elusive commodity up until book 3,

---

60. For an in-depth reading of this vision, see Wolfson, "Light Does Not Talk."

part 3, of the *Star*. But there we learn that "God is truth" (SR403). Rosenzweig means that up until then what he has been describing, in that third part of the book, is how Jews and Christians differently *see* the truth. That language may remind us of Spinoza, who understood us to *see* God by way of different attributes. For Rosenzweig, Jews see truth as a configuration of creation, revelation, and redemption that encloses them in a mitzvah-borne love relation with God. Christians see the truth as the same configuration, but carried by them to the rest of the world as the good news, or gospel. Jews live the divine love in what Rosenzweig calls eternal life; Christians bear the divine love on what Rosenzweig calls their eternal way, to everyone else. Life and way are perspectives on truth but neither captures the whole of it. The *whole* of the truth includes them both in a single image, which neither Jew nor Christian ordinarily sees. They only see it when they exit their own perspectives on truth and view it, as it were, through God's eyes. This is what the system Rosenzweig has constructed allows them to do, at least momentarily before they return to their own perspectives, for one cannot remain long in the presence of the divine face. What they see is the star of David interpreted according to Rosenzweig's system, both flaming inwardly as fire and shining outwardly as rays: the fire and rays (life and way) of love. And even this they barely see, on account of the blinding light of it, so much so that it is almost as good as seeing nothing at all—*das Nichts*[61]—in case we needed any reminder that we have not left the precincts of negative theology.

According to Rosenzweig, "everyone should philosophize some time,"[62] at least once. In illustration of that, it is important for Jews and Christians at least once in their lives to exit their own take on truth in preference for God's, bird's eye view of it, to experience what Spinoza would call the view *sub specie aeternitatis*, but which for Rosenzweig is simply to see "The Star, or Eternal Truth," the title of the last section of the last part of his book. For that vision of the star's eternal truth reveals to them the larger truth of their mutual identity. Jews and Christians are identical inverse opposites, as is any object to its mirror image. Turn a Jew inside out and you have a Christian; or a Christian outside in and you have a Jew.[63] This is indirectly evident from the vision of the star,

---

61. Rosenzweig, *Stern*, 433.

62. Rosenzweig, *Franz Rosenzweig's "The New Thinking,"* 100. Rosenzweig means this concessively, against the idea that we should philosophize all the time, which would detract from living.

63. Levinas said that Christianity is Judaism for people with pagan problems. Levinas quoted by Stroumsa, "Christianity and the God of Israel."

according to the metaphor of fire, which burns inwardly (as Jews) while shining outwardly (as Christians). When Rosenzweig superimposes a face atop the star, in accord with Num 6:24–26, it is partly with the intent of making that point. For the "mouth" of the star, which appears at the star's lowest tip, in the space of redemption, blows a kiss to the viewer. It is the kiss of the love that inaugurates reality in part 2 of the book to which the figure is sending us. But it is also the kiss that assures "the eternal victory over death," which comes at lived reality's end. This is the kiss Maimonides understood Moses to receive from God at his death. And it implies the same thing: that the receiver is at the point of transition from life in this world to the "life beyond life" (SR446).

For Maimonides, the recipient of the divine kiss of death passes into eternal life. But this is not what Rosenzweig envisions for readers who have come to the end of his book. Rather, in bold capital letters, he returns them with his last words "Into Life" (SR447). Rosenzweig admits that at the end of his book he has taken his readers to the end of life. The vision of the star is a life-ending experience. But it ends there also as fulfillment, in a space where God confronts nothing "that he himself is not" (SR406). Humanity and world simultaneously end and culminate in their final redemption, as they transpose to something that stands to life as life does to death: its end and fulfillment beyond our conceiving, as negative theology would have it, as would Sufi mysticism, when it contemplates the soul's ultimate transposition from *fana* to *baqa*.[64] Love and vision are contraries. Buber might say as much. Within love we encounter the other. Within vision we regard the other; less regard, than are captivated by. The mature Buber would doubt the value of the vision. Rosenzweig does not. In Maimonidean and Spinozan vision, the captivation with the other—Levinas might say, captivity *by* the other—becomes union with the other, who ceases to be other. And Rosenzweig suggests something like this happens to humanity and world in the final redemption. But we are not there yet, not by an eon. The vision Rosenzweig proffers at the end of the *Star* is healing and transformative. But it is only for a moment, before we return as Jews or Christians "into life," to our respective and possibly divergent lives and ways, as happens also, for Jews liturgically, at the close of Yom Kippur.

---

64. See Attar, *Conference of the Birds*, 218–20, which climaxes the poem. The passage from *fana* to *baqa* is, in the words of the book's translators, from "transmutation of self" to "everlastingness" (14).

So Rosenzweig speaks in a way that Buber does not to both the loving encounter with the other and the visionary end of all otherness. Both the lover and the mystic can share space in Rosenzweig's philosophical home. The whole of his system, and even his life, illustrates a key idea from the annals of spirituality: the notion of liminality, a concept philosophical anthropologist Victor Turner articulated in his now classic work from 1969, *The Ritual Process*. Turner theorized that rituals help us negotiate threshold moments of life when we are between social statuses, transitioning from child to adult, single to married, life to death. Those liminal moments were "betwixt and between the positions assigned and arranged by law, custom, convention, and ceremonial."[65] For Turner, those moments exude enormous spiritual charge, freed to appear in psychic space cleared of constraining social convention, even as they draw ritual to them as a way to navigate the disorientation of them. They attract to themselves a range of spiritually evocative terms dear to the heart of negative theologians: anonymity, absence, nakedness, unselfishness, silence, suspension,[66] as though the divine demands utter absence of all else before it rushes in to fill the space. But such moments occur in many spaces and times besides those Turner identifies as at birth, marriage, or death. Rosenzweig's sweeping renunciation of all worldly markers of Jewish identity, whether given by militarized land, coercive law, or national (secular) language, instates the Jewish people in a permanence of liminality—for all the paradox of that—and hence, in Turner's terms, of spirituality; to say nothing of the liminality inherent to the momentariness of love itself, the effervescence of the climactic vision that succeeds it, the flickering space between that love and that vision, the very book itself—a hothouse plant of Weimar Germany, itself a bubble that burst on the threshold of the horrors that succeeded it. Sadly, Turner, who appreciated the relevance of Buber to his thought, did not register Rosenzweig on his horizons.[67] We are all the losers for that. But then, loss is liminal too, stranded between what was and is.

---

65. Turner, *Ritual Process*, 95.
66. Turner, *Ritual Process*, 106–7.
67. I tried to make good on that missed opportunity in an unpublished lecture, "Liminality, Communitas, and Franz Rosenzweig."

Chapter 11
Conclusions

OUR STRATEGY OF NEGATION has yielded puzzle pieces of a theology of Judaism, which we have not assembled into a completed picture. Perhaps that is for another time, or for each of us to do, as inclined, on our own. We have a foundation, though, grounded in an attunement to the sufferings of nature, of history, of nation-states; to all that serves to heal, however it comes into view, whether on a near or far horizon, though likely to include heightened awareness of self and other; and to an Apophasis—let it be a capitalized abstraction—that answers for an idea of "God." Perhaps it is best to retire that word/name, as Buber implied we should. It has hazy origins in early English, perhaps connoting libation, that no longer speak to many of us. A Sufi imam once addressed a Reform synagogue on the idea of God, which drew tepid response from those assembled, until he introduced a different name for it: the Absolute, a term he borrowed from the work of the perennialist thinker Frithjof Schuon (1907–1998), though it could just have easily been from Hegel or Krochmal. A congregant later thanked the imam for renaming the God-idea in a way that brought it to life for him again. Names do matter, as Walter Benjamin and Gershom Scholem taught us, as did all the philosophers who reflected on the implications and connotations of the Hebrew names of God.

That is one small piece of a theology of Judaism that has emerged from our negations: that under different names and characterizations, the idea of God is recoverable and even available to center several kinds of spiritual life. Insofar as it is a God idea empty of describable content—whether because what it references is too close, too distant, or too deflecting of attention from itself toward our own acts—it gathers around itself a family of discursively contentless ideas that help to inform it, such as useless suffering, which negates theodicy; divine Names, which we cannot understand; Edenic language, which we cannot speak; the catastrophized self, which cannot stand; Infinity and Eternity, which respectively absent space and time and, critically for Jews: an apophatic identity. Out of a host of negatives a positive, or something like that, emerges.

That is the first building block of a theology of Judaism we might construct from our negations. Here is the second, unfolding from the first: that an affinity shows between the divine Apophasis and Jewish identity over their absence of content. This echoes the old idea of chosenness, but underminingly, by the emptiness that makes for the connection. Judah Halevi and Rosenzweig, with their own apophatically informed theories of chosenness, paved a way for us. But we would clear the space of the connection of any nameable content at all: not *amr ilahi*, not love, but simply Nothing. For all the severity of such a "chosenness," it coheres with the asceticism implicated by the exorbitant ethics we explored in chapter 7. Chosenness to the extent it operates at all, is about subtraction, not addition, as a puzzling verse from that radical Jewish text the Gospel of Matthew may imply: "From him who has not, even what he has will be taken away (Matt 13:12 RSV). But the Nothing of the connection between God and the people Israel also evokes that handshake Rosenzweig intuited between atheism and mysticism.

And that is the third building block, emerging from the second, toward a negative theology of Judaism, that, by way of Nothing, a friendly conversation arises between the philosophical and mystical traditions of Judaism. It is an old claim that a philosophically inspired religion inclines to atheism, perhaps by way of pantheism, if we follow a line of critique aimed at Spinoza. But Rosenzweig has already seen mysticism and atheism connect, as the Psalmist saw at some future time Truth and Mercy would do (Ps 85:10), which might recapitulate in biblical terms the personas of atheist and mystic. The conversation between Jewish philosophy and mysticism is already old, harking back to the Middle Ages.[1] But a modern instance of it occurred in the pre-Israeli British mandate

---

1. See Tirosh-Samuelson, "Philosophy and Kabbalah." On this point Elliot Wolfson writes "the philosophers and the kabbalists live the same kind of life, the contemplative life" (Wolfson, *Elliot R. Wolfson: Poetic Thinking*, 214).

CONCLUSIONS

of Palestine, as World War II raged. Here I draw from a memorable presentation delivered at a conference on Spinoza by French-Israeli scholar Keren Mock, about an exchange between Maimonidean philosopher Yeshayahu Leibowitz and scholar of mysticism Gershom Scholem on the relative merits of philosophy and mysticism.[2] The quoted translations given below from the Hebrew are hers.

Once in July 1941, after a bus ride together in Jerusalem over which the two conducted a conversation of high philosophic import, Leibowitz wrote Scholem with this question: "How is it that the kabbalah has so long gripped the minds and masses of Israel, whereas rationalist philosophy has remained of such limited interest to the public and its traces have barely survived a few generations?" We do not have Scholem's response preserved, but from Leibowitz's letter in return can infer what he likely said, that kabbalah was better able than philosophy to invigorate waning Jewish belief and practice because it was at heart closer to the subliminal depths of the people that originally shaped the religion.

And on that point, Leibowitz wrote:

> The sum of the matter: To counter your thesis that the kabbalah is closer to classical Judaism, I would venture to propose this opposing thesis: The kabbalah conquered the people of Israel because of its closeness to the pagan instincts against which classical Judaism struggled, but was unable to uproot. The philosophy of Maimonides didn't vanquish [prevail], for the reason that it adopted the line of the same classical Judaism that has always been and will always be the property of a virtuous few. It is not without consequence that Maimonides himself described the pure love of God as being something of which "all the sages and wise ones were unworthy but only [except for] our father Abraham" and this is also the sense of the words of Spinoza, *omnia praeclara tam difficilia quam rara sunt*, but all things excellent are as difficult as they are rare.

Leibowitz's response to Scholem is memorable if only for summoning Maimonides and Spinoza to illustrate the rationalist tradition within Jewish philosophy. It is also poignant for the concession Leibowitz ruefully makes, that kabbalah has the ascendancy over philosophy in the heart of the people Israel. But we would suggest that the very division between the two, mysticism and philosophy, attenuates at the

---

2. Mock, "Reading of the Last Sentence of the *Ethics*." That last sentence introduces the exchange between Leibowitz and Scholem that Mock discusses.

negative theological pole of Jewish philosophy. This is a gleaning from at least the rationalist and empiricist of our negative theologians, if not the pragmatists, though from them, too, to the extent their borderline atheism is, between the lines, shaking hands with mysticism. Let that be our final thought, for the hope it holds for a Judaism theologically replenished by its philosophical tradition.

Bibliography

Abuarquob, Huda, et al. "Jerusalem Crisis: What's Happening, What's Being Done, What's Needed." Lecture presented at New Israel Fund conference (virtual), May 12, 2021. https://www.facebook.com/newisraelfund/videos/306772334253724/.
Aelred of Rievaulx. *Spiritual Friendship*. Translated by Lawrence C. Braceland and edited by Marsha L. Dutton. Cistercian Fathers Series 5. Collegeville, MN: Liturgical, 2010.
Alexander, Gabriel, et al. *The Musical Tradition of the Jewish Reform Congregation in Berlin*. Program notes. Tel Aviv: Beth Hatefutsoth Records, 1997.
Altmann, Alexander. "Commandments, Reasons For." In *Encyclopedia Judaica*, edited by Fred Skolnik and Michael Berenbaum, 5:85–90. Detroit: Macmillan, 2007.
Anderson, Bernhard. *Understanding the Old Testament*. 4th ed. Englewood Cliffs, NJ: Prentice-Hall, 1986.
Arendt, Hannah. *Antisemitism*. New York: Harcourt, Brace, 1968.
Aristotle. *Metaphysics*. In *The Basic Works of Aristotle*, edited by Richard McKeon and translated by W. D. Ross, 689–926. New York: Random House, 1941.
Attar, Farid al-Din. *The Conference of the Birds*. Translated by Afkham Darbandi and Dick Davis. New York: Penguin, 1984.
Azoulay, Ariella Aïsha. *The Jewelers of the Ummah: A Potential History of the Muslim Jewish World*. New York: Verso, 2024.
Bahya ibn Paquda. *Duties of the Heart*. Translated by Moses Hyamson. 2 vols. New York: Feldheim, 1970.
Baron, Salo. "The Historical Outlook of Maimonides." In *Proceedings of the American Academy for Jewish Research* 6 (1934–1935) 5–113.
———. "Newer Emphases in Jewish History." *Jewish Social Studies* 25 (1963) 245–58.
Benjamin, Walter. "On Language as Such and On the Language of Man." In *Reflections*, translated by Edmund Jephcott, 314–32. New York: Schocken, 1978.
———. *On the Origin of German Tragic Drama*. Translated by John Osborne. New York: Verso, 1998.
———. "The Task of the Translator." In *Illuminations*, edited by Hannah Arendt and translated by Harry Zohn, 69–82. New York: Schocken, 1968.
———. "Theses on the Philosophy of History." In *Illuminations*, edited by Hannah Arendt and translated by Harry Zohn, 253–64. New York: Schocken, 1968.

———. *Toward the Critique of Violence: Critical Edition*. Edited by Peter Fenves and Julia Ng. Stanford, CA: Stanford University Press, 2021.
Ben-Sasson, H. H. "The Middle Ages." In *A History of the Jewish People*, edited by H. H. Ben-Sasson, 385–723. Cambridge, MA: Harvard University Press, 1976.
Berry, Wanda Warren. "Judaism Without Covenant: Breslauer on Buber." *Jewish Social Studies* 45 (1983) 31–42.
Biale, David. *Not in the Heavens: The Tradition of Jewish Secular Thought*. Princeton, NJ: Princeton University Press, 2010.
Bialik, H. N., and Yehoshua Hana Ravnitzky, eds. *The Book of Legends/Sefer Ha-Aggadah*. Translated by William Braude. New York: Schocken, 1992.
Bitzan, Amos. "Wissenschaft des Judentums." *Oxford Bibliographies Online*. June 27, 2017. https://www.oxfordbibliographies.com/browse?module_0=obo-9780199840731.
Blidstein, Gerald. "Capital Punishment: The Classic Jewish Discussion." *Judaism* 14 (1965) 159–71.
Blumenthal, David. *Philosophical Mysticism: Studies in Rational Religion*. Ramat Gan, Israel: Bar-Ilan University, 2006.
Bolton, Andrew. "Exhibition Tour: About Time: Fashion and Duration." Metropolitan Museum of Art, October 29, 2021–February 2, 2022. https://www.metmuseum.org/exhibitions/listings/2020/about-time.
Bolton, Andrew, et al. *About Time: Fashion and Duration*. New York: Metropolitan Museum of Art, 2020.
Boyarin, Daniel. *Carnal Israel: Reading Sex in Talmudic Culture*. Berkeley, CA: University of California Press, 1993.
Brenner, Michael. *The Renaissance of Jewish Culture in Weimar Germany*. New Haven, CT: Yale University Press, 1996.
Breslauer, S. Daniel. *Covenant and Community in Modern Judaism*. New York: Greenwood, 1989.
Brown, Francis, et al. *A Hebrew and English Lexicon of the Old Testament*. New York: Oxford University Press, 1977.
Buber, Martin. *Between Man and Man*. Translated by Ronald Gregor Smith. New York: Macmillan, 1965.
———. *Eclipse of God*. Translated by Maurice Friedman. New York: Harper and Row, 1952.
———. *For the Sake of Heaven*. Translated by Ludwig Lewisohn. Philadelphia: Jewish Publication Society, 1953.
———. *Good and Evil: Two Interpretations*. Translated by Ronald Gregor Smith. New York: Charles Scribner's Sons, 1953.
———. *I and Thou*. Translated by Walter Kaufmann. New York: Charles Scribner's Sons, 1970.
———. *I and Thou*. Translated by Ronald Gregor Smith. 2nd ed. New York: Charles Scribner's Sons, 1958.
———. *Israel and the World: Essays in a Time of Crisis*. Translated by Olga Marx et al. New York: Schocken, 1948.
———. *The Knowledge of Man*. Edited by Maurice Friedman. Translated by Maurice Friedman and Ronald Gregor Smith. New York: Harper, 1965.
———. *A Land of Two Peoples: Martin Buber on Jews and Arabs*. Edited by Paul Mendes-Flohr. New York: Oxford University Press, 1983.

———. *The Letters of Martin Buber*. Edited by Nahum Glatzer and Paul Mendes-Flohr and translated by Richard Winston et al. New York: Schocken, 1991.

———. *The Martin Buber Reader: Essential Writings*. Edited by Asher Biemann. New York: Palgrave Macmillan, 2002.

———. *On Judaism*. Edited by Nahum Glatzer. Translated by Eva Jospe. New York: Schocken, 1967.

———. *The Prophetic Faith*. Translated by Carlyle Witton-Davies. New York: Macmillan, 1949.

———. *Tales of the Hasidim*. Translated by Olga Marx. New York: Schocken, 1947–48.

———. *Ten Rungs: Collected Hasidic Sayings*. New York: Citadel, 1995.

———. *Two Types of Faith*. Translated by Norman Goldhawk. New York: Macmillan, 1951.

———. *The Writings of Martin Buber*. Edited by Will Herberg. New York: World Publishing, 1956.

Buber, Martin, and Franz Rosenzweig. *Die Schrift*. Heidelberg: Lambert Schneider, 1976.

Bulhof, Ilse. "Negative Theology as Spirituality: Deep Openness." In *Théologie Negative*, edited by Marco Olivetti, 423–41. Milan: CEDAM, 2002.

Buruma, Ian. *Spinoza: Freedom's Messiah*. New Haven, CT: Yale University Press, 2024.

Butler, Judith. *Parting Ways: Jewishness and the Critique of Zionism*. New York: Columbia University Press, 2012.

Carlisle, Clare. *Spinoza's Religion: A New Reading of the Ethics*. Princeton, NJ: Princeton University Press, 2021.

Click, Emily. "A Minister Cultivates Abiding." *Harvard Divinity Bulletin* (Autumn–Winter 2020) 15–18.

Cline, Eric H. *Biblical Archaeology: A Very Short Introduction*. New York: Oxford University Press, 2009.

"Clinton Calls for Civility, 'New Covenant.'" *Christian Century* 112 (1995) 704.

Cohen, Arthur. *The Tremendum: A Theological Interpretation of the Holocaust*. New York: Crossroad, 1981.

Cohen, Hermann. *Hermann Cohen: Writings on Neo-Kantianism and Jewish Philosophy*. Edited by Samuel Moyn and Robert S. Shine. Waltham, MA: Brandeis University Press, 2021.

———. *Reason and Hope: Selections from the Writings of Hermann Cohen*. Translated by Eva Jospe. New York: Norton, 1971.

———. *Religion of Reason Out of the Sources of Judaism*. Translated by Simon Kaplan. New York: Fredrick Unger, 1972.

———. "Spinoza on State and Religion, Judaism and Christianity." In *Spinoza's Challenge to Jewish Thought: Writings on His Life, Philosophy, and Legacy*, edited by Daniel B. Schwartz, 207–15. Waltham, MA: Brandeis University Press, 2019.

Cohen, Hillel. "Writing *Year Zero of the Arab-Israeli Conflict, 1929*." Lecture sponsored by Jewish Studies Program of Dartmouth College, July 12, 2016. https://www.youtube.com/watch?v=kHQ_SScFWuQ.

———. *Year Zero of the Arab-Israeli Conflict, 1929*. Translated by Haim Watzman. Waltham, MA: Brandeis University Press, 2015.

Cohen, Shaye J. D. *The Beginnings of Jewishness: Boundaries, Varieties, Uncertainties*. Berkeley, CA: University of California Press, 1999.

Cole, Teju. "On the Trail of Caravaggio." *New York Times Magazine*, Sept. 27, 2020, 52–67.
Collins, John. "The Zeal of Phineas, the Bible, and the Legitimization of Violence." In *The Destructive Power of Religion: Violence in Judaism, Christianity, and Islam*, edited by J. Harold Ellens, 1:11–33. Westport, CT: Praeger, 2004.
Cusk, Rachel. *Parade*. New York: Farrar, Straus and Giroux, 2024.
Daily Prayer Book: Ha-Siddur ha-Shalem. Translated by Philip Birnbaum. New York: Hebrew Publishing Company, 1977.
Dastur, Françoise. *How Are We to Confront Death: An Introduction to Philosophy*. Translated by Robert Vallier. New York: Fordham University Press, 2012.
Daum, Menachem, and Oren Rudavsky, dirs. *Ruins of Lifta*. New York: First Run Features, 2016.
Davidson, Harold. "The Active Intellect in the *Cuzari* and Halevi's Theory of Causality." *Revue des Etudes Juives* 131 (1972) 351–96.
Davidson, Herbert. *Moses Maimonides: The Man and His Works*. New York: Oxford University Press, 2005.
The Dhammapada. Translated by Irving Babbitt. New York: New Directions, 1965.
Diamond, James Arthur. "Maimonides vs. Nachmanides on Historical Consciousness and the Shaping of Jewish Identity." In *History, Memory, and Jewish Identity*, edited by Ira Robinson et al., 92–116. Boston: Academic Studies Press, 2015.
Dostoevsky, Fyodr. *The Idiot*. Translated by Constance Garnett. New York: Bantam Books, 1958.
———. *A Raw Youth*. Translated by Constance Garnett. Project Gutenberg Australia, 2014. http://gutenberg.net.au/ebooks01/0100161h.html.
Eilberg-Schwartz, ed. *People of the Body: Jews and Judaism from an Embodied Perspective*. Albany: State University of New York Press, 1992.
Einstein, Albert. *The World as I See It*. Translated by Alan Harris. The Albert Einstein Collection, v. 1. Open Road Integrated Media, 2016.
Eisen, Robert. *Judaism and Violence: An Historical Analysis with Insights from Social Psychology*. New York: Cambridge University Press, 2021.
Eisenman, Robert. *Islamic Law in Palestine and Israel: A History of the Survival of Tanzimat and Shari'a in the British Mandate and the Jewish State*. Leiden: Brill, 1978.
Elazar, Daniel. "Covenant as the Basis of Jewish Political Tradition." *Jewish Journal of Sociology* 20 (1978) 5–37.
Eliot, George. *Felix Holt: The Radical*. New York: Oxford University Press, 1988.
Fackenheim, Emil. *The Jewish Return into History*. New York: Schocken, 1978.
———. *To Mend the World: Foundations of Future Jewish Thought*. New York: Schocken, 1982.
Fagenblat, Michael, ed. *Negative Theology and Jewish Identity*. Bloomington: Indiana University Press, 2017.
Feldman, Seymour. "The Binding of Isaac: A Test-Case of Divine Foreknowledge." In *Divine Omniscience and Omnipotence in Medieval Philosophy*, edited by Tamar Rudavsky, 105–33. Dordrecht: Springer, 1985.
Feuer, Lewis. "Spinoza's Thought and Modern Perplexities: Its American Career." In *Spinoza: A Tercentenary Perspective*, edited by Barry Kogan, 36–79. Cincinnati: Hebrew Union College, [1979].

Fewell, Danna Nolan. "Stained Windows." In *The Prophetic Quest: The Stained Glass Windows of Jacob Landau*, edited by David S. Herrstrom and Andrew Scrimgeour, 87–88. University Park: Pennsylvania State University Press, 2021.

Flapan, Simha. *The Birth of Israel: Myths and Realities*. New York: Pantheon, 1987.

Fowl, Stephen. *Idolatry*. Waco, TX: Baylor University Press, 2019.

Frank, Daniel, et al., eds. *Jewish Philosophy Reader*. New York: Routledge, 2000.

Frisch, Max. *Andorra*. Translated by Michael Bullock. London: Methuen, 1964.

Gates of Prayer: The New Union Prayerbook. New York: Central Conference of American Rabbis, 1975.

Gates of Repentance: New Union Prayerbook for the Days of Awe. New York: Central Conference of American Rabbis, 1978.

Geiger, Abraham. *Abraham Geiger and Liberal Judaism: The Challenge of the Nineteenth Century*. Edited by Max Weiner. Translated by Ernst Schlochauer. Cincinnati, OH: Hebrew Union College Press, 1981.

Gibbs, Robert, ed. *Hermann Cohen's* Ethics. Boston: Brill, 2006.

———. "Postmodern Jewish Philosophy." In *Reasoning After Revelation: Dialogues in Postmodern Jewish Philosophy*, by Stephen Kepnes et al., 21–24. Boulder, CO: Westview, 1998.

Gill, David. "Greek Sources of Wisdom 12:3–7." *Vetus Testamentum* 15 (1965) 383–86.

Ginzberg, Louis. *The Legends of the Jews*. 7 vols. Philadelphia: Jewish Publication Society, 1968.

Goldstein, Rebecca. *Betraying Spinoza: The Renegade Jew Who Gave Us Modernity*. New York: Schocken, 2006.

———. *Plato at the Googleplex: Why Philosophy Won't Go Away*. New York: Pantheon, 2014.

Goldstein, Richard. "William A. Anders, 90, Who Orbited the Moon Aboard Apollo 8, Dies." *New York Times*, June 9, 2024. https://www.nytimes.com/2024/06/07/science/william-a-anders-dead.html.

Goodman, Micah. *Maimonides and the Book That Changed Judaism: Secrets of the Guide for the Perplexed*. Translated by Yedidya Sinclair. Philadelphia: Jewish Publication Society, 2015.

Graetz, Heinrich. *The Structure of Jewish History and Other Essays*. Translated by Ismar Schorsch. New York: Jewish Theological Seminary of America, 1975.

Graubart, Jonathan. *Jewish Self-Determination Beyond Zionism: Lessons from Hannah Arendt and Other Pariahs*. Philadelphia: Temple University Press, 2023.

Greenberg, Moshe. "On the Political Use of the Bible in Modern Israel." In *Pomegranates and Golden Bells: Studies in Biblical, Jewish, and Near Eastern Ritual, Law, and Literature in Honor of Jacob Milgrom*, edited by David P. Wright et al., 461–71. Winona Lake, IN: Eisenbrauns, 1995.

Guttmann, Julius. *Philosophies of Judaism*. Translated by David Silverman. New York: Schocken, 1973.

Ha'am, Ahad. *Ahad Ha-am: Essays, Letters, Memoirs*. Edited by Leon Simon. Oxford: East and West Library, 1946.

———. *Nationalism and the Jewish Ethic: Basic Writings of Ahad Ha'am*. Edited by Hans Kohn. New York: Schocken, 1962.

———. "Truth from Eretz Israel." Translated by Alan Dowry. *Israel Studies* 5 (2000) 160–81.

Halbertal, Moshe, and Avishai Margalit. *Idolatry*. Translated by Naomi Goldblum. Cambridge, MA: Harvard University Press, 1992.

Halevi, Judah. "At Night." In *Ninety-Two Poems and Hymns of Yehuda Halevi*, by Franz Rosenzweig, 12. Translated by Thomas Kovach et al. Albany: State University of New York Press, 2000.

———. *The Kuzari*. Translated by Hartwig Hirschfeld. New York: Schocken, 1964.

Handelman, Susan. *Fragments of Redemption: Jewish Thought and Literary Theory in Benjamin, Scholem, and Levinas*. Bloomington: Indiana University Press, 1991.

Harris, Jay. *Nachman Krochmal: Guiding the Perplexed of the Modern Age*. New York: New York University Press, 1991.

Hart, Kevin, ed. *The Exorbitant: Emmanuel Levinas Between Jews and Christians*. New York: Fordham University Press, 2010.

Hartman, Donniel. *Putting God Second: How to Save Religion from Itself*. Boston: Beacon, 2016.

Harvey, Steven. "Key Terms in Translations of Maimonides' *Guide of the Perplexed*." In *Maimonides' Guide of the Perplexed in Translation: A History from the Thirteenth Century to the Twentieth*, edited by Josef Stern, et al., 305–29. Chicago: University of Chicago Press, 2019.

Hebreo, Léon. *Dialogues of Love*. Translated by Cosmos Damian Bacich and Rosella Pescatori. Toronto: University of Toronto Press, 2009.

Hegel, G. W. F. *Phenomenology of Spirit*. Translated by A. V. Miller. New York: Oxford University Press, 1977.

Henderson, Bob. "The Rebel Physicist on the Hunt for a Better Story Than Quantum Mechanics." *New York Times Magazine*, June 28, 2020. https://www.nytimes.com/2020/06/25/magazine/angelo-bassi-quantum-mechanic.html.

Herrstrom, David S. "*The Prophetic Quest* of Jacob Landau." In *The Prophetic Quest: The Stained Glass Windows of Jacob Landau*, edited by David S. Herrstrom and Andrew D. Scrimgeour, 24–30. University Park: Pennsylvania State University Press, 2021.

Hertz, J. H. *The Pentateuch and Haftorahs*. 2nd ed. London: Soncino, 1980.

Heschel, Abraham Joshua. *Between God and Man: An Interpretation of Judaism*. Edited by Fritz Rothschild. New York: Free Press, 1959.

———. *Maimonides: A Biography*. Translated by Joachim Neugroschel. New York: Doubleday, 1982.

———. *The Prophets: An Introduction*. New York: Harper & Row, 1962.

Hever, Hannan. "Buber Versus Scholem and the Figure of the Hasidic Jew: A Literary Debate Between Two Political Theologies." In *Jews and the Ends of Theory*, edited by Shai Ginsburg et al., 225–62. New York: Fordham University Press, 2018.

Himmelfarb, Milton. "A Symposium: The State of Jewish Belief." *Commentary* 42 (1966) 71–160.

Hirsch, Samson Raphael. *Nineteen Letters on Judaism*. Translated by Bernard Drachman. New York: Feldheim, 1969.

Hitz, Zena. *Lost in Thought: The Hidden Pleasures of an Intellectual Life*. Princeton, NJ: Princeton University Press, 2020.

Holdheim, Samuel. "The Ceremonial Law in the Messianic Era." In *The Rise of Reform Judaism: A Sourcebook of Its European Origins*, edited by W. Guenther Plaut, 140–42. 50th anniversary ed. Philadelphia: Jewish Publication Society, 2015.

———. "A New Concept of the Sabbath." In *The Rise of Reform Judaism: A Sourcebook of Its European Origins*, edited by W. Guenther Plaut, 200–203. 50th anniversary ed. Philadelphia: Jewish Publication Society, 2015.

Hollander, Dana. "Is The Other My Neighbor: Reading Levinas Alongside Hermann Cohen." In *The Exorbitant: Emmanuel Levinas Between Jews and Christians*, edited by Kevin Hart, 90–107. New York: Fordham University Press, 2010.

The Holy Scriptures According to the Masoretic Text: A New Translation. Philadelphia: Jewish Publication Society of America, 1955.

Horowitz, Rivka. *Buber's Way to I and Thou: The Development of Martin Buber's Thought and His Religion as Presence Lectures*. Philadelphia: Jewish Publication Society, 1988.

Israel, Jonathan. *Spinoza: His Life and Legacy*. New York: Oxford University Press, 2023.

Israeli Ministry of Foreign Affairs. *The Declaration of Independence of the State of Israel, May 1948*. https://israeled.org/resources/documents/israel-declaration-independence/.

Jacobs, Jonathan. *Law, Reason, and Morality in Medieval Jewish Philosophy*. New York: Oxford University Press, 2010.

Johnson, Penelope. "Double Houses, Western Christian." In *Encyclopedia of Monasticism*, edited by William Johnson, 416–18. Chicago: Fitzroy Dearborn, 2000.

Johnson, William. *The Search for Transcendence: A Theological Analysis of Nontheological Attempts to Define Transcendence*. New York: Harper Colophon, 1974.

Kant, Immanuel. *Critique of Practical Reason*. Translated by Lewis Beck White. 3rd ed. Upper Saddle River, NJ: Prentice-Hall, 1993.

———. *Critique of Pure Reason*. Translated by Norman Kemp Smith. New York: St. Martin's, 1965.

———. *Religion Within the Limits of Reason Alone*. Translated by Theodore M. Greene and Hoyt H. Hudson. New York: Harper Torchbooks, 1960.

Katz, Steven. *Post-Holocaust Dialogues: Critical Studies in Modern Jewish Thought*. New York: New York University Press, 1985.

Keller, Catherine. *On the Mystery: Discerning Divinity in Process*. Minneapolis: Fortress, 2008.

Kellner, Menachem. "Spiritual Life." In *Cambridge Companion to Maimonides*, edited by Kenneth Seeskin, 273–99. New York: Cambridge University Press, 2005.

Kierkegaard, Søren. *Fear and Trembling*. Translated by Alastair Hannay. New York: Penguin, 1985.

Kogan, Barry. Review of *Maimonides: A Biography*, by Abraham Joshua Heschel. *Journal of Reform Judaism* 30 (1983) 70–73.

———, ed. *Spinoza: A Tercentenary Perspective*. Cincinnati, OH: Hebrew Union College, 1979.

Kornberg, Jacques, ed. *At the Crossroads: Essays on Ahad Ha-am*. Albany: State University of New York Press, 1984.

Korobkin, Daniel. "Rupture, Reconstruction, and Social Orthodoxy." *Tradition* 51 (2019) 64–69.

Kreisel, Howard. "Asceticism in the Thought of R. Bahya ibn Paquda and Maimonides." *Daat: A Journal of Jewish Philosophy and Kabbalah* 21 (1988) 5–22.

Krochmal, Nachman. "A Philosophy of Jewish History." In *Ideas of Jewish History*, compiled by Michael Meyer, 189–214. New York: Behrman House, 1974.

BIBLIOGRAPHY

Kushner, Harold. *When Bad Things Happen to Good People*. New York: Schocken, 1981.

Lefkowitz, Jay. "The Rise of Social Orthodoxy: A Personal Account." *Commentary* 137 (2014) 37–42.

Leibowitz, Yeshayahu. *The Faith of Maimonides*. Translated by John Glucker. Tel Aviv: MOD, 1989.

———. *Judaism, Human Values, and the Jewish State*. Edited by Eliezer Goldman and translated by Eliezer Goldman et al. Cambridge, MA: Harvard University Press, 1992.

———. *Notes and Remarks on the Weekly Parashah*. Translated by Shmuel Himelstein. Brooklyn: Chemed, 1990.

Levi, Primo. *Survival in Auschwitz: The Nazi Assault on Humanity*. Translated by Stuart Woolf. New York: Simon & Schuster, 1996.

Levinas, Emmanuel. *Difficult Freedom*. Translated by Seán Hand. Baltimore: Johns Hopkins University Press, 1990.

———. "Ethics as First Philosophy." In *The Levinas Reader*, edited by Seán Hand, 75–87. Cambridge, MA: Blackwell, 1989.

———. "God and Philosophy." In *The Levinas Reader*, edited by Seán Hand, 166–89. Cambridge, MA: Blackwell, 1989.

———. *Nine Talmudic Readings*. Translated by Annette Aronowicz. Indianapolis: Indiana University Press, 2019.

———. *Of God Who Comes to Mind*. Edited by Werner Hamacher and David E. Wellbery and translated by Bettina Bergo. Stanford, CA: Stanford University Press, 1998.

———. *Otherwise Than Being, or Beyond Essence*. Translated by Alphonso Lingis. Pittsburgh: Duquesne University Press, 1981.

———. "The Pact." In *The Levinas Reader*, edited by Seán Hand, 211–26. Cambridge, MA: Blackwell, 1989.

———. "Revelation in Jewish Tradition." In *The Levinas Reader*, edited by Seán Hand, 190–210. Cambridge, MA: Blackwell, 1989.

———. "Substitution." In *The Levinas Reader*, edited by Seán Hand, 88–125. Cambridge, MA: Blackwell, 1989.

———. *Totality and Infinity: An Essay on Exteriority*. Translated by Alphonso Lingis. Pittsburgh: Duquesne University Press, 1969.

———. "Useless Suffering." Translated by Richard Cohen. In *The Provocation of Levinas: Rethinking the Other*, edited by Robert Bernasconi and David Wood, 156–67. New York: Routledge, 1988.

Lobel, Diana. *A Sufi-Jewish Dialogue: Philosophy and Mysticism in Bahya Ibn Paquda's Duties of the Heart*. Philadelphia: University of Pennsylvania Press, 2007.

Lucas, Julian. Review of *How the Word Is Passed: A Reckoning with the History of Slavery in America*, by Clint Smith. *New York Times Book Review* (June 27, 2021) 13.

Lutz, Donald. "The Evolution of Covenant Form and Content as Basis for Early American Political Culture." In *Covenant in the Nineteenth Century: Decline of an American Political Tradition*, edited by Daniel Elazar, 31–47. Lanham, MD: Rowman & Littlefield, 1994.

Maimonides. *The Book of Knowledge from the Mishneh Torah of Maimonides*. Translated by H. M. Russell and J. Weinberg. New York: Ktav, 1983.

———. "Eight Chapters." In *A Maimonides Reader*, edited by Isadore Twersky, 361–86. New York: Behrman House, 1972.

———. "Epistle to Yemen." In *A Maimonides Reader*, edited by Isadore Twersky, 437–62. New York: Behrman House, 1972.

———. *Guide of the Perplexed*. 2 vols. Translated by Shlomo Pines. Chicago: University of Chicago Press, 1963.

———. "Helek: Sanhedrin: Chapter 10." In *A Maimonides Reader*, edited by Isadore Twersky, 401–23. New York: Behrman House, 1972.

———. *Maimonides' Commentary on the Mishnah, Tractate Sanhedrin*. Translated by Fred Rosner. New York: Sepher-Hermon, 1981.

———. *Sefer HaMitzvot*. Translated by Francis Nataf. Sefaria, 2021. https://www.sefaria.org/Sefer_HaMitzvot%2C_Positive_Commandments.1?lang=bi.

Mann, Thomas. *Death in Venice and Other Stories*. Translated by H. T. Lowe-Porter. New York: Vintage, 1989.

———. *Doctor Faustus*. Translated by H. T. Lowe-Porter. New York: Vintage, 1992.

Marcus, Amy Dockser. *Jerusalem 1913: The Origins of the Arab-Israeli Conflict*. New York: Penguin, 2008.

Margolin, Jean-Paul. "Aspects du surréalisme au XVIe siècle." *Bibliothèque d'humanisme et renaissance* 39 (1977) 503–30.

Marmur, Michael. "Heschel's Two Maimonides." *Jewish Quarterly Review* 98 (2008) 230–54.

Maugham, Somerset. *Of Human Bondage*. New York: Penguin, 1963.

———. *The Razor's Edge*. New York: Penguin, 1984.

McWhorter, John. "Why Scott Joplin's Ragtime Matters." *New York Times*, Sunday Review, Apr. 3, 2022, 6.

Mekilta de-Rabbi Ishmael. 3 vols. Translated by Jacob Z. Lauterbach. Philadelphia: Jewish Publication Society, 1976.

Mendelssohn, Moses. *Jerusalem and Other Writings*. Edited and translated by Alfred Jospe. New York: Schocken, 1969.

———. *Moses Mendelssohn: Writings on Judaism, Christianity, and the Bible*. Edited by Micah Gottlieb and translated by Curtis Bowman. Waltham, MA: Brandeis University Press, 2011.

Mendes-Flohr, Paul. *Divided Passions: Jewish Intellectuals and the Experience of Modernity*. Detroit: Wayne State University Press, 1991.

———. "Law and Sacrament: Ritual Observance in Twentieth-Century Jewish Thought." In *Jewish Spirituality: From the Seventeenth Century Revival to the Present*, edited by Arthur Green, 317–45. New York: Crossroad, 1989.

———. *Martin Buber: A Life of Faith and Dissent*. New Haven, CT: Yale University Press, 2019.

———. "Rosenzweig and Kant: Two Views of Ritual and Religion." In *Mystics, Philosophers and Politicians: Essays in Jewish Intellectual History in Honor of Alexander Altmann*, edited by Jehuda Reinharz and Daniel Swetschinski, 315–41. Durham, NC: Duke University Press, 1982.

Metropolitan Museum of Art. *In America: A Lexicon of Fashion*. September 18, 2021–September 5, 2022.

Meyer, Michael. "'Most of My Brethren Find Me Unacceptable': The Controversial Career of Rabbi Samuel Holdheim." *Jewish Social Studies* 9 (2003) 1–19.

Miles, Jack. *God: A Biography*. New York: Knopf, 2001.

Miller, B. J. "What Is Death?" *New York Times*, Dec. 20, 2020. https://www.nytimes.com/2020/12/18/opinion/sunday/coronavirus-death.html.

Milton, John. "Areopagitica." In *The Portable Milton*, edited by Donald Bush, 151–205. New York: Viking, 1949.

Mizrahi, Moshé, dir. *Madame Rosa*. Warner-Columbia Films, 1977.

Mock, Keren. "A Reading of the Last Sentence of the *Ethics*: From Spinoza to Scholem." *Reading Shpinoza: A Heretic in Yiddish and Hebrew*. Paper presented at a University of Wisconsin Center for Jewish Studies conference (virtual), March 18, 2021.

Morris, Benny. "The New Historiography: Israel Confronts Its Past." In *Making Israel*, edited by Benny Morris, 11–28. Ann Arbor, MI: University of Michigan Press, 2007.

Moses, Stephane. *System and Revelation: The Philosophy of Franz Rosenzweig*. Translated by Catherine Tihanyi. Detroit: Wayne State University Press, 1992.

Myers, David. "Response to Jay Harris' Reading of the Israeli Declaration of Independence." *Journal of Textual Reasoning* 8 (1998). https://jtr.shanti.virginia.edu/a-response-to-jay-harris-3/.

Nadler, Steven. *A Book Forged in Hell: Spinoza's Scandalous Treatise and the Birth of the Secular Age*. Princeton, NJ: Princeton University Press, 2011.

———. *Spinoza: A Life*. New York: Cambridge University Press, 1999.

Nauen, Franz. "Hermann Cohen's Perceptions of Spinoza: A Reappraisal." *AJS Review* 4 (1979) 111–24.

Neusner, Jacob. *Song of Songs Rabbah: An Analytical Translation*. Atlanta: Scholars, 1989.

New Oxford Annotated Bible. Edited by Hebert May and Bruce Metzger. New York: Oxford University Press, 1973.

Niebuhr, Gustav. "A Rabbi's Look at Archaeology Touches a Nerve." *New York Times*, June 2, 2001, A11.

Niehoff, Maren. *Philo of Alexandria: An Intellectual Biography*. New Haven, CT: Yale University Press, 2018.

Niehr, Herbert. "'Israelite' Religion and 'Canaanite' Religion." In *Religious Diversity in Ancient Israel and Judah*, edited by F. Stavrakopoulou and J. Barton, 23–36. New York: T. & T. Clark, 2010.

Novak, David. *Natural Law in Judaism*. New York: Cambridge University Press, 1998.

Novalis. "Monolog." In *Novalis: Philosophical Writings*, translated and edited by Margaret Mahony Stoljar, 83–84. Albany: State University of New York Press, 1997.

Ophir, Adi. "The Identity of the Victims and the Victims of Identity." In *Postzionism: A Reader*, edited by Laurence Silberstein, 81–101. New Brunswick, NJ: Rutgers University Press, 2008.

Overbye, Dennis. "The James Webb Space Telescope and a Quest Every Human Shares." *New York Times*, Jan. 29, 2022. https://www.nytimes.com/2022/01/27/science/james-webb-space-telescope.html.

———. "Webb Telescope Prepares to Ascend, With an Eye Towards Our Origins." *New York Times*, Dec. 25, 2021. https://www.nytimes.com/2021/12/20/science/webb-telescope-astronomy.html.

Oz, Amos. "The Meaning of Homeland." *New Outlook* (Jan. 1988) 19–24.

Pappé, Ilan. *Out of the Frame: The Struggle for Academic Freedom in Israel*. New York: Pluto Press, 2010.

Petuchowski, Jakob. "Abraham Geiger and Samuel Holdheim: Their Differences in Germany and Repercussions in America." *Leo Baeck Institute Yearbook* 22 (1977) 139–59.
Pew Research Center. *Jewish Americans in 2020*. May 11, 2021. https://www.pewresearch.org/religion/2021/05/11/jewish-americans-in-2020/.
Peyroux, Catherine. "Abbess and Cloister: Double Monasteries in the Medieval West." PhD diss., Princeton University, 1991.
Philo of Alexandria. *Philo*. 12 vols. Translated by F. H. Colson and G. H. Whitaker. Loeb Library. Cambridge, MA: Harvard University Press, 1929–62.
Plato. *Phaedrus*. Translated by R. Hackforth. In *The Collected Dialogues of Plato*, edited by Edith Hamilton and Huntington Cairns, 475–525. New York: Bollingen Foundation, 1961.
———. *The Republic*. In *The Dialogues of Plato*, translated by Benjamin Jowett, 1:591–879. New York: Random House, 1937.
———. *Theaetetus*. Translated by F. M. Cornford. In *The Collected Dialogues of Plato*, edited by Edith Hamilton and Huntington Cairns, 845–919. New York: Bollingen Foundation, 1961.
Poliakov, Leon. *The History of Anti-Semitism*. Translated by Richard Howard. New York: Schocken, 1974.
Pollock, Benjamin. *Franz Rosenzweig's Conversions: World Denial and World Redemption*. Bloomington: Indiana University Press, 2014.
Proust, Marcel. *In Search of Lost Time*. 6 vols. Translated by C. K. Scott Moncrieff et al. Revised by D. J. Enright. New York: Modern Library, 2003.
Putnam, Hilary. "Levinas and Judaism." In *The Cambridge Companion to Levinas*, edited by Simon Critchley, 33–62. New York: Cambridge University Press, 2002.
Rapaport, Uriel. "Jewish Religious Propaganda and Proselytism in the Period of the Second Commonwealth." PhD diss., Hebrew University, 1965.
Raz-Krakotzkin, Amnon. "'On the Right Side of the Barricades': Walter Benjamin, Gershom Scholem, and Zionism." *Comparative Literature* 65 (2013) 363–81.
Rehfeld, Andrew. "The Great American Rabbi Shortage." Interview by Yehuda Kurtzer. Shalom Hartman Institute, Apr. 15, 2022. https://www.hartman.org.il/the-great-american-rabbi-shortage/.
Reines, Alvin. *Maimonides and Abrabanel on Prophecy*. Cincinnati, OH: Hebrew Union College Press, 1970.
———. "Maimonides' Concept of Mosaic Prophecy." *Hebrew Union College Annual* 40/41 (1969/1970) 325–61.
Reinharz, Jehuda. "Ahad Ha-am, Martin Buber, and German Zionism." In *At the Crossroads: Essays on Ahad Ha-am*, edited by Jacques Kornberg, 142–55. Albany: State University of New York Press, 1984.
Rosenzweig, Franz. "Apologetic Thinking." In *The Jew: Essays from Martin Buber's Journal, Der Jude, 1916–1928*, edited by Arthur Cohen and translated by Joachim Neugroschel, 262–72. Tuscaloosa: University of Alabama Press, 1980.
———. "Atheistic Theology." In *Philosophical and Theological Writings*, translated by Paul W. Franks and Michael L. Morgan, 10–24. Indianapolis: Hackett, 2000.
———. *Briefe*. Edited by Edith Rosenzweig. Berlin: Schocken, 1935.
———. "'The Eternal': Mendelssohn and the Name of God." In *Scripture and Translation*, by Martin Buber and Franz Rosenzweig, 99–113. Translated by

Lawrence Rosenwald and Everett Fox. Indianapolis: Indiana University Press, 1994.

———. *Franz Rosenzweig: His Life and Thought*. Edited by Nahum Glatzer. Indianapolis: Hackett, 1998.

———. *Franz Rosenzweig's "The New Thinking."* Edited and translated by Alan Udoff and Barbara Galli. Syracuse, NY: Syracuse University Press, 1999.

———. "Introduction to the Jewish Writings of Hermann Cohen." Translated by Robert Shine. In *Hermann Cohen: Writings on Neo-Kantianism and Jewish Philosophy*, edited by Samuel Moyn and Robert S. Shine, 184–241. Waltham, MA: Brandeis University Press, 2021.

———. *Kleinere Schriften*. Berlin: Schocken, 1937.

———. *Ninety-Two Poems and Hymns of Yehuda Halevi*. Translated by Thomas Kovach et al. Albany: State University of New York Press, 2000.

———. *On Jewish Learning*. Edited by Nahum Glatzer. New York: Schocken, 1965.

———. *The Star of Redemption*. Translated by Barbara Galli. Madison, WI: University of Wisconsin Press, 2005.

———. *The Star of Redemption*. Translated by William Hallo. Notre Dame, IN: University of Notre Dame Press, 1970.

———. *Der Stern der Erlösung*. Frankfurt am Main: Suhrkamp, 1990.

Rubinstein, Ernest. *From Ecclesiastes to Simone Weil: Varieties of Philosophical Spirituality*. Madison, NJ: Fairleigh Dickinson University Press, 2014.

———. "Liminality, Communitas, and Franz Rosenzweig." Paper presented at Judaic Studies Section of the American Academy of Religion, San Francisco, Nov. 1997.

———. "A New German-Jewish Identity." *Aufbau* 64.7 (Mar. 27, 1998) 11–12.

———. "The Spirituality of Philosophical Judaism." *Studies in Formative Spirituality* 8 (1987) 83–95.

Rubinstein, Ernest, and Carol Sternhell, eds. *Contemplation: Humanistic Reflections by Members of The City Congregation*. New York: City Congregation for Humanistic Judaism, 2021.

Russell, Bertrand. "The Existence of God: A Debate Between Bertrand Russell and Father F. C. Copleston." In *Why I Am Not a Christian*, 138–59. London: Unwin, 1967.

Russell, John. "A Scholar's Papers." *New York Times Book Review* (Jan. 7, 1979). https://www.nytimes.com/1979/01/07/archives/a-scholars-papers-schapiro.html.

Rynhold, Daniel. "Orthodox Atheism: The Thought of Yeshayahu Leibowitz." Lecture presented at the Temple Emanuel Streicker Center, New York, May 13, 2020. http://vimeo.com/418594631.

Saadia Gaon. *Book of Doctrines and Opinions*. Abridged, edited, and translated by Alexander Altmann. In *Three Jewish Philosophers*, edited by Hans Lewy et al. New York: Atheneum, 1981.

Sacks, Elias. "Law, Ethics and the Needs of History: Mendelssohn, Krochmal and Moral Philosophy." *Journal of Religious Ethics* 44 (2016) 352–77.

Safrai, S., and M. Stern, eds. *The Jewish People in the First Century: Historical Geography, Political History, Social, Cultural, and Religious Life and Institutions*. 2 vols. Philadelphia: Fortress, 1976.

Sahih al-Bukhari. Translated by M. Muhsin Kahn. https://sunnah.com/bukhari.

Saiman, Chaim. *Halakhah: The Rabbinic Idea of Law*. Princeton, NJ: Princeton University Press, 2018.

Sand, Shlomo. *How I Stopped Being a Jew*. Translated by David Fernback. New York: Verso, 2014.

———. *The Invention of the Jewish People*. Translated by Yael Lotan. New York: Verso, 2009.

Sanders, Lionel Yehuda. "The Causes of the Alexandrian Pogrom and the Visit of Agrippa I to Alexandria in 38 CE." In *History, Memory, and Jewish Identity*, edited by Ira Robinson et al., 2–30. Boston: Academic Studies, 2015.

Sandmel, Samuel. *Philo of Alexandria: An Introduction*. New York: Oxford University Press, 1979.

Sankara. *A Thousand Teachings: The* Upadesasahasri *of Sankara*. Translated by Sengaku Mayeda. Albany: State University of New York Press, 1982.

Schechter, Solomon. "Nachman Krochmal." In *Studies in Judaism*, 321–44. New York: Atheneum, 1970.

Schelling, Friedrich. *The Philosophy of Art*. Translated and edited by Douglas Stott. Minneapolis: University of Minnesota Press, 1989.

Scholem, Gershom. "The Name of God and the Linguistic Theory of Kabbalah." *Diogenes* 20 (1972) 59–80.

———. "The Name of God and the Linguistic Theory of Kabbalah, part 2." *Diogenes* 20 (1972) 164–94.

———. "On Our Language: A Confession." Translated by Ora Wiskind. *History and Memory* 2 (1990) 97–99.

———. "Revelation and Tradition as Religious Categories in Judaism." In *The Messianic Idea in Judaism and Other Essays on Jewish Spirituality*, 282–303. New York: Schocken, 1971.

———. "Three Types of Jewish Piety." *Ariel* 32 (1973) 5–24.

———. "Who Is a Jew?" *Yearbook of the Central Conference of American Rabbis* 80 (1970) 134–39.

Scholem, Gershom, and Walter Benjamin. *The Correspondence of Walter Benjamin and Gershom Scholem*. Edited by Gershom Scholem. Translated by Gary Smith and Andre Lefevere. New York: Schocken, 1989.

Schorsch, Ismar. *From Text to Context: The Turn to History in Modern Judaism*. Waltham, MA: Brandeis University Press, 1994.

Schubert, Franz. *Schubert: The Complete Song Texts*. Translated by Richard Wigmore. New York: Schirmer, 1988.

Schwarzschild, Steven. "Two Modern Jewish Philosophies of History: Nachman Krochmal and Hermann Cohen." DHL diss., Hebrew Union College-Jewish Institute of Religion, 1955.

Scott, R. B. Y. *Proverbs, Ecclesiastes*. Anchor Bible 18. Garden City, NY: Doubleday, 1965.

Seeskin, Kenneth, ed. *Cambridge Companion to Maimonides*. New York: Cambridge University Press, 2005.

———. "Maimonides' Sense of History." *Jewish History* 18 (2004) 129–45.

———. "The Positive Contribution of Negative Theology." In *Jewish Philosophy in a Secular Age*, 31–70. Albany: State University of New York Press, 1990.

Sefaria: A Living Library of Torah Texts Online. https://www.sefaria.org.

Shazeer, Shira. "Blessing, Curse, and the Freedom to Choose." *Seventy Faces of Torah*, Aug. 7, 2018. http://hebrewcollege.edu/blog/blessing-curse-and-the-freedom-to-choose.

Shlaim, Avi. "The Debate About 1948." In *Making Israel*, edited by Benny Morris, 124–46. Ann Arbor: University of Michigan Press, 2007.
Shumsky, Dmitry. *Beyond the Nation-State: The Zionist Political Imagination from Pinsker to Ben-Gurion*. New Haven, CT: Yale University Press, 2018.
Siegel, Richard, et al. *The First Jewish Catalog: A Do-It-Yourself Kit*. Philadelphia: Jewish Publication Society, 1973.
Silberstein, Laurence. "The Renewal of Jewish Spirituality: Two Views." In *Jewish Spirituality: From the Sixteenth Century to the Present*, edited by Arthur Green, 402–32. New York: Crossroad, 1989.
Soloveitchik, Haym. "Rupture and Reconstruction: The Transformation of Contemporary Orthodoxy." *Tradition* 28 (1994) 64–130.
Sontag, Susan. "Simone Weil." In *A Susan Sontag Reader*, 91–93. New York: Farrar, Straus, Giroux, 1982.
Spinoza, Baruch. *Ethics, Treatise on the Emendation of the Intellect, Selected Letters*. Edited by Seymour Feldman and translated by Samuel Shirley. Indianapolis: Hackett, 1992.
———. *Theological-Political Treatise*. Translated by Samuel Shirley. 2nd ed. Indianapolis: Hackett, 2001.
Stanislawski, Michael. *Zionism: A Very Short Introduction*. New York: Oxford University Press, 2016.
Statman, Daniel. "Negative Theology and the Meaning of the Commandments in Modern Orthodoxy." *Tradition* 39 (2005) 58–71.
Steinberg, Michael. "1921: Walter Benjamin Writes the Essays 'Critique of Violence' and 'Task of the Translator.'" In *Yale Companion to Jewish Writing and Thought in German Culture, 1096–1996*, edited by Sander Gilman and Jack Zipes, 401–11. New Haven, CT: Yale University Press, 1997.
Steinberg, Milton. *As a Driven Leaf*. New York: Behrman House, 1939.
Steiner, George. *Real Presences*. Chicago: University of Chicago Press, 1989.
Stern, Josef. *Problems and Parables of Law: Maimonides and Nachmanides on Reasons for the Commandments*. New York: State University of New York Press, 1998.
Strauss, Leo. "Introduction." In *Religion of Reason Out of the Sources of Judaism*, by Hermann Cohen and translated by Simon Kaplan, xxiii–xxxviii. New York: Fredrick Unger, 1972.
Stroumsa, Guy. "Christianity and the God of Israel: Henri Bergson, Simone Weil, Emmanuel Levinas." Paper presented at the Harvard Center for the Study of World Religions, November 3, 2016. https://cswr.hds.harvard.edu/news/2016/11/03/video-christianity-and-god-israel.
Study Quran: A New Translation and Commentary. Edited by Seyyed Hossein Nasr et al. New York: HarperOne, 2015.
Sullivan, Meghan, and Paul Blaschko. *The Good Life Method: Reasoning Through the Big Questions of Happiness, Faith, and Meaning*. New York: Penguin, 2022.
Sutcliffe, Adam. "The Stranger as Self and Other: Georg Simmel, Hermann Cohen, and the Significance of Jewish Difference." *Jewish Quarterly Review* 111 (2021) 300–303.
———. *What Are Jews For? History, Peoplehood, and Purpose*. Princeton, NJ: Princeton University Press, 2020.

Swatos, William H. "Disenchantment." In *Encyclopedia of Religion and Society*, edited by William Swatos. Walnut Creek, CA: AltaMira, 1998. http://hirr.hartsem.edu/ency/disenchantment.htm.

The Thirteen Principal Upanishads. Translated by Robert Ernest Hume. Oxford: Oxford University Press, 1931.

Tigay, Jeffrey H. *Deuteronomy*. JPS Torah Commentary. Philadelphia: Jewish Publication Society, 1996.

Tirosh-Samuelson, Hava. "Philosophy and Kabbalah: 1200–1600." In *Cambridge Companion to Medieval Jewish Philosophy*, edited by Daniel Frank and Oliver Leaman, 218–57. New York: Cambridge University Press, 2006.

Tolstoy, Leo. *War and Peace*. Translated by Ann Dunnigan. New York: Penguin, 1968.

Turner, Victor. *The Ritual Process*. Chicago: Aldine, 1969.

Twersky, Isadore. *Introduction to the Code of Maimonides*. New Haven, CT: Yale University Press, 1980.

Underhill, Evelyn. *Practical Mysticism*. New York: Dutton, 1919.

Van Der Slik, Jack R., and Stephen J. Schwark. "Clinton and the New Covenant: Theology Shaping a New Politics of Old Politics in Religious Garb." *Journal of Church and State* 40 (1998) 873–90.

Van Ness, Peter, ed. *Spirituality and the Secular Quest*. New York: Crossroad, 1996.

Viller, Marcel, et al., eds. *Dictionnaire de spiritualité ascétique et mystique*. Paris: G. Beauchesne et ses fils, 1937–95.

Vogel, Manfred. *Rosenzweig on Profane/Secular History*. Atlanta: Scholars, 1996.

Weber, Max. "Science as a Vocation." In *From Max Weber: Essays in Sociology*, translated and edited by Hans Gerth and C. Wright Mills, 129–56. London: Routledge, 2009.

Weil, Simone. *Intimations of Christianity Among the Ancient Greeks*. Translated by Elisabeth Chase Geissbuhler. London: Routledge and Kegan Paul, 1957.

———. *The Need for Roots*. Translated by Arthur Wills. New York: Routledge, 1952, 2001.

———. *Waiting for God*. Translated by Emma Craufurd. New York: HarperCollins, 1973.

———. "What Is a Jew: A Letter to a Minister of Education." In *The Simone Weil Reader*, edited by George Panichas, 79–81. New York: David McCay, 1977.

Wiesel, Elie. *Inside a Library* and *The Stranger in the Bible*. Cincinnati, OH: Hebrew Union College-Jewish Institute of Religion Press, 1981.

———. *Night*. Translated by Stella Rodway. New York: Hill and Wang, 1960.

Winston, David. *The Wisdom of Solomon: A New Translation*. Anchor Bible 43. Garden City, NY: Doubleday, 1979.

Wolf, Immanuel. "On the Concept of a Science of Judaism." Translated by Lionel Kochan. *Leo Baeck Institute Yearbook* 2 (1957) 194–204.

Wolfson, Elliot. *Elliot R. Wolfson: Poetic Thinking*. Edited by Hava Tirosh-Samuelson and Aaron Hughes. Library of Contemporary Jewish Philosophers 11. Boston: Brill, 2011.

———. "Light Does Not Talk But Shines: Apophasis and Vision in Rosenzweig's Theopoetic Temporality." In *New Directions in Jewish Philosophy*, edited by Aaron Hughes and Elliot Wolfson, 87–148. Bloomington: Indiana University Press, 2010.

———. "Negative Theology: The Hidden Nature of God and Ultimate Reality." Interview by Jack Roycroft-Sherry. Jack Roycroft-Sherry Podcasts, October 9, 2024. http://www.youtube.com/watch?v=lPoKizvADz4.

———. "Via Negativa in Maimonides and Its Impact on Thirteenth-Century Kabbalah." *Maimonidean Studies* 5 (2008) 393–442.
Wolfson, Harry Austryn. *Escaping Judaism*. New York: Menorah, 1923.
———. "Notes on Proofs of the Existence of God in Jewish Philosophy." *Hebrew Union College Annual* 1 (1924) 575–96.
Wyschogrod, Edith. "Profligacy, Parsimony, and the Ethics of Expenditure in the Philosophy of Levinas." In *The Exorbitant: Emmanuel Levinas Between Jews and Christians*, edited by Kevin Hart, 171–87. New York: Fordham University Press, 2010.
Wyschogrod, Michael. *The Body of Faith: Judaism as Corporeal Election*. New York: Seabury, 1983.
Yerushalmi, Yosef. *Zakhor: Jewish History and Jewish Memory*. Seattle: University of Washington Press, 1996.
Younis, Rami, and Sarah Ema Friedland, dirs. *Lyd*. Brooklyn: Icarus Films, 2024.
Zadoff, Noam. *Gershom Scholem: From Berlin to Jerusalem and Back*. Translated by Jeffrey Green. Waltham, MA: Brandeis University Press, 2018.
———. "'Zion's Self-Engulfing Light': On Gershom Scholem's Disillusionment with Zionism." *Modern Judaism* 31 (2011) 272–84.

Name and Subject Index

Abel, 114, 263
Abraham, 50, 105, 109, 114–15, 126, 177
Absolute, the, 127–28, 212, 213, 221, 239n52, 244, 275
Abuarquob, Huda, 98–99
Adam, 4, 6, 136, 139, 141, 142, 158, 180n3, 223, 252
Aelred of Rievaulx, 238
Agnon, S. Y., 183
Ahad Ha'am, 85, 90–99, 101, 102
Alenu (prayer), 224
Alexandria, Egypt, 111–12, 116, 118, 154
Alexander, Gabriel, 182
allegory, 6, 113–16, 120–21, 153–54
Alliance for Middle East Peace, 98
Altmann, Alexander, 179n2
altruism, 151, 154–55, 158, 161, 163, 165, 176, 254. *See also* ethics, love
Anders, William, 3
Anderson, Bernhard, 114n23
angels, 56, 59, 107–8, 115–16, 118, 128, 132
animals, 19, 43, 66n44, 69, 139, 188–89, 190, 192
anti-Semitism, 48–49, 52, 75, 76, 111–12, 256
Apiru, 114
apocalypse, 150
apologetics, 120, 150

Arabic language, 85, 86
archaeology, 120
architecture, 202
Aristotle and
    Buber, 239
    Elisha ben Abuya, 180n4
    Heschel, 27
    Maimonides 1, 2, 3, 9, 11, 19n32, 132, 151, 187, 215
    Philo, 8
    Plato, 9, 27, 38
    Rosenzweig, 199
    Spinoza, 38, 164, 194, 250
art(s), 45–46, 107, 110, 110n15, 127, 194, 199, 201–3, 269. *See also* architecture, music, dance
asceticism. *See* self-negation
atheism and
    belief, 212, 215
    Buber, 210, 237
    ethics, 165–66, 259
    Yeshayahu Leibowitz, 208, 234, 259, 261
    Levinas, 233–34, 258, 261
    mysticism, 213, 215, 227, 276
    negative theology, 245
    social Orthodoxy, 209
    pantheism, 276
    Rosenzweig, 199, 213, 215, 244
    Spinoza, 161, 276
Attar, Farid al-Din, 273n64

Babylonian exile, 105, 125, 126, 126n60
Bahya ibn Paquda, 155–59, 161, 162, 169, 170, 172n67, 184, 192, 206, 247
Balfour Declaration, 85, 97n99
Bar Kochba, 126
Baron, Salo, 104n2, 104–5, 106, 126n58
beauty, 3, 4, 7, 46, 47, 67, 127, 187
being, 10–16, 24–26, 28, 30, 58, 89, 166n47, 174–75, 213, 223, 259
Benjamin, Walter
    on allegory, 115–16
    and Buber, 264
    on history, 106–11, 118
    on language, 137–41, 218, 223, 251, 252, 264, 275
    and Philo, 113, 115–16
    and Maimonides, 218
    and Marcel Proust, 109n15, 111, 131, 138–39, 146
    on revelation, 81n16, 137–41, 251
    and Rosenzweig, 76, 80–82, 83, 85, 86, 111, 123, 143, 145, 251
    and Gershom Scholem, 84, 130–31, 138, 143, 145, 251, 275
    and Spinoza, 251, 252
    on statehood, 76, 80–84, 85, 86, 123
    and Yosef Yerushalmi, 118
Ben-Sasson, H. H., 57n22
Bergson, Henri, 110
Berlin, Germany, 80, 180, 182
Bernstein, Leonard, 203
Berry, Wanda Warren, 72
Bezalel, 203
Biale, David, xiv, 55
Bialik, Chaim Nahman, 1nn1–2, 2n4, 95, 180n3
Bible
    and allegory, 113
    and angels, 132
    and art, 203
    on covenants, 65
    on creation, 139
    and Hebrew language, 95
    and the historical-critical method, 163–65, 256
    and State of Israel, 85
    and Jewish identity, 51
    as myth, 88, 92, 93–94, 103
    and promise and fulfillment, 14, 88
    and prophecy, 132–33, 147
    as reasoned, 168
    and revelation, 57, 132–34
    and ritual law, 179
    on the stranger, 172
    translated, 197
    and violence, 118–22
    and Zionism, 88, 102, 103
    See also individual books of the Bible, Torah
binationalism, 90, 97, 97n99
Bitzan, Amos, 124
Blidstein, Gerald, 102n111
blood, 189
Blumenthal, David, 213, 247
body, in the thought of
    Ahad Ha'am, 95
    Bahya ibn Paquda, 155–56, 157
    Buber, 70n50
    Judah Halevi, 152–53
    Yeshayahu Leibowitz, 228
    Maimonides, 10, 39, 40, 70n50, 152–53, 214, 246
    Moses Mendelssohn, 193
    Philo, 5–6, 29
    Plato, 29, 39
    Spinoza, 38–40, 42–44, 162, 163, 221–24, 251–53, 255
Bolton, Andrew, 110, 110n17
Boyarin, Daniel, 70n50
Brenner, Michael, 197n65, 202n74
Breslauer, Daniel, 65
Buber, Martin
    and Ahad Ha'am, 92–94, 98–99
    and atheism, 210, 237
    and Walter Benjamin, 264
    Judith Butler on, 101–2
    and Hermann Cohen, 170
    on covenant, 69–73, 84
    on God, 70–72, 87–88, 210, 212, 217, 234–40, 264–70, 275
    on Jewish identity, 69–73, 74, 87–90, 92, 93, 94, 101, 264–65, 268
    on law, 183–86, 210, 265, 266
    and Leibowitz, 207, 210
    and Levinas, 174, 231, 265

NAME AND SUBJECT INDEX

on ritual, 182–86
and Rosenzweig, 145, 165, 183–85, 197, 231, 240, 241, 270, 273–74
on revelation, 145–46
and Spinoza, 235, 239–40, 266, 269
on spiritual life, 263–70
on suffering, 265
on Zionism, 74–76, 87–94, 98–99, 101–3
See also I-Thou relation.
Buddhism, 3, 5, 9, 10, 18, 42, 51, 149, 161, 215, 235, 247, 248, 265
Bulhof, Ilse, 245, 248
Burrus, Virginia, 60n30
Buruma, Ian, 163
Butler, Judith, xiv, 81, 83, 101–2

Cain, 263
calendar, 187
Caligula, 111–13
Canaan and Canaanites, 118–22, 121n42
Caravaggio, 28
Carlisle, Clare, 253nn10–11
causation, in the thought of
 Bahya ibn Paquda, 158
 Buber, 266
 Ecclesiastes, 45, 262–63
 Walter Benjamin, 107
 Heschel, 24
 Immanuel Kant, 199
 Krochmal, 124, 126–27
 Yeshayahu Leibowitz, 204
 Levinas, 32
 Maimonides, 10–11, 134–35, 186–87, 216
 Haym Soloveitchik, 208
 Spinoza, 38, 42, 43, 44, 161–62, 166, 269
 Yosef Yerushalmi, 105
 See also science
Center for Jewish History (New York), 117
change, 6n14, 7, 8–9, 10, 77, 214
charity. *See* love
chosenness, 51, 59–64, 71, 94, 128, 181, 261, 276. *See also* Jewish identity

Christianity
 and Buber, 89–90, 186, 238, 264, 270
 Hermann Cohen on, 171, 256
 Judah Halevi on, 57
 Menahem Ha-Meiri on, 191n51
 and Zena Hitz, 161; in Israeli law, 84
 and Yeshayahu Leibowitz, 259–60
 Levinas on, 257–58, 259
 and Maimonides, 188
 and New Testament ethics, 150
 and Philo, 154, 155
 Rosenzweig on, 46, 50, 62, 183, 199, 201–3, 244, 272–73
 and Spinoza, 45, 164, 249, 253, 255, 256
 and Suffering Servant, 177
 and Simone Weil, 49
 and Wisdom of Solomon, 118–19
circumcision, 70, 114, 179, 180n3, 181
Click, Emily, 37
Cline, Eric, 120
Cohen, Arthur, 34–36, 45
Cohen, Gerson, 126
Cohen, Hermann, 4, 130, 165–73, 175, 212, 256
Cohen, Hillel, 98, 100–101
Cohen, Richard, 32
Cohen, Shaye J. D., 52–53
Cole, Teju, 28
Collins, John, 121
commandment(s), in the thought of
 Bahya ibn Paquda, 156, 159
 Buber, 184, 210
 Hermann Cohen, 167–68, 171
 Fackenheim, 36–37
 Samson Raphael Hirsch, 193–94
 Immanuel Kant, 166
 Yeshayahu Leibowitz, 204–8, 210, 228–30, 259
 Levinas, 233, 259
 Maimonides, 129, 131, 135, 246
 Moses Mendelssohn, 193
 Rosenzweig, 83, 142–45, 159, 194–98, 200, 203, 207, 223, 231, 241, 251, 270, 272
 Haym Soloveitchik, 208–9

commandment(s) in the thought of
      (continued)
   the Wisdom of Solomon 118
   See also law, revelation, Ten
      Commandments
Commentary (magazine), 198, 209, 270
community, in the thought of
   Buber, 72, 87–88, 89–90, 93
   Shaye J. D. Cohen, 52
   Exodus, 65
   Samson Raphael Hirsch, 261
   Yeshayahu Leibowitz, 260
   Levinas, 68
   Maimonides, 135n16, 151, 186, 190
   the prophets, 66
   Puritans, 64, 65
   Rosenzweig, 195, 198, 201, 202
   Gershom Scholem, 151
   Spinoza, 254
compassion, 3, 9, 11, 18, 41, 46, 158,
      170–71, 219, 248. *See also*
      altruism, love
Conquest of Canaan, 118–22, 121n42
contemplation, 114, 132, 133, 134, 154,
      160, 193, 245, 246–48, 253. *See
      also* meditation
contentlessness. *See* indescribability
contradiction, 32, 45, 82, 146, 147, 160,
      170, 185–86, 206, 225, 239, 268
converts, 50, 54–55, 57
Convivencia (Spain), 57
Copernicus, 250
Copleston, Frederick C., 3
cosmological argument, 215–16,
      224, 229. *See also* ontological
      argument
covenant, 51, 60, 64–73, 84, 88, 89–90,
      147, 172, 195, 244
Covid-19, 37
creation, in the thought of
   Walter Benjamin, 138–40
   Hermann Cohen, 169n56
   Ecclesiastes, 45
   Genesis, 122
   Judah Halevi, 57–58
   Heschel, 18–27
   Yeshayahu Leibowitz, 205–6
   Levinas, 31

   Philo, 1, 4–9, 16, 17, 23, 114, 224
   Maimonides, 1–3, 7, 9–12, 16, 17,
      19–21, 23, 133, 218, 219
   Moses Mendelssohn, 193
   Rosenzweig, 12–18, 22, 23, 26, 62,
      142, 145, 169n56, 198–200, 202,
      271–72
   Gershom Scholem, 136
   Spinoza, 45
Cusk, Rachel, 106

dance, 202–3
Daum, Menachem, 99–101
David, 65n43, 88, 122, 125
Davidson, Harold, 59
De Mille, Cecile B., 111
death, in the thought of
   Walter Benjamin, 107, 111, 115
   Arthur Cohen, 35, 36
   Ecclesiastes, 46, 225
   Levinas, 175, 176
   Maimonides, 17, 30, 152, 247, 273
   Marcel Proust, 146
   Rosenzweig, 12–14, 17, 30, 40, 77,
      142–43, 145, 195, 241, 273
   Spinoza, 249
decision, 61, 185–86, 230, 268
Declaration of Independence (Israeli),
      85–86, 98, 103, 123
Descartes, René, 38, 39, 40, 43, 222, 232
desire, 9, 22, 40, 41, 157, 158, 160, 162,
      166, 206. *See also* pleasure
determinism, 7, 43–44, 254–55. *See also*
      self-determination
Deuteronomy, 121
Dhammapada, 248
Diamond, James Arthur, 104
diaspora (of Jews), 92–93
disenchantment, 22–23, 26
Dostoevsky, Fyodor, 4, 237
Dowry, Alan, 97n96
dualism, 264–65, 268. *See also*
      contradiction

Earthrise (photograph), 3
Easter, 202
Ecclesiastes, xiv, 45–46, 102, 225–29,
      231, 235, 262–63

ecology, 3, 5, 17, 25
Eden, Garden of, 6, 141, 142
Egypt, 102, 109, 122, 127, 190. *See also* Alexandria, Egypt
Eilberg-Schwartz, Howard, 70n50
Einstein, Albert, 135, 187, 224
Eisen, Robert, 121–22
Elazar, Daniel, 65n42, 72, 72n60
Elijah, 261
Eliot, George, 130
Elisha ben Abuya, xiv, 180n4
Elohim, 227
Emerson, Ralph Waldo, 19
emotion, 37–45, 92, 114, 154, 157, 161–63, 214, 250, 252, 254
empiricism. *See* experience
Enlightenment, 117, 165, 192, 211
Epicureanism, 262
Esther, 54, 227
Eternal Thou, 185n35, 212, 235–36, 238, 240, 264
eternity
    as beloved, 249, 253
    of the church, 272
    as divine, 87, 221, 223, 239, 239n52, 252, 253
    as ecstatic, 111
    as indescribable, 244, 276
    of the Jewish people, 64, 78, 127–28, 272
    as joyful, 249
    of life, 273
    and perfection, 253n9
    as redemptive, 116, 195
    of truth, 164, 193, 272
    (not) of the world, 1, 2, 4, 8, 187
    See also Eternal Thou
ethics, in the thought of
    Ahad Ha'am, 94–95
    Bahya ibn Paquda, 155–61, 169, 170
    the Bible, 150
    Buber, 264
    Arthur Cohen, 35
    Hermann Cohen, 165–73, 175
    Menahem Ha-Meiri, 191
    Zena Hitz, 159–61
    Samuel Holdheim, 181

    Immanuel Kant, 165–67, 200, 205–6, 261
    Yeshayahu Leibowitz, 205–6, 231
    Levinas, 36, 173–77, 231–34, 257, 258–59, 261
    Maimonides, 150, 151–53, 155, 159, 164, 165, 219, 247–48
    Philo, 6, 153–55
    Plato, 248
    the Mishnah, 151
    Rosenzweig, 31, 177–78
    Spinoza, 43–44, 161–65, 166, 254
    Simone Weil, 177
    Elie Wiesel, 35
ethnicity and ethnicities, 53–55, 63–64, 77, 90, 120, 127–28
Eucharist, 188, 203
Euclid, 38, 161, 180n4, 250, 254
Eve, 4, 6, 142, 158. *See also* Adam
evil, in the thought of
    Bahya ibn Paquda, 157
    Buber, 75, 268
    Arthur Cohen, 35
    Ecclesiastes, 45, 225, 46
    Emil Fackenheim, 34
    Genesis, 6
    Menahem Ha-Meiri, 191
    Heschel, 21
    Levinas, 30
    Maimonides, 9–11, 152
    Philo, 6–7, 28, 112
    Spinoza, 253
    Talmud, 179
    Elie Wiesel, 35
    Wisdom of Solomon, 119, 191
    See also Good
Exodus, the, 88, 94, 105, 114, 118–20, 122, 153, 205
experience, 58, 91, 114, 145–46, 213, 241, 260, 263. *See also* vision
expression
    of (self-expressive) commandments, 204
    of God, 137, 218, 223–24, 251–53
    of ideas, 194
    as linguistic, 140–41, 143–45, 177, 195

NAME AND SUBJECT INDEX

expression *(continued)*
   of love, 84n30, 142, 143–45, 177, 195, 251
   as manifestation, 81n16, 251
   as revelation, 142, 143, 223, 251
   of self-extradition, 177
extremity and extremes, 150–66, 170–71, 176–77, 246
Ezekiel, 133, 147

Fackenheim, Emil, 33–34, 36–37, 45
Fagenblat, Michael, 211n2, 212, 245
fashion, 109–11, 140n42
Fenves, Peter, 81n17, 81n20, 83
Feuer, Lewis, 255
Fewell, Danna Nolan, 47
first fruits, 71, 118n32
Flaccus, 111–12, 116
Flapan, Simha, 122
Fowl, Stephen, 190
Frankfurt, Germany, 197n65, 203
Freies Jüdisches Lehrhaus, 197
French Revolution, 109–10, 110n15, 111
Freud, Sigmund, 101
friendship, 238–39, 254
Frisch, Max, 48–49
future, the, 107, 242, 243. *See also* past, present

Galileo, 250
Galli, Barbara, 243
Geiger, Abraham, 124, 180
Genesis, 7
gentiles, 53, 59n27, 179
Germany, 76, 79–80, 115, 180–82, 197, 202, 274
Gibbs, Robert, 28, 167
Ginzberg, Louis, 1n1, 191n52
Glatzer, Nahum, 198, 244n59, 270
God, in the thought of
   Bahya, 157n21, 158
   Buber, 70–72, 87–88, 210, 212, 217, 234–40, 264–70, 275
   Ecclesiastes, 225–27, 263
   Judah Halevi, 56–60
   Heschel, 20, 24, 26–27
   Samuel Holdheim, 180–81

   State of Israel, 85–86
   Job, 29, 49
   Krochmal, 127–28
   Yeshayahu Leibowitz, 205–8; 227–30
   Levinas, 176, 230–34, 258–60
   Maimonides, xiii, 1–3, 16, 132–34, 189–91, 211, 213–20, 246–49
   Moses Mendelssohn, 193
   Philo, 5–9, 56, 112
   Pseudo-Solomon, 119
   Rosenzweig, 12–13, 16, 60–64, 142–45, 196, 199–200, 241–44, 270–73
   Gershom Scholem, 79, 136–37
   Haym Soloveitchik, 208–10
   Spinoza, 44–45, 220–25, 249–55, 269, 270
   See also cosmological argument, names of God, ontological argument
Golden Rule, 144, 149, 169
Goldstein, Rebecca, 38, 223, 255
good
   and Buber, 212, 264, 265
   and Arthur Cohen, 35
   and Bahya ibn Paquda, 159
   and Ecclesiastes, 45, 225, 226, 228, 263
   and evil, 21, 35, 45, 225, 226, 228
   and Genesis, 263, 264
   and God, 29, 212, 265
   and Heschel, 21
   and joy, 249–50
   and human nature, 115
   and Kant, 206, 238
   and knowledge, 10, 158, 159
   and language, 264
   and the moment, 263
   and Philo, 115, 121, 155
   and Plato, 4, 132, 133, 196, 212, 248, 255
   and reason, 163, 248, 254
   and Rosenzweig, 272
   and sensuality, 121
   and Spinoza, 38, 43, 163, 249–50, 254–55
   and suffering, 45, 225

and usefulness, 43, 254, 255
and the will, 155, 206
See also evil
Goodman, Micah, 132, 134, 135, 249
Graetz, Heinrich, 117, 124
Graubart, Jonathan, 75
Greenberg, Moshe, 122n45
Guide of the Perplexed. *See* Maimonides
Guttmann, Julius, 128, 209–10

Ha'am, Ahad. *See* Ahad Ha'am
hadith, 157n21
Haim of Romshishok, 16
halacha, 36, 63–64, 149, 180, 204, 228–29, 234, 260, 262, 270. *See also* commandments, kashrut, law, sabbath
Halbertal, Moshe, 191. 214
Halevi, Judah, 56–61, 91, 92, 127, 128, 152–53, 276
Hallo, William, 18
halutzim, 91, 96, 97, 99
Ha-Meiri, Menahem, 191
Handelman, Susan, 138, 140, 141, 148
Harris, Jay, 127
Hart, Kevin, 176n80
Hartman, Donniel, 209
Hebrew language, 63–64, 64n39, 67, 78–79, 85, 95, 96–97, 136, 138, 197, 207, 275
Hebrew Union College, 182
Hebrew University, 97, 100
Hebron, Israel, 98
Hegel, G. W. F., 125, 127, 199, 201n73, 275
Helena, Queen, 54
herem (ban), 118
Herzl, Theodor, 75
Heschel, Abraham Joshua, 18–27, 135, 187, 218, 224, 253n9, 265
High Holidays (Judaism), 267. *See also* Yom Kippur
Hillel, Rabbi, 149
Hinduism, 51, 215, 247. *See also* Upanishads
Hirsch, Samson Raphael, 193–94, 196, 260–61

Hirschfeld, Hartwig, 58
historiography, academic, 105–6, 116–28
history and historians, 55, 100, 104–128, 129, 134
Hitz, Zena, 159–61, 162
Holdheim, Samuel, 180–82
Hollander, Dana, 175n77
Holocaust, 8, 33–37, 45, 49, 98, 99, 100, 105, 116, 182n15, 211, 233n33, 257
Holy Spirit, 169–70
Homer, 119
Hosea, 191, 191n52
humanity, in the thought of
    Ahad Ha'am, 96
    Buber, 89–90, 264
    Hermann Cohen, 171, 172
    Judah Halevi, 59
    Levinas, 31–33, 67–69, 259
    Philo, 5–6
    Rosenzweig, 31, 62, 63, 142, 147, 195, 201, 242, 243, 271, 273
    See also image of God, universalism
humility, 151–52, 153, 156, 158–59, 163, 187
Hyamson, Moses, 157

I Am That I Am, 56, 58, 136, 137, 168, 175, 218, 240
I–Thou relation, 69–73, 84, 87–89, 92, 94, 103, 108, 170, 182, 185, 212, 235–39, 244, 263–69. *See also* Buber, Martin; Eternal Thou
idealism, 26, 87, 93, 255
ideas, in the thought of
    Aristotle, 9n20
    Buber, 212, 264
    Heschel, 21–22
    Maimonides, 19
    Philo, 4–9, 224
    Plato, 4, 9n20, 248
    Rosenzweig, 12, 14, 22
    Spinoza, 39, 43, 221, 250–52, 254–55
    See also mind

NAME AND SUBJECT INDEX

idolatry, 1, 118, 180, 186, 189–93, 209, 254n12
ignorance, 9–11, 162, 226, 262
Iliad, 119
image of God, 5, 220, 248. *See also* humanity
imagination, 52, 128, 187–88, 202, 222
immortality, 142, 234, 238
Indefinability. *See* indescribability
indescribability of
    the absolute, 128, 185, 212, 213, 221, 231, 239, 244, 251
    the commandments, 207
    the covenant, 68, 72, 147, 244
    eternity, 221, 235, 244, 252, 275
    God, xiii, 51, 72, 84, 87, 128, 133–34, 147, 174, 190–91, 207, 211–44, 245, 252, 259, 275–76
    the Good, 132
    I-Thou relation, 69–70, 72, 84, 94, 244, 263
    infinity, 221, 244, 252, 275
    Jewish identity, xv, 48–64, 72, 84, 94,174, 207, 244, 276
    (pure Edenic) language, 140–41, 145, 244
    love, 145
    names of God, 137, 145, 218, 227, 244
    the Other, 176–77, 244
    revelation, 131,137, 147, 174, 244, 251
    the self, 147, 174, 244, 275
    suffering, 33–36, 207, 244, 276
    transcendence, 114
    (divine) violence, 83–84, 244
    See also nothing
infinity, in the thought of
    Buber, 239
    Hinduism, 51n8, 214
    Yeshayahu Leibowitz, 233, 260
    Levinas, 232–33
    the Ontological Argument, 217
    Spinoza, 221–24, 239, 249, 251–52, 255
Inquisition, 37, 164
intellect. *See* Mind
intuition, 220, 252, 255

Isaac, 114–15, 263
Isaiah, 54, 126, 176, 177, 198, 257
Islam, 57, 84–85, 93, 103, 135n16, 189, 200. *See also* hadith, Quran, Sufism
Israel, Jonathan, 165
Israel (the name), 53, 56
Israel (the people). *See* Jewish identity
Israel (the state), 48, 50–51, 55, 70n50, 73, 74–103, 122–23, 204
Israel/Palestine (the land), 61, 63–64, 75, 78–80, 85–86, 88–93, 96–103
Israelites, Biblical, 67, 68, 77, 109, 118–21, 135, 164, 171n61, 179, 189, 233

Jacob, 53, 56, 115
Jacobs, Jonathan, 158, 171
James Webb telescope, 163
James, William, 243
Jeremiah, 147
Jesus Christ, 45, 150, 238, 255n13, 256. *See also* Christianity
Jewish Catalog, The, 198
Jewish identity, in the thought of
    Ahad Ha'am, 91–98, 101
    Buber, 69–73, 74, 87–90, 92, 93, 94, 101, 264–65, 268
    Judith Butler, 101–2
    Arthur Cohen, 35
    Shaye Cohen, 52, 53–54
    Emil Fackenheim, 36
    Judah Halevi, 57–61
    Nachman Krochmal, 124–28
    Yeshayahu Leibowitz, 206, 277
    Levinas, 52, 67–69
    the Midrash, 187–88
    Amos Oz, 50
    the Pew Research Center, 149, 165
    Philo, 56, 114
    Rosenzweig, 50, 60–64, 78, 82, 184n30, 274
    Shlomo Sand, 50–52, 54–55
    Gershom Scholem, 50
    Simone Weil, 49–50
    Harry Austryn Wolfson, 48

See also indescribability of Jewish
   identity
Job, 29–30, 36, 47, 49, 102, 181, 262n31
Johnson, William A., 269n57, 270
Jonah, 54
Jonas, Hans, 34
Jonathan, 65n43
Joshua, 67
Jospe, Eva, 167, 171n61
Jost, Isaak, 55
Judah, 53, 55
Judah Halevi. *See* Halevi, Judah
Judaism, Humanistic, xiv, 227
Judaism, Orthodox, 26n46, 95–96,
   182, 183, 193–94, 208–9, 230,
   260–61
Judaism, rabbinical, 44, 50, 58, 66–69,
   95, 102, 104, 126, 130, 146, 180,
   184, 191n52, 192, 195, 205, 256,
   259. *See also* halacha, midrash,
   Talmud
Judaism, Reform, 124, 180–82, 199,
   209n87, 275
Judith, 54
Judea, 53–54, 55

kabbalah, 58, 135–38, 218, 240, 265,
   277–78. *See also* mysticism
Kafka, Franz, 245
Kant, Immanuel and
   Buber, 238
   Hermann Cohen, 4, 165–68, 171,
      172
   Heschel, 18, 21, 25, 26
   Yeshayahu Leibowitz, 205–6, 234,
      261
   Levinas, 32, 39, 232, 234, 261
   Maimonides, 133
   Rosenzweig, 199–200, 202
   Bertrand Russell, 217
   Spinoza, 39
kashrut, 179, 181
Katz, Steven, 34n19
Kaufmann, Walter, 87, 236, 240, 270
Keller, Catherine, 25
Kellner, Menachem, 257n22
Keneseth Israel, 47
Khazars, 54, 57
kibbutzim, 89–90

Kierkegaard, Soren, 177, 230, 259
Klee, Paul, 107
knowledge, in the thought of
   Bayha ibn Paquda, 156, 158, 160–61
   Buber, 70, 236
   Ecclesiastes, 262
   Judah Halevi, 58
   Yeshayahu Leibowitz, 240
   Levinas, 173, 176, 234
   Maimonides, 9–11, 39, 44, 132–34,
      152–53, 216, 252
   Moses Mendelssohn, 192
   Philo, 6
   Rosenzweig, 12, 14
   Spinoza, 161, 163, 165, 252
   See also reason and rationality,
      science
Kogan, Barry, 20n36
Kohn, Hans, 90, 92, 94n80
Korah, 82–83
Kornberg, Jacques, 91, 96n90
Korobkin, Daniel, 209
Kotzk, Chief Rabbi of, 186
Kreisel, Howard, 157, 204
Krell, David Ferrel, 12
Kristallnacht, 180. *See also* Holocaust
Krochmal, Nachman, 124–28, 275
Kushner, Harold, 29

Land for All (organization), 103
Landau, Jacob, 47
language and languages, as
   absent, 18
   agentive, 138, 143
   creative, 136, 138, 140, 264
   expressive, 137, 140–41, 143–45,
      195, 251
   inadequate, 72, 220, 228
   multiple, 67–68
   naming, 136–39, 140, 145, 146, 218,
      240, 253
   paradoxical, 34, 35, 146, 220
   presentive, 136–39, 195, 223, 251
   revelatory, 137–39, 218, 220
   sacred, 78–79
   silent, 56, 243
   translative, 140–41, 145
   unspeakable, 276
   See also Arabic, Hebrew

law, in the thought of
    Bahya ibn Paquda, 156
    Walter Benjamin, 80–83
    Buber, 183–86, 210, 265, 266
    Judith Butler, 81
    Hermann Cohen, 168, 171–72
    Ecclesiastes, 102, 227–28, 262
    Albert Einstein, 134
    George Eliot, 130
    Abraham Geiger, 124, 180
    Judah Halevi, 57, 60, 61
    Samson Raphael Hirsch, 261
    Samuel Holdheim, 180–81
    State of Israel, 84–86
    Job, 102
    Franz Kafka, 245
    Kant, 166, 205, 234
    Nachman Krochmal, 126–27
    Yeshayahu Leibowitz, 204–9, 228, 230, 234, 261
    Levinas, 67–68, 259
    Maimonides, 1, 2, 130, 134–35, 150–52, 164, 186–92, 196, 206, 219, 261
    Moses Mendelssohn, 192–93
    Philo, 120
    the prophets, 105
    Marcel Proust, 146
    the rabbis, 44, 65, 66, 67–68, 130, 150–51, 172, 179
    Rosenzweig, 63, 64, 77–78, 80, 184, 196–97, 198, 207, 274
    Saadia Gaon, 150
    Shlomo Sand, 51
    Haym Soloveitchik, 208–9
    Spinoza, 164, 261
    Leo Strauss, 130
    Simone Weil, 49
    See also commandments, halacha, Talmud, Ten Commandments
Lefkowitz, Jay, 209
Leibniz, Gottfried Wilhelm, 29
Leibowitz, Yeshayahu, 204–10, 227–34, 240, 259–62, 263, 266, 277
Léon Hebreo, 271
Levi, Primo, 8
Levinas, Emmanuel
    and atheism, 233–34, 258, 261
    and Buber, 174, 231, 265
    and Hermann Cohen, 173, 175
    on Christianity, 257–58, 259
    on covenant, 67–69, 73
    and Descartes, 232
    and Ecclesiastes, 231, 262
    on ethics, 36, 173–77, 231–34, 257, 258–59, 261
    and Fackenheim, 33, 37
    on God, 176, 230–34, 258–60
    on the Holocaust, 33, 37
    on Jewish identity, 52
    and Kant, 232, 234, 261
    and Yeshayahu Leibowitz, 230–31, 233, 259–60, 261
    and Maimonides, 231
    on reason, 45, 131, 234
    on revelation, 138, 146–48
    and Rosenzweig, 30–31, 174, 177–78, 231, 273
    and Simone Weil, 177
    and Spinoza, 39, 44, 45, 256
    on spiritual life, 256–59, 260, 261, 273
    on subjection, 179
    on suffering, 30–33, 36, 37, 45, 147–48, 174, 233
Lewandowski, Lewis, 181
LGBT+ persons, 118, 201
liminality, 148, 274
Lobel, Diana, 157n21
love, in the thought of
    Ahad Ha'am, 94
    Bahya ibn Paquda, 156, 158–59
    Hermann Cohen, 12, 168, 171–72
    Zena Hitz, 161
    Yeshayahu Leibowitz, 206–7
    Levinas, 176n80, 231, 233n33, 257
    Maimonides, 151–53, 247
    the Mishnah, 151; the New Testament, 41, 158, 257
    Rosenzweig, 62, 83, 138, 142–46, 147, 173, 174, 177–78, 184n30, 194–97, 200–3, 207, 223, 241–43, 251, 270–74
    Song of Songs, 143–45
    Spinoza, 40, 41, 163, 249, 253
    the Ten Commandments, 66

NAME AND SUBJECT INDEX

See also altruism, compassion
Lucretius, 19
lulav, 187–88
Lyd (film), 100n105

Maccabees, 54
Madam Rosa (film), 47
Maimonides
   Ahad Ha'am on, 90–92
   on Aristotle, 1, 2, 3, 9, 11, 19n32, 132, 151, 187, 215
   and Walter Benjamin, 218
   on the body, 10, 39, 40, 70n50, 152–53, 214, 246
   and Buber, 236
   on creation, 1–3, 7, 9–12, 16, 17, 19–21, 23, 57–58, 133, 218, 219
   and Ecclesiastes, 225–27
   on ethics, 150, 151–53, 155, 159, 164, 165, 219, 247–48
   on God, xiii, 1–3, 16, 132–34, 189–91, 211, 213–20, 246–49
   Heschel on, 19–21
   and Samson Raphael Hirsch, 261
   on history, 104–5, 116, 126
   on Jewish identity, 60
   on Job, 30
   on knowledge, 9–11, 39, 44, 132–34, 152–53, 216, 252
   Krochmal on, 125
   on law, 1, 2, 130, 134–35, 150–52, 164, 186–92, 196, 206, 219, 261
   Leibowitz on, 204, 227–30, 277
   and Levinas, 231, 258
   on matter, 10–11, 39, 40
   and Philo, 12, 16, 39, 40, 70n50, 153, 247–48
   and Plato, 11, 132, 133, 153, 247–48, 261
   on revelation, 2–3, 129, 131–35, 152, 159, 186, 190, 216–17, 218, 220
   on reason, 2, 20, 22, 39, 57, 60, 129, 131–33, 135, 186–88, 214, 271, 277
   and Rosenzweig, 241
   and Gershom Scholem, 151
   and Spinoza, 44, 164, 165, 220–24, 250, 252, 253, 254
   on spiritual life, 127, 134, 150, 220, 246–49, 250, 252, 254, 258, 261, 273
   on suffering, 9–11, 30, 39, 134n16, 153
   on vision, 132–33, 271, 273
Majallah, 84
Mann, Thomas, 139n37, 212
Marcus, Amy Dockser, 98
Mardi Gras, 46
Margalit, Avishai, 191, 214
Margolin, Jean-Claude, 116
Marmur, Michael, 19n31–32
marriage, 181
martyrdom, 150, 177
matter, 4, 6, 10–11, 221–22. *See also* body
Matthew, Gospel of, 276
Mauriac, François, 35
Maugham, Somerset, 4, 40, 161
McWhorter, John, 190
mediation, 58–59, 138
meditation, 42, 153, 162, 189, 263. *See also* contemplation
memory, 43, 57, 98, 104, 105–6, 111, 115, 117, 120, 127, 159, 202n74, 208
Mendelssohn, Moses, 180–81, 192–93, 196, 204–5, 206, 207, 209, 229
Mendes-Flohr, Paul, 70, 76, 209–210, 236, 239, 240n55
menorah, 47, 187, 202
Merneptah stele, 122
messianism, 94, 109, 111, 113, 134, 195
Metropolitan Museum of Art (New York), 110–11, 140n42
Meyer, Michael, 181
midrash, 1, 2, 2n4, 104, 117, 167, 187, 189
Miles, Jack, 45, 225, 227
Miller, B. J., 40
Milton, John, 3, 33
mind, in the thought of
   Bahya ibn Paquda, 156, 157
   Descartes, 39
   Judah Halevi, 153

mind, in the thought of *(Continued)*
    Maimonides, 134, 152, 246, 247
    Philo, 6, 114
    Spinoza, 38–40, 42–45, 138, 162,
        163, 221–24, 251–55
    See also body, ideas
miracles, 1, 15, 168
Mishnah, 67, 68, 151, 233
mitzvot. *See* commandments
Moab, 67
Mock, Keren, 162n32, 277
moderation, 150–53, 157, 177
monasteries and convents, 89, 154–55, 258
moon, 187
Morris, Benny, 122–23
Moses, 7, 53, 56, 67, 93, 101–2, 105, 132, 134–35, 147, 150, 151, 154, 186, 187, 246, 273
Moses, Stephane, 13n24
Mosse, George, 182n15
Moyn, Samuel, 167
Munch, Edvard, 18
music, 181–82, 182n15, 190, 202, 203, 226
Myers, David, 86
mystery, 22–27, 52, 146, 177, 186, 236
mysticism and
    atheism, 213, 215, 227, 276
    Bahya ibn Paquda, 157n21
    Walter Benjamin, 138, 139
    Buber, 236, 268
    Buddhism, 215
    Ezekiel, 133
    Judah Halevi, 58
    Heschel, 22
    the Jewish people, 56
    Maimonides, 134
    the marginalized, 118
    negative theology, xiii, 273
    Philo, 56
    philosophy, 276–77
    Plato, 4, 132
    Rosenzweig, 63, 213, 215, 274
    Gershom Scholem, 78, 136–37
    the unspeakable, 36
    See also kabbalah, Sufism
myth, 52, 86, 88, 92, 93, 103, 119, 242

names, 136–40
Nadler, Steven, 162, 164
names of God, 136–37, 145, 211, 218, 223–24, 240, 244, 253, 255, 275. *See also* absolute, Elohim, Eternal Thou, God, I Am that I Am, Nothing, YHWH
Naqba, 100–101
nation-states. *See* statehood
nationalism, 55, 76, 92–93, 95, 96n90, 171n61. *See also* binationalism
nature, in the thought of
    Bahya ibn Paquda, 158
    Walter Benjamin, 138
    Buber, 239, 266
    Heschel, 18–20, 23–25, 218
    Kant, 199, 205
    Yeshayahu Leibowitz, 204–5, 266
    Maimonides, 135, 186–87
    Philo, 1, 5, 7n16, 154
    Rosenzweig, 13n24, 142–43, 195, 198
    Haym Soloveitchik, 208
    Spinoza, 163–64, 223–24, 252–53
    See also ecology, world.
Nauen, Franz, 256n17
Nazirite, 150
negation, xiii–xv
Neoplatonism, 60
Neusner, Jacob, 189n46
New Outlook (magazine), 90, 122
Newton, Isaac, 250
Ng, Julia, 81n20
Nicene Creed, 239n52, 253
Niehoff, Maren, 113–14
Nietzsche, Friedrich, 145–46, 178
Noahide laws, 66, 172
Nothing, in relation to
    creation, 14 24, 27
    God, 56, 63, 128, 133, 215, 220, 223, 242, 276
    Jewish identity, 49, 56, 63–64, 276
    revelation, 131
    the self, 31–32
    suffering, 30
    truth, 272
    See also indescribability
Novalis, 138n31, 201n73

NAME AND SUBJECT INDEX

Odeh, Yacoub, 99
ontological argument, 144, 217–18, 221, 232, 250. *See also* cosmological argument
Ophir, Adi, 96n93
Oppenheim, Moritz, 202
other, the, in the thought of
    Buber, 69, 145
    Judith Butler, 102
    Hermann Cohen, 168, 170–72
    Hillel Cohen, 100
    the Golden Rule, 149
    Levinas, 173, 175–77, 231–34, 235, 236, 259, 261, 273
    Rosenzweig, 18, 195, 273–74
Ottomans, 84, 98
Overbye, Dennis, 163
Oz, Amos, 50, 90

Palestinians, 50–51, 75–76, 79, 84, 85, 89–90, 97–103, 122–23
pantheism, 161, 168, 224, 253, 276
Pappé, Ilan, 99
passion. *See* emotion
passivity, 16, 17, 25, 26, 30, 31, 39, 70, 114, 174
Passover, 80, 109, 114, 120, 153, 198, 201
past, the, 43, 108–11, 118, 242–43. *See also* future, present
pathos, 20–21, 258, 260–61
Patriarchs, the, 159. *See also* Abraham, Isaac, Jacob
Paul, Saint, 33, 46, 158, 268
peace, 82–83, 85, 98–99, 123, 265
peoplehood. *See* ethnicity
perfection, 9, 20, 21, 89, 116, 191, 250
personhood, 97n96, 212, 239, 264
Petuchowski, Jakob, 180
Pew Research Center, xv, 149, 165, 211
Peyroux, Catherine, 155n16
Philo of Alexandria
    on allegory, 113–15
    and Walter Benjamin, 113, 115–16
    on the body, 70n50, 153
    on change, 8–9
    on the conquest of Canaan, 120–21
    and Christianity, 154, 155
    on creation, 1, 4–9, 16, 17, 23, 114, 224
    on ethics, 6, 153–55
    and Judah Halevi, 58
    on history, 111–14
    on Israel, 56
    and Nachman Krochmal, 125n56
    and Maimonides, 12, 16, 39, 40, 70n50, 153, 247–48
    on the patriarchs, 115, 159
    and Plato, 4, 8, 28, 29, 153, 155, 248
    on pleasure, 6–7, 153–54
    and Rosenzweig, 14, 16
    and Spinoza, 7, 39, 40
    on suffering, 6, 28, 111–12, 116
    on the Therapeutae, 154–55, 247–48
    on time, 2n5, 7
philosophy and philosophers as
    biblical, 165, 168, 190
    contemplative, 57, 276n1
    (very) ethical, 152–53, 154–55, 164, 178
    fallible, 58
    heretical, 180
    non-historical, 104–5, 106
    interrogative, 225
    non-Jewish, 256
    non-legal, 130
    mystical, 276–78
    pagan, 1, 179
    prophetic, 135
    rabbinical, 1
    reason-venerating, 57, 90–91, 163
    synagogal, 101
    systematic, 199–200, 203–4
    theological, xiv
    visionary, 61, 271, 272
    Zionist, 90–91
Pirkei Avot, 151
Plato, in the thought of
    Aristotle, 9n20
    Bahya ibn Paquda, 156, 158
    Buber, 212
    Descartes, 39
    Judah Halevi, 153
    Heschel, 21, 27; Maimonides, 11, 132, 133, 153, 247–48, 261
    Moses Mendelssohn, 192

Plato, in the thought of *(continued)*
    Philo, 4, 8, 28, 29, 153, 155, 248
    Rosenzweig, 12, 14, 196, 199
    Spinoza, 38, 43, 162, 164, 194, 255, 261
    the Wisdom of Solomon, 119
pleasure, in the thought of
    Bahya ibn Paquda, 157
    Ecclesiastes, 225, 227, 262
    Philo, 6, 114, 153, 154
    Spinoza, 40, 41, 44, 162, 163, 249–50, 253
pogroms, 111–12, 116, 126
politics, 75, 99, 254, 265. *See also* statehood
Pollock, Benjamin, 244n59
poverty, 170–71, 175
pragmatism, 213, 219, 225, 227, 230, 246, 256, 259, 260, 261–62
prayer, 61, 67, 73, 96, 181, 189, 193, 204, 207, 224, 226, 246. *See also* Alenu, Priestly Blessing, Shema
present, the, 64, 108–11, 195–96, 241–42, 263. *See also* future, past
Priestly Blessing, 62, 271
processions, 202, 203
progress, 107–8, 110, 114
proletariat, 82, 83, 96, 97
promise, 14–15, 17, 105, 106, 124, 143, 262
prophets and prophecy, in the thought of
    Ahad Ha'am, 93–94
    the Bible, 29, 66, 105
    Abraham Geiger, 124
    Heschel, 20
    Nachman Krochmal, 126
    Jacob Landau, 47
    Levinas, 147
    Maimonides, 132–35, 216
    Saadia Gaon, 126
    Spinoza, 164
Proust, Marcel, 109n15, 111, 131, 138–39, 146
Psalms, 125, 248
Ptolemy, 250
punishment, 29, 65, 81, 112
Putnam, Hilary, 233

purpose, 11, 71, 94, 105, 116, 124, 127, 129, 166, 194, 199–200
Pythagoras, 8

quantum mechanics, 24, 224
Quran, 212n4

rabbis, the. *See* Judaism, rabbinical
Rabin, Itzhak, 98
Rapaport, Uriel, 54n20
Rashi, 21
Rauf, Feisal Abdul, 200n72, 275
Ravnitzky, Yehoshua Hana, 1nn1–2, 2n4, 180n3
Raz-Krakotzkin, Amnon, 99
reason and rationality, in the thought of
    Ahad Ha'am, 90–91
    Bahya ibn Paquda, 156, 158
    Buber, 184
    David Blumenthal, 213
    Hermann Cohen, 165–68, 171, 172
    Abraham Geiger, 180
    Judah Halevi, 57, 58
    Heschel, 21–23, 27
    Samuel Holdheim, 181
    Kant, 21, 32, 165, 205, 206
    Kierkegaard, 230
    Yeshayahu Leibowitz, 230
    Levinas, 45, 131, 234
    Maimonides, 2, 20, 22, 39, 57, 60, 129, 131–33, 135, 186–88, 214, 271, 277
    Moses Mendelssohn, 193
    Philo, 7n16, 113, 121
    Plato, 132, 196, 248
    Rosenzweig, 14, 178
    Saadia Gaon, 129, 150
    Spinoza, 39, 41, 44, 45, 161–63, 164, 224, 254, 271, 277
redemption, in the thought of
    Walter Benjamin, 109, 110, 115–16, 141
    Rosenzweig, 31, 194–95, 198–202, 203n75, 243, 271–73
Rehfeld, Andrew, 182
Reines, Alvin, 135
Reinharz, Jehuda, 96
relationship, in the thought of

NAME AND SUBJECT INDEX

Buber, 69, 71, 74, 84, 88, 89, 184–85, 217, 235, 240, 265–66
Hermann Cohen, 168–70
Levinas, 67, 235
Maimonides, 241
Rosenzweig, 13–17, 22, 31, 62, 145, 169, 241, 242, 243, 244
See also I-Thou relation
revelation, in the thought of
Walter Benjamin, 81n16, 137–41, 251
Buber, 70, 145–46, 174, 183, 217
Arthur Cohen, 34, 168, 172n66
Ecclesiastes, 226–27
Judah Halevi, 57
Heschel, 218
kabbalah, 135–37
Yeshayahu Leibowitz, 205–6, 207
Levinas, 138, 146–48, 174, 176
Maimonides, 2–3, 129, 131–35, 152, 159, 186, 190, 216–17, 218, 220
Philo, 153, 154
the rabbis, 126, 129–30, 132
Rosenzweig, 62, 138, 141–45, 147, 194–96, 198–201, 202, 223, 251, 270–72
Saadia Gaon, 129
Gershom Scholem, 130–31, 135–37, 223, 251
See also Sinai, Mount
Rittenberg, Dasha, 99
ritual, xiv–xv, 47, 61, 67, 70n50, 130, 154, 178, 179–210, 244, 259, 274
romanticism, 138, 143, 201n73
Rome, 54, 111–13
Rorty, Richard, 266
Rosenzweig, Franz
on art, 46–47, 201–3
and atheism, 199, 213, 215, 244
and Walter Benjamin, 76, 80–82, 83, 85, 86, 111, 123, 143, 145, 251
and Buber, 145, 165, 183–85, 197, 231, 240, 241, 270, 273–74
on Christianity, 46, 50, 62, 183, 199, 201–3, 244, 272–73
on Hermann Cohen, 168, 169, 170n58, 172–73

on commandment, 83, 142–45, 159, 194–98, 200, 203, 207, 223, 231, 241, 251, 270, 272
on creation, 12–18, 22, 23, 26, 62, 142, 145, 169n56, 198–200, 202, 271–72
on death, 12–14, 17, 30, 40, 77, 142–43, 145, 195, 241, 273
on God, 12–13, 16, 60–64, 142–45, 196, 199–200, 240, 241–44, 270–73
and Heschel, 21–22, 23, 26
on history, 104, 106
on Jewish identity, 50, 60–64, 78, 82, 184n30, 274
on law, 63, 64, 77–78, 80, 184, 196–97, 198, 207, 274
and Yeshayahu Leibowitz, 207
and Levinas, 30–31, 174, 177–78, 231, 273
on love, 62, 83, 137–38, 142–46, 147, 173, 174, 177–78, 184n30, 194–97, 200–3, 207, 223, 231, 241–43, 251, 270–74
and Maimonides, 241
and Plato, 12, 14, 196, 199
on redemption, 194–95, 198–99, 201, 202
on revelation, 62, 138, 141–45, 147, 194–96, 198–201, 202, 223, 251, 270–72
on ritual, 183–84, 194, 198–203
and Gershom Scholem, 78–79, 141, 143, 251
and Spinoza, 194, 243, 256, 271, 272
on spiritual life, 270–74
on statehood, 77–78, 80, 82, 85, 102, 123
on suffering 18, 31, 46–47, 106, 142, 201
on Zionism, 76–78
Rossi, Solomon de, 203
Rudavsky, Oren, 99
Ruins of Lifta (film), 99–101
Russell, Bertrand, 3, 217
Russell, John, 4
Ruth, 54
Rynhold, Daniel, 208, 229, 233

Saadia Gaon, 129, 131, 150
sabbath, 47, 50, 150–51, 154, 179, 181, 187, 192, 194, 198, 200, 201
Sacks, Elias, 124
sacrifice, 48, 119, 119n33, 188–89, 227
Safrai, Shmuel, 112n20
Said, Edward, 101–2
Saiman, Chaim, 130
saintliness, 151–52, 155, 157, 166, 176n80, 258
Samuel, 77
Sand, Shlomo, 50–51, 54–55, 64n39, 86, 206
Sankara, 247
Sarah, 50, 52
satan, 262n31
Saul, King, 20
Schechter, Solomon, 124
Schelling, Friedrich, 12, 201n73
Scholem, Gershom
  and Walter Benjamin, 84, 130–31, 138, 143, 145, 251, 275
  on secularized Hebrew, 78–79
  on the state of Israel, 79–80, 86, 98
  on Jewish identity, 50
  and Yeshayahu Leibowitz, 277
  and Maimonides, 151
  on names, 136–37, 240
  on revelation, 130–31, 135–37, 223, 251
  and Rosenzweig, 78–79, 141, 143, 251, 275
Schopenhauer, Arthur, 201n73
Schorsch, Ismar, 117n27
Schuon, Frithjof, 275
Schwarzschild, Steven, 125n56, 126n60, 127
science
  and Aristotle, 11
  and Bahya ibn Paquda, 158n21, 159
  and Einstein, 135
  and Heschel, 23, 24
  and historiography, 105, 117–18, 125
  and Judah Halevi, 152
  and Kant, 167, 199
  and Yeshayahu Leibowitz, 204
  and Maimonides, 11, 132, 134–35
  and Haym Soloveitchik, 208
  and Spinoza, 37–38, 39, 161, 162, 163, 249, 250, 255
Scott, R. B. Y., 45, 262
Schubert, Franz, 46, 181, 203
secularism
  as atheistic, 199
  as Hebraized, 78–79
  as Jewish, xiv, 36, 59, 168, 182, 183n21, 201, 206, 208, 209, 230, 245, 270
  as (non)Jewish, 50, 55
  as Ecclesiastical, 45, 227
  as Israeli, 85–86
  as profaning, 85–86
  as spiritual, 269
  as Zionist, 94–96
Seeger, Pete, 226
Seeskin, Kenneth, 104n2, 211n2
self-Determination, 38–40, 42, 44, 173, 221, 250–51, 253–54
self-Negation
  as altruistic, 151, 155, 158, 161, 163, 165, 248
  as ascetic, 154–62, 166, 206, 234
  as biblical, 102, 150
  as commanded, 204
  as ethical, 154–55, 173, 175–78, 232–33
  as Jewish, 102
  as loving, 144, 151, 195
  as Mosaic, 102
  as prayerful, 246–47
  as revelatory, 147–48, 232
  as spiritual, 248
  as Zionistic, 84
senses, the, 114, 121, 157, 160, 216, 224, 227, 247. *See also* pleasure
Septuagint, 8n18
Shabbat. *See* Sabbath
Shavuot, 198
Shekhina, 58
Shelley, Mary, 3
Shema (prayer), 187, 199, 200, 268
Shlaim, Avi, 122
Shumsky, Dmitry, 97n99
Silberstein, Laurence, 266

NAME AND SUBJECT INDEX

Sinai, Mount, 58, 65, 67, 88, 126, 129–30, 132, 153, 186. *See also* revelation
silence, 63, 200, 220, 226, 243, 248, 264, 274
Simon, Leon, 94, 96
slavery, 108, 109
Smith, Ronald Gregor, 240
solitariness, in the thought of
    Bahya ibn Paquda, 157
    Buber, 90
    Samson Raphael Hirsch, 261
    Levinas, 30–33, 147
    Maimonides, 247
    Moses Mendelssohn, 192
    Philo, 154
    Rosenzweig, 12–18, 22, 30–31, 142, 202, 242
    See also relationship
Solomon, 122, 164
Soloveitchik, Haym, 159, 208–9
Song of Songs, 62, 143–45, 194, 198, 241, 242
Sontag, Susan, 177
Sorel, George, 81n20, 82n24
soul, in the thought of
    Ahad Ha'am, 92
    Bahya ibn Paquda, 157, 158n21, 159
    Walter Benjamin, 83
    Buber, 268
    Buddhism, 51, 215
    Ecclesiastes, 226, 262
    Hinduism, 51, 214–15
    Samson Raphael Hirsch, 193
    Yeshayahu Leibowitz, 260
    Levinas, 148
    Maimonides, 214
    Marcel Proust, 138
    Philo, 4, 6, 113, 114–15, 153, 156
    Plato, 4, 39
    Rosenzweig, 194–95, 207
Spinoza, Baruch
    and atheism, 161, 276
    and Walter Benjamin, 251, 252
    on the Bible, 93, 163–65
    on body and mind, 38–40, 42–45, 138, 162, 163, 222, 224
    and Buber, 235, 239–40, 266, 269
    and Christianity, 45, 164, 249, 253, 255, 256
    and Hermann Cohen, 166, 256
    on determinism, 43–44, 254–55
    on emotions, 38–45, 161
    on ethics, 43–44, 161–65, 166, 254
    on God, 44–45, 220–25, 249–55, 269, 270
    and Yeshayahu Leibowitz, 261, 277
    and Levinas, 39, 45, 256
    and Maimonides, 44, 164, 165, 220–24, 250, 252, 253, 254
    and pantheism, 161, 276
    and Philo, 7
    and Plato, 38, 43, 162, 164, 194, 255, 261
    on reason, 39, 41, 44, 45, 161–63, 164, 224, 254, 271, 277
    on ritual, 180
    and Rosenzweig, 194, 243, 256, 271, 272
    on self-determination, 44
    on spiritual life, 45, 163, 249–56, 258, 261, 269, 273
    on suffering, 37–45, 249, 250
spiritual life, and the thought of
    Bahya ibn Paquda, 156, 157, 159n26
    David Blumenthal, 213
    Buber, 239, 263–70, 273, 274
    Ecclesiastes, 227, 262–63
    Einstein, 135
    Judah Halevi, 57
    Samson Raphael Hirsch, 260–61
    Kant, 261
    Nachman Krochmal, 127
    Yeshayahu Leibowitz, 259–61
    Levinas, 256–59, 260, 261, 273
    Maimonides, 127, 134, 150, 220, 246–49, 250, 252, 254, 258, 261, 273
    Philo, 155
    Rosenzweig, 270–74
    Haym Soloveitchik, 159n26, 208n84
    Spinoza, 45, 163, 249–55, 256, 258, 261, 269, 273
Star of David, 46, 271–73
statehood, 74, 76–86, 123, 126n60, 164
Statman, Daniel, 209

Steinberg, Michael, 80
Steinberg, Milton, 180n4
Steiner, George, 159
Stern, Josef, 131
Stern, Menahem, 112n20
Stoicism, 39, 42, 113
strangers, 64, 67, 171–75, 198
Strauss, Leo, 130, 169
Stroumsa, Guy, 257
sublime, 18, 20, 22–25, 94, 166, 207
Sufism, 157n21, 247, 273, 275
suffering, in the thought of
    Bahya ibn Paquda, 157
    Walter Benjamin, 107–9, 111, 115–16
    Buber, 265
    Arthur Cohen, 34–36, 37, 45
    Hermann Cohen, 166n47, 170–71
    Ecclesiastes, 45–46, 225, 262
    Emil Fackenheim, 33–34, 36–37, 45
    Judah Halevi, 153
    Heschel, 20–21, 26
    Job, 29–30
    Nachman Krochmal, 126–28
    Levinas, 30–33, 36, 37, 45, 147–48, 174, 233
    Maimonides, 9–11, 30, 39, 134n16, 153
    Philo, 6, 28, 111–12, 116
    the prophets, 20
    Rosenzweig, 18, 31, 46–47, 106, 142, 201
    Spinoza, 37–45, 249, 250
    Simone Weil, 106
    Elie Wiesel, 35
Suffering Servant, 150, 177, 257
Sukkot, 187–88, 198
Sulzer, Salomon, 203
Sutcliffe, Adam, 60n28, 171–72
Swatos, William H.
symbolism, 193–94
synagogues, 47, 48, 101, 181–82, 182n14, 203, 275

Talmud, 67–68, 117, 150, 167, 205, 256, 258
Tanak see Bible
Tefellin, 183
teleology, 38
Temple (Jerusalem), 95, 112, 113, 126, 181, 227
Ten Commandments, 66, 70, 79, 144, 156, 191n52, 196, 203, 211, 229
Ten Commandments (film), 111
Teresa of Avila, 257
Tertullian, 2
theodicy, 10, 29, 33, 44, 46, 105, 112, 120, 124, 127–28, 134, 234, 257, 258, 265. See also Evil
Therapeutae, 154–55, 247–48
Thirteen Attributes of God, 219
Thirty Years War, 115, 116
thought. See mind
Tigay, Jeffrey H., 119n33
Tikkun (magazine), 122
time and temporality, 2, 3, 6, 7, 78, 107–11, 138, 192–93, 202, 241–43
Tirosh-Samuelson, Hava, 276n1
Tolstoy, Leo, 235
Torah
    and art, 203
    and Canaanites, 118, 119, 121
    and chosenness, 59–60
    and contemplation, 154
    and covenant, 65, 67, 68
    and creation, 2, 206
    and dance, 203
    and ethics, 156–57, 172n66, 179
    and faith, 229, 230
    and German translation, 185n35
    and God, 205, 229, 230
    and humanity, 68
    and Israel, 56
    and law, 124, 150, 184, 186, 230
    and Moses, 152
    and name of God, 137
    and Nazarites, 150
    and obedience, 233
    and polysemy, 156
    and revelation, 58, 205, 206
    and ritual, 159, 179
    and Sabbath, 154
    and scrolls, 202
    and study, 154, 205, 246

NAME AND SUBJECT INDEX

and time, 104
  See also Bible, commandments, law
tragedy, 31, 46
translation, 140–41, 145, 165, 197
Turner, Victor, 274
Twersky, Isadore, 150, 155n15

Underhill, Evelyn, 268
unintentionality, 109–11, 116, 131, 185
United Nations, 122, 123
unity, 170n58, 184–86, 212–14, 217, 224, 265, 268–69, 273
universalism, 66–68, 70, 73, 89–90, 166, 195, 201, 261
Upanishads, 51n8, 214, 217, 228, 247
Usque, Samuel, 126n58

Van Ness, Peter, 269
violence, in the thought of
  Ahad Ha'am, 92
  Walter Benjamin, 80–84, 106–10, 115–16
  Israeli Declaration of Independence, 85–86
  Deuteronomy, 121–22
  Levinas, 173, 258
  Philo, 111–12, 120–21
  Post-Zionist thinkers, 122–23
  Rosenzweig, 77–78, 80–82, 85, 106
  Gershom Scholem, 79
  Spinoza, 254
  Simone Weil, 106
  Wisdom of Solomon, 118–20
vision of
  the cosmos, 59, 115–16, 132–35, 255
  God, 56, 60–61, 62–64, 133–34, 135–37, 271
  Goodness, 43, 250
  truth, 273–74
  See also mysticism
Vogel, Manfred, 203

War of Independence (Israeli), 122–23
Webb telescope, 18
Weber, Max, 22–23, 24
Weil, Simone, 49–51, 106, 119, 177

wholeness, 69–73, 92, 94, 185–86, 238, 267–70, 272
Wiesel, Elie, 35, 171, 172
wine, 188, 189
Winston, David, 119–20
wisdom, 29, 47, 125, 135, 136, 150, 151–53, 161, 164, 225, 248
Wisdom of Solomon, 118–20, 191
Wissenschaft des Judentums, 117, 124, 126, 180
Wolf, Arnold Jacob, 209n87
Wolf, Immanuel, 117, 123, 124, 125
Wolfson, Elliot, xiv, 212n2, 213, 216, 220, 276n1
Wolfson, Harry Austryn, 48
Wolpe, David, 120
wonder, 24, 26–27, 225
world
  as beloved, 194–95, 243
  as changing, 7, 8, 17
  as configural, 271
  as deathly, 17, 145, 194
  as deniable, 246
  as disenchanted, 22–23
  as (not) eternal, 1–2
  as fragile, 3–5, 16, 17–18, 23
  as grand, 159
  as image of God, 5
  as it is, 204
  as linguistic, 136, 138–39
  as pre-existent, 13–18, 22, 31
  as mysterious, 23–27
  as profane, 115
  as reason-resistant, 22
  as redeemed, 273
  as relational, 13–17, 22, 145, 199
  as spiritual ladder, 251–52
  as stressful, 264–65
  as in vain, 45
  See also cosmological argument, creation, nature
World War I, 76, 77, 80, 81, 98, 107, 110n15
World War II, 258, 277
Wyshogrod, Edith, 174, 176
Wyshogrod, Michael, 70n50

Yemen, 134n16
Yerushalmi, Yosef, 105–6, 117, 118, 124, 126, 126n58
YHWH, 137, 218, 223–24, 227
Yigdal (hymn), 191, 214
Yom Kippur, 30, 63, 183, 195, 201, 244, 273

Zadoff, Noam, 80
Zionism, 64n39, 74–103, 123, 211
Zunz, Leopold, 117

Ancient Document Index

Hebrew Bible

Genesis

1–3	58
1	136, 248, 264
1:1	19
1:2	16, 31, 180n3
1:5	8
1:7	2
1:9	5
1:11	5
1:26	7, 87
1:28	5, 155
9:1–17	66
9:5	66
9:9	66
9:15	66
12:1–3	114
17:10–14	70
22	102
24:63	114
32:29	56

Exodus

3:14	56, 136, 137, 168, 218, 240
6:3	137
15:11	133
15:25	189
19:5	60, 65, 70, 72
20:2	66, 144, 230
20:11	187
21:2	74
22:21	171
22:26–27	171n59
23:4	74
23:20–33	67
23:31–33	121n42
24:7	65, 179, 233
33:20	63, 271
34:6–7	219
34:11–17	121n42

Leviticus

19:9–10	171n61
19:18	144, 168, 171
24:5	188
25:8–13	171n59
25:13	74
25:23	74

Numbers

1:46	57, 68
5:11–31	67, 188
6:1–21	150
6:24–26	271, 273
6:25	62
12:3	152
16:32	82–83
16:33	83

ANCIENT DOCUMENT INDEX

Deuteronomy

4:39	156
5:1	68
6:5	207
6:6	207
7:2	118
10:19	156
11:19	68
12:31	119
14:2	60
20:8	102
22:1–3	150
27:8	68
27:11–26	67
28:1–68	67
28:1–14	65
28:15–68	65
30:11,14	150

Joshua

8:30–35	67
8:33	67
8:35	67

1 Samuel

8:4–19	102
20	65n43

1 Kings

19:12	261

Esther

8:17	54

Job

2:9	29
4:17	29
9:22	47
38:2–3	174, 176
42:7	29

Psalms

85:10	234, 276
92	203
96:9	187
120–34	248
121:1	248
123:1	248
132:4	248

Proverbs

8:30	136

Ecclesiastes

1:2	46
1:18	225, 262
2:2	225
2:13	225
2:18–19	45, 226
2:24	225
3:1–8	226
3:4	225
3:11	45, 226
3:12	262
4:2	225
4:17	227
5:1	226, 227
5:5	225
5:7	226, 231
5:18	225
6:2	225
6:7	225
7:13	225
7:15	45, 225
7:24	226
7:28	226
7:29	225
8:13	225
8:14	225
8:15	225
8:17	45, 226
9:2	226
9:4–5	225
9:11	226
10:8–9	225
10:8	45

11:5	226
12:1–7	46
12:1	45, 225
12:10	226
12:13	227, 228, 262

Song of Songs

1:2	143, 144
1:4	144
1:7	144
8:6	143
8:14	143

Isaiah

6:8	176, 211
11:6	198
19:25	66
42:1–4	150n4, 257

Jeremiah

2:3	71
31:33	206

Ezekiel

1:4–28	133

Amos

9:7	66

Apocrypha

Wisdom of Solomon

12:5–6	119
12:12	119
14:23–24	191

New Testament

Matthew

5:38	150
13:12	276
6:25–53	150
20:16	150

1 Corinthians

13	41
13:4–7	158

Rabbinic Writings

Mishnah

Avot 2:16	233
Avot 5:10	151
Sotah 7:5	68

Babylonian Talmud

Avodah Zarah 17a–b	189
Eruvin 13b	146
Shabbat 31a	149
Shabbat 118b	150n5
Sotah 37a–b	67
Ta'anith 7a	205n79
Yoma 67b	179
Yoma 69b	189

Genesis Rabbah

4:6	2

Leviticus Rabbah

30:12	188n45

Song of Songs Rabbah

7:7	189n46

Mekilta de-Rabbi Ishmael

Exod 15:9–10	104
Exod 20:12–14	192n52

Philo

De Abrahamo (On Abraham)

202	28

De Congressu Quaerendae Eruditiones Gratia (On Mating for the Purpose of Education)

168–70	154

In Flaccum (Flaccus)

65–68	111–12
109	112
146	112
170	112
190–91	112

De Fuga et Inventione (On Flight and Finding)

136	28

Hypothetica (Suppositions)

6:5–8	121

De Iosepho (On Joseph)

143	28

Legatio ad Gaium (The Embassy to Gaius)

2	113
182	113
196	113
371	113

Legum Allegoriae 3 (Allegories of the Law 3)

68	153
73	5
186	56

De Migratione Abrahami (On the Migration of Abraham)

20	114
25	114
140	115
223	114

De Opificio Mundi (On the Creation of the World)

4	7
6	7
7	1
12	7
23	4
25	5
26	2n5, 7
29	4
31	5
38	5
76	7
80	7n16
100	8
134	6
151	6n14
154	6
166	6
172	5

Quaestiones et Solutiones in Exodum (Questions and Answers on Exodus)

1:15	153

Quod Deterius Potiori Insidiari Soleat (The Worse Attacks the Better)

153	56

De Sacrificiis Abelis et Caini
(On the Sacrifices of Abel and Cain)

16	154
63	153

De Somniis (On Dreams)

1:72	121

De Vita Contemplativa
(On the Contemplative Life)

2	154
25	155
58	154
64	154
71	155
78	154
85	155
89	248
90	154

www.ingramcontent.com/pod-product-compliance
Lightning Source LLC
Chambersburg PA
CBHW030433300426
44112CB00009B/989